THE AUTHOR

NINE TROUBLED YEARS

VISCOUNT TEMPLEWOOD

D.C.L., LL.D., Litt.D.

(THE RT. HON. SIR SAMUEL HOARE)

GREENWOOD PRESS, PUBLISHERS
WESTPORT, CONNECTICUT

Library of Congress Cataloging in Publication Data

Templewood, Samuel John Gurney Hoare, 1st Viscount,
    1880-1959.
    Nine troubled years.

    Reprint of the 1954 ed. published by Collins,
London.
    Includes index.
    1.   Templewood, Samuel John Gurney Hoare, 1st
Viscount, 1880-1959.   2.   Statesmen--Great Britain--
Correspondence, reminiscences, etc.   3.   Great Brit-
ain--Politics and government--20th century.
4.   Great Britain--Foreign relations--20th century.
I.   Title.
DA566.9.T4A33   1976   941.083'092'4   75-36363
ISBN 0-8371-8633-1

Originally published in 1954 by Collins, London

Reprinted with the permission of William Collins Sons & Co., Ltd.

Reprinted in 1976 by Greenwood Press,
a division of Williamhouse-Regency Inc.

Library of Congress Catalog Card Number 75-36363

ISBN 0-8371-8633-1

Printed in the United States of America

DEDICATION

To my wife, without whose advice I could not have written this or any of my books, without whose help I could not have achieved anything in public life, and without whose sympathy the difficulties and troubles that I am describing might have been intolerable.

Preface

I HAVE tried in this volume to describe my personal impressions of the many crises that rocked the world between 1931 and 1940. The main sources upon which I have drawn are the notes and papers that I regularly kept at the time, and the many official documents that have since been published. A volume of memoirs is in the nature of things egoistical. This is my answer if it is thought that I have overstated the part that I played in the politics of a confused period. I do not claim to have written a history, nor do I pretend that my conclusions are impartial. Having been jointly responsible for the Cabinet decisions during almost all these nine years, I am naturally anxious at least to explain, and, if possible, to justify them. I am equally ready to admit that we all, and not least myself, made mistakes. It was a time when no one's record was free of faults. My account may in any case add to the evidence upon which a considered verdict can be given, either now or in the future. It will be seen that I have resisted the temptation of giving definite answers to questions that are probably unanswerable. Could, for instance, the war have been prevented, or was it inevitable? And if it was inevitable, were all our efforts to avert it misguided? I have said neither " yes " nor " no." I have tried rather to give an account of the conditions in which the Mac-Donald, Baldwin and Chamberlain Governments were working, and my own reactions to them. Others if they wish can draw conclusions that may not only affect past history, but may well prove useful for the present and future conduct of affairs.

Of the many friends who have helped me, I would particularly mention Mrs. Neville Chamberlain and Miss Hilda Chamberlain, who have not only given me the benefit of their advice, but have placed at my disposal any papers and letters in their possession that bore on my book.

Several of my former colleagues in Whitehall have assisted me in revising particular chapters, Sir Findlater Stewart, for instance, my Indian memories, Sir Robert Craigie my account of the Anglo-German Naval Treaty, Lord Vansittart the tangled story of the Abyssinian crisis, and Lord Halifax and Sir Alexander Cadogan the Munich negotiations and the events that followed the Prague *coup*. I wish to thank them for their invaluable help, and at the same time to make it clear that they are not on that account responsible for the opinions that I have expressed.

In another direction, Mr. R. Bassett has placed at my disposal his unrivalled knowledge of the disarmament movement between the two wars.

Finally, I am grateful to Mr. Charles Eade for allowing me to make general use of some articles that I wrote in the *Sunday Dispatch* on the Abdication of King Edward VIII, to Mr. Victor Gollancz for letting me describe my views on capital punishment in much the same words that I used in my book, *The Shadow of the Gallows*, and to the executors of the late Lord Lothian for agreeing to the inclusion of the letters that he wrote to me from Washington in the first year of the war.

TEMPLEWOOD

July. 1954.

Contents

PART THREE

Return by Sea to Whitehall

PART FOUR

Munich, Prague and War

Part One

INDIA, FEDERAL AND UNITED

CHAPTER I

Summer Storm

THE END of a Parliamentary session is very like the end of the summer term at school. Everyone has been counting the days to the holidays, and making plans for the longest break of the year from routine work. Unfortunately, a spiteful providence has so dispensed the affairs of the world that most of the crises have recently come to a head in the month of August, the very month when Whitehall and Westminster are packed up on a care and maintenance basis. Awkward and sometimes dangerous consequences have resulted from this annual exodus from London. Just when there is a need for quick and resolute decisions, Ministers are scattered, Parliament is in recess, and the Press, reflecting the general relaxation, is chiefly interested in Loch Ness monsters and beauty queens. It is against this incongruous background that many of the chief events of the last forty years have been enacted. It was certainly the case in 1931, the year that I have chosen for the start of this volume of memoirs.

When Parliament adjourned before August Bank Holiday, only a very few members who were in the confidence of the Treasury and the Bank of England were seriously worried about the immediate future. I myself had been warned by Benes the previous summer, when I was visiting Prague, that financial trouble was threatened in Austria, but I had then thought of the danger as one of the many that so often came and went in Central Europe. Benes's forebodings had since been confirmed by the failure of the old-established Credit Anstalt in Vienna and the spread of the financial crisis to Germany. Even so, the Labour Government gave little heed to the warning of Montagu Norman, the Governor of the Bank of England, and the world at large went on its way as if the crisis affected only Austria and Germany. Indeed, it is interesting now to remember that upon the rare occasions when Parliament took any notice of it, members were only interested in the question of financial help for Germany, and altogether indifferent to the need of protecting ourselves against an economic collapse. No one listened to Norman's prophecies of trouble. Exhausted by his fruitless efforts to rouse public opinion, he broke down in health and left the country for a long rest.

There had been a slight and passing stir over the gap between public expenditure and revenue towards the beginning of the session. A debate in the House of Commons on February 11 had induced the Government to appoint a departmental committee of inquiry under the chairmanship of an insurance magnate, Sir George May, and composed of five leaders of finance and industry and two of Labour. In spite of this move for economy, Snowden's budget speech gave no ground for panic. The May Committee started its work in due course with little public attention directed to it, and ninety-nine members of the House of Commons out of a hundred regarded it as no more than a routine expedient for helping the Treasury to balance the next budget. Its Report at the end of July came as a shock both to politicians and the public. The recommendations that were accepted by all the members of the Committee except the two Labour representatives were based on the assumption that the budget expenditure would exceed the revenue by no less than £120 millions, and that to obtain a balanced account it was necessary to cut the pay of government servants, civil and military, local and central, to reduce unemployment benefit, commonly known as the dole, by 10s. a week, and to impose further drastic taxation. Whether by chance or design, the Report was not published until Parliament had adjourned. Was the Government anxious to avoid an embarrassing debate when their supporters had already made their plans to leave London? Or was the reason nothing more sinister than the demand upon the time-table of the government printer? Whatever was the right answer, I have always thought that if the Chancellor of the Exchequer had wanted a debate before the House adjourned, he could easily have arranged for the Report to be in members' hands a few days earlier. In any case, when once the Report was published, the Government saw the amber, if not the red light, and a Cabinet committee consisting of the five principal Ministers was at once appointed to consider the recommendations and their embarrassing reactions.

Yet, although gold was leaving the country at the rate of £2 millions a day, the members of the Cabinet, having appointed the committee, left London, and the House of Commons was shut down for the summer until the normal date for re-opening in the autumn. The Government supporters were relieved that they had survived another precarious session, and the Opposition were satisfied that, after the recess, they would find the Ministry weakened by internal dissension and external pressure.

The exceptional heat made all the more agreeable the long holiday that was in everyone's mind. MacDonald, the Prime Minister, hurried to his beloved Lossiemouth, Baldwin made a leisurely progress across France to his annual cure at Aix, and Neville Chamberlain started upon his regular fishing season in the Highlands. In accordance with my own invariable practice, I retired to Norfolk, where I spent the first days of August playing tennis in the Cromer Tournament.

It was on August 11 that I was suddenly called back from the games of Arcady to the problems of Westminster. An urgent message reached me from Geoffrey Lloyd that the flight from the pound was getting out of control. Lloyd had been my Parliamentary Private Secretary until Baldwin, realising his many abilities, took him from me for himself. With a keen flair for forecasting political movements, he had often given me accurate warning of future events. His was advice that could not lightly be set aside. Moreover, it was confirmed within a few hours by the announcement that the Prime Minister and Baldwin had both returned to London for a conference in Downing Street. It was clear to me that the financial trouble had suddenly become more acute, and that I had better go to London for the day to see for myself what was happening. I was not expecting an immediate crisis, particularly as MacDonald and Baldwin, after a short talk, returned to their holiday resorts. I therefore did no more on August 19 than take a day return ticket to London for a journey of inquiry. It was a sudden surprise to me when my train was stopped at a wayside station, and the stationmaster came running down the platform with an official telegram from No. 10 Downing Street, asking me to attend a three-party conference on the following day, and adding that Neville Chamberlain was expecting to see me that evening at the Carlton Club. It was obvious that my day ticket would have to be extended. As a matter of fact, my journey was to be the start of a new chapter in my political life, during which I was to hold six of the highest offices under the Crown, and be involved in fourteen years of almost incessant ministerial work. Perhaps it is a wise dispensation that hides from us so great a part of the future view. None the less, it involves certain minor inconveniences. If I had imagined that I should be back in London in the middle of August, and should not see the country again for many months, we should not have shut up our London house and sent away my secretary for her holiday. As it was, throughout these critical days, Chamberlain, whose house was also shut, and I met in our bedrooms in the annexe of the Carlton Club. The main building of the club was closed for cleaning, with the result that he and I used a small restaurant in Sloane Square for luncheon and dinner. These trivial details are worth mentioning, as they bring into relief the uncomfortable background of an August crisis.

When I arrived at the Carlton Club, Chamberlain explained to me the history of the telegram. Baldwin, having taken no particular interest in the Downing Street meeting, had seized the first opportunity for going back to Aix, and had left him with full powers, but with no instructions, for dealing with the crisis. Upon the strength of this general authority, Chamberlain, with whom I had worked on intimate terms for nearly ten years, had chosen me as his colleague for the three-party conference that MacDonald had decided to summon. As the conference was to meet the next day, he proceeded to give me a description of the swift course of events since Parliament had adjourned, and of the urgent need for immediate and drastic action, if the pound was to be saved.

In spite of a credit of £50 millions from the Federal Bank and the Bank of France, gold had been pouring out of the country. The high officials of the Bank of England had bluntly told the Government that if the Budget was not balanced, and British credit restored, we were faced with a financial and economic crisis of unprecedented gravity. The Cabinet was deeply divided as to whether or not the necessary programme of retrenchment and austerity should be accepted. Snowden, the champion of sound finance, was having a fierce struggle with several of his colleagues; the Prime Minister was doubtful of his party's support for any resolute move, and Thomas, the Sancho Panza of MacDonald's Don Quixote, was all for broadening the Government's back if it was to carry a heavy burden of popular criticism.

Chamberlain's mind was already made up. It was clear and definite, as was always the case with him on questions of finance and economics. The problem was the immediate re-establishment of the country's credit. Foreign countries were convinced that excessive expenditure and loose administration were drifting us into bankruptcy. How, he asked, could their confidence be restored? The answer was obvious—only by balancing the Budget by means of drastic economies and heavier taxation. Any hesitation or partial measures would plunge us into the worst of all worlds. They would excite discontent at home without stopping the flight from the pound abroad.

This was the background of our first conference on August 20. We met in the Cabinet Room in Downing Street, the Prime Minister with Snowden on his right and Thomas on his left, Samuel, Donald Maclean, Chamberlain and myself facing them. Snowden began with a compromise proposal that omitted the insurance cuts. He was obviously speaking to the Cabinet brief, and made no effort to conceal his personal opinion that it did not go far enough. Chamberlain at once declared that what was proposed was completely inadequate. The meeting adjourned, to be followed by two others in which the struggle within the Cabinet became more apparent. In the meanwhile, we heard that the T.U.C. had put an absolute veto on any pay and salary cuts, and any reductions in the dole. Snowden, supported by Thomas, was obviously ready to accept Chamberlain's requirements. MacDonald, who certainly did not disagree with his two colleagues, was nervous of undertaking the responsibility of a decision that at least half his Cabinet and all the T.U.C. opposed. Even when he implied at the last of the conferences that he was ready to break with the dissidents and carry on as best he could, it was clear to me that he felt that the task would be beyond his powers. His doubts became even more evident when, after the last meeting, he asked Chamberlain and me to talk to him alone in his upstairs sitting-room. It was late in the evening, and the room was almost dark when, for many minutes, he soliloquised to us about his own troubles and the country's need of an all-party effort. His words, like the atmosphere, were obscure, but the conclusion that Chamberlain and I drew from them was the same. He had decided to resign, and to advise the King to send for the party leaders for consultation as to the next step. Having no instructions from Baldwin, we could give him no advice, least of all on the question of his own resignation.

Events followed quickly on the lines that we had foreseen. Within a few hours, the King was back in London from Balmoral. When he had left London, he had intended to carry out his usual programme of a few days at Sandringham, followed by several weeks at Balmoral. When the crisis seemed to be coming to a head, he was still at Sandringham, and on the eve of his journey to Scotland that had been fixed for August 21. Should he change his plans and stay within easy reach of London? A royal journey by special train in the holiday season involves many complicated arrangements. Was it necessary to cancel them? The Prime Minister advised against any change of plan. Postponement might create the very panic that the Government wished to avoid. The King accepted MacDonald's advice, and decided to leave for Scotland. As soon, however, as he reached Balmoral, the crisis had become more acute, and he saw at once that he must return to London. The royal train was therefore ordered for the return journey the next day. The decision was his own, and in no way prompted from London. His common sense, or perhaps his uncommon touch for assessing the value of people and events, convinced him that the King's place was in London.

It took longer to dislodge Baldwin from Aix. He returned, however, in time for conferences with the Prime Minister and the leaders of the Conservative Party on the 23rd. Just as he had been content to leave Chamberlain in complete control of the negotiations, so he was equally content to accept *en bloc* the results of our talks. The impression that he made on us when we discussed the crisis in the rooms of the Conservative Research Department in Great Queen Street was that the last thing in the world that he wished was either a return to office or the end of his holiday. " Having destroyed one coalition," he did not, as he continued to repeat to us, " wish to form another." Only if a National Government was really inevitable, was he ready to take his part in it. Chamberlain and I were inclined to be impatient when we saw him so reluctant to take the only course that seemed to us possible. Our impatience became irritation when the King, on MacDonald's advice, sent for him the next morning and he could not be found. The result was that Samuel saw the King in the morning, and Baldwin only in the afternoon, after Samuel had already opened the way to a coalition. It may well be that this timing suited Baldwin, who may have wished to come in at the end of the play. True to type, he had waited for the last moment to intervene, with the result that the scene was altogether set when he decided that the moment had come to walk on to the stage. While Chamberlain and I had been working night and day in the August heat of London, he had been peacefully meditating, like Montaigne in his tower in Guienne, upon the strange course of human affairs that was turning him, the leader of the Conservative anti-coalitionists, into the principal figure in a coalition government. When I come to sum up his characteristics, I shall include amongst his chief qualities the power to wait for the right moment. In this case, without the full use that he made of it, the formation of a Three-Party Government might have been impossible.

From my memories of these anxious days, three other impressions have been left with me. First, Philip Snowden's hard and immovable determination to balance the Budget at any cost. His doctrinaire, radical mind was inspired by an unquestioning belief in the infallibility of a balanced budget, whilst his whole nature rebelled against the political evasions and complacent generalities of many of his ministerial colleagues. From start to finish in our talks he was never deflected from the course that he had set himself, nor, I believe, was he ever blind to the destination to which it was undoubtedly leading him, much as he disliked it. My first memory, therefore, of these inter-party discussions is of the alert, dogmatic and explosive Chancellor of the Exchequer, irritated by the Ossian-like complexities of MacDonald, shocked by the Rabelaisian levities of Thomas, always intent upon his own single purpose, a balanced budget—a " sea-green incorruptible " who regarded most of his own colleagues as fools, and who never disguised the fact that he did not suffer fools gladly.

My second memory is of Chamberlain's clarity of mind. From the first moment he exactly gauged the situation. Like Snowden, he saw that nothing short of a balanced budget was of any use, and that therefore no compromise could be accepted. His grasp of detail made his interventions particularly effective. Samuel, equally well instructed and " always damned relevant," as Arthur Balfour had once philosophically remarked, was equally firm against any compromise. It was indeed fortunate that he and Chamberlain were the two principal representatives of the Liberals and Conservatives. Lloyd George was ill, and Churchill, another former Chancellor of the Exchequer, was out of the country, and after his break with Baldwin over India, out of the confidence of the Conservative Party. Neither of them would have been as well fitted as were Chamberlain and Samuel to deal with the intricate problems of finance and the personal prejudices that complicated the work of the conference.

My last memory has none of the hard outline of the first. It is of the obscurity that enshrouded all our technical discussions about the flight of gold. No one could tell us what to expect from day to day. Like Baldwin, the Governor of the Bank of England was out of the country. If, however, he had been in London, I do not believe that he could have given us any more definite information than we had from the Deputy Governor, Sir Ernest Harvey, and his colleague, Sir Edward Peacock. When we asked what was likely to happen to the flow of gold, their answer was that, as they were dealing with a factor as subtle and sensitive as national credit, it was impossible to estimate the volume and the course of the flight from the pound. So far from dominating the situation or plotting a bankers' ramp, the representatives of the City whom we constantly saw throughout the crisis were as uncertain about the flight of gold as we were ourselves, and were most reluctant to intervene in any political discussion. The sum total of their advice was " Balance the Budget." With the detailed methods that Chamberlain and I had been pressing at the conference they did not concern themselves, nor did they ever attempt to exercise any pressure upon the Government or the Opposition.

The suggestion was equally groundless that undue pressure was being exerted from Washington. The American Government, pledged to isolation and reeling under the blows of the economic crash, showed no sign of wishing to be directly involved in the British crisis. As a matter of fact, the Federal Bank was debarred by its constitution from making loans to foreign Governments. Any loan, therefore, that we might need, had to be negotiated privately between the Bank of England and an American financial house, and not between British and American officials. This was the reason for the intervention of the great financial house of J. P. Morgan. When the Bank of England asked on what terms the firm would make a loan, the obvious answer was returned that " the indispensable condition was a balanced budget." The reply was in no sense an ultimatum; it was no more than a statement of the fact that a private loan could only be raised if the borrower was solvent. From what Chamberlain and I were told at the time, the Cabinet wrongly jumped to the conclusion that the Americans were trying to dictate to them. There was no ground for this resentment. The only dictation during the crisis came from the T.U.C. when they put an absolute veto on the main economies.

Whilst at first we had some reason for thinking that the Cabinet would accept the necessary cuts, and even be prepared to impose duties for restricting imports, we soon realised that the rift in the ministerial ranks made it impossible for MacDonald to obtain the support of all his colleagues. He seemed at one time to think that he could carry with him the majority of his Ministers, including Morrison. None the less, he made no special effort to bring over to his side either the dissidents or the hesitants. I gathered the impression that he was himself so perplexed that he shrank from any attempt to persuade his colleagues to join him in an uncharted adventure. When he finally made his decision, he was only able to bring to the new Government a handful of supporters.

It was probably because of his small following that he at first wished to resign and recommend the King to send for Baldwin. Baldwin was against taking office in a minority, and having to hold a General Election so soon after the last. It was because of his reluctance that MacDonald eventually agreed to become Prime Minister of a Three-Party Government. Snowden has since declared in his memoirs that " MacDonald set about the formation of the National Government with an enthusiasm which showed that the adventure was highly agreeable to him." I can only say that throughout the whole of the week's discussions I never saw the least sign of any desire on MacDonald's part to become the Prime Minister of a Three-Party Government. His talk to Chamberlain and me was of resignation, and it needed considerable persuasion to dissuade him from throwing in his hand.

It has also been suggested that the King used undue influence in persuading him to form a National Government. All that I heard at the time contradicted the truth of this suggestion. During the whole crisis the King carried out his constitutional duties with a meticulous precision. He was neither for nor against any particular kind of administration. The constitutional duty that he scrupulously fulfilled was to see that there was a government to meet the crisis, and to receive advice as to its composition. It was on the advice of the Prime Minister that he consulted the Conservative and Liberal leaders, and he did so for the unanswerable reason that they alone could ensure a majority in the House of Commons. MacDonald, though he still talked of resignation, had already decided in favour of a National Government before he saw the King. The King at once accepted his advice, and gave him, as he would have given to any Prime Minister, his moral support in the process of forming it.

MacDonald, having worked himself up into taking his critical decision, at once relapsed into a mood of doubt and depression. When he appeared at the Privy Council for the swearing in of the new Cabinet, he looked so mournful in a black tie and frock coat, that the King laughingly said to him: " You look as if you were attending your own funeral. Put on a white tie and try to think it is your wedding." From that day onwards the King never ceased to hold up the Prime Minister's hands.

Within a remarkably short space of time the formalities were completed, and the Three-Party Government, the first in British history, duly installed. It was not a coalition in the full sense of the word. Created for the single object of balancing the Budget and re-establishing stability, its programme was strictly limited, and there was no attempt to build a common platform of general policy. Its origin dominated its whole existence. It was the financial crisis that had brought together MacDonald, Baldwin and Samuel, and financial recovery was the sole object for which they and their followers had made an alliance. The Budget had to be balanced, and great economies imposed, whatever might be the sacrifices that a policy of drastic deflation involved. The small Cabinet of eleven ministers, MacDonald, Sankey, Snowden and Thomas from the Labour Party, Baldwin, Chamberlain, Cunliffe Lister and myself from the Conservatives, and Samuel, Reading and Maclean from the Liberals, was to be an emergency

Committee of Public Safety for dealing with an immediate crisis. I became Secretary of State for India, and was able to continue the interest in Indian affairs that had already involved me in the first Round Table Conference.

I shall never forget the spontaneous outburst of enthusiastic support that greeted Snowden's appeal in the House of Commons for sacrifices to meet the crisis. The same ruthlessness that he had shown in publicly exposing the cowardice of many of his former colleagues, he applied to the need for further taxation. No Chancellor of the Exchequer ever excited as many cheers by reducing taxation, as Snowden by the increased burdens that he was imposing. Within the next few days the British public was standing in queues outside the offices of the Inland Revenue for the purpose of paying the new taxes, although they were not due for several months.

Throughout these hectic days, not a thought was given to the cloud that, though only the size of a man's hand, was appearing on the distant horizon. Without our noticing it, the Locarno chapter of reconciliation had come to an end. Briand and Stresemann had just died, and Hitler, an unknown Austrian adventurer, had forced his way into public attention by winning in September more than a hundred seats in the Reichstag. Although at the time there was justification for ignoring these happenings in foreign countries, and for concentrating our undivided attention on economic recovery, historians will look with a sardonic smile at one of the first acts of the National Government—the reduction of our meagre expenditure on defence by £8 millions, and one of its immediate results, the mutiny of naval ratings at Invergordon, at the very moment when Nazism was first showing its ugly head in Germany. Austen Chamberlain, with the disinterested patriotism that always marked his public life, had refrained from pressing his claim to be a member of the Cabinet, and had accepted the post of First Lord of the Admiralty without a Cabinet seat. "What a delightful office," he said to me when we met one morning in Hyde Park. "Unlike the Foreign Office, the Admiralty runs itself and the First Lord need not worry about it." Within twenty-four hours, the astonished world heard the news of the first mutiny in the Royal Navy since the Mutiny of the Nore. First, the collapse of the British pound, next, the collapse of the British Fleet—the almost simultaneous downfall of the two

Arks of the British Covenant—this was how it struck our friends and foes. They did not stop to learn the details of the affair at Invergordon. If they had, they would have known that it was incompetence amongst senior officers in Whitehall, rather than disloyalty on the lower deck, that had turned the Service cuts into a burning grievance. The fact, however, that the cuts were accepted as necessary by practically everyone except the aggrieved crews, showed not only the gravity of the financial crisis, but also the general feeling that military security was of little account compared with economic recovery. The crisis, by adding economic to moral and political arguments, had, in fact, intensified the demand for disarmament. It was only a few weeks before the fall of the Labour Government that Field-Marshal Sir William Robertson, the very embodiment of the British fighting spirit, had presided at a great meeting at the Albert Hall to protest against the burden of armaments.

In cutting down the expenditure on the fighting services, we were carrying out an almost unanimous popular mandate. In the autumn of 1931, no one could foresee the course of future events in Germany. The fact, however, remains that we were reducing our armed forces at a time when, if we had known what we have since learnt from bitter experience, we should have been starting to increase them. Concentrated with an amazing singleness of purpose upon the task of economic recovery, we were submitting to heavy cuts in salaries, wages and benefits, civil and military alike, and were so intent upon our own affairs that we had no time to listen to any strange sounds on the Continent that not even a trained ear could yet understand.

CHAPTER II

Three Ministers and a King

THIS WAS the background of the stage to the front of which I had suddenly stepped. Hitherto, I had been for the most part in the wings. Five years at the Air Ministry had tended to keep me isolated in the field of defence. It was while we were in opposition after 1929 that Baldwin had first begun to use me for more general affairs. At one time, he persuaded me to be Treasurer of the Conservative Party; at another, to lead the Conservative delegation at Lord Ullswater's Three-Party Conference on Electoral Reform; at another, to speak on foreign affairs in several debates in the House of Commons.

Chamberlain, to an even greater degree, had availed himself of my help in his many plans of social reform for the future. This widening of my political horizon brought me into the Shadow Cabinet of half a dozen ex-Ministers who controlled Conservative policy during MacDonald's second government. It was then that Baldwin asked me to represent the Conservative Opposition on the first of the Indian Round Table Conferences. Although I had previously spoken in several Indian debates, this was the beginning of my close connection with Indian questions, and my entry into the very centre of the Inner Cabinet's discussions. This was the position when the crisis of 1931 swept me into the conference that created the National Government, and into the small Cabinet of eleven members. Whilst Indian affairs then became my principal occupation for the next four years, my former associations with the Air Ministry kept me interested in another question that was very prominently in the public mind—the question of disarmament. From 1931 to 1935, there was scarcely a meeting of the Cabinet or the Committee of Imperial Defence in which disarmament was not discussed in one form or another. The British world, as I shall show in greater detail in a later chapter, was almost solidly behind the demand for smaller armaments. In any description, therefore, of the years between the wars, the pressure for disarmament is a constant factor of the first importance that must never be forgotten. I intend, therefore, to deal with it in some detail, even though it may seem tedious to a generation that is now demanding greater military strength.

Before, however, I become involved in its intricacies, I must make a sketch of the three main characters on the new stage, Ramsay MacDonald, Stanley Baldwin, and Neville Chamberlain. Two of them, MacDonald and Baldwin, had already been Prime Ministers. The third, Chamberlain, was already Baldwin's accepted heir, and was to be his successor as Prime Minister in six years' time.

The influence of personality is one of the most enthralling studies in politics. I had seen in my own experience the extent to which it enters into every phase of British public life. At one time, the demand is for a colourless leader, and Bonar Law is chosen in preference to Walter Long or Austen Chamberlain; at another, for a dynamic war Prime Minister, and the emotional Lloyd George takes the place of the classical Asquith. Then comes the inevitable reaction, when the peaceful personalities of Bonar Law and Baldwin harmonise better with the general sentiment than the brilliant qualities of " the man who won the war."

Baldwin's character in particular was as well suited to the chapter of recovery after a great war as Walpole's had been two centuries before. With his successor's personality I shall deal later in detail. At this point I restrict myself to saying in a single sentence that in 1937 the country was clamouring for a complete contrast to Baldwin's tranquillity, and in Neville Chamberlain it believed that it had found the man whom it wanted.

Having made these general observations, I will try to sketch the three men who dominated the political stage in 1931: Mac-Donald, Baldwin and Chamberlain. No personalities could have been more unlike. If I apply a single word of description to each of them I would say MacDonald was the romanticist, Baldwin the humanist, and Chamberlain the analyst. MacDonald's sensitive nature made him feel instinctively rather than see clearly the difficulties that faced him. Baldwin's human heart gave him a

power that on great occasions made " the whole world kin."
Chamberlain's analytical mind broke down the problems of
government into their constituent parts and fixed on the points
that really mattered.

I begin with MacDonald the romanticist. I had never known
him personally before I entered his Government. When I was
first elected to Parliament at the beginning of 1910, his striking
appearance had immediately impressed me. He always spoke
from below the gangway, where he sat amongst the small group
of Labour members, most of whom had been returned by the
help of Liberal votes. Whilst his fine voice and dramatic pose
always attracted the attention of the House when he rose to
speak, it was often difficult to unravel his meaning from the
tangle of his sentences. Snowden's distilled logic and Thomas's
boisterous sallies brought members back from the lobby and
smoking-room when MacDonald's involved adumbrations sometimes made them leave the Chamber.

By the time that he became the Prime Minister of the National
Government, MacDonald was already a tired man. How tired,
it was difficult for those of us to realise who had not faced the
hard road that led Labour leaders to the Treasury Bench. Forty
years before, he had been walking the streets of London as a
penniless boy in search of work, and when he found it as the
secretary of the Cyclists' Touring Club, it was at ten shillings a
week for addressing envelopes. There had followed an obscure
chapter of ceaseless struggle, during which he was actively
engaged on the various plans that produced in 1893 the Independent Labour Party. Two years later he stood for Parliament,
as the Independent Labour candidate at Southampton, and was
crushingly defeated. Throughout this early period, he seems to
have shown both the faults of the qualities and the qualities of
the faults that were to become more conspicuous as he became
great. Being both proud and sensitive, he could never bring himself to the complete acceptance either of his colleagues or even of
his own programme. With the Fabians, he was for Independent
Labour, with Independent Labour, for the Fabians. I can only
speak from hearsay of the period, but I gather from his friends
that as long as his remarkable wife, Margaret Gladstone, was
alive, this excessive eclecticism was to a great extent kept under
control. After her death, and as he became older, it showed

itself more frequently. The result was that he never seemed to be a hundred per cent for or against any one course of action. The pale cast of his complicated thought was apt to tone down the colour of his generous sentiments, and to obscure both his intentions and the words with which he expressed them.

In spite of these hesitations he undoubtedly played a notable part in the political life of the country. As one of the founders of the Parliamentary Labour Party, he was chiefly responsible for winning a place for Labour in the great world of politics and public opinion. If he had not possessed remarkable qualities, he would have irrevocably lost any influence that he ever possessed by his pacifist opposition first to the South African War, and subsequently to the War of 1914. Yet, within a short time of each of them, he was back again in public life, a leading figure and a politician of growing importance. When Labour came into power in 1923, it was he and not Clynes, Henderson or Lansbury who became its first Prime Minister. Having become Prime Minister, he showed both tact and judgment. In particular, he succeeded in lowering the international temperature. The *détente* that followed the end of the Curzon-Poincaré wrangles gave him the chance of improving Anglo-French relations, whilst his love of tradition was a valuable antidote against the irresponsible anarchism of some of his followers. The history of his first Labour Government was to a great extent repeated in his second. If, however, he had his successes in both, in both also there were the same failures from want of decision. The first Ministry was brought down by the fumbling over the Campbell case, in which the Executive committed the unforgivable sin of meddling with the Judicature; the second, by the failure to deal in time with the symptoms of national bankruptcy. It was typical of the unexpectedness of British politics that the man whose chief fault in office had been hesitation, became for the third time Prime Minister at a moment of unprecedented crisis, when the most resolute action and the most fearless decisions were urgently needed. He himself seems to have been conscious of the incongruity of his position. During the Three-Party Conference before the formation of the National Government, he spoke more than once to Chamberlain and myself of his wish to resign. He spoke of it again when Baldwin returned from Aix and a new Government had to be formed. Although he continued in office for a further period of four years,

I had the feeling that he was always in doubt as to whether to stay or go. The result was what might have been expected. The ingrained habit of hesitation kept him in office after his eyesight and health had failed. It would have been better if he had made way sooner for Baldwin, and brought a period of obvious transition to an end.

My more intimate dealings with him were almost entirely concerned with India. He regarded himself as an expert on Indian affairs. He had played a useful part in one of the Royal Commissions that had visited India, and he had many friends amongst Indian political leaders. None the less, he was often reluctant to agree to definite decisions upon Indian questions. I have several letters written in his own hand warning me against some course of action without suggesting to me any alternative. It was probably this elusiveness that made Gandhi dislike him. Gandhi, as I shall later describe, saw at once through any veil that was intended to conceal anything from him. MacDonald, by nature very sensitive, shrank from exposing his whole mind, not because he wished to mislead, but because he wished to keep his inner thoughts to himself.

In his general conduct of Cabinet affairs and his relations with his colleagues, he always struck me as a dignified chairman with an impressive manner, scrupulously polite to everyone, but none the less giving us the impression that he knew more than any of us, though he did not wish to disclose the sources of his greater knowledge. The result was that, though the Cabinet and the Conservative Party were entirely loyal to him, and no one wished to displace him, least of all Baldwin, he never inspired the complete trust that he would certainly have acquired if his own character had been more simple and open. As it was, he filled very adequately a place in our public life for which no one else was at the time exactly suited. It was then essential to create the framework of a Three-Party Government into which to fit the unpopular programme of national austerity. Neither Snowden nor Thomas, left to themselves, could have brought the necessary contribution to it, whilst the Conservatives and Liberals were more likely to work together under a Labour chairman and on a three-party programme than under one of their own leaders. The weakness in MacDonald's position was the lack of any substantial support from the rank and file of his former party. The Labour

Ministers and Members of the House of Commons who supported
the National Government could be counted on two hands. None
the less, the Government that was formed and the Prime Minister
who took office were the best available in the peculiar circumstances of August, 1931. It is therefore both unjust and illogical
for those who welcomed him as Prime Minister of the new
Government to criticise him for the faults that he had been
known to possess for many years, and that he subsequently showed
in his four years of office. The country wished to have him at
the time. He reluctantly responded to the call, and his help was
considerable in tiding us over a critical period. Many of those
who now disparage his qualities are for the most part actuated by
political resentment or personal spite on account of the landslide
that, in December, 1932, almost obliterated the Labour Party at
the polls.

Of the three chief personalities in the Government, he was,
as I have suggested, the romanticist. As sensitive as Fergus
McIvor in *Waverley*, his vivid imagination made him see all the
difficulties that beset any course of action. If it sometimes confused his arguments, it none the less kept him responsive to the
needs of the time, and gave him an engaging touch in all his
dealings with his Ministerial colleagues. We realised as vividly
as he the difficulty of his position. Like Lloyd George, he had lost
his own party, and was the Prime Minister of a Government
mainly supported by Conservatives. No doubt he had the uneasy
feeling that he was a captive in a gilded prison. I hope and
believe, however, that his suspicions gradually abated under
Baldwin's friendly influence.

Baldwin, the humanist, was the very colleague that Mac-
Donald needed for restoring his self-confidence, and encouraging
him when characteristic hesitations weakened his grip. Baldwin,
in fact, was exactly the man for keeping together a Three-Party
Government. When the historian of the future defines his place
in British history, I believe that it will be this indispensability
that will put him amongst our great Prime Ministers. He was
indispensable for freeing the Conservative Party from the toils of
Lloyd George in 1922. While others took the active parts in this
political drama, he kept at the back of the stage and seemed to
me, a private member, who was at the time in close contact with
Bonar Law, to be aloof and almost indifferent to what was

happening. Then came the Carlton Club meeting, at which he made the first notable speech of his career. His plain and simple statement that Lloyd George's word could not be trusted completely demolished in a single sentence the arguments of Balfour, Birkenhead and Austen Chamberlain, three of the most skilled debaters in British Parliamentary history. Without it, I doubt whether Bonar Law would have pulled up his coalition anchor and sailed out into the Conservative sea. I had been with him late on the previous night, and he was then still disinclined to break with Lloyd George. It was Baldwin's rather than his own speech that settled the issue of the day. Baldwin had waited until the critical moment before acting, and when finally he intervened, the result was decisive.

His second intervention was equally effective. For month after month he had refused to intervene in the coal strikes that were so seriously compromising economic recovery during his second Ministry. The culmination had been the General Strike of 1926. Here again, he seemed to be doing nothing. I was a member of the Cabinet Committee that met each day at the Home Office to deal with the crisis. In the chair sat Joynson-Hicks, the very embodiment of a Victorian Home Secretary, frock-coated, eloquent, determined to rise to a historic occasion. On one side of him were Churchill and Birkenhead, no less conscious of the magnitude of the crisis, and bent upon bringing it to an end by bold and dramatic action. On the other side was John Anderson, the Permanent Under-Secretary of the Home Office, an outstanding Civil Servant as yet unknown beyond Whitehall, but already showing the solid qualities of imperturbable resolution and sound judgment that were afterwards to distinguish his great career. From the first meeting of the Committee it was evident that he very well understood what should be done, and that, if left to himself, he intended to do it. Baldwin, on the other hand, not only did not attend the Committee, but remained singularly detached from its decisions. It was only when the moment arrived for making the choice between war and peace that he came into action. When there was a clamour for unconditional surrender, he made it clear in his broadcast to the nation on May 12 that he was for peace on fair and generous terms, and against any vendetta. The General Strike ended, and once again he had shown that he was indispensable.

The third great occasion came in August, 1931, when history repeated itself. Baldwin kept aloof until the last possible moment. As I have already described, he was at Aix during the meetings of the Three-Party Conference. During all our discussions he never once communicated with Chamberlain or me. When it was clear to us that MacDonald's resignation was imminent, he still delayed his return to London. Even after his arrival, he was reluctant to take a hand in the final development. Just as in 1924 he had hesitated to turn out the Labour Government on the Campbell case, so in 1931 he seemed unwilling to undertake again the burdens of office. His disinclination had the effect of making the part that he eventually took in the formation of the new Ministry appear both inevitable and disinterested. Without the delayed action of his intervention, there might have been no National Government.

Of the fourth occasion when he was once again indispensable, I shall write more fully when I come to the year 1936 and the Abdication of King Edward VIII. Here I will only say that what appeared to be months of inaction made his final intervention irresistible.

For a Minister to be indispensable once in his career is a rare achievement. For Baldwin to have been indispensable upon four occasions of first-class importance is a feat unique in the history of British Prime Ministers. In each of them he played his part in his own way. If he had been a performer on the stage or the radio, he would have had the same signature tune for all his chief appearances. The motif would have been very English and very simple, perhaps one of Cecil Sharp's country dances. Yet in point of fact his personality was by no means as simple as it seemed. Although he was born a townsman, his best role was as the lover of England's green and pleasant land. He had never been a classical scholar, and as he told me himself, he could not read a Latin or a Greek text. Yet, there was no one living who could better express the classical tradition or make a more delightful classical allusion. In spite of these apparent incongruities, his stock-in-trade was never sham or imitation; it was part of himself, just as his pipe was the pipe of a genuine pipe smoker, and not the stage property of a public man wishing to be advertised. When he broadcast, he gave the impression of an English countryman sitting at the end of the day in a comfortable chair in friendly conversation with two or three of his old friends. As a matter of fact, the talk that seemed to flow so naturally had been very carefully prepared. Sitting, or, as some thought, sleeping over his pipe, he had meditated for hours over what he intended to say, with the result that when he said it, every word had become a part of his own nature. In contrast with Lloyd George and Churchill, he never seemed to be speaking to great crowds. Yet, behind the outward intimacy, there were hidden a complicated personality, and a unique instinct for seizing a great opportunity. It is significant that for all this appearance of simplicity, he was the only politican of his generation who, when drawn into conflict by Lloyd George, the most astute of tacticians, never failed to emerge triumphant.

Just as he was less simple than he seemed, so also was he less tolerant than his easy geniality suggested. His prejudices were strong and persistent. His chief dislike was fixed on Lloyd George, and extended to many of the members of the Lloyd George Coalition. Of Birkenhead he disapproved, Churchill he mistrusted, Beaverbrook he definitely disliked. Although force of circumstances made him the principal member of two coalitions, and he worked patiently and loyally with his Labour and Liberal colleagues, his suspicion of all coalitions was never removed.

The result was that the few intimate friends that he possessed were, with the exception of Tom Jones, anti-coalitionists. Willie Bridgeman, at one time Home Secretary and at another First Lord of the Admiralty, was typical of them. He, like his leader, seemed more simple than he really was. Like him, he had an unerring touch for the business of the House of Commons, and the same kind of English humour, so different from French wit, that helped it through difficult debates without undue trouble. No Minister was more popular, and his engaging smile and unruffled temperament were priceless assets to any Government. The two had much the same tastes. To both of them Lord's Cricket Ground was the happy isle of perpetual bliss. Whilst Bridgeman had played cricket well enough to play for Eton and Cambridge, Baldwin's interest in the game was academic and detached. Cricket, that he had never himself played with any success, appealed to him on account of its particularly English characteristics. The game was played on green grass; it was leisurely and traditional; team spirit inspired it; a pleasant chapter of English history recorded its achievements. Whenever, therefore, there was a chance, he escaped from Downing Street, usually accompanied by Bridgeman, and found his way to the roof of the Pavilion at Lord's. Sometimes I went with them. Once, I remember, it was a very hot day, and within a few minutes of our arrival, both of them were sound asleep. When they woke up after about a quarter of an hour, Baldwin seized my knee and said to me in a rapturous voice: " Isn't this splendid, Sam? There is nothing like a good game of cricket."

In great affairs, Baldwin habitually trusted Bridgeman's judgment. A crisis would arise, an appointment would need to be made, a difficult situation would have to be surmounted. Baldwin would talk over the question with his principal colleagues, but in the end, it would be Bridgeman's opinion that he would nine out of ten times accept. When the Conservative Party and all the popular Press were clamouring for his resignation of the party leadership in the spring of 1931, Bridgeman, alone of his colleagues, advised him to pay no attention to the agitation. I remember the evening of March 1, when Chamberlain told me that Baldwin had definitely resigned. We walked together up and down the Terrace of the House of Commons, discussing the action that the new leader would have to take to put life into the policy and machinery of the party. Everything then seemed fixed. Yet, by the next morning, Baldwin had determined not only to hold his ground, but to make a vigorous offensive against his critics. The chief reason for the sudden change had been Bridgeman's eleventh-hour advice. The leading article that was already set up in *The Times* office headed " Mr. Baldwin Withdraws " had hastily to be destroyed.

The result of this unexpected change was equally typical of Baldwin's career. Having been in the lowest political depths, he was soon again upon a political pinnacle. Within a few months of what seemed to be his impending collapse, the part that he reluctantly took in forming and maintaining the National Government re-established him as the most popular and respected figure in British politics. Just as the General Strike had regained for him the country's affection after the previous chapter of unpopularity, so the financial crisis of 1931 raised him from the disrepute into which he had fallen only a few months before, and made him once again the national leader.

The same alternation between the depths and the heights was to follow in December, 1935, when the Abyssinian crisis almost destroyed his position, and the Abdication a few months later in 1936 made it stronger than ever before.

This series of extreme vicissitudes would never have been expected in a life that seemed so equable and serene. But here again was another evidence of the complexity of his character. Knowing his own reserves of strength, he advisedly preferred to wait for the darkest day and the final attack before he went into serious action. The British Fabius Cunctator was always ready to lose the first battle, because he was convinced he would win the last.

Being so sure of himself, he never fully realised that during his long term of office the field of action, and with it, the tactics and strategy that were required, was changing. Whilst he was humanising politics in England, Hitler was brutalising them on the Continent. Whilst he showed his wisdom by going slow at home and gaining time for heated tempers to cool, his Fabian tactics were only a sign of weakness in Hitler's eyes. The fact was that he never understood foreign countries. Like Sir Edward Grey, he spoke no foreign language, and had little or nothing in common with foreigners. It was this insularity that obscured his view of the changing world. A totally new chapter had begun with Hitler's advent to power, and a new technique of government was needed to deal with it. It was doubly unfortunate that MacDonald remained Prime Minister after his physical strength had failed, and that Baldwin, having waited too long for the succession, continued to wear the crown in a period that had completely altered from the conditions of his former reigns. History offers many examples of kings and ministers who ruled too long. Reigns that continue beyond the period of their usefulness are bad both for the rulers themselves and their successors. When a change is known to be coming in the political world, there is a risk of inaction and hesitation until it comes. Although MacDonald's health and Baldwin's expressed intention to resign made inevitable two successive changes in the Premiership, both lingered on the stage after they had finished their parts. It meant also that Chamberlain, Baldwin's successor, was kept year after year waiting in the wings.

As it was, Baldwin was able to lay down his office after the

Abdication crisis and the coronation of the new king with a halo
of final success around his head and the grateful acclamations
of the whole country resounding in his ears. The fact that he left
behind to his successor a task of overwhelming difficulty in the
field of foreign affairs does not invalidate his claim to have been
one of the great peace-time Prime Ministers of the country.

I come to the third dominant figure in the National Government of 1931, to Neville Chamberlain, whom in distinction to Mac-
Donald the romanticist, and Baldwin the humanist, I have called
the analyst. With Neville Chamberlain I had much more in common than with either MacDonald or Baldwin. Perhaps on that
account I could better understand his successes and failures and
sympathise with his final troubles. We shared several of our
tastes, for instance, our love of country life and country sport.
Whilst he had taken to shooting in later life, and I had started
upon it before I was ten years old, his characteristic concentration
upon everything that he did had made him a good shot and an
expert sportsman, learned in the lore of the woods and fields.
Each season we met in several country houses, where we came
to know each other better than was ever possible in Whitehall and
Westminster. Meetings such as these showed us how closely our
habits and minds corresponded. We were both very hard workers,
who needed a definite plan for our work. We could neither of us
be idle for a moment. Perhaps it was in both of us a weakness
that we were never able to do nothing. " What a pity," said
Talleyrand of Napoleon, " that he is not lazy." Being very
efficient, Chamberlain had, as he said himself, " no capacity for
looking on and seeing other people mismanaging things." Of his
planning there is no better example than the programme that he
made for the Cabinet in November, 1924, for the reform of local
government. It was a five-year plan to cover the whole field of
health, housing, local taxation and rating, and to be carried out
methodically by twenty-five Bills neatly spaced over each succeeding session of the five-years Parliament. No previous Minister of
Health or President of the Local Government Board had ever
contemplated so ambitious a task. Chamberlain not only convinced a doubtful Cabinet of its advantages, but passed the whole
programme through Parliament in little more than four years.
Without his remarkable grasp of detail, his achievement would
have been impossible. From start to finish it involved an almost

interminable series of administrative problems. The result was to display the remarkable talent for administration that had already made his reputation on the Birmingham City Council. The Ministry of Health and the Exchequer provided an unlimited opportunity for still further applying it. His critics sometimes thought that this grasp of detail made him undertake work that ought to have been left to his permanent staff. I am sure, however, that his reforms between 1924 and 1929 would never have been carried through if it had not been for his knowledge of detail and the use that he made of it. When, however, I come to describe his work as Prime Minister, I shall have to admit that he would have been less open to criticism if he had not been so deeply involved in the details of administration.

Like him, I was never happy in opposition when once I had held office, and like him also, I hated Parliamentary elections. The interest of politics for both of us was doing things. When, therefore, we were out of office, we occupied ourselves with the holding of inquiries and the making of plans for future action. Each of his social reform bills was based on the report of a party committee aided by chosen experts. I was a member of most of the committees, and it was no doubt my interest in a constructive programme for the Conservative Party that made him later write to his sister in 1923: " Hoare and I are the only Socialists in the Government."

A mentality such as his was equally far apart from the easy-going quietism of Baldwin and the introspective hesitations of MacDonald. Although a man of great personal modesty, Chamberlain was not tolerant. His likes and dislikes were even stronger than Baldwin's, so strong, in fact, that they sometimes led him to mistaken decisions, and when he became Prime Minister, to some bad appointments to responsible posts. He had none of Baldwin's appeal to other men's feelings. " I like your old man Baldwin," Lloyd George once said to me. " I could work with him." He could never work with Chamberlain. Whilst it was the humanist's touch that made Labour hang on Baldwin's words, it was the analyst's accuracy that, reacting against Labour's reluctance to face unpleasant facts, made the Trade Union leaders regard Chamberlain as a bitter enemy, when in actual practice he was a pronounced radical reformer far to the left of many of them and most of his own party.

These, as I saw them, were the characteristics of the three founding fathers of the first two National Governments. It is to their credit that in spite of their differing characteristics, they worked loyally together for several years, and kept the wheels of government working smoothly and efficiently.

Without, however, an outside influence of very great importance, it is doubtful whether they could have co-operated for so long a time. This influence came from the help and advice of a wise constitutional King. When people speak of a constitutional monarchy, they rightly think of a king who acts solely on the formal advice of his Government. The other side of his duties, his own informal advice to his Ministers, is apt to be underrated or ignored. Yet, in the case of a King who has gained wide experience during many years of office, the reverse stream of advice from the Crown to the Ministry is scarcely less essential to good Parliamentary government. There could be no better instance of the value of this advice than the experience of 1931. The crisis exhibited the scrupulous care with which George V avoided any word or action that went beyond his constitutional powers, and at the same time gave the party leaders the help of his sound judgment. I have already described how, throughout the critical days of August, he neither started the idea of a change of Ministry nor put pressure on the party leaders to have one, how he remained at Balmoral until the views of MacDonald, Baldwin and Samuel had crystallised the idea of co-operation, and how, when he acted, it was on the constitutional advice of the Prime Minister. Should it then be assumed that he did no more than put a rubber stamp on a decision that had already been taken? Any such conclusion would be altogether contrary to the facts. From what I was told at the time, I am convinced that if the King had not been able to encourage the party leaders at the critical moment, MacDonald, whose hesitations were painfully evident, would have resigned, and Baldwin would unavoidably have been forced to form a one-party Government. As it was, the King, knowing that all three party leaders were in favour of a National Government, was able to hold up their hands and support them by practical advice based on his long years of political experience. Better than any other British sovereign, he was qualified to fill the role of impartial intermediary between the party leaders. He had twice before presided over inter-party conferences, once in 1910 soon after his accession, when the attempt failed to settle the constitutional battle between the two Houses, and again, on the eve of the First World War, when a similar attempt was made to settle the Irish question. If these two conferences had failed, the fault was not the King's. In the third case, in 1931, he succeeded, and was able to anchor the ideas that were already floating in the minds both of the Prime Minister and many men and women in the country.

MacDonald's temperament needed a friend's encouragement. In the King, he found an adviser who was ready to give him a definite and straightforward answer to the questions that were worrying his over-sensitive mind. The advice was not only that of a capable man of the world, but also of someone who had lived and acted through many political crises.

Surprising as it may seem, MacDonald and the King had much in common. Both were traditionalists. For the King, it was the tradition of a routine that never varied, and was founded on the established habits of a long line of constitutional sovereigns and the rigid training of the Royal Navy. For MacDonald, it was the romance of the past blending with the confusing present and the misty future. MacDonald required the sure and certain support that the solid royal background could give him. There was nothing snobbish in his attitude. It was far less incongruous than Chatham's obsequiousness to George II. MacDonald's traditional respect for the historic Crown was all the deeper for his personal respect for its actual wearer. It was indeed fortunate that the first Labour Prime Minister was able to prove by his friendly relations with the King, that the Crown was much more than an aristocratic perquisite.

King George was, in fact, both by character and training, supremely fitted to play to the full his constitutional role in the new chapter that began in 1910 and came to a climax in 1931. To add to his influence, he was fortunate in his two most intimate advisers, Stamfordham and Wigram. Both were not only paragons among private secretaries, but men of singleness of purpose and untiring energy who never failed to keep their master in contact with the main currents of public opinion. Of Stamfordham's wisdom I had seen many evidences when I was Secretary of State for Air in the Bonar Law and the first two Baldwin Governments. I remembered particularly the part that

he played at the time of Bonar Law's resignation in 1923. He
had then made it his business to collect the best available opinion
on the question of the succession. It was Bridgeman's advice that
chiefly influenced him in advising the King to send for Baldwin
rather than Curzon. I was flattered at the time when he asked
my opinion; it was symptomatic of the care that he took over all
his duties, that he went to the trouble of consulting, amongst many
others, one of the younger Ministers. For more than twenty years
he served his master with a loyalty and skill that could not be
surpassed. At the time of which I am writing, he had just died, and
had been succeeded by Clive Wigram, who had for some years
held the post of Assistant Private Secretary.

Wigram was indeed the ideal successor to this remarkable
man. Both of them had entered the royal service on their own
merits. Bigge had become known to Queen Victoria as an able
gunner officer who had been the close friend of the Prince Imperial. Wigram, one of the remarkable public servants produced
by the Indian Army, had been introduced to the Prince of Wales
in 1904 by Sir Walter Lawrence. The plans were then being
made for the Prince's first visit to India, and Lawrence was asked
to be the chief of the royal staff. His one condition for accepting
the offer was that he should have " a certain Wigram " for his
assistant. " Who is this wonderful Wigram? " asked the Prince.
Lawrence answered that he had been one of Curzon's aides-de-
camp, and had won golden opinions for his efficiency. The
Prince agreed, and from that day until the King's death in 1936
Wigram was his inseparable companion, adviser and friend.

Master and secretary had the same direct and normal outlook
upon the world. Both were ready to state their views simply and
vigorously. Both took the most methodical pains in carrying out
their duties. Wigram was especially valuable in keeping contact
with life outside the Palace. He was at home and at his ease in
many worlds. Being a first-class athlete, he was in touch with all
the principal phases of British sport and athletics, never missing,
for instance, a Cup Final or a Test match at Lord's. As a keen
soldier, he was the intimate friend of the service chiefs and many
regimental officers. Popular with politicians of the Left as well as
the Right, and no less popular in London society, he could quickly
draw upon any channel of information that would be useful to
the King. Even more fully than Stamfordham, he realised the

need of the most intimate liaison between Buckingham Palace and Whitehall. There were few days in the week when he would not be found in Downing Street or Whitehall, gathering on all sides information from Ministers and officials. Under his dispensation the King's private office ceased to be an exclusive corner of the Palace, and became one of the most important links in the whole chain of Government. True, however, to the spirit as well as the letter of the Constitution, it was never permitted by master or secretary to encroach upon the preserves of Parliamentary Government.

As in his golf and his tennis, Wigram never put a foot wrong. Trusted by his master, and the friend of all sorts and conditions of men and women, he played a part in public life that was all the more effective for its complete loyalty to the King and its no less complete indifference to any personal advantage. It was indeed fortunate that he was at hand when the novel experience of the first National Government was on trial.

It was the men whom I have just described who were the chief actors in the drama of 1931. Two other well-known names might have been expected on the playbill. Yet neither Lloyd George nor Churchill, whose dramatic talent would have found ample scope in the unwinding of the plot, took part in the performance. The reason was that both were out of favour with the public. Lloyd George had frittered away his great position in fractious quarrels and at this time was laid low by a severe operation. Churchill, who had broken with Baldwin and his colleagues over India, was lost in the political wilderness. No one even suggested that they should be associated in any way with what was happening. Providence had probably been kind. Neither of them would have fitted into the MacDonald-Baldwin-Samuel combination. Providence must also have had another motive for keeping Churchill out of the play. If he had taken part in it in 1931, there might have been no alternative leader for the country in 1940.

CHAPTER III

The Round Table Conference

WITH the formation of the National Government I found myself installed in one of the old-established offices of Whitehall. In my five years at the Air Ministry I had spent much of my time and energy in meeting the attacks of the many critics who wished to abolish it. At the India Office, my task was very different. In an atmosphere steeped in tradition the need was to keep the peace rather than to fight, to harmonise the Parliamentary democracy of London with the bureaucracy of Delhi, to reconcile the Conservative demand for security with the repeated promises of self-government to India, and to mitigate the communal bitterness that obstructed at every turn political and social progress in India. Never was any Minister given a more inspiring opportunity, nor faced with a longer list of tangled questions.

It was fortunate that I already had some knowledge of Indian affairs. As long before as 1922 I had been pushed into Indian controversies. It was the time when the Lloyd George Coalition was obviously crumbling. Of the many causes of discontent that shook the Government, anxiety over India was then one of the most acute. The Rowlatt Act for the suppression of terrorism, the Amritsar debate over General Dyer's order to fire on the mob, the resignation of Edwin Montagu, the second Secretary of State to resign within four years, and, not least, the failure to attract new recruits to the Indian Civil Service, had irritated and excited both the Right and the Left. It looked, indeed, as if the machine of government in India would break down for want of the political support to direct it and the manpower to work it. The Services upon which the whole system depended were running down at an alarming rate. Many of the older officials, fearing the uncertainties of the future, were prematurely retiring on pension, and young recruits were not coming forward to fill the many vacancies in the *cadre*. Something had to be done at once to reassure the schools and universities that produced the candidates. It was accordingly arranged by Peel, the Secretary of State, and Winterton, the Under-Secretary, that Lloyd George should make a speech on the Appropriation Bill to encourage the Services, and that I, as an active back-bench member, should start the debate and create the background for the Prime Minister's intervention. The India Office having provided me with the details of the case, I made my speech in accordance with the plan. Not so Lloyd George, who, in his newly-stirred emotion for the Indian Civil Service, let himself go, and describing the Services as the " steel frame " within which the Government was set, delighted the die-hards with a speech that sounded like Kipling adapted to the House of Commons. Whilst Indian opinion was outraged, his bold words undoubtedly helped recruitment; they left me, however, with an even stronger feeling than I had before that he was strangely insensitive to the atmosphere of India, and scarcely less out of touch with the general feeling in the House of Commons. The debate, however, gave me a new and lasting interest in Indian questions that, during the next nine years, I was able to extend in several directions.

First, for example, in 1926, after I became Secretary of State for Air, when I was able to start the air service from London, and to open it with my wife, by making with her the first civil air flight ever made from Europe to India.

Next, in the autumn of 1929, during the controversy over Irwin's notable statement on Dominion Status. This almost forgotten incident is worth describing not only for the light that it throws upon the opinion of the time, but for the effect that it subsequently had on British politics.

Irwin was a friend of many years' standing whose serene career I had always admired. His striking personality, easy and distinguished manners, human and humane outlook on life, had, since his Oxford days, marked him out for great positions. Essentially a peacemaker, it was his mission as Viceroy to humanise the Government of India after Reading's chapter of rigid cere-mony and cautious legalism. It was typical of him that almost his first word to his military secretary had been " we are in India to keep our tempers." The overriding need at the time was for Indians as well as British to take an active part in the next constitutional advance. The appointment of the Simon Commission in 1927 for considering the next step had made this need more than ever urgent. For reasons good or bad Birkenhead, the Secretary of State, had chosen for the inquiry a small Parliamentary body of seven members taken exclusively from the two Houses. Indians deeply resented their exclusion from an inquiry that affected their whole future. Irwin, therefore, had not only to soothe their irritated nerves, but to recreate some measure of Indian goodwill towards any new proposals. Gandhi, in particular, needed to be convinced of our sincerity, if Congress, the only organised political force in India, was to be diverted from its policy of frontal opposition.

Montagu's famous declaration of August 20, 1917, upon which every subsequent proposal had been based, seemed clear enough. "The policy of His Majesty's Government with which the Government of India are in complete accord is that of the increasing association of Indians in every branch of the administration and the gradual development of self-governing institutions with a view to the progressive realisation of responsible government in India as an integral part of the British Empire." To Indian politicians, however, convinced that they could and should govern their own country at once, it left the immediate future in obscurity. Every word of the formula was scrutinised with the ingenuity of medieval schoolmen. What was meant by the ' progressive realisation of responsible government '? Why had Lord Curzon changed the original draft of ' self-government ' into ' responsible government '? What was the difference between responsible government and Dominion status? Hailey, the ablest of the Viceroy's advisers, had unintentionally deepened Indian suspicions by speaking in the Legislative Assembly of possible gradations of Dominion status, and had quoted Southern Rhodesia as a Dominion of limited scope.

There was a further reason for some pronouncement by the Viceroy. The Simon Commission, aided by the Central Indian Committee composed of representative Indians, was nearing the end of its work, and although Congress was threatening a renewal of civil disobedience, there were signs of a desire amongst influential Indians to co-operate in the making of the new constitution. It seemed wise to encourage this movement by a clearer statement of British intentions. There followed, therefore, a series of discussions between the Viceroy, Simon and the Prime Minister as to whether such a statement should be made, if so, in what form, and whether the terms of reference of the Commission should be extended to include the question of an All-India Federation of which the Indian States would form a part. The result was general agreement on the extension of the Commission's terms of reference and on the proposal of a Round Table Conference to include Indians. As to the statement on Dominion Status, Simon, who at first seemed ready to accept it, finally came down definitely against it. Reading and Lloyd George, who were also consulted, were even more strongly opposed to it. Baldwin, however, supported Irwin. He implicitly trusted the Viceroy's judgment, and his natural instincts were always more liberal on Indian questions than those of the two Liberal leaders.

MacDonald ignored the Liberal opposition, and the statement was made on October 31, 1929, after Irwin's return to India from his discussions in London. It took the form of an official communiqué to the Indian *Gazette*. The governing sentence came after a reference to the Montagu-Chelmsford reforms.

" In view of the doubts which have been expressed both in Great Britain and in India regarding the interpretation to be placed on the intentions of the British Government in enacting the Statute of 1919, I am authorised on behalf of His Majesty's Government to state clearly that in their judgment it is implicit in the declaration of 1917 that the natural issue of India's constitutional progress as there contemplated is the attainment of Dominion Status."

These words, that seemed to me unobjectionable, started an explosion that left a lasting mark on British and Indian politics for many years. Whilst their effect was excellent in India, in Great Britain the use of the sacred and ritual phrase of Dominion Status became the shibboleth that divided Churchill from Baldwin, and the diehards from the main body of the Conservative Party. The two lawyers, Birkenhead and Reading, were horrified at a layman's use of words that had acquired an exact and legal meaning in the Statute of Westminster. How, they asked, could India, with its communal differences, its many languages and religions, its Indian States and British Indian Provinces, and last but not least, its inability to defend itself, ever become a Dominion after the manner of Canada, Australia and South Africa? The Conservative Shadow Cabinet was at once summoned. We met in an uncomfortable room in the Conservative offices in Palace Chambers. Criticism of the statement, started by Birkenhead and supported by Austen Chamberlain, at once became very bitter. Baldwin obviously approved of Irwin's action. He had, in fact, already agreed with it in principle at the time of the discussions between Irwin, Simon and MacDonald. He had not, however, then seen the actual words in their final form, and when MacDonald sent them to him, he was already on his way to his annual cure at Aix, and could not or would not give them his careful attention. His answer, therefore, to MacDonald was a perfunctory agreement provided that Simon also agreed. Mac-Donald and Benn, the Secretary of State, thereupon authorised the Viceroy to make the statement without obtaining Simon's approval. Not unnaturally, Simon was greatly annoyed. Baldwin also had been placed in a difficulty. His condition had been ignored, but none the less, as he fully approved of the statement, he had no intention of repudiating it. All that he could do in the circumstances was to sit back, listen to Birkenhead's scathing criticisms, and obtain a letter from MacDonald in which it was made clear that the Viceroy's words meant no change in British policy. I also failed to see anything either new or revolutionary in the statement, and I took two early opportunities in the House of Commons to pay a tribute to the Viceroy's wisdom.[1]

Soon afterwards, after more than two years of exhaustive work, the Simon Report was published in two instalments on June 10 and June 24, 1930. The first volume contained a superb survey of Indian conditions. Simon himself wrote most of it, though I gathered that he was greatly helped by Attlee and Findlater Stewart. The second volume contained the recommendations. Was it the complexity of the problems, or the political conditions of the time, or the extreme caution of the seven members of the Commission that left several questions unanswered? Whatever was the reason, the recommendations failed to give a definite lead on more than one critical question and to satisfy any substantial body of Indian opinion. In British

[1] December 18, 1929. May 20, 1939.

circles their immediate effect was to strengthen the widely held belief that responsible government in the Provinces should be tried out before it was extended to the centre. My correspondence with Irwin made me doubt from the first whether reforms that did no more than grant provincial autonomy could satisfy an Indian demand for full equality of status. Baldwin, who had no doubts at all, was convinced that if we were to keep India within the Commonwealth, we must be prepared to go much further and faster than most of his colleagues were ready to agree. It was no doubt because we thought alike, that he asked me to be one of the Conservative representatives on the Round Table Conference.

The Conference, consisting of 89 delegates, 57 from British India, 16 from the Indian States, and 16 representatives of the Government and the Opposition in the two Houses, met in the following November and was opened by King George V in St. James's Palace. The Conservative delegation, Peel, Zetland, Oliver Stanley and myself at once met the principal Indian representatives. It was immediately clear to us that any slow-motion plan of gradual advance was impracticable. A complete change had come over the picture during the delegates' voyage from India to England. Someone, no one knew exactly who it was, had started the idea of an All-India Federation, not as a shadowy ideal, but as the basis of an Indian constitution to be established at once. Liberals, Princes, Hindus, Moslems, Sikhs, Untouchables, were irresistibly swept along in the new tide, and when they arrived in London, left us in no doubt that the Simon plan of provincial autonomy, however wise in theory, was impracticable without some measure of responsibility at the centre. Whilst I agreed generally with the Indian view, I could not be blind to the formidable difficulties in the way of setting up a responsible government for a sub-continent of many races and religions, and I pointed them out as clearly as I could in the principal committee of the Conference. My arguments seemed only to strengthen the Indian demand, and to prove to me that there was not a single one of the 89 Indian delegates who was prepared to accept the main Simon recommendation without simultaneous changes in the central government. The Princes, in particular, stated in so many words that they would only federate with a responsible Indian Government. I immediately insisted with both Baldwin and my Conservative colleagues on the significance of a new and unexpected development, that had not been contemplated in the Simon Report or in the despatch of the Government of India that had commented upon it. The Shadow Cabinet of the Opposition, composed of all the principal ex-Ministers, had not met since the controversy over Irwin's speech. In its stead, there were frequent meetings of a small Business Committee to which Baldwin invited Chamberlain, Churchill, Hailsham, Peel, Oliver Stanley and myself. It was to this committee that I reported the movements of the Conference, and argued in favour of accepting the demand of an All-India Federation. I developed my views in a memorandum in which I tried to show the advantages of federation and the kind of safeguards that were needed to ensure its security. Churchill greatly resented any suggestions of responsibility at the centre, however carefully safeguarded, and it was soon evident that he would not remain a member of a committee that accepted my view and supported federation. This was the origin of his breach with Baldwin, and his relentless opposition to the Government of India Act.

As I was one of the principal participants in the battle over India that raged from the day on which he left the Business Committee in 1931 to the final passage of the India Act in 1935, I am not an impartial judge of his action. None the less, I may perhaps make two comments. From the point of view of India, the consequences were altogether bad. His formidable opposition embittered a constitutional discussion that should have been kept free of recrimination. It delayed by many months and perhaps years the passing of the Act, when every day's delay compromised the chance of settlement. If the Act had reached the Statute Book in 1933 instead of 1935, I am convinced that it would have been in effective operation before the war started. Even more serious than delay was the atmosphere created by years of Parliamentary wrangle, during which Churchill was constantly attacking and I as constantly defending the safeguards in the Bill, with the inevitable result that Indians came to believe that instead of giving them the fullest possible opportunity for obtaining responsible government, we were intent upon tying them up in a strait-jacket.

So much for the immediate result of Churchill's breach with

Baldwin on India. But there was a further consequence that, though it does not affect this chapter, had a lasting effect upon British history. The breach over India drove Churchill into opposition during the next seven years. Whilst I do not attempt to assess the loss and gain of this long sojourn in the wilderness, the outstanding fact remains that his action, by separating him from his Conservative colleagues, left him free and untrammelled to fight his great campaign of resistance to Hitler, and to become, amidst general acclamation, the alternative Prime Minister when Chamberlain resigned. Was Providence redressing the balance that had been grievously shaken by his Indian obsessions by throwing into the scales the overwhelming weight of his war services?

After this aside I must return to the main story. The Round Table Conference that opened on November 12, 1930, held three sessions, and continued in being until the end of 1932. The personnel varied from year to year. Jinnah, for instance, came to the first two sessions but not to the third; Gandhi only to the second; the Princes to the first two, but only their Ministers to the last. Changes of this kind did not, however, alter the character of the experiment. For the first time in history we were trying to work out, in full co-operation with representative Indians, the details of a constitution that was sooner or later to give India full self-government. So far from clinging to power, we were actively assisting in the ending of the British Raj. All the skill and experience of Whitehall and Delhi were engaged in producing a gigantic plan that, when it was carried out, would mean the end of the careers of the British officials who were helping to make it. Never once, however, during all our discussions was there any sign of official obstruction to what we were doing. Indeed, as I shall show later, Hailey, the ablest amongst all his civilian colleagues, was one of our most valued helpers in finding methods for making the great change. Could there be a better example both of self-abnegation, and devotion to the India that they had served, than this willingness to make ready the way for their successors in power?

The Conference started like most large conferences in some confusion. MacDonald and Benn, the Secretary of State, had been so anxious to leave a free field to the Indian delegates that they had not prepared a detailed agenda. It was in these first days that

Sankey, the Lord Chancellor, was able to give free play to his talent for compromise and conciliation. His appearance in the various committees, with a shawl round his shoulders and preceded by an usher from the Lord Chancellor's office carrying a rug, for he was extremely nervous of draughts, created the atmosphere of a motherly talk round the fireside, rather than the disputations of a Constituent Assembly.

The keynote of the Conference was at once struck by the Princes who, one after another, declared their newly-found belief in All-India Federation. Amongst them were several remarkable personalities. The most notable was Bikaner. When he spoke in vigorous and almost too fluent English, his fine figure and resonant voice dominated the Federal Structure Committee. His record, both in peace and war, had marked him out as one of the leading figures in the British Empire. I had already seen some of his achievements in a State that, before his time, had been little better than Sind desert, when I went with the Viceroy to one of his famous shooting parties in 1927. The staff work with which he had then managed a hundred and fifty guests and arranged the morning drives, at which over five thousand Imperial sand grouse were killed, had left on my mind the most vivid impression of a veritable Napoleon of organisation. The Princes could not have had a more impressive spokesman for the Federal proposal. When I listened to him, I was more than ever convinced that the future of the central government was not only the cardinal question of the Conference, but that an All-India Federation was a practicable proposition.

It was the Hindu intellectuals from British India who put both substance and theory into the Federal conception. Three of them, Sapru, Sastri and Jayakar, amazed me by their subtlety of thought and their power to express it in perfect and eloquent English. They seemed to me to be the lineal descendants of the best type of our own Victorian liberals. I was told that their political importance in India was very small. None the less, I remained convinced that their indirect influence was very great, and that just as they had made it possible to work the 1919 reforms, so their support was indispensable for any new Constitution.

On the Moslem side of the table, the two outstanding leaders were the Aga Khan and Zafrulla Khan. Of the first, so much has

already been written that there is little new that I can add to the
description of one of the strangest and most remarkable personalities of contemporary history. Pope, Prince, accomplished
man of two worlds, eastern and western, equally well known on
the racecourse, in the casinos of Europe, and the mosques of
Africa and India, a consummate diplomat and an untiring peacemaker, the Aga at once took a foremost place at the Round Table.
His fellow Moslems made him their leader, and the Hindus joined
with them in choosing him as the chief spokesman of the whole
Indian delegation.

Later, I was to see more of him after I became Secretary of
State. It was then that I was able to recommend the rare distinction of the Crown of India for the Begum, his mother, and to
arrange for her journey to London to receive it at the hands of
the King. If the son was notable, this old lady was unique. A
Princess of the Ruling House of Persia, she was as astute as she
was devout, following, and helping to control from her house in
Bombay, both the spiritual and mundane affairs of the Grand
Council of the Ismaili Community. Her strict habits of Purdah
and her great age, for she was already nearly ninety, created
difficult problems for her first journey to Europe. We had, for
instance, to arrange for a Purdah aeroplane, and when she
arrived in London, the only visits that she permitted herself were
to Buckingham Palace and our house. Never did my wife Lady
Templewood and I have a more enthralling visitor. Small and
fragile, heavily veiled, but keenly alert to the world outside Purdah,
she kept us spellbound with her lively conversation. Of her son, she
told us much, particularly of his education. His long lineage from
Fatima and Ali, the Prophet's daughter and son-in-law, and his
high status as the ecumenical head of a widely-spread religious
community, had inspired her with the wish to make him the best-
educated man in the world. She had accordingly chosen for him
the most accomplished teachers that she could find in both the
east and the west. To one of them, a German Jesuit, she testified
her special gratitude for the stimulus that he had given to her
son's thirst for knowledge.

Soon after her London visit she returned to Bombay, and
falling ill, decided in accordance with the practice of devout
Ismailis, to be taken to Iraq in order to die in the sacred city of
Nejef. Death overtook her in Baghdad, and ended the long life

of one of the most remarkable women of our time. So remarkable, in fact, that I must be excused if I have interjected an account of her into my description of the Round Table Conference. It has not been irrelevant. Her son, thanks to the training and education that he had received through his mother's wisdom, proved himself well equipped to take the lead among his Indian colleagues.

The other notable Moslem, Zafrulla Khan, was of very different origin and outlook. Zafrulla was a successful lawyer from the Punjab who, in spite of the fact that, being a member of the Amadiya Sect, he was never fully acceptable to many orthodox Moslems, soon acquired an exceptional influence in the Conference by his clear mind and grasp of complicated detail. It was he and the Aga who contributed most to our discussions from the Moslem side of the table. As Jinnah sat with them, it might have been imagined that he would have given the lead to his delegation. It is true that he intermittently took a prominent part in the debates, but many of us could never follow the movements of his volatile mind. He never seemed to wish to work with anyone. Was he in favour of All-India Federation? We could not tell for certain, though it is worth remembering that he never then suggested the division of India and the creation of Pakistan. Was he in favour of provincial autonomy without change in the centre? Sometimes he gave us the impression that he did not wish to go beyond provincial autonomy, and at other times, that he demanded responsible government both in the centre and in the Provinces. It was this elusiveness that made it difficult for us to co-operate with him, or for him to give any clear lead to his Moslem colleagues.

Throughout the discussions the Indian delegates showed a remarkable knowledge of the almost countless questions involved in the framing of a constitution for four hundred and fifty million human beings of many races, languages and religions. The debates were often tedious. This is always the case when delegates feel that they must do full justice to their clients' briefs. None the less, the Round Table in St. James's Palace was the symbol of a common purpose. Was it the joint feeling that the great achievement of a united India must be preserved with its efficient administration, its incorruptible officials, its impartial justice and its religious tolerance? Whatever was the reason of the success of the first session of the Conference, our deliberations undoubtedly showed a large measure of agreement amongst the delegates in favour of a united All-India Federation. We were, therefore, able to recommend the general lines of a new Constitution based on full autonomy in the Provinces, a responsible Federal Government at the centre, and certain safeguards, which we hoped would be transitory, to ensure them. The vague idea of Federation, that had first floated through the ship that brought the Indian delegates to London, had been given substance and form in a series of concrete proposals.

As I read again the notes that I made at the time, I have since wondered whether we should not have been wiser to have followed the precedent of the Indian Round Table for dealing with the federation of Rhodesia. For Asians and Africans alike, it is status that chiefly matters. Free discussion between equals is the best way of creating an atmosphere of friendly understanding, even when full agreement is unattainable. The long discussions between East and West, Moslem and Hindu, Brahmin and Untouchable, gathered round the table in St. James's Palace, were a convincing example of the value of friendly debate.

Having made considerable progress, the Conference adjourned on January 19, 1931, until the following September 7.

CHAPTER IV

Gandhi

IT WAS within a few days of the reassembly of the Conference that I had become Secretary of State for India in the newly-formed National Government. Irwin had already brought about a dramatic change in Gandhi's attitude. Hitherto, Gandhi and Congress had not only refused to take part in the Conference, but had inspired and directed a formidable campaign of Civil Disobedience that was endangering the whole future of Indian reform. The boycott of British goods, the non-payment of taxes, and the indirect encouragement of terrorist outrages showed only too clearly their power to obstruct any constitutional settlement by agreement. The Viceroy and his advisers felt that a great and perhaps final effort should be made to bring Gandhi to the Round Table, and induce Congress to co-operate. Irwin possessed the qualities that were needed for a reconciliator. Alone of the Viceroys who had dealings with Gandhi, he saw the springs that gave the Mahatma his astounding power. His own upbringing had taught him where to look. His father, the second Lord Halifax, sensitive, affectionate and alert, was an ascetic after the manner of Ignatius Loyola, deeply religious, socially attractive, transparently sincere. These were the qualities without which it was impossible to understand the man whom Churchill despised as a "half-naked Fakir."[1] I do not know whether Irwin knew that he had inherited many of his father's qualities for dealing with a

[1] It was "also alarming and also nauseating to see Mr. Gandhi, a seditious Middle Temple lawyer, now posing as a fakir of a type well-known in the East, striding half-naked up the steps of the Vice-regal Palace, while he is still organizing and conducting a defiant campaign 'of civil disobedience, to parley on equal terms with the representative of the King-Emperor." (Speech to the West Essex Conservative Association. February 23, 1931).

man who was ascetic, saint and astute politician. I imagine that being by nature very modest, he did not. He did, however, decide to meet Gandhi face to face, and discuss with him patiently and simply the differences that were keeping them apart. The meeting that took place in the second half of February, 1931, lasted for three weeks. The very thought of the Viceroy closeted in Delhi with the leader of the civil disobedience campaign infuriated the diehards, whether Conservative or Liberal, and gravely disturbed many experienced Indian officials. The irritation and impatience grew with every day that the conversations continued. Indeed, so great was the prejudice against the talks that the full scope of the agreement that ended them on March 5 never received due credit. The many days of discussion in which Gandhi had welcomed the chance of setting out all his grievances had, in fact, resulted in his acceptance of a place at the Round Table when the Conference resumed its sittings, and an undertaking to call off civil disobedience, and the boycott of British goods.

These two results of Irwin's personal intervention created a more favourable atmosphere for the second meeting of the Conference in September, and counteracted to some extent Indian suspicions of a Conservative Secretary of State. It was obvious that since the outburst of the diehards against Irwin's pronouncement on Dominion Status, Indian opinion was suspicious of British Conservatives. Indians never fully understood that the diehards were a minority in the Conservative Party and that Baldwin's influence was much greater than Churchill's. It was, therefore, necessary for me from the start of my new office to do what I could to remove this suspicion, and convince the Indian delegates that I was as strongly in favour of All-Indian Federation as any of them. It was not an easy task. On the one hand, there was an influential section of my own party watching my every word and action, lest I should surrender the essentials of power, on the other, the sensitive Indian minds that noted in an instant the least deflexion from the road to Dominion Status. The difficulties on the two fronts loomed all the larger as the day approached for Gandhi's arrival in London. Many of my Conservative friends and supporters resented his invitation to the Conference. Nor were they all reactionaries. It is difficult, more than twenty years afterwards, to appreciate the depth of feeling that the murders of Indian civilians and policemen had excited against the author of the programme of civil disobedience. Whilst himself disapproving of rioting and murder, the movement that he had started had undoubtedly undermined the respect for law and order, and encouraged, however unintentionally, many irresponsible young men and women to attack officials who were patiently and loyally carrying out their duties. It was not surprising that British resentment was deep and bitter against the man who seemed to be mainly responsible for these hideous crimes.

How was I to act in face of this widespread feeling? What should be my attitude to the man who was hated as fiercely as he was loved? How was I to obtain his invaluable help in the making of the Constitution without turning against me not only the Moslems and the Untouchables who regarded him with unconcealed suspicion, but the many Conservatives who still viewed with doubt and dislike the changes that I believed to be necessary for India? These were some of the most difficult questions that I have ever had to face in half a century of public life.

The answers had not always been made easier by Gandhi's many friends in England. The fervour and veneration with which they received their patron saint had turned the spotlight of public attention on to everything that he said or did. Some of them were not always discriminating in their attentions. Wishing for instance, to supply him with goat's milk, they were reported to have bought him two he-goats. In the very delicate situation in which I found myself I would have preferred quiet and confidential talks without any publicity. As it was, our meetings were bound to be known to the world, and to give rise to every kind of surmise that would outrage the feelings of the Right, who regarded him as a rebel and a traitor, and excite the fears of the Left, who suspected me of obstructing the mission of a saint.

In the India Office we had made every possible arrangement for his stay in London. Rooms were made ready for him in a West End hotel, and two detectives posted from Scotland Yard to watch over his safety and prevent his being annoyed by the crowds of sightseers. When we heard that he preferred to stay with his friends in Kingsley Hall, Bow, we readily agreed, and arranged for his regular transport between the East and the West End. In Bow, he lived in the midst of a small community of pietists who, though bound by no rule, lived a life of self-denial and good works. Neither they nor he altered the strict habits of their lives during the three months that he was in London. Their social and religious work continued as before, but with the added interest of Gandhi's share in it. He had his fixed hours of prayer, the first at three o'clock in the morning, and the second at half-past six in the evening, his silent day every week, and his early walk at six o'clock in the morning. Neither the social life of London, even when Charlie Chaplin visited him in Bow, and Bernard Shaw talked to him in a Knightsbridge flat, nor the work of the Round Table Conference was allowed to change his daily routine. It was typical of his regular habits that he would never miss a meeting of the Conference, even on his ' silent day,' but that he would attend without speaking and occasionally pass me a note to explain the way that his mind was working.

This was the man who, whatever his opponents might say to the contrary, held one of the master keys to the book of the Constitution that we were trying to write. How was a Conservative Secretary of State, surrounded by all the conventional proprieties of Whitehall and Westminster, to negotiate with this holy man, this Staretz in *khaddar*, who seemed more interested in his simple friends in Bow than in the constitutional discussions in St. James's Palace?

Gandhi, whose manners were superb,[1] at once asked to see me. I imagine that, having given up hope of any help from the British Conservatives, he made the request principally out of politeness. I looked forward to the visit with some trepidation. It was a very cold autumn afternoon when my magnificent Royal Marine messenger showed him into the Secretary of State's room in the India Office. He was in his habitual *khaddar*, and looked even smaller and more bent than his pictures had shown him. His sharp, penetrating eyes seemed to take immediate possession of the whole room in a glance. His bony knees and toothless mouth would have made him look ridiculous if they had not been completely overshadowed by the dominating impression of a great personality. There was fortunately no moment of embarrassment between us, or any difficulty in starting the conversation. He was

[1] As a young man, when he first visited London, he bought himself a frock-coat and learnt the violin and dancing in order to share the tastes of his English friends.

shivering with cold in clothes that could not have been more
unsuitable for an English autumn, and I had a magnificent fire
ready at hand. It was this fire of coals that warmed his stiff knees
and thawed the ice-pack that separated us. From his pleasure in
the fire we passed easily to the leading question of his co-operation.
I was clear in my own mind that I was not prepared to obtain it
by false pretences, and that there must, therefore, be no reservations or equivocations in what I said to him. As I spoke, I
remembered Dostoievsky's description of the visit of the Kara-
mazov family to the Staretz Zosima, and the ignominious result
of their attempts to hide their motives from a very astute holy man.
I was determined not to make the same mistake. Accordingly, I
told him as clearly and definitely as I could that I sincerely wished
to see responsible government in India, that I believed that I could
have a Bill passed that would make this possible, but that in view
of British public opinion, Conservative anxieties in Parliament,
and not least, Communal fears in India, I could not promise
Gandhi or anyone else immediate Dominion Status. I went on
to say that law and order must be maintained if there was to be
any constitutional advance, and that terrorism was as fatal to
Indian aspirations as it was to British understanding. Having
done my best to remove any cause of future misunderstanding
between us, I ended by saying: " You may very well think that
there is so great a gulf between your demand for immediate independence and my gradual approach to Dominion Status that it is
a waste of your time to go on talking to me. If you do, I shall
perfectly understand, and certainly not regard it as discourteous
if you do not visit me again to continue our conversation. If,
however, you still think it is worth while, I am always ready
and willing to see you, and I shall welcome further discussions
within the framework that I have just described."

Gandhi at once responded to my approach. He was obviously
relieved that there was to be no make-believe between us. With
an eye and mind as pointed as a needle he penetrated in a
moment any sham or imitation. More than once in London he
had already shown his impatience with some of his over-zealous
admirers who said that they agreed with him when he knew that
they did not. Others had tried to convert him. " I am so well
accustomed to it," he observed after meeting Lloyd George and
Lady Astor, " people of so many religions have tried to convert

me to their own. It is very good of them, of course. It has
helped me a great deal because they all quote the finest things in
their religion; they give me the greatest literature. I get
acquainted with its best interpretation, and that is very good for
me. I learn a great deal that way." In my case he was relieved
to find a Secretary of State who did not pretend to agree with
him when in reality he did not, or to convert him to some new
belief when he had no intention of being converted. The result
was a series of very frank discussions between us, and the start
of a friendship, shown by many letters, all of them written in a
beautiful flowing hand, that continued until his tragic death.

Shortly after this first meeting there was to be an afternoon
party at Buckingham Palace for all the Round Table delegates.
Would Gandhi go to it? And if he accepted, how would the
leader of civil disobedience be received by King George V? The
answers to both these questions were in some doubt. To clear
up the second, I asked the King for an Audience. His Majesty's
reaction was much as I had expected. " What! Have this rebel
fakir in the Palace after he has been behind all these attacks on
my loyal officers? " Although this outburst was the first answer
to my question, it was by no means the King's last word. Having
let off steam, he started to discuss the arrangements for the party,
to which he at once assumed that Gandhi would be invited. It
was only towards the end of the Audience that he had a slight
return of his earlier irritation when he protested against having
" the little man " in the Palace with " no proper clothes on, and
bare knees." However, His Majesty was finally mollified, and
an invitation without any conditions as to clothes was sent to
Gandhi, and it was immediately accepted.

It was arranged that at the party I was to fetch up Gandhi
at a suitable moment for presentation to the King. When the
time came, Gandhi's *khaddar* made it easy for me to find him
amongst the black coats and ceremonial clothes of the delegates.
When I presented him, there was a difficult moment. The King
was obviously thinking of Gandhi's responsibility for civil disobedience. However, when they were once started, the King's
simple sincerity and Gandhi's beautiful manners combined to
smooth the course of the conversation, though more than once
I became nervous when the King looked resentfully at Gandhi's
knees. When the conversation was drawing to an end, the King,

the most conscientious of monarchs, evidently thought that it was his duty to warn Gandhi of the consequences of rebellion. Just, therefore, as Gandhi was taking his leave, His Majesty could not refrain from uttering a grave warning. " Remember, Mr. Gandhi, I won't have any attacks on my Empire! " I held my breath in fear of an argument between the two. Gandhi's *savoir faire* saved the situation with a grave and deferential reply. " I must not be drawn into a political argument in Your Majesty's Palace after receiving Your Majesty's hospitality." They then took leave of each other as friendly guest and host. A very honest King, and a great diplomat, I thought to myself, and what exquisite worldly manners the unworldly possess!

In the Conference, Gandhi made three claims, each of which was fiercely contested by the majority of the other delegates. First, he asserted that Congress alone represented political India; secondly, that the Untouchables, being Hindus, could not be segregated from the main body of Hinduism; and thirdly, that Hindus and Moslems could and should live together in a united India without separate electorates and special safeguards for minorities. His chief opponent was Dr. Ambedkar, the representative of the Depressed Classes, who insisted that the millions of Untouchables needed separate constituencies and rigid protection. The two men never ceased to dispute with each other. Ambedkar was a very able advocate of the Old Bailey type, fluent, audacious and aggressive. Gandhi's reaction must have intensely irritated him. Completely indifferent as to whether he was repeating what he had already said many times before, or as to whether his audience was bored or hostile, Gandhi would go over the whole of his case in a low voice, and with his head bent down so that it was often difficult to hear him. The hour brought no stop to his flood of words. Once, I remember his beginning a two-hours' speech at one o'clock in the morning.

It was clear from the first day of the Conference that the Communal question would dominate all our discussions. As the plans for self-government began to take form, Communal fears and suspicions became more acute, so acute, in fact, that at one time the Moslem delegates seemed anxious to make sure of the Provinces in which they had a majority, and to leave unreformed the Central Government in which federation would place them in a minority. The diehards were quick to make capital out of this fundamental breach in the plan of All-India Federation. Without Communal agreement, or at least a Communal *modus vivendi*, the proposed reforms would be impracticable. Why, therefore, should we not postpone constitutional reform until Indians were agreed amongst themselves as to what they really wanted?

Churchill had been convinced by this argument when he came to my room in the House of Commons, to press the case for Provincial Autonomy without any change at the Centre. Whilst I would gladly have kept out of the Communal controversy and left it to Indians to settle it for themselves, I saw from what was happening in the Conference that they would never do so, and that to postpone self-government at the Centre until they were agreed, was simply a way of saying that self-government was permanently impracticable. I had, therefore, to tell him that it was not practically possible to hold up responsibility at the Centre until Indians settled their own differences.

I had also to convince MacDonald that if we wished the Conference to continue, the British Government had to intervene. Not unnaturally he was at first anxious to avoid the hornets' nest of Communal troubles. However, he soon saw the need to act, and agreed to make a statement, in which he undertook that the British Government would give a decision upon Communal electorates if the Communities failed to agree among themselves. This pledge involved a most delicate inquiry and a most dangerous decision that were certain to cause discontent in all the Communities. None the less, it was the only alternative to a breakdown of the discussions. So far, therefore, from falling back upon the policy of *divide et impera* with which we had so often been unfairly charged, we decided at great risk to build a bridge over which we hoped to bring Indians together and make it possible for ourselves to withdraw from our Imperial Raj.

For the next six months the India Office and the Government of India were, in consequence of this promise, together engaged upon what was called the ' Communal Award,' under which the 1523 seats proposed for the Provincial Assemblies were allocated to the various communities. When the details were announced in August, the inevitable criticism in India was concentrated upon two points. First, the Sikhs, a martial community with a stirring history behind them, resented Moslem predominance in the

Punjab, and Congress, personified in Gandhi, refused to accept the segregation of the Depressed Classes from the main Hindu community. Whilst nothing could be done to mollify the Sikhs, a Hindu crisis was averted by the Poona Pact between Gandhi and Ambedkar, by which the Depressed Classes, under the threat of Gandhi's ' fast unto death,' abandoned their separate electorates in exchange for double the number of seats in joint electorates. Taking into account the complexity of the insoluble problem that faced us, it may fairly be said that the Award was generally regarded as an honest attempt to break the Communal deadlock, and that it opened the way to the start of responsible government.

I must, however, go back to Gandhi, and describe what happened at the end of the Conference and after his return to India. As soon as he realised the strength of the opposition in London to his conception of a united India without safeguards for the minorities, he became very restive, and more than once looked like walking out of the Conference. I did my utmost to dissuade him. I had many talks with him that not only enabled me to have a better understanding of his mind, but gave me an interesting insight into his methods of work. As to his mind, I soon saw that it was quickly sensitive to emotional appeal. He was certainly not the relentless and scheming conspirator that many of my friends imagined. He would seem for a time completely rigid and immovable, then suddenly something would excite his feelings and make him change his mood. Time after time in his career an emotional impulse impelled him to take an unexpected step. In 1921, for instance, he called off the civil disobedience campaign within a few weeks of its starting when he heard of the massacre of the police at Chauri Chaura. He could not bear to think of the horrible sufferings of loyal men who, within their lights, were trying to do their duty. So, also, in his meeting with Irwin, it was the feeling that he liked and trusted the Viceroy, rather than any detailed arguments about constitutional reform, that made him sidetrack the official policy of Congress. It seemed also, from what he said to his friends both in London and India that he liked me, even though we often disagreed.

" Sir Samuel " (this was his description of a talk with me to one of his most faithful friends, Miss Muriel Lester) " said that he might appear to be a hard man, he might even be called in after years a bad man, but he would rather appear as hard and as black as anyone liked to declare, than that anyone should ever be able to say of him that he promised things that afterwards he failed to perform." " Ah "—these were the words that he used to me and repeated to her—" I can meet you, Sir Samuel, I shake hands with you over that. It's a point of unity between us, your truthfulness. Thank you."

His emotions had overcome his mental resistance to a Conservative Secretary of State. I believe that if I had been able to say to him: " Take Dominion Status at once without any safeguards," we should not only have found him one of our best friends, but he would immediately have offered us in return all the safeguards in the Government of India Bill and many more besides if anyone had wanted them. Of course, I could not make any such offer. My responsibility to the other Indian communities and interests made it impossible. Besides, it would have run counter to our conception of self-government as a continuing process based on actual experience, rather than a gift, settled once and for all in an Act of Parliament. In this respect, Gandhi and I represented two different outlooks. As an Eastern, his eye was on the final principle rather than on the steps to be taken to achieve it; mine, on the steps that would make the achievement possible. Agreement between East and West, whether in the field of theology or of politics, has often been compromised by the determination of one of the parties to begin at the end, and of the other to begin at the beginning. In spite, however, of this deep-rooted difference, Gandhi and I came to understand each other better in each succeeding talk.

None the less, there were inevitably several difficult moments in the discussions between a Secretary of State who was wondering how he could manœuvre a vast and contentious Bill through Parliament, and a saint who was impelled by singleness of purpose and confidence in his own divine mission to demand the full and immediate satisfaction of his claims. There was always a risk that some difference of opinion would start him on a ' fast unto death,' a sanction that he applied more than twenty times in his career. It was also difficult to keep steady the quicksilver of his mind. One morning he told me of the mental processes that led to his decisions.

> " When I wake up in the morning "—these were his words—" I say to myself, I am starting a new experiment. It may well be that I shall have to scrap the other daily experiments that I have been making. But I must go on experimenting and trying out day by day what is good."

It was this daily trial by experiment and error that accounted for much of what seemed incoherent in his attitude. For those of us who were negotiating with him, it is not surprising that this very individual outlook on the day's work made it difficult to understand the sudden changes in his opinions.

The important fact, however, was that he and I parted the best of friends at the end of the Conference. In spite of his fulminations against our offer of a Communal Award and our arguments for safeguards, he left London in a friendly mood. He had arranged to visit Rome on his return journey, not to see Mussolini, the Duce, but Signora Montessori, the woman Pope of educational reform. A few days before his departure he asked me whether he could take with him his two detectives. They had made such friends with each other in London that he wished to give them a pleasant holiday in Rome, after all the trouble that they had taken on his behalf in London. The Home Secretary readily agreed, and together the three left England. In Rome, the usual crowd of admirers gathered round the Mahatma. His stay was so short that there was no time for any set programme, least of all for press interviews. It came, therefore, as a totally unexpected shock to him when, in the ship that took him from Italy to India, he heard a wireless message from Rome describing a fictitious interview that he was said to have given to Gayda of the *Giornale d'Italia*. According to this notorious enemy of the British Empire, Gandhi had made the following declaration:

> " The Round Table Conference has been for Indians a long and slow agony. It has, however, served to make quite clear the spirit of the Indian nation and of its leaders, and to unmask the true intentions of England. He was returning to India to restart at once his struggle against England, which was to take the form of passive resistance and the boycott of British goods. He considered that the boycott would prove a powerful means of rendering more

acute the British crisis already difficult through the devaluation of the currency and unemployment."

When I heard a report of the interview, I was horrified and amazed. He had just sent me two silver watches as presents for his detectives, and a letter of friendly greeting. The threat attributed to him was so unlike his parting words to me in London that I at once telegraphed for its confirmation. The answer came from Gandhi himself, to the effect that he had made no such statement, and that the reported interview was a fake. Whilst this disclaimer brought me great relief, the harm was unfortunately done. The lie, like calumny in Don Basilio's famous song in *The Barber of Seville*, had already spread over the world, and had been accepted in London and Delhi as clear proof of Gandhi's irreconcilable opposition. " We always told you so," said the diehard critics. " We always knew that he was our bitterest enemy."

In the meanwhile, an evilly disposed Providence was destroying in India the better feeling that I had hoped we had created in London. Trouble had broken out on the North-West Frontier with the Red Shirts, Gandhi's chief Moslem supporters, while in the United Provinces the Congress organisers, who disapproved of his moves towards conciliation, had started a no-rent campaign that was already threatening the whole basis of law and order. Willingdon, who had succeeded Irwin as Viceroy, felt bound to act. The result was recourse to the Ordinances under which suspects could be summarily arrested and detained. By the time that Gandhi reached Bombay, Abdul Ghaffar Khan, the leader of the Red Shirts, was in prison in Peshawar, and Nehru, together with several of his Congress colleagues, in prison in Allahabad. The combination of the fictitious interview with the renewal of civil disobedience and the arrests that it involved, seemed to have frustrated all our efforts for peace. Gandhi, in a speech that he made in Bombay on his arrival replying to a welcome, at once announced a return to civil disobedience, on the pretext of the measures taken by the Government of India. Even so, he paid a generous tribute to the British Government in general, and to me in particular for our efforts in the Conference. These were his words:

" Whilst I could not say that the Round Table Conference or the Prime Minister's declaration has offered anything that would positively satisfy Congress, I would say that there was an honest effort on the part of the British Ministers to understand the Indian situation, although they could not appreciate the Indian viewpoint as I conceive it. . . . I am here to testify that of all the Ministers I had the privilege of meeting I found the Secretary of State for India to be an honest and frank-hearted Englishman. I had no difficulty in understanding what was at the back of his mind, and every interview with him brought me nearer to him, and we parted as the best of friends, as I did with all the other Ministers."

Willingdon had felt that he could not ignore Gandhi's threat at a time when disorder was spreading dangerously in two key provinces. He therefore ordered his arrest under a Bombay Ordinance of 1827.

So ended the effort started by Irwin and continued by me for keeping Gandhi at the Round Table. In the third session his place was empty. Thenceforth he persisted with his plans for non-co-operation, and either attacked or ignored the work of the delegates in London. When the Bill eventually passed after four years of detailed discussion, he told the Viceroy that he had never read it. His way and ours had definitely parted.

Was the Viceroy right to bring to an abrupt end the short chapter of co-operation with this elusive and potentially dangerous leader? The question raised one of the difficult problems that was always recurring in the India Office, the relation between the Secretary of State and the Viceroy, in other words, between Parliamentary government in London and bureaucratic administration in Delhi. I knew enough of Indian history to realise the danger of a clash between the two. The ghosts of Curzon and Brodrick still haunted the Secretary of State's room in Whitehall. By instinct also, I was for leaving the man on the spot the greatest possible liberty of action. The Government of India had become much too complicated to be administered from London. I was therefore very reluctant to press my views when I knew them to be contrary to the Viceroy's wishes. In this case, I was by no means sure that the Viceroy was not right. He and his Council were convinced that law and order could not be guaranteed with Gandhi at large and civil disobedience rampant over India. If I made any criticism, it would be that Willingdon did not, like

Irwin, understand Gandhi's personality, and on that account underrated his power. The arrest of " the little man," as he always called him, would, he believed, stop the trouble. He and Gandhi differed so completely from each other that it would have been a miracle if they had understood each other. On the one hand, the accomplished man of the Western world, the most engaging product of Eton, Cambridge and Westminster, in his beautifully cut grey suit and I Zingari tie, on the other, the toothless seer with his *khaddar* and spinning wheel. It was not surprising that when Gandhi asked after his arrest for a personal interview, the Viceroy refused his request, unless he first abjured civil disobedience. I would guess that Irwin would have seen him without any condition. What would then have happened, I cannot say. One thing, however, was clear. The arrest showed the difficulty of keeping together the companions of the Round Table, and at the same time maintaining law and order in India.

CHAPTER V
"The Monstrous Boat"

So MUCH for two of the horses that I was trying to ride. But there was a third, and in some ways, the most difficult to manage. There was the British Parliament, through which every detail of the new Constitution had to be steered. Although I could not yet foresee the full magnitude of the task, I already knew enough to realise that the Bill would be immensely long and complicated, and many milestones would need to be passed before I reached my journey's end. There would have to be a third session of the Round Table Conference, then a Joint Select Committee of the two Houses, and finally, the Bill itself. The task before me seemed to be almost insuperable. I comforted myself with some words from the Memoirs of Sir Philip Francis. He was describing a supper with Warren Hastings when the conversation turned upon Robinson Crusoe:

> " Hastings seemed lost in a reverie, in which I little expected that Robinson Crusoe could be concerned. At last, he gravely declared that he had often read the book with singular satisfaction, but that no passage in it had ever struck him so much as where the hero is said to have built a monstrous boat at a distance from the sea, without knowing by what means he was to convey it to the water. ' And, by jove,' said Hastings, ' the same thing has happened to myself a hundred times in my life.' "

How was I to get the monstrous boat not only to the sea, but across it to its final destination?

The first stage was to manœuvre it past the third Round Table Conference. The more clearly I saw the length of the journey, the more sure I was of the need to have my hands free for the drafting of the Bill. The Conference was therefore brought to a close after only five weeks in order that I should be able to move without delay to the next stage of a White Paper setting out the Round Table proposals, and a Joint Select Committee of both Houses to consider them.

The White Paper was circulated within three months of the ending of the Conference. It poured breath into the dry bones left by the years of continuous discussion. The two hundred paragraphs contained in it represented the maximum of agreement that it was possible to obtain between Indians and Indians and Indians and British. The drafting was a *tour de force* of the staff of the India Office, in which they were effectively helped by their colleagues in Delhi, and by Maurice Gwyer, the Treasury Solicitor in London. Without Gwyer's inexhaustible knowledge of constitutional law, the work would never have been accomplished in the time or with the same success.

In less than three weeks after the publication of the White Paper, I introduced the motion to appoint sixteen members of the House of Commons to a joint Select Committee of both Houses. In the short interval, however, I passed through many difficult moments. But before I deal with them, I must describe the office in which I was working and some of the men who were my colleagues in London and Delhi.

As soon as I took possession of the Secretary of State's delightful room overlooking the lake in St. James's Park, I felt myself in congenial surroundings. Not only did the history and tradition of the office make a warm appeal to my Conservative instincts, but there was something reassuring in the ripe experience of the staff, much of which had been gained in India at first hand.

The Permanent Under-Secretary of State was Findlater Stewart, one of the many Scots[1] who have done so much to build and govern the Empire. He had recently succeeded Arthur Hirtzel, a notable scholar for whom the Greek and Latin classics were an inspiring guide through the forest of Indian problems. Stewart's experience in Whitehall had been widened by his two years as Secretary of the Simon Commission. There was no side of Indian life that he did not understand, and no crisis in Whitehall

---

[1] Although Scottish exports had become more varied, Sir Walter Scott's remark that " the only two exports from Scotland were our cattle to Smithfield and our sons to India," had still an element of truth.

that ever ruffled his equable mind or disturbed his balanced judgment. Amongst all the many Civil Servants who have helped me in my various departments, Stewart stands out pre-eminent as a dependable counsellor and friendly colleague. No one could have fitted better than he into an office that was still filled with the memories of the East India Company and the Scots who had served it.

If Stewart was the *beau idéal* of a civilian adviser, my two Parliamentary Under-Secretaries represented the best of both Houses of Parliament. Lothian came to me as one of the Liberals who joined the National Government in 1931. I was offered the choice between him and a well-known party politician. I had no doubt in my mind as to which I should choose. Round Table Conferences and the framing of a Constitution for four hundred and fifty million human beings were certain to bring out the finest of his great talents, and I knew from our many years of personal friendship how well we should work together. Indians of all sorts and conditions liked him, whilst his years with Milner in South Africa and his subsequent studies of Commonwealth problems had given him an exceptional knowledge of constitutional theory and practice. Three special inquiries in India were about this time contemplated in the Round Table discussions, the first, into the franchise, the second into the financial relations between the Federal Centre and the Federal Units, and the third, into the question of the financial position of the Indian States in a Federation. On my recommendation, Eustace Percy took charge of the Financial Committee, J. C. C. Davidson of the States inquiry, and Lothian, the vast and intractable problem of the franchise. The result of his Committee's investigations was a proposal to enfranchise about 27 per cent of the adult population of India. More valuable, however, than the specific proposals was the sympathetic atmosphere that his engaging personality and obvious sympathy created wherever he went. It was indeed a heavy blow to me when he resigned his office at the time that Samuel and the Liberal Ministers left the MacDonald Government over Imperial Preference. Lothian himself was so entirely enthralled by his Indian work that he was most reluctant to resign. Indeed, he told me, when the first rumours of a final rupture were becoming prevalent, that whatever his colleagues decided, he intended to remain in office. It was only after several days of reflection that loyalty to his Party forced him to give up a post that he not only greatly enjoyed, but filled with rare distinction.

I had then to find a new Under-Secretary to fill his place. I was already overwhelmed by the complexities of the Constitution and the difficulties of sorting them out in a Bill that Parliament would pass. There was no time to train an ignorant newcomer, and no place for anyone who did not already understand something of Indian problems. I felt that if I was to succeed, I must have as a colleague an Under-Secretary who knew both me and my methods of work, and even more important, what to avoid in dealing with very susceptible Indians. For my purpose I saw the ideal Under-Secretary in my Parliamentary Private Secretary, Rab Butler. Rab had come to me by inheritance. In the old days of the Air Ministry my guide, philosopher and friend had been his uncle, Geoffrey Butler, one of the members for Cambridge University. I never had a better friend than Geoffrey, nor an adviser who gave me wiser guidance. Those who were with him at Cambridge or in the House of Commons will never forget his delightful wit, lively imagination and unsurpassed talent for making friends, particularly amongst the young. Permanently lame, physically delicate, the superb quality of his spirit kept his life at boiling point. As my Parliamentary Private Secretary at the Air Ministry, he inspired Trenchard and me with the right conception of the Auxiliary and University Squadrons. In the University his philosophy of Tory Democracy re-established Conservatism as a dominant force. His own college of Corpus Christi he put in the forefront of all the colleges. In the Conservative Party he was on the point of playing a notable part when Baldwin invited him to become Chairman of the Conservative central organisation. It was indeed unfortunate that at the last minute the appointment fell through, and that shortly afterwards, while still a young man, he died of an incurable complaint. His last words to me when I visited him on his death-bed were: " Look after my nephew Rab, and help him in his newly-started political career."

This was the history of my taking the future Chancellor of the Exchequer as my Parliamentary Private Secretary. Of all the good advice that his uncle gave me, none was better than that contained in his dying wish. The nephew had the very qualities that I needed. Descended through a long line of academic notables, the son of one Indian Governor and the nephew of another, both of whom had made great reputations, he possessed a well-trained and imperturbable mind that could digest a mass of disjointed facts and remain clear and unconfused. Having excelled at school and in the University in many examinations, he had learnt how to fix his mind upon a given subject. Never had this power of concentration been more necessary than in face of the vast mass of constitutional details that confronted me in the India Office. I could see this need at every turn. When, therefore, the Conservative Whips came to me and tried to impose upon me the kind of Member who could read a written answer with a pleasant manner and evade awkward supplementary questions in the House of Commons, I grew impatient and insisted with Baldwin that I must have as Under-Secretary of State someone capable of grasping every detail of a very complicated subject, and that the only possible choice was my Parliamentary Private Secretary, Rab Butler. Baldwin, chiefly because he liked young men, and not because he was then aware of Butler's qualities, let me have my way.

Thus began three years of the closest possible co-operation with my Under-Secretary, and more important still, his own expanding career, to which he has added so many achievements. If Lothian had been able to give me ideas, Butler was pre-eminently able to give me facts. His methodical and analytical mind sorted the chaff from the corn, whilst his academic training helped us both to see a very detailed picture as a single whole.

Stewart, Lothian, Butler—no Minister ever had three such good companions in a great adventure. Behind them was the *corps d'élite* of the men whose predecessors had formed the first Civil Service and carried on a great tradition for more than a century. Sustained by this support, I felt that I could face the future, not indeed with confidence, for there were too many snares and pitfalls on every side, but at least with the healthy cold feet that are needed for a long march on a rough road.

After these few sentences of tribute to my chief helpers, I must continue my story of the struggle for the new Constitution with a sketch of the building in which I was working, and the unique character of the department of which I had become head.

A great administrator, Sir Charles Lyall, had described the

India Office as " comfortable and convenient, but rather depressing." I suppose that he was thinking of the dark corridors and stairs that had resulted from the changes in the architect's plan. The original intention had been a Gothic building. The Derby Government approved of the plan, but before the work started, Palmerston and the Liberals returned to office. The new Ministers regarding Gothic as symbolic of Conservative feudalism, and inspired by the generous sentiments of the Italian *Risorgimento*, insisted instead upon a Renaissance exterior. The inside of the building, however, they left in the gloom of a Gothic cathedral, although they intended the glass-covered court and the Council Chamber to rival the *piano nobile* of an Italian palace. In spite of this confusion of styles, many of the living-rooms in the office justified Sir Charles Lyall's description " comfortable and convenient." They certainly possessed one great advantage over the rooms in the neighbouring departments. Almost without exception they contained mahogany furniture and contemporary pictures from East India House, the historic home of the East India Company. When, as President, I presided over the India Council, I sat in the throne-like chair that had always been occupied by the Chairman of the Directors of the Company, with my Vice-President next to me in a smaller chair expressly made by Chippendale. The walls of my room were covered with a superb set of Moghul and Rajput paintings. In other rooms were Zoffanys of Asaf-ad-Dowla of Oudh and one of his Ministers, painted during Zoffany's Indian tour, and, most curious of all, a portrait of Byron's famous servant,[1] Giovanni Battista Falcieri, who, after his master's death, drifted penniless to England, became Disraeli's valet, and ended as a messenger in the peaceful haven of the newly created India Office. In the upper storeys of the building was housed a magnificent oriental library containing unique Sanskrit, Arabic, Persian and Chinese treasures. The spirit of Sir William Jones, first and perhaps greatest of British Orientalists, still inspired the researches of the many students who worked in it. Finally, on the ground floor, at the foot of the grand staircase, was a marble statue by Flaxman of Warren Hastings, the founder of all Civil Services, and the true creator of the Indian Empire.

The staff were very proud of its treasures, and watched over

[1] See *The India Office* by Sir Malcolm Seton.

them with scrupulous care. Once, when Curzon removed some of the best pieces of furniture to his room in the Foreign Office, the Council of India rose up in fury and demanded their immediate restitution. Being a corporate body that owned the contents of the office, and therefore free from all interference from the Office of Works, they could not be gainsaid, and the furniture was returned.

In the midst of these memories and associations I felt that I had entered a temple of tradition. The great office over which I was presiding was the direct successor of the small company of Gentlemen Adventurers who, in 1665, had engaged " half a dozen youths of mean parentage who could write good hands and shall be willing to be employed upon all occasions without murmuring," and twenty years later had settled their pay at £10 a year, whose successors had appointed Warren Hastings as a bookkeeper in the export warehouse in Madras, who had endured for generations the civil wars of the Court of Governors, survived many inquests, and finally been superseded in 1859 by a Secretary of State fully responsible to Parliament. As the outward sign of this long continuity, the records of young Indian civilians were still kept in the massive Bond Books entitled *The Company's Servants Abroad.*

In later years these memories of a fascinating past came back to me with an added vividness, when I studied in detail the history of the Spanish Indies. As Ambassador in Spain, I had many opportunities of visiting Seville, and admiring the majestic seat of the lost empire. Instead of the Company's ramshackle City office where Charles Lamb drowsed over business ledgers and wrote his private letters in office time, instead of the sober India Office, its successor, where the Secretary of State worked amidst the quiet mahogany furniture of a merchant's house, I found the vast and splendid Renaissance Palace of the Indies, its walls glistening with the gold from the New World, and panelled with the many-coloured woods in which South America abounds. Never was there a more magnificent Government office, nor a more impressive setting for the dignified and meticulous instructions that week after week were drafted for the three Spanish Viceroys in the newly-established Empire. The great building embodied the conception of a centralised régime based on definite moral and religious principles of government. The aim, about which there was no doubt, was a new Spanish Kingdom, Catholic like the Kingdoms of European Spain, and equipped with all the institutions of Church and State that the Mother Country possessed. Nothing could be more different from the India Office and the system of government that it represented. Our Indian Empire had been created empirically and almost by chance. No preconceived theories had dominated its administration, no claim to permanence had ever been made for it. Some time, but not in this description of my four years at the India Office, I will try to develop at greater length the train of thought that is started by a comparison of the two régimes. It is not, however, irrelevant to state here that my Spanish researches confirmed the line from which I never deviated as Secretary of State. I was always convinced that a distant bureaucracy cannot control in detail a sub-continent thousands of miles distant. The Spaniards made the attempt. Their motives were excellent. Their desire to protect the Indians from exploitation was far in advance of the times. Yet, they failed, as I felt sure that we should also fail if we tried to dictate from Whitehall every act and decision of Indian government.

Differing in every way from the *Consejo de Las Indias* in Spain, the India Office, as the successor of John Company, was also unlike the other great offices in Whitehall. It possessed its own system of accounts, its own auditor, and its own surveyor, whilst its Secretary of State had a special position that distinguished him from the other Secretaries of State. Constitutionally, he possessed the ' Power of Superintendence, Direction and Control ' of all Indian affairs. In other words, he could in theory direct almost every movement of the huge machine of Indian government. Only in two respects were his powers limited by statute. For decisions concerning the finance of India and the security of the Secretary of State's services, such as the Indian Civil Service, it was necessary for him to obtain the concurrence of the Council of India, the small and expert board of experienced officials who constitutionally advised him in London. It might, therefore, be supposed, in view of the immense powers that he possessed, that his relation to the Viceroy resembled that of the Prime Minister to the Sovereign, the one possessing all the power, the other, all the pomp. In practice, the position was very different. The Viceroy stood for much more than pomp. He presided at his

Council's meetings, supervised the Indian Services, and himself retained in his Council the portfolio of the Political Department that dealt with the Indian Princes. Even without these specific duties, he was bound as the man on the spot, to take an active share, often the most active share, in Indian administration. The days were long past when a small group or a Minister in London could attempt to control the daily course of Indian affairs. The more complicated became Indian needs, the more necessary it was for the Secretary of State to curtail his powers of direction and control. Convention helped to make a rough and ready line between the London and Indian spheres of power. Legislation that transferred certain activities of government to Indian hands, turned the nebulous line into a more defined frontier. History also, as I have already observed, had its influence in showing how disastrous it was when the Secretary of State and the Viceroy failed to agree. A clumsy pen at one end and a too fluent pen at the other had sometimes strained to breaking-point relations between London and Delhi. A safe text for me to follow was Dalhousie's letter to the President of the Board of Control on June 29, 1854:

> " My experience has taught me that men who correspond over a space of 10,000 miles should watch their pens, for ink comes to burn like caustic when it crosses the sea."

Fortunately for me, I found in Willingdon, the Viceroy, an experienced Indian Governor and one of the most charming men of his generation. His Governorship of Madras had left the pleasantest of memories in Indian minds, and his good looks, agreeable manners and social talents had made him many friends in East and West alike. For the next three years we wrote to each other every week, and although we never concealed our occasional differences, came to understand each other in a way that was only possible between real friends.

After a somewhat rough start our two caravans settled down on their respective roads. While he did not involve himself in the complexities of the new Constitution, I did my best to leave him a free hand in his daily administration of British India and his dealings with the Princes in Indian India. The first jolt, that at one time looked like leading to a breakdown, came within a few days of my taking office. On the morning of September 20 the Prime Minister broke the news to me that we had been forced off the gold standard. I could not have been more shocked. As a member of one of the oldest banking families in the City, I had been brought up to regard the gold standard as a fundamental law that could never be altered. Besides, as one of the Conservative representatives in the recent discussions in Downing Street, I felt that repudiation not only threatened our influence throughout the world, but stultified the chief claim of the new Government. When I went home after my interview with the Prime Minister, I was, according to my wife, almost in a state of collapse. I have mentioned this personal detail as it shows not only that my fears and forebodings were unjustified, but that in 1931 a change that ten years later would have been regarded as a normal operation with a managed currency, appeared at the time to be a sign of the end of the world.

As the rupee was tied to sterling, it was necessary, if chaos in India was to be avoided, to make an immediate decision as to the future of the Indian exchange. There was not a moment to be lost. The announcement that we in London were leaving the gold standard was to be made in Parliament within a few hours. I at once summoned the India Council as the body constitutionally responsible for Indian currency and exchange. The members were unanimous that the rupee must remain tied to sterling if the stability of Indian finance was to be maintained and the Indian cultivator protected from exploitation. As it was necessary to act within a matter almost of minutes, we telegraphed instructions to this effect direct to the currency officials in India, as well as to the Viceroy himself. The Viceroy, who could not be expected six thousand miles away to realise the extreme urgency of the crisis, not unnaturally felt that he had been short-circuited. Fortunately, however, our decision was soon justified by the results. From the day that we made it, the rupee retained a stability that would have been lost by any other decision, and gambling in exchange was stopped. Within six months the rate of Indian borrowing fell from $5\frac{1}{2}$ per cent to 4 per cent, and Indian credit stood higher than at any time for twenty years. When the improvement showed itself, the Viceroy was amongst the first to admit that we were right, and to congratulate us on the result.

One of the results of the currency crisis was the friendship that I started with two representatives of the City, who each in his own way exercised considerable influence upon the decisions of the Government. The first was Montagu Norman, the Governor of the Bank of England, the second Catto, the chairman of the great enterprise of Andrew Yule and Company in Calcutta and Bombay, and Norman's successor in Threadneedle Street. Norman was in the habit of calling at No. 10 Downing Street on his way home from the City in the late afternoon for a talk with Baldwin, his intimate friend. He would then come on to the India Office and discuss with me the movements of the rupee. We soon came to know and like each other. I was attracted by his intriguing personality. In many ways the most orthodox of financial experts, he delighted in appearing unconventional, and in protecting himself with a screen of mystery from the common world. In point of fact, his mind worked along well-established lines, just as the tastes that endeared him to Baldwin were those of an old Etonian who possessed a cultured mind and respected great traditions. Catto was of a different type. He was one of the many hard-headed Scots who had made a splendid career in India, but unlike Inchcape, his fellow countryman, had made it by conciliation rather than frontal attack. I was to find his help of no little value during the whole of my time at the India Office. Indians trusted him, and in the new chapter of British-Indian relations, his velvet glove was better suited to the new conditions than the iron hand of the earlier pioneers.

Within a few days of the crisis over sterling, a second controversy seemed likely to strain even more severely the relations between Whitehall and Delhi. Like the British Government, the Government of India was faced with the difficulty of balancing a budget that the economic slump had thrown completely out of gear. One of the Viceroy's proposals was a cut in the pay of the Indian Civil Service that seemed to us disproportionate to the rest of the budget, and disastrous to the future of a service upon which we depended not only for the good government of India, but also for support in the chapter of constitutional reform. A Cabinet, specially summoned to consider the two views, authorised me to insist upon a modification of the cuts. There followed some hours of acute crisis in which it seemed likely that there would be resignations either in London or Delhi. In the end, however, the Viceroy agreed to a compromise, and I breathed again when the second danger that threatened my first days in office was removed.

Subsequently, my relations with Willingdon were easy and friendly, though a difference of outlook was sometimes inevitable. Our letters show that we both understood the boundaries of our respective spheres. The Viceroy's responsibility was for the daily maintenance of law and order, peace and quiet; mine, for the passage of a complicated and very vulnerable Bill through a Parliament that was dominated by a large Conservative majority. The world from his windows in Delhi looked very different from the Whitehall and Westminster upon which mine looked out. For him and his advisers British India filled the immediate prospect; Indian India was too far distant to be included in the view. For me, an All-India Federation was not only an immediate possibility, but the only practicable plan for reconciling a Conservative Parliament to responsible government at the centre. Yet, although this difference of view continued to exist, we managed to get on well together, and to round many difficult corners on the uneven road to constitutional change.

We were able, for instance, to check by resolute and joint action the endemic plague of terrorism that had ravaged India, and particularly Bengal, since the emergency measures that had supplemented the ordinary law, had been repealed under the Montagu-Chelmsford reforms. From 1924 to 1931 there had been a grim and growing series of terrible outrages. Loyal officers like Lowman, the Inspector-General of Police in Bengal, Peddie and Burge, the District Magistrates of Midnapur, Garlick, the Sessions Judge of the Twenty-Four Parganas, and many other devoted servants of the Crown had been murdered, often by boys and girls, sometimes, also, when the British officials were taking a friendly part in games and social gatherings. A bomb exploded under the Viceroy's train. Three Governors, Jackson, Anderson and de Montmorency, only escaped by a miracle from attempts on their lives. The vernacular Press incited and applauded these crimes, and the Calcutta Municipal Council regarded their perpetrators as national heroes. British opinion was deeply stirred over their rising number and increasingly savage character. The reports, particularly from Bengal, were in the Viceroy's words 'extraordinarily disquieting.' Many were saying that we ought not to give self-government to a country that had so little respect for law and order.

Faced with this situation, the Viceroy and I made the suppression of terrorism our first and paramount duty. On his side, he at once took steps to strengthen the morale of the police, and to arrange for the active co-operation of the army in the campaign against the terrorists. Perhaps even more important, he succeeded in inducing the Legislative Council of Bengal to replace the Emergency Ordinances against terrorism by permanent legislation. On my side, I was able to take two special steps to help in addition to the general support that I was giving him. In order to show the importance that I attached to the Indian police, I appointed Sir Charles Tegart, the celebrated police chief in Bengal, to the Council of India, and broke a precedent under which no police officer had ever before been appointed to the Council. Secondly, I persuaded Sir John Anderson, an unrivalled expert in questions concerning law and order, to allow me to recommend his name for the Governorship of Bengal. The result of our joint action was that, by 1935, terrorism had been practically stamped out in India. For the three years previous to 1931 there had been an average of five serious outrages every month. By June, 1935, when my partnership with the Viceroy came to an end, they had been completely stopped.

We had much the same record of success in our dealings with civil disobedience. When I took office there were between 23,000 and 24,000 men and women in prison for civil disobedience offences. The effect of the double policy of firm government and constitutional reform brought the number down to 76 at the time that I was passing the Government of India Bill through the House of Commons. Even Churchill, my irreconcilable opponent, could not ignore the spectacular change that had come over the Indian scene. " The Secretary of State," he told the House of Commons, " is like a cow who has given a good pail of milk, but," he added, remembering the other side of my dual policy, " has then kicked it over." He refused to admit the influence for good brought about by the constitutional proposals. Without them, Indian public opinion would never have veered to the support of law and order.

It was undoubtedly difficult to hold the balance between police measures and constitutional needs. If we had wished to suppress Indian nationalism, we could, I feel sure, have succeeded. We should not have destroyed it, but we could have broken its political power for many years by a concentrated effort of resolute repression. It was this effort that neither the British public, nor Willingdon nor I was prepared to make. Sympathising with Indians in most of their political aspirations, we restricted police methods to a minimum and inevitably made it possible for Gandhi and Congress to carry on their political campaign almost without let or hindrance.

Nor, though we had great temptation, did we interfere with the established processes of the law. The Indian Code had been drafted by men who intensely believed in the value of personal liberty. The result was the provision of every kind of safeguard for the accused. Delays and appeals were multiplied. The ingenuity of Indian lawyers made the most of every statutory enactment. Conspiracy cases dragged on for years, and often in the end finished with acquittals on technical points or inconclusive verdicts. If we had refused to respect the motives of the many Indians who believed in Swaraj in much the same way as the Italians of the *Risorgimento* believed in national independence, we should have swept away the protection that a more peaceful era had given them, and introduced the method of courts martial and summary justice. Not only did we maintain the established system, but the idea of changing it never entered our minds.

CHAPTER VI

The Making of a Constitution

M OST FORTUNATELY we were able to rely throughout these
troubled times on several remarkable public servants. I
pick out three of them—Anderson for his work in Bengal,
Brabourne for his work in Bombay, and Hailey for his expert
knowledge of Indian administration.

Anderson's subsequent career has given him a high place in
British public life. At the time that I recommended him for the
Governorship of Bengal, the world still knew little of him.
I had twice seen his abilities at first hand, once, when he was in
Dublin Castle in virtual charge of Irish affairs in 1920, and I was
Chairman of the Government Committee dealing with the needs
of the Southern Unionists; and again, as I have already described,
at the time of the General Strike in 1926, when as Under-
Secretary of State at the Home Office, his was the power behind
several ministerial thrones. No man was more experienced in
problems of administrative efficiency. Stewart and I at once
thought of him when the end of Stanley Jackson's term of office
made a vacancy in the Governorship of Bengal. Would he be
ready to leave a safe and distinguished career in the Home Civil
Service for the risks of a temporary Governorship in the most
disturbed Province of India? Would the Home Secretary and the
Treasury make it possible for him if he wished to go to Bengal?
In due course, but not without much consideration, the answer
" yes " came to both these questions. The wisdom of our choice
was very soon justified. The Services in Bengal had been gravely
shaken by the repeated terrorist crimes. It had even been found
necessary to evacuate some of the worst areas and to leave them at
the mercy of the criminals. It was clear that if the machine of

government was not to collapse, a strong and experienced hand was needed to control it. In Anderson, the officials felt that they had not only an expert who understood the needs of the police, but a trained administrator who could master a difficult problem in the shortest possible space of time. Within a few months he took control of a very critical situation. By improving the intelligence services he was able to obtain reliable information for his campaign against the terrorists. Even more important, by organising the closest possible co-operation between the police and the army, he was able to concentrate the full force of the Government on the strategic points. When his Governorship came to an end, his notable achievements in Bengal had marked him out for other great posts. With the clouds of war gathering round us, and the need for fuller protection against air-raids becoming more urgent, Chamberlain, on my advice, appointed him first, Lord Privy Seal, and secondly, Minister of Home Security for dealing in particular with the new and baffling problem of civil defence.

Soon after Anderson's appointment to Bengal, Sykes' period of office came to an end in Bombay. Bombay needed not so much a professional administrator as an alert and accomplished man of the world who would get on equally well with the politicians, the business community, the social workers, and last but not least, the many friends and supporters of Gandhi. Looking round for someone who possessed the needed qualities, I thought at once of my Parliamentary Private Secretary, Micky Knatchbull, the Conservative Member for Ashford, soon to succeed his father as Lord Brabourne. Since his entry into Parliament in 1932, he had made many friends on both sides of the House, and whenever he spoke, had exhibited a quick mind and sensitive touch. When Rab Butler ceased to be my Parliamentary Private Secretary on becoming Under-Secretary of State, I asked him to take the vacant place. He proved so helpful to me that I afterwards had no hesitation in recommending him for Bombay. The only difficulty was that he was comparatively unknown. The King, who took a very keen interest in Indian appointments, had never seen him. The Whips in the House of Commons thought of him only as a new boy who should be kept at work on the back benches to learn the job of a county member. Baldwin had other names in his mind. However, I prevailed. He was duly appointed

Governor, first of Bombay, then of Bengal, and when his life was prematurely cut short at the height of his powers, he had already achieved as successful a career as any Indian Governor in modern times. Fortunate in his many gifts, fortunate also in his wife, he would have made an equally good Viceroy if he had lived to complete the chapter that I had started for him. I have mentioned Lady Brabourne not because she has also been one of our personal friends, but because the joint partnership in Bombay and Calcutta was a standing example of the value of a good wife in great positions. The winning of a double event is perhaps not so rare in public life as it is on the racecourse. Yet, when the double event is brought off, how great are the stakes that are won. In this case, both husband and wife were equally good. Their combined qualities not only fostered friendly feeling between British and Indians in the two Provinces in which they worked, but notably enhanced the standing of two historic posts. Together they proved the value of pleasant and agreeable manners in public life.

Thirdly and lastly in my gallery of successful Governors, I place Malcolm Hailey, a man very different from both Anderson and Brabourne. In contrast to Anderson, the prudent, efficient and successful Scot, and to Brabourne, the accomplished Kentish squire, Hailey seems at first sight colourless and intangible. Behind a quiet and unassuming exterior, however, is a mind of rare temper, unswerving courage, and a passion for work that never tires. I first knew him when he was Governor of the Punjab, and I stayed with him and his Italian wife in the Lahore Residency that had once been a Moslem mosque. I felt at once the influence of his personality. In the streets of Lahore he was everywhere greeted as a friend and neighbour who understood at first hand the individual needs of the men and women in his Province. The more difficult were the problems, the more he welcomed them with an unflagging vivacity. Never relying exclusively on files and minutes, he liked both to see things and do things for himself. When the plague was ravaging the Province, not only did he organise the relief measures, but took so active a part in the day-to-day work that upon one occasion he carried an infected corpse to burial and himself caught the disease.

In Delhi, where he held the highest posts in the Viceroy's Council, he had the opportunity of showing his talent for politics.

Each new task stimulated his interest and exhibited the versatility of his mind. " Hailey, Hailey, Lord God Almighty," murmured one of his colleagues as he saw him passing easily from finance to law and order, and from law and order to constitutional reform. There was nothing that he could not do.

When, therefore, I needed an expert from India to help me in the preparation of the Government of India Bill, he was the obvious choice. No one could have been a better guide to me in the tangled maze through which I was groping my way. This part of his work will become apparent when I come to write of the Joint Select Committee and the passage of the Bill through Parliament. At this point I mention him as one of the last of the great Indian civilians who, generation after generation, did honour to themselves and their country by their devoted service and unassailable integrity. Hailey has fortunately made a treaty with time never to grow old. The qualities for which I knew him are still as conspicuous in his reports upon African problems as they were in the days when we worked together on the Indian Constitution.

These three men, each in his own way, supplemented in India the work that Stewart, Lothian, Butler and I were trying to do in London. Having suggested their characteristics, I must return to the story of the constitutional discussions in London.

The Communal Award removed the principal obstacle on the side of British India. In Indian India, however, there were still doubts and hesitations about the conditions on which the Princes were prepared to accede to the Federation. Their first flush of enthusiasm had faded when they came to realise that they could not join a Federal system and still retain their sovereignty unaffected. They were jealous of each other, and possessed no effective body for reaching corporate decisions. The Chamber of Princes that had been intended to represent their views was boycotted by some of the principal rulers, and for long periods and at critical times never met.

I had countless interviews with those of them who came to London. Time after time I pointed as a warning to the fate of the Princes in Germany. The trouble was that many years of paternal supervision by the Political Department in India had left them with little initiative. One of them said to me: " In the past, my ancestors sat on hard saddles. Now we sit on silk divans. We have become soft." Others, like Ranji, could talk of nothing except their financial grievances against the Government of India.

In the case of the Maharaja of Alwar, who called himself " a philosophic prince," and claimed to be directly descended from the Sun God, it was difficult to decide whether he was more mad than bad or more bad than mad. His visits to London put me in great difficulty. As a Ruling Prince, he had the right to be received by the King, and the King, who knew all about his misdeeds, firmly refused to receive him. Alwar, being diabolically clever, made the most of grievances of this kind, and would descend frequently upon me with his complaints. On one of his visits he produced a copy of a letter that he had written to his divine ancestor expressing contrition for his sins, and asking for heavenly guidance. His divine descent prohibited him from touching leather, and as the chairs in my room had leather seats, there were always moments of embarrassment before we could begin to talk. When the obstacle of the leather had been evaded or surmounted, he would produce two silver clocks and put them on the mantelpiece. " You see," he would say, " I do not trust a single clock to check the time of my conversation with you. I have therefore brought two." Another of his habits was to drop his handkerchief in order that the Secretary of State should pick it up. My response was either to ring the bell for the messenger, or leave it to him to pick up for himself. Alwar was a bad ruler who was always making trouble both with his subjects and the Government of India.

It should, however, be said in justice to the Princes generally that many of them were men of real mark, who were anxious to attract efficient Ministers to their States. Their Diwans, such as Akbar Hydari from Hyderabad, Mirza Ismail from Mysore, and Krishnama Chari from Baroda, were conspicuous in the various conferences for their outstanding ability. If these excellent Ministers had been given a freer hand by their masters, there would have been none of the alarms and excursions that gave so much encouragement to the diehards in England and India.

The worst of these agitations came at a very critical moment in the discussions about Federation. Without a word of warning a meeting of Princes in Bombay passed a resolution that appeared to repudiate the Federal proposals. Churchill at once took advantage of a situation that had providentially played into his hand, to make one of his most formidable attacks in the House of Commons on the whole conception of Federation. In the meanwhile, the King, who was intensely interested in everything that concerned India, and convinced that All-India Federation was the right policy, was greatly incensed by the Princes' action. He was at the time recuperating from his recent illness at Compton Place, Eastbourne. As he wished to see me at once, I went there for the night, and had the opportunity of discussing Indian questions with him for many hours. There was no party in the house—only the King and Queen, a lady-in-waiting and Wigram. Our talk began in the evening and started again the next morning, when I went to the King's room at 8.30 a.m., and found him already surrounded by red boxes and Government papers. His annoyance with the dissident Princes had increased overnight, rather than diminished. " I won't see them when they come to London. Why should they come to London at all and spend a lot of money? Tell them to stay in their States and look after their own subjects." It was clear that he regarded very seriously his responsibilities as King-Emperor. He knew many of the Princes individually, and had visited their States. His love of sport had taken him to remote corners of Indian India, and given him vivid glimpses of local life. Indeed, I always thought that it was Indian sport more than anything else that first awakened and then stimulated his very close interest in Indian affairs. His attitude to the Princes was that of a sympathetic but severe father who knew and understood his family's weaknesses and was determined to bring up his sons in the way that they should go. As to what he thought of the Princes' behaviour in Bombay, he left them in no doubt. The Viceroy was at once instructed to notify them of the Imperial displeasure, while they on their side let it be known that they had not really repudiated Federation, and that their resolution had not meant what it said. None the less, in the period between the end of the Round Table Conference and the final passing of the Bill, their hesitations were a serious obstacle in the way of speedy progress with the Constitution.

Any hindrance of this kind was very embarrassing in view of the character of the Parliamentary procedure through which the Bill had to pass. The steps still to be taken before the proposals could find a place on the Statute Book were marked by a ceremonial exactitude that was not allowed to depart in any way from the accepted ritual for making Parliamentary Constitutions. First, there had to be a White Paper, setting out in detail the proposals, next, its discussion and approval in both Houses of Parliament. Then, a motion, also in both Houses, and necessary in each separate session, setting up a Joint Select Committee for considering the White Paper and for making recommendations on which a Bill could be drafted. Here again, Parliamentary approval in both Houses was needed for the Committee's recommendations. Lastly, the introduction of a Bill based upon the maximum of agreement available between Indians and Indians, British and Indians, British and British, that had been reached after many years of continuous discussion.

The debate on the White Paper on March 17, 1933, produced one of the fully staged battles in Churchill's Seven Years' War against the reforms. The result was a three-to-one victory for the Government, but an unmistakable warning of the diehard determination to continue the fighting to the bitter end.

The next stage in the campaign ended in much the same way. Both Houses approved with large majorities the appointment of the Joint Select Committee, and named their respective members to serve on it. Behind the scenes, however, there had been many difficulties to surmount before I could ask for the necessary Parliamentary approval. The House of Lords was very much on its dignity as to the personnel and powers of the Committee, whilst the House of Commons wanted a larger representation of its own members. I myself would have preferred a small body of about six to represent both Houses, but I was eventually forced to agree to a Committee of thirty-two to be divided equally between the two Houses. A long discussion then began as to which members should be selected. Salisbury, although not in office, was by far the most influential member of the House of Lords. He was also the most effective and respected leader of the diehards, whilst the rank and file of the Conservative Party trusted him more than anyone except Baldwin. He had therefore to be placated as far as possible at every turn. Could I persuade him to join the Committee himself? Could I induce him to select for his diehard colleagues peers whose advice would be useful in the Committee? Hoping to make him say " yes," I saw him many times, and at last persuaded him both to join the Committee and to recommend certain of his best supporters to serve on it. Upon the question of the membership, he at first objected to my suggestion that Archbishop Lang should be invited as the representative of the Christian communities in India. Whilst he finally withdrew his opposition, he never disguised his feeling that the inclusion of the Archbishop of Canterbury in a constitutional inquiry was unprecedented and incongruous.

The other difficult question that we had to settle concerned the chairman. Salisbury was obviously suspicious of any nominee of the Government. By a process of elimination we eventually fixed upon Peel, a former Secretary of State for India, no longer a Minister, and already showing independence from official influences. Peel accepted the invitation, and it was arranged that the Archbishop and Salisbury should propose and second his appointment to the chair at the first meeting to be summoned for the afternoon of April 25 at 2.30. All seemed to be happily arranged when I was unexpectedly called out from the Cabinet in the morning of the day when the Committee was to meet, to be told by Stewart that Peel had been ordered to bed with a severe attack of phlebitis, and would not be available. What could we do to replace him? The Committee was due within an hour and a half, and we should be playing into the hands of the diehards, who were bent upon discrediting the proceedings, if we had no one to propose for the chair. Stewart and I went hurriedly through the list of the members, and came down in favour of Linlithgow, who had most creditably presided over the Royal Commission on Indian Agriculture. We drove at once to his house in Chesham Place, and persuaded him, not without some difficulty, to agree to replace Peel. Having obtained his consent, we still had a few minutes in which to conciliate the Archbishop and Salisbury, who were expecting to propose Peel. Neither of them was at all pleased at the change. However, they eventually agreed within a few minutes of the start of the Committee, and Linlithgow was duly voted to the chair. Thus ended the second of my troubles over procedure. I have described them in some detail as they illustrate two of the minor difficulties in a long Parliamentary process. More than this, the crisis over the chairman discloses the unexpected workings of chance and providence in political affairs. If Peel had not been immobilised by phlebitis, Linlithgow would not have been chairman, and if Linlithgow had not been chairman, he would have been given no

opportunity to exhibit the qualities that subsequently made
Baldwin recommend him for the Viceroyalty.

Twenty representative Indians from British India and seven
from the India of the Princes were appointed as assessors to the
Committee. Constitutionally they could not be full members of
a body that was exclusively composed of Members of Parliament.
For the earlier meetings that mainly concerned procedure, the
British members, therefore, sat alone. When the Indians arrived,
the Moses Room in the House of Lords was filled to overflowing.
The British side embodied almost all the available Parliamentary
experience upon Indian affairs, whilst the Indians from British
India and the States represented the main currents of Indian
opinion in favour of co-operation. The chairman and most of the
members did everything possible to make it easy for the Indians
to take an active part in the general discussions and the examination of witnesses.

Salisbury was honestly convinced that our proposals were
based on false sentiment, and had never been fully thought out.
He regarded me with distrust and a certain measure of somewhat
patronising pity, as the principal author of a mad scheme. In
order to expose the hollowness of the Federation and the ignorance
of the Secretary of State, he at once demanded that I should be
the principal witness. I of course agreed, and in due course submitted myself to a cross-examination by the thirty-two Members
of Parliament and the twenty-seven Indian assessors that continued for nineteen days, during which I answered more than
10,000 leading and supplementary questions. Whilst the questions
and answers covered every known problem of Provincial Autonomy and All-India Federation, it is interesting to remember that
no one, either British or Indian, raised the possibility of the
division of India. The idea of Pakistan had not passed beyond
the romantic mind of a Moslem poet, and the very name,
Pakistan, was practically unknown.

With Stewart on one side of me, Hailey on the other, and
Croft, my invaluable private secretary, behind me, I exposed
myself like some up-to-date St. Sebastian to a rain of arrows
from every side. In my case, the onslaught did not end in
martyrdom. I knew very fortunately by this time the answer to
most of the questions, and I was able not only to repel the arrows,
but to throw back many of them into the enemy's camp. Not

a little due to my excellent advisers, I was therefore able to survive the ordeal, and to feel at the end that the interminable process of question and answer had not only cleared up many of the complexities of the Constitution, but had shown that the plan had been fully considered in every aspect.

The Committee sat almost continuously from April, 1933, until November, 1934, holding 159 meetings and examining 120 witnesses. The only considerable break in the sittings was during the spring of 1934 when there occurred an interruption so strange and unexpected that it needs a chapter to itself.

CHAPTER VII

Churchill's Attack

B Y THE spring of 1934 we had made considerable progress, and there seemed a good chance of the work being finished by the summer recess. The factor of time was very important. Every month that the long-drawn-out inquiry continued, endangered the goodwill that had been created in India by the Round Table atmosphere, and stimulated the diehard opposition in England. There was a further reason for speed; the twenty-seven Indian assessors were all busy men who wished to return to their activities in India. It was consequently a matter of general regret when it was found necessary in the early summer to suspend the Committee's meetings for several weeks. The reason was an intervention by Churchill in the form of a charge that Derby and I had committed a serious breach of Parliamentary Privilege amounting " to a high crime and misdemeanour meriting the utmost severity against the offender."

On April 15 Churchill and I were both lunching with Philip Sassoon. I had then no suspicion of any sudden attack. It was therefore a complete surprise to me when the next day I received the following letter:

> " *Chartwell*,
> " *Westerham, Kent*
> " *April 15, 1934*

" MY DEAR SECRETARY OF STATE,

" I have apprised Mr. Speaker of my intention to seek his ruling upon the question of Privilege which has arisen out of the proceedings of the Joint Select Committee upon Indian constitutional reform. Evidence has been placed in my possession showing that the Indian Section of the Manchester Chamber of

Commerce completed their evidence for the Joint Select Committee about the middle of June, and a hundred copies were sent to the Secretary of the said committee for circulation to its members preparatory to the hearing of the evidence which had been fixed for June 30. A member or members of the Joint Select Committee used influence with the Manchester Chamber of Commerce to procure the withdrawal of the evidence, and the substitution of evidence which differed materially from that which had already been deposited with the Secretary of the Joint Select Committee. The altered and substituted evidence was in fact rendered at the end of October and heard by the Committee on November 4 and has since been published.

" Information at my disposal shows that you were cognizant of these proceedings which I am advised constitute a breach of the privileges of the House of Commons, and are in any case most irregular and regrettable.

" I send you this notice in order that you may be in your place and have previous notice of my intention.

" Yours sincerely,
" WINSTON S. CHURCHILL."

When I read this strange ultimatum, I could not understand what it meant. I had not, however, to wait long for an explanation, as Churchill raised the question in the House of Commons the same afternoon. The story that he told was to the effect that Derby, a member of the Joint Select Committee, and I, also a member, had brought pressure to bear upon the Manchester Chamber of Commerce to withdraw the *précis* of evidence that they had already sent to the Committee, and to substitute for it different evidence. A picturesque and presumably sinister detail in the charge was his account of a dinner that Derby had given in Derby House for bringing together the witnesses appointed by the Chamber of Commerce and Runciman, the President of the Board of Trade, and myself. As ten months had elapsed since these events were supposed to have happened, it was not possible for me at a few hours' notice to be ready with the full details for rebutting the charge. I remembered, however, enough of what had happened to be able to say that Churchill had " discovered one of his mare's nests," and that I should welcome a full inquiry that would undoubtedly show how fantastic was the whole story. The House was bewildered, many members were inclined to believe that there must be some ground for so serious a charge, and the Speaker agreed that there was a sufficient *prima facie* case for an inquiry. Two days later, when Churchill formally proposed that my conduct should be considered by the Committee of Privileges, the resolution was unanimously accepted. The Lords agreed that Derby's part in the affair should also be examined.

At first sight the charges seemed to me so groundless and irresponsible that they could quickly be laughed out of court. Upon further thought, I realised the harm that they might do to the case for the reforms if they were not fully answered. Churchill claimed that the Government was using every kind of secret pressure for pushing through a Bill that no one really wanted. He had already gone so far as to throw doubts on the integrity of the Government of India by suggesting that only those who supported the reforms were given promotion.[1] He was now making an even more serious charge of undue pressure against the sacred rights of the High Court of Parliament. If he could substantiate it even to a slight degree, he would destroy all the intricate processes that we had undertaken for making the new Constitution.

Members of the House of Commons have always been jealous guardians of Parliamentary Privilege, and it is easy to excite their suspicions over any alleged breach. What exactly came within the definition of Privilege was not always clear to a layman, and the body of precedents on which it was based applied for the most part to conditions that had greatly changed. There was no code to define Privilege and no court of appeal other than the House of Commons to adjudicate on it. From start to finish, therefore, Parliamentary practice controlled its application. The doubts and complexities that were inherent in any system of this kind convinced me that, however groundless was Churchill's charge, I must take it very seriously. For the next three months, therefore, I devoted practically all my time to the preparation of a reply that would be so complete as to be decisive.

The Privilege of the House of Commons was regarded as based on a Resolution that has always been passed unanimously at the beginning of every session. It runs as follows:

[1] " For five years past," he had told the House of Commons, speaking of the Federal plea on March 29, 1933, " the high personnel of India has been continuously arranged with a view to securing men who would give a modern and welcome reception to this sort of proposal."

1. That if it shall appear that any person hath been tampering with any witness, in respect of the evidence to be given in this House or any Committee thereof, or directly or indirectly hath endeavoured to deter or hinder any person from appearing or giving evidence, the same is declared to be a high crime and misdemeanour; and this House will proceed with the utmost severity against such offender.

2. That if it shall appear that any person hath given false evidence in any cause before this House or any Committee thereof, this House will proceed with the utmost severity against such offender.

The Resolution was originally passed in 1701 as a safeguard against perjury and intimidation during the conduct of elections and the hearings of election petitions. Cases were then frequent in which voters and witnesses were bribed or kidnapped and prevented from giving evidence to Parliamentary Committees. Later, when the House of Commons abandoned its rights to decide election petitions, the offence of tampering with witnesses became much rarer, only eight being recorded since 1701. Of these later cases, the most notorious was one of 1809 connected with the selling of commissions in the army by Mrs. Clark, the lady of the Duke of York's affections. Mary Anne Clark was a lady of very extravagant tastes who required much more than the Duke's penurious allowance for her needs. She kept twenty servants, of whom three were excellent *chefs*, in a big house in Gloucester Place, and entertained her friends on the Duc de Berri's gold plate and with wine glasses that cost two guineas each. Towards meeting her household bills, she started a well-organised business for selling commissions in the Army, of which her protector was Commander-in-Chief. The trade brought in large sums of money, and to make the scandal worse in official eyes, undercut the established prices asked by the War Office. The best part of a whole session was devoted to her iniquities. The House resolved itself into Committee, and spent many weeks in examining witnesses, Mrs. Clark in particular, whose unconventional and disrespectful repartees greatly shocked the Honourable Members. Towards the end of the inquiry it transpired that a certain Rev. W. Williams had written to Mrs. Clark, who was in the process of giving her evidence, advising her to leave the country, and promising that, if she agreed, she would be " well provided for."

The reverend gentleman was at once apprehended for committing a breach of privilege on the ground that he had tampered with a witness to a House of Commons Committee. When he was brought to answer the charge at the Bar of the House, it at once became apparent that he was half-witted, and the case was dropped.

Two later precedents concerned witnesses who had been victimised for the evidence that they had given before House of Commons committees upon certain industrial disputes.

None of these cases seemed to have the least bearing on my dealings with the Manchester Chamber of Commerce. The Manchester Chamber of Commerce had always been in close contact with the India Office. The textile industry of Lancashire, created by the Indian market, was acutely sensitive to any changes in the Indian tariff on cotton goods. There had recently been increases in the Indian import duties for revenue purposes, and these, coming at a time when Japanese competition and the Swaraj boycott of British goods were crippling British trade, involved both the India Office and the Board of Trade in continuous correspondence with the Chamber of Commerce. The discussions became more intense as the new Constitution took shape. Some of the Lancashire leaders looked to working agreements between themselves and the Indian mill-owners for protection against unfair competition, others felt that the making of the new Constitution provided an opportunity for ending the Fiscal Autonomy Convention, under which the British Government undertook to accept any tariff arrangements that were agreed between the Viceroy and the Legislative Assembly. Both these views were strongly pressed at the time. When the Chamber asked for my comments, I made it as clear as I could that there was no chance whatever of any British Government abrogating the Fiscal Autonomy Convention that had for many years been accepted by every British party. I also let it be known that while the Government would not intervene in the friendly talks that had already begun between British and Indian mill-owners, I was convinced that it was only by way of negotiation that Lancashire could hope for better trade. The diehard members of the Chamber were disturbed by my answer, and succeeded in weighting the *précis* of evidence that was to be given to the Joint Select Committee in favour of restricting any future Indian Government's liberty of fiscal action. A memorandum on these lines was sent to the Joint Select Committee on May 23. As the Committee's programme was already full, its consideration was postponed until the autumn. In the meanwhile, Sir William Clare Lees, the representative of the Lancashire mill-owners, and Mr. H. P. Mody, the representative of the Indian mill-owners, had transferred to India negotiations that had begun in England, and were making satisfactory progress towards a working agreement. Sir William Clare Lees, seeing that the draft evidence of the Chamber would stultify his efforts for a friendly *modus vivendi*, telegraphed his anxieties to Manchester. The result was a request from the Chamber of Commerce to the Secretary of the Joint Select Committee for the withdrawal of the original *précis* of evidence and the substitution of a more conciliatory memorandum. I myself had no part in this request. It was entirely the result of the representations of a leading member of the Chamber of Commerce to his colleagues.

The dinner at Derby House, around which Churchill gathered so black a cloud of suspicion, was an entirely normal event in view of the interest of Lancashire in the proposed Bill, and of Derby's unique position in the County Palatine. Derby, reluctantly but very patriotically, had agreed to serve on the Joint Select Committee, primarily in order to watch over the interests of Lancashire. His influence was so great with his Lancashire neighbours that there was no important question that concerned them, on which they did not ask his advice. In their dilemma over the Fiscal Autonomy Convention, they naturally went to him at once, and he no less naturally suggested a dinner-party at Derby House, where they could meet and have a friendly talk with the President of the Board of Trade and the Secretary of State for India. This was the origin of the meeting between us. We had a delightful dinner, Derby, rubicund and genial, talked enthrallingly of the crops and the weather, Aintree, Epsom and Ascot, and towards the end we had a general exchange of views about India. The evidence to be given to the Committee was never mentioned, and I did no more than re-state my opinion that it was not practical politics to try to abrogate the Fiscal Autonomy Convention, and that negotiation, not compulsion, was the only method of progress.

Many of these details had gone from my mind when Churchill

made his attack. They had appeared to me so normal that there was no need to give them a second thought. However, my office and I were forced to spend many weeks of valuable time in checking and presenting them to a committee composed of ten of the most important men in the country, including the Prime Minister, the Leader of the Opposition, the Attorney-General and Austen Chamberlain, that held no less than sixteen lengthy sittings to consider them. I myself spent two days giving evidence, during which I answered scores of questions. I shall never forget my feelings of irritation whilst I waited in the upstairs passage outside the House of Commons Committee room to be summoned for my cross-examination, as if I were a prisoner outside the court room in the Old Bailey.

The inquiry, of course, ended as it was bound to end, in a unanimous verdict that there had been no Breach of Privilege. When the Report came up in the House on June 13, the debate fizzled out in the dinner hour with a unanimous approval of the Committee's verdict, but not before Simon and Amery had torn Churchill's charges to pieces. Amery at one point picturesquely described Churchill as impelled by the irresistible motive of *Fiat justicia, ruat coelum.* "Translate," shouted members from all sides. " If I can trip up Sam, the Government is bust," came back his ready rendering.

True, I had not been tripped up, but weeks of valuable time had been wasted in refuting groundless charges during which the Joint Select Committee had been adjourned and therefore prevented from finishing its work before the end of the session. Not only was it necessary to have the Committee reappointed by motions of both Houses in the new session, but the weeks lost were never recovered in what was to prove a struggle against time. Churchill's raid, therefore, though it may not have achieved its original objective of destroying the Bill, succeeded in imposing a delay that had a lasting effect upon the whole course of the campaign. I suppose that he felt fully justified in his relentless opposition. The splendid memories gathered round the Indian Empire blinded him to the changes that had come about since the days of Clive, Wellington, Lawrence and Kipling. The India that he had served in the Fourth Hussars was the India of polo and pig-sticking, of dashing frontier expeditions, of paternal government freely accepted, and the great White

Empress revered as a mysterious goddess. "Settle the country, make the people happy and take care there are no rows," the words of Henry Lawrence to his band of brothers, still seemed to him sufficient for maintaining the British Raj. How deeply I sympathised with his *nostalgia* for a glorious past! I also had steeped myself in Indian history, and I had been profoundly moved—as profoundly moved, I believe, as he—by the unsurpassed record of British achievement. The long list of great names was deeply engraved on my mind. The record, unique in all history, of power exercised with mercy and justice, enthralled my imagination. If the effect was so strong upon me, I could well imagine the irresistible influence that it had upon Churchill's love of colour and veneration of brave deeds. It was clear that he sincerely believed his fight to be a crusade in a great cause; the issue in his eyes was too serious to neglect any manœuvre that might help him to victory. The affair of the Committee of Privileges, that seemed to many so mischievous and irresponsible, was to him a perfectly defensible movement in a campaign carried on with the full rigours and ruses of war. If he had looked more to the future and less to the past, the grim struggle into which he had thrown himself would have assumed a very different aspect in his mind's eye.

The Joint Select Committee reported to Parliament on November 22, 1934, after holding 159 meetings and hearing 120 witnesses. The Report had been carried by nineteen votes to nine, the minority being made up of five diehards who thought it went too far, and four Labour members who did not think that it went far enough. Whilst it did not substantially differ from the proposals in the White Paper, it contained three not unimportant changes. For direct election upon a limited franchise for the Central Assembly, it substituted indirect election by the Provincial Chambers; it strengthened the provisions against terrorism, and clarified the restrictions upon economic discrimination for political objects. There followed a three days' debate in the House of Commons on December 10, 11 and 12, ending in a four-to-one majority for the Government, and the second reading of the Bill embodying the recommendations of the Report on February 7, 8 and 11, carried by 404 to 133.

The Bill was inevitably of such unprecedented length and complexity that, without a timetable, it would have taken years to pass.[1] I therefore had several discussions with the chief spokesmen of the two Oppositions in order to make an arrangement for the allocation of Parliamentary time for the three stages of Committee, Report and Third Reading. We eventually agreed upon thirty days for Committee, four days for Report, and two for Third Reading. The pattern of these long debates became standardised as soon as the procedure started to operate. Butler or I would explain towards the opening of the proceedings some constitutional provision. Churchill would then fall upon us with a furious attack, and having discharged his artillery, would retire until later in the evening, when he would resume his offensive. This protracted engagement reminded me of an eighteenth-century campaign in which the conventional methods of attack were obstinately followed for months on end without any marked effect on the beleaguered fortress. The Bill remained intact, and eventually reached the Statute Book on July 24. By the time of the Third Reading I had left the India Office and become Foreign Secretary. I had, however, seen the 473 clauses and 16 Schedules through all the critical stages, and I had made the greater part of the 1951 speeches that, with their fifteen and a half million words, had filled four thousand pages of Hansard.

These facts and figures were recalled to me shortly after the Third Reading when Austen Chamberlain presented me with a sumptuous volume entitled *The Government of India Act*, *by Sam Hoare*. There, bound in morocco and tooled with gold, were the clauses and schedules over which I had toiled so incessantly, and there also, the signatures of the scores of helpers who, inside and outside Parliament, had joined with me in " conveying the monstrous boat to the water."

And what was the result of all our labour? The vital provision of the Act, the All-India Federation, was never brought into operation. The unity of India was eventually destroyed. The breach between Churchill and the Conservative Party was made so wide and deep that it took four years and a world war to bring them together again. All this is true. Yet, when I look not only at the past, but also at the present and the future, I am more than ever convinced that these years of concentrated endeavour were worth while. There was, first of all, the value of a great

---

[1] Churchill, in his picturesque language, called it " a gigantic quilt of jumbled crochet work, a monstrous monument of shame built by pigmies."

Parliamentary achievement. I do not mean the achievement of the Secretary of State for India. I was so well briefed by my advisers that I was bound to succeed. I am thinking rather of the years of Parliamentary debate. Never was there a better example of government by Parliamentary discussion. The full ritual of Parliamentary procedure was followed in every detail, the three sessions of the Round Table Conference, the expert inquiries in India, the White Paper, the Joint Select Committee, and finally, the Bill, debated in every detail and passed without any closure of discussion. If the essence of democracy is government by debate, Parliament was never exhibited in a more truly democratic light.

There was another result that was even more important. The comprehensive Constitution contained in the Act proved an invaluable quarry for the construction of the new governments in India and Pakistan. Without the Act, and the countless inquiries that went to make it, both the new States would have started upon their chapter of independence with no text to guide them. As it was, they found in existence a provincial administration that they could accept at once, a division between central and local government that could easily be adapted to their needs, a system of justice developed and brought up to date in the Act, and last but not least, a corps of public servants, Indian and British, central and local, defined and reinforced by the Act, who could be trusted to work the machine of government. I doubt whether the transfer of power could ever have taken place with so little administrative upheaval without the framework of the Act that had cost us so many years of discussion and controversy.

Nor were these years of friendly discussion valueless in another respect. The goodwill that they created between British and Indians was a continuing asset of great importance. Men are very inhuman if they can meet year after year without making friends with each other. Questions also that have seemed intractable tend to thaw in the milder atmosphere of personal intercourse. Although, therefore, Indian opinion was dissatisfied with the Act, individual Indians in the passing of it made friendships and contacts that convinced them of our goodwill. An asset of this kind may be intangible, but it none the less weighs heavily in the scales with which I test the results of our protracted efforts.

I have left to the end of my summing-up a result of a very

different kind—the rupture between Churchill and the Conservative Party. I was as much astonished at his bitterness as amazed at the brilliant and ruthless way in which he delivered his attack. Practically alone and with little effective support from his diehard followers, he maintained the opposition not only in the House of Commons, but in meetings of the Conservative Party and demonstrations in the country. In the periodical conferences of the National Union of Conservative Associations he was particularly formidable. These great gatherings, filled with the party's front-line troops, eagerly responded to emotional appeals, and Churchill's rhetoric stirred to the depths both their passionate devotion to the Empire and their resentment against any attempt to disrupt it. It was then that Baldwin and Churchill most dramatically crossed swords, for Baldwin took little part in the debates on the Bill in the House of Commons. Churchill's eloquence never disturbed Baldwin. Quietly and confidently he would, sentence by sentence, bring the meeting back from the exciting realms of fancy to the hard road of sober fact. I do not know whether he had ever heard of the instruction of the Court of the East India Company upon their methods of correspondence. " Humdrum is our style," was their laconic remark to their young writers. Baldwin's speeches on India, like his broadcast talks, were all the more effective for the complete contrast that their simple and direct English made with Churchill's flood of words. However brilliant was the unflagging force of Churchill's offensive, it was Baldwin's combination of humanity, common sense and quiet confidence that invariably won the day.

Of the wider effect of Churchill's opposition, I have already spoken. If it did not prevent the Bill from becoming law, it prevented it from becoming law in time. How serious was this delay, few realised in 1935. The long delay encouraged disillusionment both here and in India, the cracks that were obvious from the start became wider, the initial drive behind the inspiring conception of an All-India Federation weakened. Even so, the Princes on their side were, by 1937, unmistakably accepting Federation as a necessity, and British India, in spite of the official opposition of Congress, was steadily moving towards the acceptance of the Act. Could we have pushed them harder? I have often asked myself this question. I suppose that if we had been living in 1800, we should have found no difficulty in bringing them into an All-India Federation. We should have directed on them the kind of barrage of threats, honours and rewards that had broken down the opposition of the Irish Parliament to the Union. The times, however, had changed, and we could not adopt the methods that Pitt had used with such determined purpose. Nor could we entice them into a Federation on false pretences. Our aim was a real and not a paper Constitution. If they were not wise enough to see the advantages of a system that gave them security in exchange for some part of their sovereign powers, we could neither tempt nor force them. None the less, I believe that if greater efforts had been made in Delhi to explain the advantages of Federation, we could have obtained the voluntary assent of a sufficient number for starting the Federation before the war.

As it was, it was the war that cut short the slow process of agreement, and the victories of Japan that swept away the ground upon which the Constitution had been built. If only we could have had a longer breathing space between the passing of the Act and the outbreak of war, we should, I am convinced, have seen the Constitution in action, and with it, the magnet-like attraction of an established system. The needed interval could have been obtained by shortening the period of preliminary discussions. It was in this respect that Churchill's opposition was so disastrous. It was his diehard campaign that made it impossible to move more quickly.

Once again, the impact of British politics had affected the conduct of Indian affairs. Whilst in the eighteenth century it had been Indian politics that for many years dominated the British Parliament, it was British politics at the time of the Government of India Act that chiefly frustrated agreement on a united India.

Part Two

ABYSSINIA AND RESIGNATION

CHAPTER VIII

Policy Without Power

MACDONALD HAD for some time been a sick man. His eyes sorely troubled him, he read with difficulty, and his handwriting had become very shaky. It was obvious not only to his colleagues but to the world at large that he could not remain Prime Minister. His resignation, therefore, on June 7, 1935, came as no surprise to anyone. There had already been much canvassing, not about his successor, for Baldwin had always been accepted as the next Prime Minister, but about some of the offices, particularly the Foreign Secretaryship. The feeling of frustration over British foreign policy had been shown in the constant attacks upon Simon. In the years that immediately followed Hitler's rise to power, no British Foreign Secretary could have escaped criticism. Without military strength to back his policy, and with public opinion set upon peace, he was expected somehow or other to reconcile the French demand for security with the German claim of equality for status, and to persuade more than fifty governments in Geneva to accept a plan of disarmament. Simon's penetrating mind was much too acute to ignore the contradictions and illogicalities that lay behind the façade of platitudes at Geneva and the backbiting of critics at home. He would not have been human, still less a great lawyer, if he had not sometimes seemed hypercritical in dealing with questions upon which the world at large preferred resounding generalities, and in analysing questions upon which scarcely anyone was ready to face the answers. Just as the British public had grown tired of Curzon and Austen Chamberlain in the ten years after the First World War, so in the spring of 1935 there was a widespread outcry for a new Foreign Secretary. The choice seemed gradually to be narrowed down to Eden and myself. Eden had shone at Geneva, where most of the older stars were fading. Everyone liked him, particularly his personal following amongst the younger Conservatives, and he had made many friends amongst Continental statesmen.

As for myself, I had been isolated from foreign affairs by my four years' hard labour in the India Office. Since the first Round Table Conference in 1931 I had thought of nothing but India. Weeks would sometimes pass when my work either in the Department or in the many conferences with Indians would even prevent my attendance at the Cabinet. Red boxes filled with urgent Indian papers would barricade my table and leave no room for their rivals with the Foreign Office telegrams. I cannot imagine that any Minister's mind had ever been more intently set upon a single purpose. When, therefore, the change of government took place, I had not given a thought to the Foreign Office, and until my name came to be widely mentioned, I did not look beyond my end of the corridor that joined the two Departments. In the meanwhile the older Conservatives thought Eden either too young or too emotional, and wished for someone with a wider experience of the great Departments of State, whilst a large section of the Press, particularly *The Times* under Geoffrey Dawson's leadership, hoped that after my many years of reconciling Indian differences, I might succeed in bringing France and Germany together in Europe. In view of this trend of opinion, I was not altogether surprised when, two days before MacDonald's resignation, Baldwin asked me to see him. He had not then decided upon his choice. Two great offices needed to be filled, the Foreign Secretaryship and the Viceroyalty of India. He was anxious that I should be given one of them, but he was doubtful which it should be. Which would I prefer? I told him at once that both on political and personal grounds I would prefer India. In India I felt at home. I had made countless Indian friends from Gandhi to the Princes. I knew the details of the many constitutional problems, and it was the chief ambition of my political life to turn the Government of India Act into a living All-India Federation.

On personal grounds also, I was attracted by the few months of respite that the Indian appointment would give me before the new Viceroy was installed. The strain of the Round Table Conference, the Joint Select Committee and the months of

Parliamentary debate had left their mark upon me. Upon several occasions I had suddenly fainted, once, for instance, at a cinema with Philip Sassoon, once again, at the Glyndebourne Opera, and finally, during the Report Stage of the Government of India Act, I had collapsed for several days with an attack that narrowly escaped pneumonia. It was no light task to steer through Parliament an Act of 478 clauses and 16 schedules, with Churchill, the greatest Parliamentarian of the time, in relentless opposition. In my case, these four years of incessant work had left me physically weak and mentally tired. I not only needed a rest, but also time to acclimatise myself to the world from which I had been detached by my almost Trappist seclusion in the India Office. These considerations I put to Baldwin. His response was a knock on the table with his pipe, and a promise to think them over. When I saw him again the next day, his mind had definitely moved towards the alternative of the Foreign Office. I gathered that he had consulted several friends, including Lothian and Geoffrey Dawson, and that they had pressed it. They had found him more than half-converted to their view, and it needed little further persuasion to convince him. He accordingly offered it to me, though he added that if I refused it, he would still offer me India. Wisely or unwisely, I accepted the offer.

The Foreign Office is the most difficult of all departments. Since the end of the First World War, no Foreign Secretary, with the possible exception of MacDonald, could claim to have made a success of his period of office. Curzon had ended with a breach in the Anglo-French front; Austen Chamberlain, when once the golden dawn of Locarno was ended, had faded into obscurity; Henderson, though he pleased his party, had tied up none of the ragged ends that irritated the world. To Simon's difficulties I have already alluded. It should be noted that all these Ministers were men of mark, and that without exception they found to a greater or lesser extent the obstacles too many and too great for any real success. Was it that the problem of satisfying at one and the same time both the British public and many foreign governments was insoluble in the years between the wars?

Certainly the solution had been made more difficult by the vast increase in the number of people who had to be satisfied. Castlereagh had only to consider Metternich, Talleyrand and Alexander the First. With Wellington's victorious army to support his policy there was no need to give a thought to what the lesser people were saying and thinking. Even with the more general interest in foreign affairs that developed during the nineteenth century, foreign policy continued until the First World War to remain the close preserve of a few experts. A Foreign Secretary had not continually to be looking over his shoulder at an excitable public, nor had he to carry on his diplomatic negotiations in the glare of international assemblies filled with the representatives of fifty or sixty governments. Not only had his constituency increased to an unmanageable size, but the new practice of frequent public meetings in Geneva had transformed its character.

Success, in these conditions, had become almost unattainable, even without a further and principal cause of difficulty that particularly affected British Ministers. To a much greater extent than in any other great country we had reduced our military strength to so low a point that there was no effective support for our foreign policy. No British Foreign Secretary could hope to succeed when other governments had begun to question our influence in the world. However much the fact was concealed, the ultimate success of Victorian Foreign Ministers had depended upon the supremacy of the British Navy. As long as the fleet was unchallenged, there could be no world war, and no quarter of the globe in which British ships of war could not sustain British prestige. Thanks to our traditions of moderation and common sense, this great power had been used with the utmost discretion. But there it was, in the background, an ever-present help in time of trouble, giving weight to a British Minister's policy in the councils of the world.

The fundamental change that had taken place since the First World War was the loss of the military power, without which foreign policy becomes hesitant and opportunist. It was military weakness rather than the faults of this or that Foreign Secretary that was predominantly responsible for the dismal failure of much that happened between the two wars. Having successfully re-sisted the challenge of the German Fleet in 1914, we waited too long in the twenties and thirties before taking up the even more dangerous challenge of the German Air Force. Was it any wonder that foreign governments paid less attention to us, and that Hitler and Mussolini came to write us off as a Great Power? How this state of affairs came about, is a key question in any account of these years. If the final acts of the drama that ended in 1938 and 1939 are to be understood at all, it is therefore necessary to tell in some detail the story of the disarmament movement in Great Britain between the wars. It is a tiresome chapter, and may now seem singularly unreal. None the less, it is not only the necessary preface to the record of my own months at the Foreign Office, but an indispensable guide on the road from Versailles to Munich. I am therefore interpolating at this point a description of the way in which a well-intentioned British public accepted a policy of unilateral disarmament, and left its Foreign Secretaries in a vacuum of words and promises.

The demand for disarmament began naturally and commendably after the First World War. The men and women who had basked in the warm sunshine of Victorian peace, were convinced that what they had been told was " the war to end war " had been a unique and abnormal aberration in human affairs, and that money spent on great armaments was needlessly wasted. Having been brought up in a typically Victorian family, whose traditions had for many generations been Quaker, Evangelical, and family banking, I fully shared this feeling. I well remember my father's horror at the outbreak of war in August, 1914. To him it was like the Great Flood, an overwhelming catastrophe, so terrible that it could not conceivably be repeated in the world's history. His feelings represented the general attitude of the country. When the war ended, there was a universal belief that as the world would never again be so mad and bad, another Armageddon was impossible. We had behaved in much the same way after every great war. It was so after the War of the Spanish Succession, when Walpole's maxim of *quieta non movere* was accepted by a world that was sick to death of fighting. It was so after the Napoleonic Wars, when the anti-militarist feeling became so strong that Wellington declared that the only way in which he could keep any soldiers at all was by hiding them in Ireland. After 1919, the revulsion was all the stronger for the far heavier losses of men and treasure that the country had suffered.

A very British characteristic reinforced this semi-pacifist tradition. We are bad haters. Having been reluctantly drawn into a fight, we wish to forgive our enemies as soon as it is finished, and forget their evil deeds. We go even farther, and introduce into our international dealings the same kind of mentality that we show in our games. When our side wins the match, we often carry generosity to the losing side to such a point that we seem sometimes to glorify defeat more than victory.

The tendency to forgive and forget was further strengthened by the wish to be freed from the financial burden of armaments. There was nothing new in the cry for an axe on the Service Estimates. Criticism of defence expenditure had persisted throughout most of the nineteenth century, and proved the chief stimulus to the peace movements that always stirred the fervour of the Liberal Party. The Conservatives had also been affected by it. Sir Robert Peel, in particular, true to the business traditions of his family, set the example to his party when, in 1841, he declared himself strongly in favour of great reductions in defence expenditure, although at the time the Army and Navy scarcely existed. Since then, the world of commerce and finance had been heavily on the side of national economy, and had found its text book in 1920 in the recommendations of the Geddes Economy Committee.

Even Churchill was not immune from these influences. His record at the Treasury between 1924 and 1929 proved him to be a Chancellor of the Exchequer who maintained the most rigid doctrine of economy, and applied it with a relentless hand to all military expenditure. Even the Navy, his first love, was sacrificed to the new goddess of economy. Not content with reducing the very modest estimates proposed by the Admiralty, he was anxious in 1927 to stop the construction of all new cruisers, and Bridgeman, the First Lord, had the greatest difficulty in persuading him to agree to a programme that fell far short of the Navy's needs. Towards the Air Force he was even more severe. The efforts of Trenchard and myself to persuade him to agree to the next stage of our modest scheme of Air Force expansion were unavailing. The programme of fifty-two squadrons for Home Defence that had been regarded in 1923 as the barest minimum, was pushed into the distant future, with the inevitable result that a crushing handicap was placed on us in the race for air parity in later years. I do not blame Churchill for his action. As a Cabinet colleague I accepted it. Nor do I criticise his responsibility for the instruction issued to the Defence Departments that they should continue to base their estimates on the assumption of a period of ten years of peace, although I think that

he was misguided in withdrawing the time limit that had previously
restricted the formula to a single ten years period. The unlimited
formula certainly embarrassed MacDonald when he became the
Prime Minister of a semi-pacifist Government in 1929. " How
can I change the formula, with Henderson as my Foreign
Secretary, and many of my colleagues opposed to all military
expenditure? " was the anxious question that he put to one of
his closest advisers. MacDonald was in a real difficulty. Unlike
some of his colleagues, he already saw the clouds on the international horizon. He saw also how, when once the time limit
had been withdrawn, it was difficult for any Government, and
almost impossible for a Labour Government, to re-impose it,
short of an immediate threat to peace. In the twenties, neither
governments nor electors foresaw the dangers ahead, and apart
from MacDonald's doubts, Churchill's unlimited formula was
generally approved at the time. It expressed, in fact, an almost
universal desire to make hay while the sun shone.

So sure, indeed, were we of the virtues of disarmament that
we easily became irritated with other countries, and particularly
our former allies, the French, when they did not agree with us.
Anti-French feeling became very strong. Annoyance with our
former allies went very near to becoming affection for our former
enemies. The Press, in and out of season, clamoured for equality
of status for Germany ; Lloyd George's most applauded speeches
were those in which he attacked the French for their obstinacy in
insisting upon military security; the opinion of the Left was
definitely pro-German and anti-French, whilst many Conservatives thought the French unreasonable.

Moral fervour of a strength not to be exaggerated put further
life and power into the political agitation. The meetings held by
the League of Nations Union and the other organisations that
supported disarmament, became semi-religious services. I
attended many of them. They began and ended with prayers
and hymns, and were throughout inspired by a spirit of emotional
revivalism. To many foreigners who were always on the look out
for examples of British hypocrisy, it seemed that, having won our
Empire by force of arms, we were principally interested in preventing any challenge to our right of possession. Criticism of this
kind, although it was easily intelligible in the circumstances
amongst peoples whose national security was threatened, or whose

aspirations had not been satisfied, did not do justice to the profound desire of the British people for a new chapter of international peace.

As in the case of all great movements, the campaign gathered into its ranks men and women with varied motives. The leading figure was undoubtedly Robert Cecil, whose sincerity, singleness of purpose and political talent were of supreme value to his followers. Like many crusaders, his eyes were so entirely fixed upon the Holy City that he did not always take into account the obstacles on the road that led to it. If his colleagues pointed them out to him, he was apt to regard their warning as a sign of lukewarmness in the campaign. As a matter of fact, we were just as anxious as he to stop the threatening race of armaments, and eliminate the increasing horrors of war. None the less, he continued to distrust us, and finally resigned from the Baldwin Government in 1927. Thenceforth, he became the Savonarola of the movement, the preacher who condemned the sins of his fellows, and prophesied the judgment to come.

The combination of all these forces, moral, political and religious, created so strong a volume of opinion in favour of disarmament that no government, right, left or centre, could resist it. The more fully, however, the question was discussed in detail, the more complicated it appeared. The chief obstacle in the way of progress was a fundamental divergence of view between the Germans and ourselves. We believed that armaments were a necessary evil, the extent of which it was essential to reduce as much as possible. They, on the other hand, regarded them as the outward and visible sign of a country's greatness. This difference of outlook had been clearly brought out in the discussions between the British and German Governments before the First World War, when the German Emperor in 1909 told the British Ambassador in Berlin that:

" It was a point of national honour in Germany that the naval programme should be completed, and that no discussion on this subject with a foreign government could be tolerated. Such a proposal would be contrary to the national dignity, and would give rise to internal troubles if the government were to accept."

Yet we, no less than Sir Edward Grey, continued to believe that our conception would eventually persuade the Germans to drop theirs. The many documents that have now come to light prove that Hitler unreservedly accepted the Emperor's view, and regarded large armaments as the essential evidence of Germany's position as a Great Power in the world.

The reconciliation of the British and German views was made much more difficult by the unhelpful attitude of the other Great Powers. Hoover was not prepared to involve the United States in the European wrangle. The Russians were engaged in their favourite sport of fishing in troubled waters. The French, although we sometimes succeeded in modifying their intransigent attitude, never abandoned their demand for security as the preliminary to any reduction of military forces. Having lost the guarantee of the United States and Great Britain, they fell back upon proposals for making more precise the general obligations of the Covenant. This was the history of the Draft Treaty of Mutual Assistance in 1923, and the Geneva Protocol for the Pacific Settlement of International Disputes in 1924. The Treaty and the Protocol would in practice have involved our automatic intervention in the event of any aggressive threat against the settlement of the Treaty of Versailles. Both were rejected with the full approval of the Commonwealth Governments, the one by the Labour Government of 1924, the other by the Baldwin Government of 1925. Having obtained neither Treaty nor Protocol, and despite the Locarno Pact of 1925, the French fundamentally objected to any disarmament, although from time to time they modified their rigid opposition. Wishing to avoid the charge that they alone were holding up progress, they concentrated their case not upon the frontal issue, but upon the many complexities with which the question was inevitably involved. Their argument took the form of showing that piecemeal disarmament was impracticable, and that it was therefore impossible to isolate one part of it, for instance, air armaments or the ' knock out blow ' or the size of aeroplanes, from the other parts connected with army, naval and industrial capacity. They maintained in particular that the reduction of military aviation involved the international control of civil aviation, and that, if there was to be any general disarmament, an international police force must first be created for ensuring peace. Logically they were right, militarily also there were powerful arguments against any piecemeal treatment. Latin logic, in this case well documented and based on expert opinion, was almost unanswerable. None the less, as the whole front was too wide to be taken by general assault, it seemed wiser to us to select a particular point for the beginning of the offensive, and then to continue the advance by stages. Ours was the typically British method of ' line upon line, here a little, there a little '; theirs, the typically French conception of a single plan, one and indivisible, that could not be carried out by instalments. The result of the French argument was to embed any discussions in a mass of detail from which they were never extricated.

The British public refused to pay attention to these technicalities, and assumed that they were merely French pretexts for avoiding any action. No credit was given to the British Government for its persistent efforts to find a bridge between the French demand for security and the German claim for equality, nor was there any appreciation of the fact that we were not engaged upon a unilateral action, but upon an attempt to reach a general agreement that was acceptable to both France and Germany. The result was the inevitable fate of the peacemaker between two irreconcilable combatants. We were abused alternately by each side, whilst the British public was apt to assume that our failure to obtain an acceptable plan was due to the half-heartedness of the British Government and the supposed machinations of the armament industry. Much of the criticism was concentrated upon MacDonald, when he became Prime Minister of the National Government, and upon Simon, when he became Foreign Secretary. In point of fact, MacDonald, pacifist by origin, was indefatigable in his efforts to obtain an agreement. More than once he personally intervened to save the League discussions from complete breakdown. Simon, also a man of peace, devoted his acute mind and exceptional powers of advocacy to the same end. None the less, both were violently attacked for not producing the impossible, and Simon in particular was unjustly held up to obloquy as the cunning lawyer who was splitting hairs in a case that he really did not wish to win.

The agitation had the unfortunate effect of not only reducing British strength, and with it British influence, but of convincing the Germans, not of our good intentions, but of our increasing inability to protect our own interests. Of the weakening of our defences, there was no better evidence than our repeated delays in carrying out the air programme of 1923. The programme had been three times delayed, with the result that our defences were notoriously insufficient at their most vulnerable point. By 1931, we had actually sunk to fifth place in the list of Air Powers.[1]

Just as the Germans realised our weakness in the air, so the Japanese noted our weakness on the sea after the Washington Conference of 1921 and the Naval Treaties of 1930. To add to these outward and visible signs of what appeared to be our declining power, the Labour Government of 1929 to 1931 stopped the work upon the fortifications of Singapore. The Chiefs of Staff, who at this time regarded the Japanese danger as by far the greatest that threatened us, declared that the fortress was left absolutely defenceless.

It was in these years that I became more directly involved in the controversy. As Secretary of State for Air in the Bonar Law Government of 1922, I had been convinced of the need for putting a check on the arms race. Trenchard, the Chief of the Air Staff, with an eye that always looked far into the future, exactly expressed what I thought when he bluntly declared that the invention of aviation was a disaster for the human race. Short of total abolition, the need was to find some method of controlling it. It seemed to me that the best chance was to concentrate upon plans for preventing what then appeared to be the chief danger to civilised life, the ' knock out blow.' The need as I saw it was to prevent the lightning defeat of a peaceful country by a sudden and overwhelming attack from the air. If the ' knock out blow ' could be made more difficult, an aggressor would be less likely to attempt it, and world opinion would have time to mobilise. To eliminate or at least to lessen the risk, therefore, the first and most urgent step in any advance towards disarmament was the reduction in the number and size of bombers. This was a view that ran counter to the French thesis of 'all or nothing.' Baldwin, attracted by my argument, asked me to be one of the Conservative representatives on the Three-Party Committee of the Committee of Imperial Defence that MacDonald set up in March, 1931, " to

[1] *List of Air Powers*   *First Line Aircraft*

France	..	..	..	..	.. 1,320
Italy	..	..	..	..	.. 1,100
U.S.A.	..	..	..	..	.. 1,050
Russia	..	..	..	..	.. 1,000
Great Britain	..	..	..	..	800

(700, if India is excluded)

advise as to the policy to be adopted at the forthcoming Disarmament Conference."[1]

The Committee provided a remarkable example of inter-party co-operation on a vital question of Imperial policy. Only once before had the Opposition been formally brought into the full confidence of the Government of the day upon a vital question of defence. This was in 1908, when Asquith invited Balfour to attend the meetings of the Committee of Imperial Defence during the discussions upon the creation of the Expeditionary Force for the Continent. The precedent could not have been more encouraging. Balfour's help was invaluable to Asquith, and when war came in 1914, it ensured in Parliament an agreed strategy and an Expeditionary Force capable of mobilisation. I have always thought that fuller use should have been made of a procedure that enabled the Government to obtain the co-operation of the Opposition upon a great issue of national safety. Successive Prime Ministers have, however, been reluctant to revive it. With Baldwin, the chief reason was his fear of having Lloyd George in the inner confidence of the Government. With Chamberlain, it was the feeling that the Opposition would only embroil and frustrate the Government's policy. In any case, the Committee appointed by MacDonald worked exceedingly well, and although it represented very different points of political view, ended after ten meetings in a series of agreed resolutions. MacDonald proved an excellent chairman, and Lloyd George, faced with the actual facts of the situation, soon settled down to a responsible discussion of the many complicated problems that he had ignored in his public speeches. The Committee accepted my view as to the danger of the ' knock out blow,' and specifically stated that " the military forces of nations, whether personnel or material, available at the outbreak of war should be limited in such a way as to make it unlikely for an aggressor to succeed with a ' knock out blow.' "

Much the most important of their recommendations, however, was that in which they explicitly repudiated unilateral disarmament. " Any further reduction of British armaments could

---

[1] The Committee, which was fully representative of the three parties, consisted of the Prime Minister, Snowden the Chancellor of the Exchequer, Henderson the Foreign Secretary, Thomas the Dominions Secretary, Shaw the War Secretary, Amulree the Air Secretary, Alexander the First Lord of the Admiralty, Robert Cecil, Austen Chamberlain, Inskip, Eden, Lloyd George, Herbert Samuel, Lothian and myself.

only be undertaken as part of an international agreement containing comparable reductions by other Powers, and after taking into account the particular obligations and dangers of each country." In other words, the three parties agreed for the first time that there was to be an end of what was called ' disarmament by example,' which in practice had meant the unilateral reduction of British strength. By agreeing to this change of attitude, the leading members of the Opposition declared themselves against peace at any price.

Although the Committee's recommendations were never specifically discussed in Parliament, they formed the basis of the Prime Minister's speech on June 29, 1931, in a debate that showed that they represented the general feeling of the House of Commons, Government and Opposition alike. Indeed, the only dissentient voice was Churchill's. Churchill not only saw no good, but much harm in any Disarmament Conference. " The discussions about disarmament have been a cause of friction and ill-will." We alone had disarmed and had " exposed ourselves to real danger." The speech, the first of his great Philippics, brought down upon his head a flood of criticism, including the singularly inept observation of the *New Statesman* that he was " the oldest old woman in Europe." At the time, he stood alone among public men, an *Athanasius contra mundum* both in and out of Parliament.

The Prime Minister's proposals were a year later embodied and expanded in a White Paper on July 7, 1932, and became the text that our delegates followed at the Disarmament Conference until it ended in failure in 1935. The debate in June, 1931, had shown the general agreement between the Opposition and the Government. By July, 1932, however, the political atmosphere had changed after the fall of the Labour Government, and the unanimity that had been the outstanding feature of the 1931 debates had finally disappeared.

CHAPTER IX
The Parting of the Ways

IT WAS the political crisis, following the economic crash, that disrupted the united front. Within little more than a month, the British world was thinking of nothing but the flight from the pound, and the Labour Government that had sponsored the agreed disarmament proposals was out of office. On the Government side, the question of disarmament at once gave place to the immediate need for preventing an economic collapse. On the Opposition side, the Labour resentment against the Prime Minister's action undermined any attempts at further co-operation. The Labour Party, that had been ready to support MacDonald's attitude as long as he was the Prime Minister of a Labour Government, was not prepared to continue it when he became the Prime Minister of a coalition. It would have been better if the defeat of Labour had not been so overwhelming. A stronger and more representative Opposition would have been less irresponsible. The result was that for the next eight years the controversy over armaments became one of the most bitter and unreasonable in British politics. If the Government proposed any increase, the pacifists attacked it, and if it did not go to war with the dictators, they equally attacked it.

The Opposition, reduced by the October Election to a handful of Labour members, with the pacifist George Lansbury, the only ex-Cabinet Minister left in the House of Commons to lead them, showed its fierce hostility to its former leader by attacking a part of the Government programme that was not only surrounded by every kind of international difficulty, but was ready to hand as a rallying point for all the discontented forces in the country. If Arthur Henderson, the President-elect of the Disarmament

Conference, had been the leader of the Opposition instead of Lansbury, it might have been possible to prevent the disarmament movement degenerating into an agitation against all military expenditure. As it was, the Labour propaganda, ostensibly started in support of the Disarmament Conference, became increasingly pacifist, and culminated the following summer in the unanimous resolution of the Miners' Federation at Scarborough in favour of a general strike if ever the British Government went to war.

All this time there continued from critics as distant from each other as Lloyd George and *The Times* a persistent demand for full equality of status for Germany. Hitler's growing power seemed only to strengthen the general sympathy with German claims. The new and unconventional leader had no terrors for the pacifist propagandists. When the Reichstag elections showed a fall in the Nazi vote, Professor Laski, then one of the major prophets of the left, jumped to the conclusion that the danger of dictators had passed.

" The day when they were a vital threat is gone. Hitler never amounted for much except as a symbol . . . a second-rate actor with no real policy . . . not even the gift for action . . . a mere product of events. The men behind him—the big industrialists who subscribed to his funds—pull the strings and he dances. . . . Everything he has done has always been a pose arranged for him behind the scenes. His orations, his shrill threats, his passionate denunciations, reveal no mind of any sort. They have the heavy air of a lesson learned by a man who is being schooled to look like a Mussolini in German dress. . . . Accident apart, it is not unlikely that Hitler will end his career as an old man in some Bavarian village who, in the Tiergarten in the evening, tells his intimates how he nearly overturned the German Reich. Strange battle cries will struggle to his lips; and he will mention names that trembled at his name. But his neighbours will have heard the tale so often that they will shrug their shoulders and bury their faces deeper in their mugs of Pilsener to hide their smiles. The old man, they will think, is entitled to his pipe-dreams. It is comforting to live on the memory of an illusion."[1]

While the Left was declaring that the appearance of Hitler gave no cause for anxiety, the Conservatives were, for the first time, beginning to realise the danger of our weakness in the air.

[1] *Daily Herald*, November 21, 1931.

Baldwin, with the best intentions in the world, increased rather than allayed the anxieties of both camps. Wishing, no doubt, to emphasise the terrible power of the new arm and the need to restrict it, if civilisation was to survive, he included in an impressive speech on disarmament on November 10, 1932, some sentences that subsequently became notorious.

" I think it is well also for the man in the street to realise that there is no power on earth that can protect him from being bombed. Whatever people tell him, the bomber will always get through, and it is very easy to understand that, if you realise the area of space. I said that any town within reach of an aerodrome could be bombed. . . . The only defence is in offence, which means that you will have to kill more women and children more quickly than the enemy if you want to save yourselves."

Both sides in the controversy immediately made their own use of his words, the Opposition for the purpose of claiming that air defence was now admitted to be useless, Churchill and the small band that worked with him, for that of criticising the Conservative leader for adopting a defeatist attitude towards British weakness in the air.

I very well remember the debate. It was one of those occasions when Baldwin dominated the House of Commons. Pulling out the deeper stops in the fine organ of his voice, he gave full scope to his own peace-loving traditions and beliefs. His words were not based on any technical knowledge, still less on any report from the Chiefs of Staff. Nor, I feel sure, had he considered the possible reactions of what he was saying. He was making an emotional appeal to the young men of the new generation, and warning them that unless they found some means of controlling the instruments of destruction, civilised life would be destroyed. In the circumstances of the moment, his speech had the paradoxical effect of strengthening the extreme demand for the abolition of all air forces on the ground that they were useless.

It was against this murky and confused background that the Disarmament Conference had met in Geneva in February, 1932, after eight years of preliminary discussion. It was widely felt at the time that the opening should have been postponed on account of the Japanese aggression in Manchuria. No Government, however, dared to flout public opinion by recommending delay.

According to Benejs, whose word carried particular weight in the League, and whose views were shared by the French Government:

> "A less opportune moment for a conference could not be conceived —at the same time, no government could suggest postponement without creating misunderstanding."

The Conference, therefore, assembled, but in an atmosphere of war and rumours of war.

The Japanese seized the moment for a new act of aggression in China. The first session was actually adjourned for an hour in order to give the Council an opportunity for considering the Japanese attack upon the Chinese quarter in Shanghai. I took part in the incongruous scenes that followed, as the chief representative of the Government of India. Nothing could have been more depressing than the generalities that were uttered by one speaker after another, and the realities that were only too evident in the world outside. On the one hand, there were impressive services in the principal Church, and a relay of inter-denominational preachers, including Archbishop Temple, the presentation of Bibles by the ' Maison de la Bible ' to each of the delegates, and a long series of speeches in a grim hall that re-echoed the never-ending perorations. On the other hand, there was the firm conviction in the minds of many of us that so long as the French demand for security and the German demand for equality of status could not be reconciled, there was little hope of a successful ending to the Conference. I described my feelings in the following letter that I wrote to the Prime Minister, who was in a nursing-home after an operation on his eyes:

> " *India Office,*
> " *Whitehall, S.W.1.*
> " *4th February, 1932*
> " I got back from Geneva last night, very glad to have escaped from its curiously artificial and neurotic atmosphere. Moreover, as you will have seen from the telegrams, all was safe in Jim's[1] keeping. He was indeed tremendous. Metternich in Vienna and Dizzy in Berlin paled into insignificance beside him. The hand of destiny had fallen upon him, and not a moment of the day or night was without his meetings with European statesmen or Empire

---

[1] J. H. Thomas, Secretary of State for the Dominions and Head of the Commonwealth Delegation at the Conference.

delegates. Do not think when I say this that I am criticising him. He did excellently, and as long as he does not get it into his head that he and Geneva are necessarily moving the world, he will continue to do it excellently.

" I have never been to a Council meeting in Geneva, although I once attended one in Paris. Certainly, the Geneva surroundings were depressing, the atmosphere of a conservatory without the heat on, and the curious medley of delegates and stray spectators. I thought that the Chinese and Japanese delegates would have a scrap. Instead of this, the Chinese said nothing, and the Jap, Sato, being very astute, made a statement saying that the move of Great Britain and America was the one thing that the Japanese Government desired, as it would entirely substantiate the Japanese contentions as to what had been happening.

" After a short interval we all, and many more, adjourned to the Bâtiment Electoral, the grim hall in which the Disarmament Conference was to take place. I do not know if you have ever spoken there. If so, I think that you will agree that there are few more dismal buildings in Europe. There was little or no ventilation; and to cope with the bad acoustics, a kind of veil had been drawn over the ceiling and windows. The delegates sat in alphabetical order in the body of the hall, their technical advisers in the lowest tiers around them, and in the galleries an army of savage-looking women, most of them representatives of pacifist societies from the Middle West. To give the affair the atmosphere of an American Presidential meeting, there was a veritable battery of cinema machines that enfiladed the platform, whilst Henderson was so much surrounded by loudspeakers that I could only see the top of his head.

" The Conference began late and with no ceremony. Henderson, Eric Drummond and Philip Baker appeared on the platform together, Philip Baker sitting in a chair directly behind Henderson. We then had to endure an hour and five minutes of the stodgiest speech to which I have ever listened. Pertinax told me that originally it was a much more live affair, as Philip Baker had put into it all his pet propositions, but that the Archbishop of York had virtually made Philip Baker's speech on Sunday in his sermon in the Cathedral, and the secretariat were nervous of some of the stuff in it. Accordingly, a great deal of Philip Baker's had been cut out, and wads of dreary stuff about the number of committees that had been formed, and the procedure that they had adopted in dealing with disarmament had been put in instead. Henderson remained seated the whole time and read it in a good but monotonous voice. Before he had been at it twenty minutes I do not believe there were fifty people in the room listening to him. This was the less to be wondered at as copies of the speech had already been distributed to the delegates in English and French.

" Finding the proceedings very tedious, I interested myself in looking at my fellow delegates. Behind me were the Italians, talking loudly and critically about everything that was happening. A little way on my left, for we were seated alphabetically and I, being India, was with the I's, was the representative of the Hedjaz, dressed as an Arab sheik. He was the only delegate in fancy dress. In the front row were the Afghans. We asked the Afghans why, Afghanistan not being a member of the League, they had come to the Disarmament Conference. They told us that they were short of arms, and that they thought at a Disarmament Conference there would be a chance of picking up second-hand munitions cheap. Behind me, in the R's, I saw the Russians, Litvinov in particular, and Radek, who, having been refused entry into Switzerland as a newspaper correspondent, had got himself in as a delegate. At last the meeting came to an end and we struggled out, dazed and weary, into the fresh air. You will see from all of this that you did not miss much by not being present at the opening. Sometime or other I greatly hope that you will be able to speak, as although I have made these criticisms of what has happened, I none the less feel that this curious body, half Congress, half mass meeting, might rumble into some important action. In any case, if we cannot get on with it, we cannot get on without it."

As soon as the discussions began, the old differences became even more apparent. I became so weary of the wrangle that I left Geneva as soon as I could. Plan after plan was proposed— according to Churchill there were no less than fifty-six plans— only to be rejected or submerged in technical arguments. The proposals that gathered the greatest measure of support were the recommendations of our own 1931 Committee with the condition added to them of a probationary period during which Germany would be deprived of military aircraft. Simon, supported by Eden, his Under-Secretary, was tireless in his efforts to obtain general acceptance of the British scheme. MacDonald reinforced them by going to Geneva on March 16, 1933, to press it upon the Conference. Eventually, after much discussion, it was accepted on June 7 as the text for further discussion. The Conference then adjourned. Interest passed from Geneva to Berlin. Hitler, whose appointment as Chancellor was, in the words of the *News*

Chronicle, " on the whole, a good and necessary thing," made it immediately clear that he would oppose any kind of discrimination against Germany, but that, according to Walter Layton, who had just visited him, he was ready to accept " any form of armaments control that was applied to all alike."

The French were at this moment involved in one of their almost monthly Cabinet crises. The fall of the Sarraut Government had been followed by the most dangerous riots that had been seen in Paris since the Commune. In England, the disarmament movement had drifted into a landslide towards unconditional pacifism. On October 4, the Labour Party Conference came out officially for peace at any price by supporting the July resolution of the Miners' Federation by a further undertaking:

" To pledge itself to take no part in war and to resist it with the whole force of the Labour Movement and to seek consultation forthwith with the Trade Union and Co-operative Movements with a view to deciding and announcing to the country what steps, including a general strike, are to be taken to organise the opposition of the organised working-class movement in the event of war or threat of war, and urges the National Joint bodies to make immediate approaches to endeavour to ensure international action by the workers on the same lines."

Not a word, it will be noticed, was said about collective security. It was a crude and unreserved declaration in favour of complete pacifism.

Ten days afterwards, on October 14, Hitler withdrew from the Disarmament Conference as a protest against any differentiation in the treatment of Germany. Neither this provocative challenge nor his treatment of the Jews and the German Trade Unionists made any difference to the attitude of the Opposition. When a by-election took place in East Fulham on October 25, immediately after the German withdrawal, the Labour candidate fought the contest upon a denunciation of the Government for proposing any rearmament.

" I am asking for votes for peace and disarmament; my opponent demands armaments and preparations for war."

" I would close every recruiting station, disband the army and dismiss the air force. I would abolish the whole dreadful equipment of war and say to the world, ' Do your worst,' " was the message to the electors of Lansbury, the Leader of the Opposition.

The electors were swept into the pacifist wave, and a Conservative majority of 14,521 turned into a minority of 4,840. Three weeks after this staggering victory for peace at any price, Samuel, with his Liberal followers, went into formal opposition. " We are profoundly dissatisfied with the course of events on disarmament " was the conclusion with which Samuel justified his decision.

It was at this point that Baldwin, greatly shaken by the Fulham result, made another of the *obiter dicta* that more than once in his career confused both his friends and foes. Answering a Conservative demand for completing the Air Force Programme of 1923, he made the cryptic observation:[1]

" One of my difficulties here, and of anyone indeed who has to speak on this matter, is that they cannot tell all they know. It is impossible. If I were to stand here and to say where the difficulties are, and who the people are who raise those difficulties, it would be perfectly impossible ever to advance one inch with regard to disarmament. One's lips are sealed."

The phrase " sealed lips " was never to be forgotten by the Opposition, and was to give the inimitable Low a ready-made subject for his Goya-like ruthless caricatures.

The year 1933 ended in Great Britain amidst a strident clamour for disarmament at the very moment when the rift between Germany and France was becoming wider, the chances of agreement at Geneva more remote, and the threat of German militarism more formidable.

The next year, 1934, saw the climax of the movement. The Opposition voted against all the Service Estimates, and in March, Robert Cecil and the League of Nations started the campaign that afterwards came to be known by the misleading label of the Peace Ballot. The country was systematically canvassed in the autumn by 500,000 volunteer workers on behalf of a committee that represented more than twenty powerful organisations, and a questionnaire circulated to many millions of men and women.

The replies were what the questioners expected. The only hesitation in answering " yes " was shown over Question 5, where

[1] House of Commons on November 29, 1933.

the vote for military as compared with economic sanctions fell by more than three millions.[1] The so-called ballot emphasised the already obvious fact that the country stood for peace. The questions had, however, been so worded that they had no bearing on the actual state of the world. They gave the impression that we could depend on collective security when four of the Great Powers held aloof, and they kept discreetly in the background the need for British rearmament. The real question that should have been asked: " Do you support British rearmament in the interests of peace? " was carefully avoided. The result was a strengthening of all the pacifist influences at a time when peace was being threatened, and an encouragement to the complacent in their belief that no special effort was necessary to strengthen British defences. The Opposition at once exploited the situation for an attack on the Government for increasing the Air Force, and failing to make quicker progress in the disarmament discussions in Geneva.

The Ballot had an even more unfortunate effect on the Continent. At the very moment when France on the one hand was being weakened by a series of political crises, and Hitler on the other was consolidating his power in Germany, the impression was spread abroad that England was for peace at any price.

In the meanwhile, Hitler and Goering had come into the

[1] The detailed analysis of the Ballot was as follows. The figures were announced by Viscount Cecil at the Albert Hall on June 27, 1935.

Question 1. Should Great Britain remain a member of the League of Nations?

Yes	No	Doubtful	Abstentions
11,090,387	355,888	10,470	102,425

Question 2. Are you in favour of an all-round reduction in armaments by international agreement?

Yes	No	Doubtful	Abstentions
10,470,489	862,775	12,062	213,839

Question 3. Are you in favour of an all-round abolition of national military and naval aircraft by international agreement?

Yes	No	Doubtful	Abstentions
9,533,558	1,689,786	16,976	318,845

Question 4. Should the manufacture and sale of armaments for private profit be prohibited by international agreement?

Yes	No	Doubtful	Abstentions
10,417,329	775,415	15,076	351,345

Question 5. Do you consider that, if a nation insists on attacking another, the other nations should combine to compel it to stop by

(a) economic and non-military measures?

Yes	No	Doubtful	Abstentions
10,027,608	635,074	27,255	855,107

(b) if necessary, military measures?

Yes	No	Doubtful	Abstentions
6,784,368	2,351,981	40,893	2,364,441

Total votes: 11,599,165 (27.9 per cent of total number of voters over 18 in Great Britain and Northern Ireland).

On Questions 5a and 5b the statement " I accept the Christian Pacifist attitude " was allowed as an alternative to the answer " Yes " or " No." On Question 5a, 14,121 votes of this kind were recorded, and 17,482 on Question 5b.

open. There was no longer any doubt as to their determination to obtain parity in the air with the least possible delay. The Conservative Party, that at first had been sceptical about the importance of air power, now became more keenly alive to the growing danger.

The clash between the views of the Government and the Opposition came to a head in a debate on July 19, 1934, when Baldwin outlined the programme of forty-one new squadrons for Home Defence. Although the increase included several squadrons that should have been formed years before under the 1923 plan, and was the barest minimum for national safety in the troubled state of Europe, Labour's reply was a vote of censure on July 30. The Prime Minister's defence was once again one of those speeches in which, whilst seeming to think aloud, he made use of words that were not fully understood at the time or ever forgotten in subsequent years.

" Let us never forget this; since the day of the air, the old frontiers are gone. When you think of the chalk cliffs of Dover, you think of the Rhine. That is where our frontier lies."

The idea behind these sentences was sound, but if it was not to be misunderstood and misrepresented, it needed careful explanation. In its abrupt and unexplained form, it confused the debate and irritated our Continental neighbours.

The battle that was now developing on two fronts, continued even more fiercely after the announcement of the figures of the Peace Ballot. To the Labour attack on the Government from the Left was added a counter-attack by Churchill from the Right. Whilst Labour wanted no armaments, Churchill continued his active campaign for more by moving an amendment to the Address on November 18 demanding a bigger and quicker programme. It was in the debate that followed that Baldwin made two assertions that led in future years to continual controversy. The first was that, contrary to many rumours, Germany was not rapidly reaching parity in the air with Great Britain; the second, that we should never accept a position of air inferiority. These are his words:

" It is not the case that Germany is rapidly approaching equality with us. All that I would say is this, that H.M. Government are determined in no conditions to accept any position of inferiority with regard to what air force may be raised in Germany in the future."

The Air Staff, in advising Baldwin to make this statement, were anxious to contradict the exaggerated stories that were then current as to the growth of the Luftwaffe. Having suffered from the slow motion of the British expansion, it was no doubt difficult for them to believe it possible for any new force to outstrip British strength in the near future. Parity seemed a standard easy enough for us to maintain, but still difficult for Hitler to reach. It was against this background that Baldwin made a pronouncement that certainly gave the impression that the position was not as serious as was actually the case.

While he was defending our very modest expansion, French opinion hardened against any reduction of armaments. Barthou, the new Foreign Minister, was definitely opposed to any concessions to Germany as long as French security was in danger. The complete deadlock reached at Geneva was followed by the French Minister's visits to the capitals of the Little Entente for the purpose of strengthening the *cordon sanitaire* round Germany's eastern frontiers. His assassination at Marseilles brought this chapter of French policy to an abrupt end before it was possible to test the strength of the French alliances in Central and Western Europe.

Laval, who succeeded him as Foreign Minister, was less likely to be intransigent towards German claims. French security was none the less his main objective. His approach to it, however, differed from his predecessor's. In his case, it began at the Italian end. French security needed a friendly Italy that would not only free the French Army for protecting the eastern frontier of France, but would help to maintain the independence of Austria, and French influence in Central Europe and the Balkans.

In Great Britain, the early months of 1935 witnessed an intensification of the partisan battle. The Left continued to clamour for disarmament. The insignificant increase of £4 millions in the Service Estimates, carefully explained and justified in a White Paper of March 5, brought down upon the Government a barrage of Opposition abuse. Herbert Morrison, for instance, whose party had just withdrawn the L.C.C. grant from the School Cadet Corps, declared in Bermondsey on March 13 that:

" Toryism as represented by the National Government had resumed its historic role as the party of militarism and aggressive armaments."

Even so open-minded and balanced a Liberal as Lothian was writing in *The Times* on March 11 in support of the German claim for equality, and describing the inoffensive phrases in the White Paper as " an inadvertent carry over from pre-equality days."

In spite of these attacks the Government persisted along its parallel lines of appeasement and gradual rearmament, the line of appeasement being much the more popular of the two. Whilst a White Paper on Defence described the line of rearmament, two of Simon's moves were intended to advance the line of appeasement. On February 3, an Anglo-French declaration reaffirmed Anglo-French solidarity, and on March 25, he visited Hitler for a comprehensive discussion of all the outstanding questions with Germany. The date that had been arranged for the visit proved to be most unfortunate. A few days before it was to take place, Hitler publicly repudiated the chief restriction of the Versailles Treaty and announced the reintroduction of conscription and the formation of an army of thirty-six divisions. The question at once arose as to whether it was right to proceed with the Berlin meeting after the Führer had so flagrantly flouted not only the Peace Treaty, but also the Anglo-French Pact, that only a month before had pledged Great Britain and France to oppose any unilateral repudiation of Treaty obligations.

The Times, expressing a widely held view, and bent upon bringing Germany back to the Disarmament Conference and co-operation with Great Britain and France, insisted that the visit should be carried out, and that nothing but harm would be done to the cause of peace by agreeing with the French proposal to take the question of German conscription to the League of Nations.

After weighing the arguments for and against the visit, the Government came to the conclusion that it was best, on the whole, that the visit should take place in spite of Hitler's provocation. Simon and Eden accordingly went to Berlin, and for two days discussed with Hitler the whole field of Anglo-German relations. On the first day Hitler insisted that he was the most reasonable person in the world, and was only asking for peace and justice in the matter of armaments. All that he needed was fair treatment— an army the size of the French Army, parity of air force with either of the British or French Air Forces, and a fleet a third of the size of the British Fleet. As to multilateral pacts in Central and Eastern Europe, he was against them on the ground that the German people would never undertake any obligation to fight on the side of the Bolsheviks. In any case, they were unnecessary, as there was no threat to peace nor any possibility that Germany would declare war on Russia, nor was Austria threatened by anyone.

On the second day, the question of an Air Pact for restricting the uncontrolled increase of air power was the main subject of discussion. Simon outlined our proposals—immediate air action against an aggressor, a prohibition of the bombardment of civil targets, and an agreed restriction of air armaments after a Pact was signed. It was at this point that Hitler, who seemed inclined to give them favourable consideration, incidentally observed that the German Air Force had already reached parity with the British. Our own staff never accepted this claim, and took the view that he was bluffing to impress Simon. Whether this was so or not, the remark profoundly disturbed British public opinion, and became the subject of many debates in Parliament.

Upon the question of naval armaments, Hitler was more forthcoming. On no account, he declared, would he build a fleet in competition with the British. He was ready at once to agree to a conference in London, when he would propose to restrict the German Navy to thirty-five per cent of the British strength.

Apart from the promise about the German Navy, the talks were inconclusive. Whilst they confirmed the view that Hitler would not or could not take any military action for a period of some years, they gave no ground for the continued complacency of public opinion in Great Britain. Nor did they make any less urgent the need for strengthening the Anglo-Italian front in the impending conference at Stresa. It is, however, significant of the general feeling in support of a *rapprochement* with Germany that *The Times*, once again insisting on its central objective of German appeasement, was obviously doubtful of the wisdom of an Anglo-Italian meeting. It is to MacDonald's credit that he came out strongly against this one-sided attitude, and in an article of April 27 in the *News Letter*, the weekly paper of the National Labour Party, severely criticised the Germans for their intransigent militarism, and the Germanophiles in this country for their blindness in swallowing the German case.

How necessary was his protest, appeared a few weeks later, when a hymn of praise went up in response to the speech that Hitler made in the Reichstag on May 21. In it he declared himself to be a man of peace who would faithfully carry out Germany's international obligations. Upon points of detail, he followed closely the lines that he had set out in the conversations with Simon. The effect was exactly what he intended. All the pacifist forces in Great Britain were at once mobilised against the Government's rearmament proposals. The Parliamentary Labour Party immediately decided to vote against the air programme, and, backed by the Trade Union Congress and the National Executive of the Party, demanded a special international conference to take advantage of Hitler's magnificent offer. The religious leaders in the country were equally insistent that we should welcome with open arms Hitler's approach. Archbishop Temple and Dean Inge were for once found to be in agreement. " Hitler," wrote the Archbishop to *The Times*, " has made in the most deliberate manner offers which are a great contribution to the secure establishment of peace." " What an admirable letter! " responded the Dean three days afterwards. When Baldwin ventured to say a word of caution and to point out that the collective security of peace was still endangered by the absence of four Great Powers from the League, Herbert Morrison, using a metaphor that subsequently created an unfortunate precedent for Chamberlain, declared to the Fabian Society on May 24 that

" The Government had either lost the boat or was in danger of losing it, and that Baldwin had missed the opportunity for a big, inspiring and mighty gesture."

It was conveniently forgotten that all the most burning questions of Europe were still unsettled. The German sword was hanging over Austria's head, and Austrians were saying that Hitler's speech was nothing more than a blind for an impending *coup*. Yet the agitation against British rearmament went on more fiercely than ever before, and disarmament proved to be the most effective cry at by-elections.

Should the National Government in these circumstances have taken up the challenge and with or without a mandate embarked in 1933 or 1934 upon a full-scale programme of rearmament?

Churchill in 1936 attacked Baldwin for failing to act in these years even though he had no mandate.[1] The National Government had undoubtedly an overwhelming majority, and it could be urged plausibly that a great rearmament programme could have been pushed through Parliament. The description, however, that I have given of the public attitude to armaments shows how formidable would have been the opposition to any such attempt. Organised labour would have resisted it, the general body of electors would have felt that they had returned the National Government on false pretences, the Conservative Party, whilst ready to support moderate increases in defence expenditure, was not yet prepared for a complete change of policy. In 1933 and 1934 it was not practical politics for the National Government, returned on the economy mandate of 1932 to reverse its whole policy and concentrate on a programme of arms. Should, then, MacDonald have asked the King for a Dissolution, and the electors for a new mandate? For good reasons MacDonald rejected the idea of a general election. The National Government had still three years to run, its majority in the House of Commons was overwhelming, and its programme of economy not yet completed. Faithfully reflecting the general opinion of the country, the Cabinet believed that war was neither imminent nor inevitable. The King would certainly have objected to granting a Dissolution in these conditions. If the Prime Minister had persisted, and the King had eventually withdrawn his opposition, the Government that forced an election that seemed both premature and unnecessary, would have been swept from power, and a pacifist successor put in its place.

[1] See Appendix, p. 193.

CHAPTER X

The
Anglo-German Naval Treaty

IT WAS in these conditions that I went to the Foreign Office. The Government was still substantially the National Government of 1932, though Baldwin had made some changes in MacDonald's personnel. The economy mandate still bound it, for there had been no General Election. The country was still under the illusion that British policy did not need military support, that our prestige was as unassailable as in the days of Queen Victoria, and that Hitler and the Japanese would collapse before us. A consistent policy was impossible without power behind it, and there was no chance for at least three years of any rearmament programme giving us the military forces that we needed. Collective Security, the panacea of the Labour Party, had ceased to be either collective or secure. The United States was outside the League and dominated by extreme isolationism. Germany, Italy and Japan were flouting the Covenant and starting to form a definitely hostile *bloc*. The Manchurian crisis of 1931 had clearly shown that unless we could rely on military help from the United States, we could not risk war in the East while the threatening clouds were gathering in the West, and that Congress had no intention of agreeing to combined military action against Japan or any other Great Power. The best, therefore, that I could hope for in my new post, was to avoid frontal crises until we were strong enough to overcome them. In the meanwhile, the public, having failed to realise the consequences of our military weakness, still expected a British Foreign Minister to behave like Palmerston with the Victorian Fleet at his beck and call.

In my new post I found myself faced with a long list of questions that needed answering at once. The first concerned my relations with Eden. He had established for himself so notable a position both in Geneva and Westminster that his loss would have been very serious to the world at large as well as to Great Britain. I myself was most anxious that he should not leave the Foreign Office. Baldwin agreed with me, and asked me to see him and persuade him to continue as an assistant Minister whose chief duty would be League of Nations affairs. As a result, Eden and I had a friendly meeting, and all that seemed to be needed was a formula that, while avoiding the creation of a dyarchy within the Foreign Office, gave the assistant Minister a definite sphere of work and an adequate status in the Government. I not unnaturally expected Baldwin to define a *modus operandi* that might well irritate personal susceptibilities if its settlement was left to the two parties directly concerned with it. He would not, however, involve himself in the details, and merely passed me a pencil note at a Cabinet meeting, asking me " to settle them direct with the young man." In the meanwhile, he authorised a notice to the Press stating that Eden had been appointed " Minister without Portfolio for League of Nations Affairs." The Law Officers at once intervened to say that a Minister with a special Portfolio could not be a Minister without Portfolio. The result was an immediate change in the description that, insignificant in itself, gave the impression of fumbling at the start of a new chapter. Eden and I, however, aided by a wisely worded draft suggested to me by Findlater Stewart, were able to agree upon our respective activities, all the more easily as he realised better than anyone the danger of a divided sovereignty in the Foreign Office, and I was most anxious to give him the fullest possible scope for his great talents. Even so, there were critics of the arrangement, particularly Austen Chamberlain, who feared a division of ministerial responsibility.

Baldwin's dislike of detail had left behind another difficulty. He had told Eden that if he went on at the Foreign Office, he would make Cranborne, his Parliamentary Private Secretary, an Under-Secretary of State. Cranborne was in every way qualified for the post, and the Foreign Office needed another Under-Secretary. Baldwin, however, did not realise that special legislation was needed for carrying out his promise. The result was that within a few days of entering my new office, I had to pilot a

Bill through the House of Commons in the face of not a little criticism, and at a time when I was overwhelmed with urgent questions, such as the Anglo-German Naval Agreement, that needed an immediate answer.

How often during these days I wished myself back in my turret room in the India Office where, surrounded by advisers who were all agreed upon the same policy, I could devote myself to a single purpose. The contrast between the two wings of the great block of Government offices could not have been greater. The Ministers' rooms, although only separated by a passage, were poles apart. In the India Office, there was the intimacy of a small study, the comfort of the eighteenth-century mahogany from East India House, and the delight of the Persian miniatures from Moghul Delhi; in the Foreign Office, a vast and draughty saloon with windows too big either to shut or to open, a writing-table in the middle of the room that made conversation difficult, and the atmosphere of a pretentious hotel lounge. Being very sensitive to my surroundings, I was at once depressed by the change. I was still more disturbed by what seemed to me to be the rarefied atmosphere of my new environment. Everyone seemed to be over-excited. There appeared to be no generally accepted body of opinion on the main issues. Diametrically opposite views were pressed upon me, and sometimes with the intolerance of an *odium theologicum*.

It has been said that this restless state of affairs was due to the attempts of Warren Fisher, the permanent head of the Treasury, to absorb the Foreign Office into the general administrative system of the Civil Service. Warren Fisher, who often discussed with me questions of organisation, undoubtedly thought that the efficiency of the Foreign Office compared badly with that of the rest of the Civil Service. If he wished to make changes, it was because he believed that the other offices were attracting more ability than the Foreign Office. I could not judge whether he was right or wrong. I am, however, certain that while I was Foreign Secretary, there was no foundation for the charge that he interfered in the administration of the Office, still less that he dictated foreign policy to anyone. He was a great patriot, whole-heartedly engaged at this time, with Vansittart as his chief colleague, in preparing plans for intensifying British rearmament. I doubt if Whitehall has ever produced two such vivid personalities, each fired with the same consuming spirit. The reports of the Defence Requirements Committee, composed of the Chiefs of Staff and the heads of the great Departments of Whitehall, bear witness to the crusading fervour that these two remarkable men put into the campaign for strengthening our defences. The divisions that I found in the Foreign Office were not due to any meddling by the Treasury. They were the result of the general feeling of frustration, created by the repeated failure of a foreign policy without adequate force to support it.

Vansittart felt intensely this atmosphere of division and defeatism. It was his mission to dissipate it. From the first moment, I came under the influence of his singleness of purpose. His creed was short and undeviating. He firmly believed in the reports of Hitler's aggressive plans, he was certain that the only method of blocking them was by British rearmament, and that as British rearmament would take years to complete, the immediate need was to gain time and strengthen the allied front. Coming as I did from the distant world of India, the fervid recitation of his faith at first shocked me. I had not before realised the imminence of the German danger, and the slowness of our rearmament programme. Hitler had appeared on the scene when I was thinking of Gandhi, the German Air Force had developed when I was struggling with the complicated accounts of the Indian contribution to Imperial Defence. As for air parity, a new term that meant different things to different people, I had not yet brought myself to believe that the Royal Air Force would not maintain its superiority in numbers, training and equipment over an upstart Luftwaffe. Once convinced, however, I threw all the influence that I possessed into the double campaign for more arms and more time. Vansittart's fertile mind and unequalled knowledge of European politics and personalities were invaluable to me, whilst my more conventional methods may have been useful to him as a supplement to his sparkling *tours de force*. In Ralph Wigram, one of the younger members of the staff, he found a brilliant lieutenant to support his campaign for time and arms. Together, we started with very little light around us upon a new chapter in the encircling gloom. Vansittart's refrain never ceased to ring in my head. " We are terribly weak. We must gain time for becoming stronger. Only military strength will stop Hitler, and at present we do not possess it." These convictions, so far from being theoretical, or elaborated in the vacuum of a Whitehall office, were not only founded upon actual facts, but needed to be applied immediately to two concrete cases, the Anglo-German Naval Agreement and the Abyssinian crisis.

The Naval Agreement was waiting to be signed. Should we sign it? Mussolini was already moving great armies into Abyssinia. Should we make a final effort to prevent the rupture of the Allied front in face of an aggressive Hitler? The answers to both these questions bristled with complexities, and to understand, let alone to justify our attitude, it is necessary to follow closely the course of events that led up to our final decisions. Many of the details may now be as tedious as the story of disarmament that I have already described. Nearly twenty years have passed since we were struggling with them, and subsequent history has changed the focus in which we then saw them. There is a further reason for forgetting them. The world of to-day is bored and irritated by the *pièces justificatives* of former Ministers. Whilst I fully admit these objections against stirring the dead leaves left by past storms, I none the less believe that we may sometimes find beneath them deposits that still have their use. In any case, it is profitable to follow in retrospect and stage by stage two controversies that brought into the open some of the most difficult problems of the years between the two wars.

The very first paper of importance that I found in my Foreign Office tray was the draft of the Anglo-German Naval Agreement. Ribbentrop was already in London waiting for its signature. Behind it was a long history of naval negotiations that had continued intermittently since the Washington Conference of 1921, when the naval powers had for the first time agreed upon the limitation of their fleets. Since then, there had been periodical attempts to extend the agreement. Once, in 1927, when the discussions were transferred to Geneva, they had given rise to some most unfortunate recriminations between the Americans and ourselves. This episode confirmed the view that the question of naval limitation was best treated away from Geneva and apart from the questions of land and air disarmament. Naval problems were very different from the problems of armies and air forces, and the countries concerned with them could be counted on one hand. This being so, it was generally agreed that the method of the Washington Conference should be continued, and that the

British Government should be responsible for organising the periodical meetings of the naval powers. By 1935 one of these meetings had already taken place in London in 1931, and another was due in 1936, when all the limitations upon a race of naval armaments would come to an end unless some new agreement could be made. The prospect of unrestricted expansion was particularly formidable. The existing navies were obsolete, and replacement, much worse unchecked expansion, threatened national bankruptcy. As early, therefore, as 1934 the British Government started discussions with the other naval powers with the object of making some agreed plan for the Conference due to take place in London in 1936. In the meanwhile, the Germans had unquestionably begun to build a fleet beyond the limits of the Versailles Treaty. As the naval powers had no intention of stopping them by force, the potential strength of the German Fleet became an essential factor in the problem. It was not, therefore, surprising that when we asked the Americans, the Japanese, the French and the Italians for their preliminary views as to the size of fleets, they all declared that they must know more about the German programme before they could answer. It was to obtain this information that Simon was authorised by the Cabinet to raise the question of naval construction with Hitler when he saw him in February, 1935. In answer to Simon's inquiry Hitler had categorically declared that he was ready to agree that the German Fleet would not exceed thirty-five per cent of the British. The three Staffs, particularly the Naval Staff, regarded the offer as supremely important. Not only did it provide a firm basis for the 1936 Conference, but it ensured us a superiority over the German Fleet twice as great as we had possessed in 1914, and avoided a race of naval armaments that would beggar the British Treasury. The Chiefs of Staff declared in so many words that although our greatest danger was then Japan, we could only send the main fleet to the Far East if we were sure both of the French Fleet and of a great superiority over the German Fleet in European waters. This superiority could be guaranteed by the limitation offered by Hitler.

These arguments seemed to us unanswerable, and we at once urged them upon the other naval powers. The American and Japanese Governments replied that they saw no objection to the German proposal, while the French unofficially told us that we had better go ahead without asking them for a formal answer. It was on the strength of these replies that we invited Hitler to send a delegation to London to discuss the details of a formal agreement. Hitler then publicly announced his offer in a mass demonstration on May 21, and immediately afterwards agreed to send Ribbentrop and a delegation of naval experts to London in the first week of June. As it turned out, this was the very moment when MacDonald was resigning and I was entering the Foreign Office.

Our delegation consisted of Robert Craigie, the Foreign Office expert upon naval treaties, and two senior naval officers. Craigie had the great advantage of being *persona gratissima* to the Naval Staff. From the days of the Washington Conference he had specialised in naval questions, and had at his fingers' ends every technical detail that affected qualitative and quantitative limitation. He and the Admirals understood each other. Nothing in the negotiation escaped his methodical and well-instructed mind. Ribbentrop was accompanied by Admiral Raeder and one or two other naval officers.

The background of the Conference was no secret to anyone. All the naval powers knew its history and understood its consequences. Hitler's speech on May 21 had made his offer reverberate round the world, and our readiness to welcome it was not only well known, but generally approved. We wished, however, to obtain the official blessings of the other naval powers before we signed an Agreement. Our first intention, therefore, was to begin the Conference with a discussion of the details, and to postpone formal acceptance of the thirty-five per cent ratio until we received the answers of the other Governments. Ribbentrop made this procedure impossible by insisting upon the settlement of the ratio as the preliminary condition of any detailed negotiation. When the question was put to the Cabinet, it was agreed that no question of procedure should block the discussion, but that we should not actually sign until we had given the other naval powers a further opportunity to give us their views. We accordingly telegraphed to them urgently on June 7.

The American Government replied at once that they left the decision entirely to us; the Japanese, that they had no objection to the agreement. The Italian, already irritated with us over Abyssinia, avoided a direct answer by declaring that all armament questions should be considered together, whilst from the French we had no official reply, although we knew that they still disliked any unilateral agreement with Germany. Laval, who had recently become President of the Council, was occupied with one of the internal crises in which he revelled, and would not give his mind to our urgent request for his Government's answer. Faced in these circumstances with the choice of making an agreement that seemed to us to benefit the Allies, and particularly the French, who were guaranteed a thirty per cent superiority over the German Fleet, or of losing another chance of restricting German rearmament, I urged the Cabinet on June 11 to authorise the signature of the Agreement. I pointed out that not only did it guarantee to the British Fleet a decisive superiority over the German Fleet in European waters, but that it also saved the French and Italians from a German rivalry that, if it was not checked, was certain to defeat them. There were two further advantages; first, an undertaking, greatly valued by our Naval Staff, to exchange full information as to programmes and construction, and secondly, an extension of the overall thirty-five per cent ratio to cover each category of ship. I admitted that the most vulnerable provision in the document concerned submarines. The Germans were to have the immediate right to a ratio of forty-five per cent of British submarine tonnage, and an ultimate right to parity. The Naval Staff, however, believing at the time that we had mastered the submarine danger, did not object to this concession. Indeed, they saw some advantage in it, as it was expressly agreed that any additional submarine tonnage would mean a corresponding reduction in the tonnage of the rest of the German Fleet. And most important of all, the German undertaking was accompanied by a formal acceptance of the International Rules of Submarine Warfare. The Cabinet readily accepted my recommendation, and I was authorised to sign. Even so, we postponed the actual signature until the 18th to give the French further time for expressing their official view. When they still failed to answer, we could wait no longer. The signature, therefore, took place at the Foreign Office on June 18, but without any pomp or circumstance. Ribbentrop had wished to turn the occasion into an impressive ceremony for the glorification of his country, and still more, a personal triumph for himself. I had no intention of pandering to his vanity. I regarded the Agreement as nothing more than a practical arrangement for gaining time and reducing the risks that faced Europe in general, and Great Britain in particular. Accordingly, there was no special publicity to mark the final act. Only the members of the two delegations were present, and the speeches that Ribbentrop and I made were restricted to the barest exchange of conventional compliments.

In the meanwhile, we kept the Opposition informed of the course of events, with the result that on June 21 George Hall put a question on the subject to the First Lord of the Admiralty. The answer declared that the German offer was " of great importance since it holds out the possibility of averting for all time the threat of naval rivalry between Germany and this country." The Opposition did not seem to be unduly worried over the Government's action, and postponed any detailed discussion to a debate on the Foreign Office and Admiralty Votes.

Before, however, the discussion took place, two developments embittered the question. First, a virulent anti-British agitation in Paris, and secondly, one of Lloyd George's marauding forays against a British Government that he detested. The French Press, looking for an opportunity to attack us over our opposition to Mussolini's Abyssinian aggression, abused us for breaking the united front that we had proclaimed on February 5, 1934, and cemented at Stresa only a few months before. A special brand of venom was added to their bitterness when they declared that, whilst we were ready to give our naval secrets to the Germans, we refused them to the French. The truth was that the Germans had offered us an exchange of naval information on the basis of reciprocity, that the French could have the same facilities on similar conditions, and would in any case be given full information when they came to London for discussions at the Naval Conference. The French irritation, incongruously fomented by the Francophobe and Germanophile Lloyd George, came to a head in the House of Commons in a Foreign Affairs debate on July 11, and an Admiralty debate on July 22. As I had made my first important Foreign Affairs speech at the opening of the July 11 debate, the detailed answer to Lloyd George's attack was left to Eden. In a very effective speech he pointed out that the Agreement marked a long step forward in the cause of disarmament, that it gave us a sixty-five per cent superiority over the German Fleet, and the French a thirty per cent superiority in contrast to the thirty per cent inferiority with which they had started the war of 1914. The answer satisfied almost everyone except Lloyd George who, unappeased, returned on July 22 to the charge on the Naval Vote. Upon this occasion he was answered by the First Lord, Eyres Monsell, in one of the best speeches that I ever heard in the House of Commons. In it, he made it clear that the Naval Staff on naval grounds entirely approved of the Agreement, and that we had much to lose and nothing to gain by rejecting it. At one point he quoted with great effect the conclusion of the President of the Foreign Affairs Committee of the French Senate.

" Have we not perhaps irritated our friends for the last few years with our everlasting mania for linking into a whole all the questions under discussion in order to solve any of them? If the ' multi-lateralism ' dear to our bureaucrats has hitherto resulted in nothing but trivial arguments, is it not understandable that the British should prefer less dilatory methods than those which have resulted in the rearmament of Germany, not to 35 per cent but to 130 per cent of the French Army? "

The debate ended with a vote of 247 to 44 in favour of the Government, with Churchill voting in the majority, even though he had criticised us for not obtaining the formal agreement of all the Allies before we signed. Parliamentary criticism then died down. Even in France, where the anti-British Press continued to rage, an arrangement that guaranteed the French Navy a decisive superiority over the German, and allowed the French Government full freedom to build a fleet as strong as they liked, did not on second thoughts seem too bad a plan. Laval told Eden, who went to Paris to explain our case, that he quite understood the British position, and did not object to the ratio, but that owing to the public outcry, he would have to wait a few weeks before sending his experts to London to discuss the forthcoming Naval Conference. When Léger insisted upon the gravity of the breach of the Versailles Treaty and our failure to use it to greater effect as a bargaining counter, Eden rounded upon him with a retort that was never answered.

" Did M. Léger think that Part V of the Versailles Treaty that restricted German armaments was now worth anything as a bargaining counter? . . . Our case was that we circumscribed

Germany's powers and did not give Germany any new powers.
We could not postpone the naval question for a general agreement
on all armaments that might never be made. . . . The fact that
Hitler was ready to accept the international rules for submarine
warfare was of great value to France and Great Britain."

Mussolini, whom Eden saw immediately after his interview
with Laval, did not criticise the terms of the Agreement, but
claimed that he ought to have been more fully consulted about
it. He seemed, however, to have been impressed by the fact that
the German naval authorities thought the thirty-five per cent
ratio too small for Germany, and that the Agreement had been
made by Hitler on his own initiative and against the advice of
his experts.

These discussions confirmed my view that we were right to
seize the opportunity of restricting one very important side of
German rearmament. Vansittart strongly supported me. With
neither of us was there any question of placating Hitler. Seeing,
however, Hitler's growing strength in the air and on land, and
our serious weakness, we were forced to play for time. The
Agreement might not last for ever—no international agreement
was ever permanent—but it would at least have the effect of
slowing down the construction of a formidable German Fleet and
giving us time to rebuild and strengthen our own. Having taken
this first step, we hoped to follow it up with an Air Pact on the
basis of parity for ourselves, France and Germany, and we
believed that we were more likely to succeed with the second stage
when once we had shown Hitler that an agreement upon naval
armaments was possible. The alternatives were either drift or
preventive war. No one in Great Britain or France was prepared
to go to war with Germany in order to stop German rearmament. A preventive war, therefore, was out of the question. The
alternative of drift had let him build up an army as strong as the
French, and an air force as strong as ours. French politics had
already stopped agreements that would have restricted the
German Army to 300,000 men and the Luftwaffe to 300 first-line
machines.

The Naval Conference was due to take place in London in a
few months' time, and if any agreement was to be reached at it,
it was essential to define and fix the German position. Whilst
these reasons in favour of the Agreement seemed to us to be

overwhelming, we were fully conscious of the criticisms against the procedure that we had to use for making it. The Agreement meant the official acceptance of the already notorious fact that Part V of the Versailles Treaty was obsolete. It was a bilateral pact between the Germans and ourselves that followed negotiations in which the French had not taken part. The discussions ended after a few days, with a document signed by Ribbentrop and myself on behalf of our two Governments, and did not give much time for the further exchange of explanations between the Allies. A negotiation of this kind could easily be made to look like a hole-and-corner affair carried on behind the backs of our French friends. The fact, however, was that there was no other way of making an agreement that we regarded as of exceptional value both to the French as well as to ourselves. When we consulted Laval, he was obviously reluctant to send us an answer. Indeed, he gave us throughout the impression that he was ready to accept an accomplished fact, and did not wish to be asked to give a definite reply to any official Note.

Looking back at the rush of these events that almost over-whelmed me within a few hours of my becoming Foreign Secretary, I feel neither regret nor doubt as to the course that I then took. Has subsequent history condemned my judgment or changed my mind? So far from weakening the conclusions that I reached at the time, it has confirmed them. As a footnote, therefore, to my description of the negotiations, I add these facts that have come to light in the official German documents published since the war.

When war broke out in September, 1939, the German Fleet was amazingly weak and unready.[1] It consisted of two old

---

[1] *The Führer Conferences on Naval Affairs* (issued by the Admiralty) and *Hitler's Strategy* by F. H. Hinsley (Cambridge University Press, page 241). The German Surface Fleet in September, 1939.

Battleships: *Schlesien* and *Schleswig-Holstein* (both unfit for operations outside the Baltic).

Battle Cruisers: *Gneisenau* and *Scharnhorst*.

Pocket Battleships: *Admiral Graf Spee*, *Admiral Scheer* and *Deutschland* (renamed *Lutzow* in 1940).

8-inch Cruisers: *Admiral Hipper* and *Blücher*.

6-inch Cruisers: *Konigsberg, Nürnberg, Leipzig, Köln, Karlsruhe, Emden.*

Small vessels included 22 destroyers, 20 torpedo-boats and 20 E-boats.

As to the underwater fleet, there were never more than seven or eight U-boats at sea throughout 1940. Yet two million tons of British and Allied shipping was destroyed. If Hitler had given to submarine building a priority parallel with the priority that he gave to the Luftwaffe, our losses would have paralysed our whole war effort.

battleships, two battle cruisers, three pocket battleships, eight cruisers, twenty destroyers and fifty-seven submarines, of which only twenty-six were capable of operating in the Atlantic. Admiral Raeder was gravely perturbed by the state of affairs. The Agreement had, in fact, meant so heavy a handicap upon the German Navy that in his view it needed another five years before it had any hope of tying down the British Fleet. In the meanwhile, to quote his own words, " The U-boat arm was much too weak to have any decisive effect on the war, and the surface forces could do no more than show that they knew how to die gallantly."

The Agreement had undoubtedly slowed down German naval construction. Between 1935 and 1939 Hitler could, with little difficulty, have expanded his shipbuilding yards and faced a race in all three fields of land, air and sea. As it was, he persuaded himself that if he left the command of the sea to us, we would leave the command of the land to him. The fact that our motive in making the Agreement was very different from his, did not affect the actual result. We agreed to the ratio in our own interest, and not because we were willing to appease him or ready to divide the world with him. We were convinced that a check upon German naval expansion would at the best steady the precarious balance of power in Europe, and at the worst, give us time for our own rearmament. Nor was our decision due to any naïve belief in Hitler's goodwill, and still less in any permanent affection that he might have for us. In point of fact, apart from exceeding the limits in the construction of a battleship, he carried out the provisions of the Agreement for nearly four years, and only repudiated them after our guarantee to Poland in the spring of 1939. When war broke out, the German Fleet had not even reached the thirty-five per cent ratio, and until the Agreement was denounced, the German Naval Staff had, unlike the Russian Naval Staff, continued to exchange information with us as to the plans and progress of their construction. The result was a state of what Admiral Raeder called " almost complete unpreparedness " on the German side in the following September, whilst we and our Allies had been able to adapt our plans to the developments of the German programme, and gain four precious years for strengthening our own fleet.

I now leave the description of the Naval Agreement for the

even more controversial story of the Abyssinian crisis. Both have running through them the same central thread. Each alike records the efforts made by Vansittart and myself to gain time and build up our strength in face of Hitler's growing threat.

CHAPTER XI

The Abyssinian Crisis

THE BLACK cloud that overhung Abyssinia had made me hurry the Anglo-German naval negotiations. As with the Agreement, so with Mussolini's threats, delay was too dangerous to risk. If a calamity was to be avoided, the new Foreign Secretary had to act at once, and in a field that had already been trodden flat by marching and counter-marching.

The trouble had been brewing for many years. Ever since the partition of Africa in the second half of the nineteenth century, the Italian claim to special interests in Abyssinia had been accepted by the Great Powers. The country bordering on the colonies of Eritrea and Italian Somaliland seemed not only to successive Italian Governments, but also to the whole Italian people, destined for Italian colonial development. Colonial expansion was regarded, particularly by the unsatisfied countries, as the outward sign of a Great Power, and the Italians were convinced from the success of their overseas emigrants in other parts of the world that they could hold their own as a colonising race in Africa with the French, Germans and British. The British Government always admitted and frequently promoted the Italian aspirations. At the time of Fashoda, when we and the French were on the brink of war with each other, it suited us to encourage Italian influence on the east coast of Africa, and particularly in the neighbourhood of the head waters of the Nile. In the Triple Agreement of 1906 between ourselves, the Italians and the French to determine the respective zones of interest of the three Powers, whilst the French restricted their claims to the Djibouti Railway, and we to the area of Lake Tsana, the Italians were given what amounted to a predominant position in large tracts of the country, together with a concession to build a railway joining their two colonies. The Italian Government, therefore, could rely upon international agreements in support of their claim to a specially favoured status.

Even more important in Italian eyes than international concessions was the belief that national prestige was at stake. For nearly fifty years a humiliating disaster had been unavenged. No Italian had forgotten General Barattieri's terrible defeat by the Emperor Menelik at Adowa in 1895, and the massacres and mutilations that had followed it. Much worse than Majuba in British memories, " the scar, yes, the shameful scar of Adowa," as d'Annunzio described it, had left a black mark on the national life that every Italian was determined to wipe out. The First World War both delayed the day of vengeance, and failed to satisfy the Italian demand for territorial gains. In the meanwhile, the Abyssinian Government continued to show its inability or unwillingness to carry out its promises or prevent frontier incidents. We also had found the Abyssinians bad neighbours. The Amharic Government of Addis Ababa had little authority over the tribes and races of the south and west, Gallas, Somalis, Leiba and Shifta wandering gangs, disloyal Rases, anti-Christian Moslems, Arab slave traders and intriguing adventurers, who one and all did much as they liked in this remnant of medieval Africa. However good the intentions of the Emperor, his writ scarcely ran beyond the limits of his palace. The result was a long chapter of clashes and complaints that irritated all three Treaty Powers and particularly infuriated the Italians.

The final incident that brought this precarious situation to a head happened in the second half of 1934. We were engaged at the time in trying to delimit the frontier between British Somaliland and Abyssinia. Colonel Clifford, the chief of our Mission, arrived in the course of his duties with eighty men of the Somaliland Camel Corps in the vicinity of Walwal, one of two forts that, though they had been in Italian occupation for five years, had never been formally included in Italian Somaliland. The three Governments, the Abyssinian, the Italian and the British, whose territories converged at this point, had left the frontiers undefined and the nomad tribes free to move to and from the wells that in this case were situated in what had been recognised in fact as a part of the Italian colony. A crowd of Abyssinian tribesmen gathered around Colonel Clifford's survey party. Their appearance made the local Italian commander believe that he was threatened with a hostile attack. Having only a handful of native troops, he telegraphed for reinforcements. In due course the reinforcements, amounting to 350 Askaris, arrived, together with two aeroplanes that appeared from the ground to be pointing machine-guns at Colonel Clifford's party. It afterwards transpired that the supposed machine-guns were cameras for photographing the position. Colonel Clifford, having made a vigorous protest and carried on a heated correspondence with the Italian commander, eventually withdrew from the area in order to avoid a serious international clash. His departure was the signal for the Abyssinian camp followers, who had tacked themselves on to the British party, to attack the Italian fort. In the confused fighting that followed, the Italian native troops, for there were no Europeans involved, suffered heavy casualties. Mussolini at once seized upon this typical frontier incident to inflame the already strong resentment against the Abyssinian Government by demanding an unconditional apology, a substantial indemnity, and a final settlement of the frontier. The Emperor replied by claiming that the dispute came within the terms of the 1928 Treaty of Friendship under which Italo-Abyssinian differences were to be referred to arbitration. Mussolini repudiated the claim, and at once proceeded to reinforce the Italian garrison in Eritrea, call up new classes in Italy, put 50,000 troops on a basis of full mobilisation, and make no secret of his intention to attack Abyssinia. In support of the punitive action that he clearly intended, he could point to many precedents from the past. Had not the British Fleet bombarded Alexandria, and the British Army pursued the Mahdi to the frontier of Abyssinia? Had not the French and the Spanish made their wars of conquest in Morocco? Had not a British General occupied Magdala, at the time the capital of Abyssinia? All this was perfectly true, but Mussolini, who always lived in the past, ignored the change that had come over the world since the First World War. It was of no account to him that his own Government, together with the French Government, had insisted in 1923 upon the admission of Abyssinia into the League of Nations. Halifax, the British representative at Geneva, supported by the Australian, Norwegian and Swiss Governments, had opposed it on the ground that the Emperor was not in effective control of the country, and that slavery and the slave trade were still rampant. The opposition failed, and Abyssinia became a Member State in full enjoyment of the rights and responsibilities included in the Covenant. An attack, therefore, upon Abyssinian territory involved the various League sanctions against aggression. After he had supported Abyssinian admission to the League, Mussolini's argument that the Covenant did not apply to Africa, convinced no one, nor his further contention that the Abyssinian Government, having failed to carry out its obligations, ought to be expelled from the League, when in actual practice the Emperor had made some improvement between the time of the League Resolutions and the Walwal incident.

Whatever were the arguments on both sides, and however weak the Italian case, a frontier incident in an African desert seemed likely to involve Europe and the world in a very serious crisis. Could we, we asked ourselves, settle Walwal as we had settled Fashoda, and prevent a remote and unknown corner of Africa from becoming the starting point of a general conflagration? It was to stamp out the dangerous spark that we made every kind of effort in the ensuing months. Even if we had wished, we could not look the other way and evade the consequences. Apart from our obligations to the League, we had to safeguard our vital interest in the upper waters of the Nile that gathered in Abyssinian territory at Lake Tsana, and upon which Egypt depended for its existence. We also believed that our traditional friendship with Italy enabled us to influence Italian opinion and bring pressure upon Mussolini at a time when he shared the Italian suspicion of all Germans and personally could not bear the sight of Hitler. No doubt, our influence would have been much more effective if from the start we had been vigorously supported by the French Government. French pressure upon Mussolini was, however, most unlikely. Laval had only in the previous January reached a Franco-Italian reconciliation over African questions, and was now in no mood to endanger what he believed to be a military alliance between France and Italy. As the French Government would not intervene, the responsibility fell upon us.

The very first days, therefore, in my new office I devoted to long discussions with Vansittart and Eden as to what, if anything, we could do. I remember particularly two afternoons that I spent with Vansittart, the one at my house in Cadogan Gardens, the other at his house at Denham, in which we went over the problem in all its phases. The basic facts were stark and ineluctable. First, Hitler's strength was becoming daily more formidable, and his intentions more unabashed. Secondly, Japanese aggression threatened us with war in the Far East when we were not strong enough to resist Hitler in Europe and at the same time fight in the Pacific. Thirdly, it was essential to British security to have a friendly Italy in the Mediterranean that would both guarantee our lines of communication to the Far East and make it unnecessary for the French to keep an army on the Italian frontier. Fourthly, and as a favourable pointer towards the maintenance of Anglo-Italian co-operation, Mussolini was at the time on very bad terms with Hitler, his rival dictator. The murder of Dolfüss at a moment when members of the Dolfüss family were actually staying with him in Italy, the anti-Italian provocations of the Austrian Nazis, and the claim in *Mein Kampf* to the absorption of Austria into the Nazi Reich, had brought about the concentration of Italian divisions on the Brenner, and driven the Duce to open abuse of the Nazi régime. Hitler, of whom he had formed the lowest opinion when they met the previous June at Venice, was, in his own words, " a horrible sexual degenerate, a dangerous fool. . . . Thirty centuries of history allow the Italians to regard with supreme indifference certain doctrines taught by the descendants of people who were wholly illiterate in the days when Cæsar, Virgil and Augustus flourished in Rome." The attitude that such outbursts exposed, seemed to show that the Stresa front still held against German pressure. In any case, we decided to do what we could to prevent its crumbling. Perhaps we were too optimistic. Perhaps we did not sufficiently realise the contrast between Mussolini's outlook and ours. In his eyes, a war, particularly a colonial war in Abyssinia, was good in itself both for his régime and the Italian people. Complete victory would, he believed, come quickly, and with it, the opportunity to bring back his armies to Europe in time to meet Hitler's attack in the future. To us, the diversion of Italian troops to a remote corner of East Africa, still worse, the breach of the Stresa front that the expedition involved, meant a great and threatening accession of strength both to the Japanese in the East and to Hitler in the West.

Perhaps, also, I somewhat lightly flattered myself with the feeling that my past associations with the Duce might still have some effect upon him. Many years before, I had had personal contacts with him that led me to think that he might listen to me. It was the time of the catastrophe of Caporetto when I was a staff officer in charge of certain branches of military intelligence on the Italian front. The whole front seemed to have been irrevocably broken. From Udine to Naples the roads were filled with crowds of deserters on their way home from the war that had apparently ended. In Rome, the pro-Germans and the war-weary were in the complete ascendant. It was then that one of my staff told me of the editor of *Avanti*, the Socialist paper in Milan, who might help to stop the *débâcle*. " Chi é questo Benito Mussolini? " I still have a copy of my note of inquiry that began with these words about a man of whom few in England had ever heard. The answer was that he was a powerful mob leader in Milan who had helped to bring Italy into the war, and was then hesitating on which side of the barricades he would fight. A little timely help might keep him on our side. I at once telegraphed to Sir George Macdonagh, the Director of Military Intelligence in London, and asked him to authorise me to approach this unknown agitator. He agreed, and gave me the means of subsidising a resistance movement. " Leave it to me," was the answer that Mussolini sent back through my intermediary, " I will mobilise the *mutilati* in Milan, and they will break the heads of any pacifists who try to hold anti-war meetings in the streets." He was true to his word, the Fasci of the *mutilati*, the prototypes of the Fascisti who marched on Rome, made short work of the Milanese pacifists. When in after years I met the Duce, he reminded me of our work together in the days before he was great, and when I was a young Lieutenant Colonel of the General Staff and he, a Socialist agitator. No doubt I was foolish to imagine that an almost forgotten incident of many years before would influence the dictator. Yet, as almost anything was worth trying, I did my best in the personal letters that I sent him to remind him of my work for Italy during the First World War. Once or twice he seemed to respond either in long and rambling letters or in personal messages transmitted to me by Grandi, the Italian Ambassador. One of these messages was so unlike an official communication that Grandi, after reading it to me, described it to me as " a psychological and not a diplomatic document."

Something more, however, was needed than the personal memories of the past for influencing a mind that was only open to material arguments. Was it possible to find some inducement of this kind that might at least open the way to further negotiation? It was upon this question that my talks with Vansittart and Eden constantly turned. Somehow or other we had to find a card of re-entry in a hand that was almost lost. This was the history of the proposal that Eden took with him to Rome for ceding to Abyssinia a narrow tract of territory in British Somaliland as an outlet to the sea in compensation for substantial Abyssinian concessions to the Italian demands. It was while staying with Philip Sassoon during the week-end of June 16 at Trent that we three agreed on the offer. We at once telegraphed to Perth in Rome, and asked for his opinion. His answer was altogether favourable, and the Cabinet, although somewhat taken aback by the suddenness of the move, approved both the proposal and Eden's journey to Rome to explain it. It was then that the first of a series of premature and unauthorised disclosures compromised our efforts. A Sunday paper published the outline of the plan, and what was more serious, a Cabinet inquiry discovered that the information had been given to it by the Parliamentary Private Secretary of one of the Ministers. When I pressed Baldwin to take some action against the culprit, he evaded the unpleasant duty. As it was, the disclosure at once excited an agitation against the transfer of any British territory to the Italian dictator, even though it was desert in Somaliland. The House of Commons was up in arms, and one of my first afternoons as Foreign Secretary was spent in meeting an enfilading fire from both the Right and the Left, the one opposed to any cession of British territory, the other opposed to any accommodation with a potential aggressor. Mussolini was equally unreceptive. He was violently opposed to the concession of any port to Abyssinia, and told Eden in so many words when he arrived in Rome, that Laval had promised him a free hand.

" I interjected ' economically,' "—to quote Eden's description of the conversation. " Signor Mussolini replied that might be so far as a written document was concerned, but since he had yielded to France 100,000 Italians in Tunis, and received in return half a dozen palm trees in one place, and a strip of desert which did not contain a sheep in another, it must be clear that he had understood that France had disinterested herself in Abyssinia. I contested this, telling Signor Mussolini that when Monsieur Laval had described in Geneva his interview with Signor Mussolini, he had insisted that France had only given a free hand to Italy in economic matters, and that he had added to Signor Mussolini: ' Vous avez des mains fortes. Faites attention,' making it clear that French goodwill did not apply to other than economic enterprises. At this, Signor Mussolini flung himself back in his chair with a gesture of incredulous astonishment."

This lively interchange of arguments did not augur well for any agreement, and there seemed to be no chance either of a compromise to persuade the Duce or a deterrent to frighten him. He and Eden did not conceal the extent of the differences that separated them or the personal dislike that they felt for each other. The result was the complete failure of our first attempt at a *détente*. Mussolini was convinced that in pressing upon him the obligations of the Covenant we had at the back of our minds the ulterior motive of ousting Italy from Abyssinia. The fact that we had not raised the question at the Stresa Conference in April before I went to the Foreign Office, made him all the more suspicious. When each delegation took their Abyssinian experts, and we never asked for the question to be placed on the agenda, he jumped to the conclusion that either we did not regard it as important, or that we had some secret reason for not discussing it. The explanation of our silence was our reluctance to force an issue that might break the Allied front. None the less, the effect on Mussolini was undoubtedly bad, and even at the risk of endangering the front, we should have done better to insist on a full discussion.

Certain other factors were hardening Mussolini's attitude. One of them affected the most sensitive side of a dictator, his *amour propre*. He had asked us in January for a statement of our interests in Abyssinia, and had expected the kind of quick answer that he received as to French interests from Laval. Instead, it took us many months and a long inquiry by an expert committee under Sir John Maffey before we gave him an official reply. In the meanwhile, the Italian Secret Service succeeded in photographing in the British Embassy in Rome, the Committee's Report, and divulged the fact that our experts were not worried over Italian predominance in Abyssinia so long as the head waters of Lake Tsana were safe. The Report, together with several other confidential documents that were also secretly photographed in the Embassy, strengthened Mussolini's belief that we were playing a double game with him.

After the abortive meetings in Rome, there followed many weeks of incessant efforts to find some new way round the *impasse*. At first, we tried the path of arbitration. Under the 1928 Treaty, Italy and Abyssinia were under an obligation to settle their disputes by arbitration. Whilst Abyssinia was anxious to use the method accepted in the Treaty, Mussolini refused on the ground that it was impossible to submit to arbitration a dispute with a country that had shown itself to be uncivilised and anarchical. The furthest that we were able to push him was to agree to a League inquiry into the Walwal incidents. The Committee's Report, when it appeared, increased rather than weakened his objections to a more general arbitration. The two Italian and two Abyssinian representatives, and the neutral chairman, all agreed that the Italians were not to blame for the incidents, and that the Abyssinian local authorities, by allowing the concentration of troops in the neighbourhood, had given them ground for believing that they were about to be attacked. The conclusion was that, from the international point of view, no responsibility could be placed on either side for a series of accidental circumstances. The Report, if it did not help towards a solution of the dispute, at least tended to lower the rising temperature.

Pending its publication, we had also been trying another line of advance. We in London were in favour of a meeting of the three Powers under the 1906 Treaty, and a Tripartite discussion of the new situation. Mussolini was against a meeting. So, also, was Laval, and rather to our surprise, Perth, who throughout wished to avoid a direct issue with Mussolini.

As three-Power action was impracticable and the French wished to keep out of the controversy as much as possible, the brunt of the negotiations inevitably fell upon us. This was not of our choosing. So far from being drawn into them from any wish or intention, we realised from the start that we could not have been engaged upon a more thankless and embarrassing task. The issues, were, however, so serious that we could not stand aside. Italy was an essential part of the western front, and the Covenant of the League the basis of our foreign policy. We could not sacrifice either without grave danger to ourselves and Europe, and were bound to intervene actively in the attempt to reconcile their conflicting demands.

This was the problem that faced us, and it raised questions that had to be answered at once. Mussolini had already 600,000 troops under arms in Italy, and an army of 250,000 in East Africa that was only awaiting the order to invade Abyssinia.

The world at large was either ignorant of the impending danger or convinced that some expedient would be found for averting it. In Rome, Perth had, on his own initiative, suggested to Mussolini a plan for giving Italy the kind of status in Abyssinia that we enjoyed in Egypt, and had urged us to bring the greatest possible pressure on the Emperor to accept whatever concessions were necessary for a settlement. In Geneva, Avenol, the Secretary-General of the League, was openly advocating an Italian mandate for the whole country. In Paris, Laval was relying on his January agreement with Mussolini for avoiding any serious rupture between France and Italy. Every day that passed was making it more difficult to find any compromise that could stop an act of flagrant aggression against a Member State of the League. Continental statesmen flocked to London to ask our advice. I remember particularly the talks that I had with the two leaders of the Little Entente, Benes and Titulesco. No two men could have provided a greater contrast in appearance. Benes, small, almost insignificant, self-effacing but very persuasive; Titulesco, with Mongol cheek-bones, as extravagant in his words as in his tastes, constantly boasting of an influence in Central Europe that, though it was substantial, was by no means as great as he claimed. Differing in manner and approach, they agreed in the conclusion that they both expressed to me, that at all costs we must keep a solid Anglo-French front. Titulesco admitted that we might find it difficult. He had just seen Laval, who was " tending more and more to collaboration with Italy." Their conversation had ended with a retort of which Titulesco was very proud. " You are not a statesman," were his last words to Laval, " you are a tendency." Even so, both the Czech and the Roumanian insisted that we must preserve Anglo-French solidarity.

One or other of the Ambassadors in London was continually waiting to see me. Ambassador Bingham, in his evident anxiety to mobilise American opinion on our side, suggested a meeting of the governments that had signed the Kellogg Pact. I was attracted by the proposal, but it came to nothing, as Cordell Hull, the Secretary of State, was not prepared to take any effective part in it. Corbin, the French Ambassador, a trained and cultured diplomat of the Quai d'Orsay school, made no secret both of his difficulties and his fears. If he sometimes seemed to me reserved and almost despairing, I knew that the reason was his consciousness of French political divisions and Laval's habitual elusiveness.

Most frequent of all were the visits of the Italian Ambassador, Grandi. Grandi undoubtedly wished to see a compromise that would avoid an Anglo-Italian breach. Not only was he an Anglophile at heart who had taught himself English in order to qualify for the London Embassy, but he nursed a feeling of resentment against Ciano, who had supplanted him in Rome and become the champion of Italian chauvinism. But unlike Balbo, the adventurous airman whom he in some ways resembled, he never, so long as he was in London, dared to force his views upon the Duce. Balbo would break into the Palazzo Venezia, sit on Mussolini's sacred writing-table with a pipe in his mouth, and shout his arguments at the top of his voice. I could never imagine Grandi, for all his look of an Italian *condottiere*, telling his master exactly what he thought of his mad policy. It is, however, fair to say that if in 1935 he adapted his London dispatches to suit Mussolini, he made full amends in 1943 by giving the *coup de grâce* to the Fascist régime.

Besides seeing the Ambassadors, I had many discussions with the High Commissioners of the Dominions. Torn between their loyalty to the League and their opposition to European commitments, their words were words of warning rather than advice, but the meaning behind them was clear enough—their governments were not prepared to go to war on the Abyssinian issue.

Parallel with these diplomatic discussions were the many audiences that I had with King George V and a succession of interviews with the party leaders. King George was a sick and worried man. The thought of another war was a constant nightmare to him. " I am an old man. I have been through one world war. How can I go through another? If I am to go on, you must keep us out of one," was the gist of the many talks that

I had with him. I had never seen him so grievously worried. After he left London at the end of July he summoned me to Sandringham for a further discussion of the crisis. Once again we went over the same ground without finding any new light to guide us. He then left for Scotland in a state of grave anxiety. Always constitutionally correct, he was most careful to refrain from any interference with the Government's policy. He could not, however, disguise his deep anxiety and his consuming desire for some compromise that would avoid war. No less than the King, all the Ministers were against war, and so, also, was the country when it was faced with the actual danger of its near approach.

It was at this time that Eden and I interviewed in turn the party leaders, and Churchill, Austen Chamberlain and Robert Cecil, as the outstanding representatives of non-official opinion. Lloyd George, rather to my surprise, came out strongly against any unilateral action on our part. When I told him that none of us were contemplating it, he seemed immensely relieved. What was needed, he declared, was collective action, and by collective action he particularly meant Anglo-French co-operation. Churchill's advice was also against unilateral action. The substance of it was: " Go as far as the French will go, take them along with you, but remember their weakness and don't make impossible requests to Laval. It is doubtful whether the French will go as far as economic sanctions, but that is no reason for not pressing them. The real danger is Germany, and nothing must be done to weaken the anti-German front. The collapse of the League will mean the destruction of the instrument that may be chiefly effective as a deterrent against German aggression."

Attlee, Lansbury, Samuel, Cecil and Chamberlain all insisted on the need for genuinely collective action based on full Anglo-French co-operation. When Cecil urged us to repeat our declaration of loyalty to the Covenant, I implied that I was contemplating a further statement on the subject, but that I was anxious at the moment to avoid getting out of step with the French. Though I did not say so, I had already in mind the speech that I intended to make to the Assembly of the League in Geneva in a few weeks' time. Whilst these interviews did not add anything new to the situation, they at least confirmed me in the belief that there was general approval of the double policy that I was pursuing, of negotiation with Italy and respect for our collective obligations under the Covenant, based on Anglo-French co-operation.

Twice already the House of Commons had approved this double line, once: on July 11, when I had used the carefully chosen words:

> " As things are, and as long as there is an effective League, we are ready to take our full share of collective responsibility. But when I say collective responsibility, I mean collective responsibility."

And once again, on August 1, when I insisted that:

> " War between Abyssinia and Italy would be wholly bad, whoever won."

It was during these weeks that a faint ray of hope flickered on the dark horizon. Although Mussolini had refused to take part in any formal Conference of the three Powers under the 1906 Treaty, he at least agreed to allow informal talks in Paris between French, British and Italian representatives. Eden and Vansittart accordingly went to Paris and spent two days with Cerutti, the Italian Ambassador, and Laval and Léger in an attempt to find a *modus vivendi*. The result was at first sight little more than another disclosure of the Italian demands. Mussolini categorically insisted upon the unconditional annexation of all the non-Amharic territories, and an Italian mandate for the rest of the country. Eden and Vansittart made it perfectly clear that we could not accept these demands, and in face of Laval's obvious attempt to play the intermediary between ourselves and Italy, repeated that it was not an Anglo-Italian, but a League of Nations controversy, in which we were engaged. Léger, who saw that Mussolini was making impossible demands, inclined to a plan under which the League would be requested to give a joint mandate to Italy, France and Great Britain for the whole of Abyssinia, and at the same time, obtain the Emperor's approval by the cession of an outlet to the sea. As we objected to a mandate in any form, we made a counter-proposal on three lines, first, an exchange of territory in which Abyssinia would cede certain extensive tracts to Italy in return for an outlet to the sea; secondly, an economic zone in which Italian interests would be predominant; and thirdly, a League framework in which these arrangements would be carried out. Whilst our plan produced no immediate result, it undoubtedly impressed the Italians and kept open the possibility of a compromise. The experts in the Ministry of Foreign Affairs in Rome, who were much more cautious than the Fascist politicians in the Ministries of the Colonies and Propaganda, were ready to work upon it, provided that they were left to themselves. That the general lines were sound was further proved by the fact that it was taken as the starting point in all the subsequent discussions at Geneva.

CHAPTER XII

My Geneva Speech

I MUST now bring the story back to London, where throughout August I had been catching at every straw that was blowing towards peace, and at the same time preparing for a possible storm. A violent campaign in the Italian Press, particularly in Mussolini's paper, the *Giornale d'Italia*, had stirred up in Italy a vicious feeling against Great Britain, and an emotional excitement in support of war. Secret reports came to us from several sources that Mussolini was planning what was called a " mad dog act " against Malta and the fleet in the Mediterranean. The rumours were so persistent that we could not neglect precautions to forestall the risk. Accordingly, we ordered the two battle cruisers with a support of three other cruisers and some smaller craft to Gibraltar, and shortly afterwards, on the advice of the Naval Staff, withdrew the main fleet from Malta, where it had no anti-aircraft defence, to Alexandria.

Parliament had now adjourned, the Cabinet had fixed its next meeting for October 2, and Baldwin was on the eve of his annual visit to Aix. Even Neville Chamberlain, who seldom took a foreign holiday, had left for Switzerland. With some difficulty Eden, Vansittart and I caught the Prime Minister before his departure and obtained his general approval of what we were trying to do. With the principal Ministers out of reach, I felt dangerously isolated. To make matters worse, immediately after seeing Baldwin, I was immobilised by what appeared to be an attack of arthritis in one of my feet. Besides, therefore, feeling very ill, I was prevented from going either to Paris or Geneva, where important discussions were taking place. It was in these circumstances that I wrote on August 18 to Chamberlain, the Chancellor of the Exchequer. As the letter explains the position at the time, I quote it at length:

"I am adding this personal note to the papers that have been sent to you about the Abyssinian controversy. I am exceedingly sorry to trouble you in Switzerland. It is, however, inevitable that there should be a Cabinet on or about the 27th and I should very much hope that, intolerably inconvenient though it may be, you could come back for it. Stanley has promised to return and it seems to me to be essential that you should be there.

"I believe that we have done everything possible to keep in step with the French and to do nothing to provoke the Italians. None the less, at the time of writing it looks to me as if the Italians will be entirely unreasonable, and as a result there will be a first-class crisis in the League at the beginning of September. It is urgently necessary for the Cabinet to consider what, in these circumstances, our attitude should be on two assumptions: (1) that the French are completely with us; (2) that the French have backed out. It is equally urgent for the Cabinet to consider what preparations should be made to meet a possible mad dog act by the Italians. As to the latter question, I have been in great difficulties. On the one hand, I was anxious to suggest no action which would even give the impression of provocation to the Italians or of war to the British public. On the other hand, I have been very nervous of leaving undone anything that might make a mad dog act more dangerous. In the circumstances it seemed to me that I could do no more than get the Chiefs of Staff and the Planning Committee to investigate the position, and to leave it to the Cabinet to decide upon what action should be taken. I am having the reports circulated to the Cabinet and you will be receiving them in this bag. It seemed to me even at the risk of a dangerous period of delay best to defer any action until the Cabinet.

"As you may imagine I have received little or no help from other quarters. Stanley would think about nothing but his holiday and the necessity of keeping out of the whole business almost at any cost. Ramsay has written me a curious and almost unintelligible letter warning me of all the dangers that surround us, generally taking the side of the Italians and making the amazing suggestion that the Italians are likely to be our great Empire rivals in the future and will almost certainly be stronger than ourselves.

"Outside the Cabinet public opinion has been greatly hardening against Italy. Papers like the *Birmingham Post* are getting very restive over the arms embargo[1] and over the ineffectiveness of the

[1] The Tripartite undertaking to prohibit the transit of arms to Abyssinia.

League. I see myself the making of a first-class crisis in which the Government will lose heavily if we appear to be repudiating the Covenant. When I say this, I do not mean that I have changed my views since we both discussed the question in London. What, however, I do mean is that if we adopt Stanley's attitude of indifference or Ramsay's alarmist and pusillanimous surrender to the Italians, we shall get the worst of every conceivable world. Our line, I am sure, is to keep in step with the French, and, whether now or at Geneva, to act with them. I may add that Eden or Vansittart or both of them are going to see Stanley at Aix some time this week. Send me, if you feel inclined, any suggestions or criticisms that occur to you."

In answer to this appeal Chamberlain arranged to return to London. In the meanwhile, I persuaded Baldwin at least to have a meeting at the end of the month of all the Ministers within reach of London, if he was still not prepared to summon a full Cabinet.

Having retired to bed in Norfolk with my bad foot, I had plenty of time to meditate upon my troubles with a mind made the more alert by the shooting pains of my complaint. In my search for some new line that would encourage my colleagues, strengthen the Geneva front, and possibly give Mussolini the chance to withdraw from his threatening position, it seemed to me that the best hope lay in shifting the controversy from the political ground to the economic. This was the line that the Economic Conference of 1931 had tried to follow for strengthening the forces of world peace, and if it had not been for the American defection, it would almost certainly have led to concrete results. In the present case, the real needs of Italy were economic and not political, however much Mussolini might declaim to the contrary. Why should I not revive the excellent programme of free access to raw materials that had been in abeyance since the Economic Conference broke up in failure? Lugard, the greatest of our colonial administrators, supported my idea. Neville Chamberlain had already accepted it in his conception of a free trade zone for the Central African colonies of the European Powers on the lines of the Congo Basin. Vansittart at the Foreign Office at once saw its application to the Italian demands, and was strongly in favour of my giving it a foremost place in British policy. The first step, before putting it to the Cabinet, was to obtain the approval of the Treasury and the Board of Trade. As the Chancellor of the Exchequer was entirely in favour of it, no opposition was to be expected from that side of Whitehall. On the other side of the street, Runciman and the Board of Trade were at first not so forthcoming. Was there not already free access to raw materials for anyone who could pay for them? What exactly did I mean by it? To questions like these I gave much the same answer that we had given in 1933, with the added argument that since then the demand for a freer distribution of raw materials had grown everywhere, and particularly in the countries that possessed little or no colonial territory. I do not claim that I converted all the doubters. I did, however, succeed in obtaining general approval from my colleagues for including the proposal in our programme. I was already turning over in my mind the kind of speech that I should make to the Assembly of the League in September, and the authority to include a paragraph on materials gave the right orientation to my ideas. The success of the speech seemed to me to depend upon whether or not I could give the League some kind of future programme. The general feeling, inside as well as outside the Foreign Office, was at the time painfully defeatist over the League and its future. " It is practically dead, and it is no good trying to revive it," was the verdict of many of my most influential advisers. Whilst I clearly realised that I might be forced to accept this view, I wished to resist it until the last possible moment. There might still, I thought, be a chance of putting new life into its crippled body. I accordingly determined to make a revivalist appeal to the Assembly. At best, it might start a new chapter of League recovery, at worst, it might deter Mussolini by a display of League fervour. If there was any element of bluff in it, it was a moment when bluff was not only legitimate but inescapable. Accordingly, with Vansittart's invaluable help, I made the first draft of the Geneva speech that subsequently created so considerable a stir. It was finished about the time that Baldwin returned from Aix for the meeting of Ministers. Runciman had already approved the paragraph about raw materials, and Chamberlain had throughout helped me with the text. I own that I was pleased with it, as it seemed on the one hand to explain our double policy of negotiation with Italy and loyalty to the League, and on the other, to give the League a programme for an expanding future. Armed with a copy, I hurried off to

Chequers to show it to Baldwin. When I arrived, we talked of the delights of Aix and the English countryside. We walked round the garden and we had tea. Then, remembering something about Geneva, he said to me: " You have got a speech to make, and you have brought me the draft. Let me have a look at it." When I gave it to him, he gave it a quick glance, and said, on handing it back to me: " That is all right. It must have taken you a long time to make it up," and that was all. Though the answer seemed to me scarcely adequate to the importance of a comprehensive statement of policy, and his casualness damped any personal vanity that I possessed, on second thoughts I was not dissatisfied. At least his perfunctory acquiescence showed confidence in his Foreign Secretary and enabled me to go ahead on the lines that I had set out. That was what I wanted, and the way was open for the next chapter. Should I be well enough to see it through? The Assembly was due to meet at the beginning of September, and if the French and the British were to keep in step, it was necessary for me to have a preliminary discussion with Laval in Geneva. My doctor looked anxiously at the programme, and particularly at the strain involved in the journey to Switzerland. However, I went ahead with my plans, and the Air Ministry adapted a military machine with devices that made it possible for me to keep on my back during the flight. I survived the journey without mishap, and installed myself in some noisy and uncomfortable rooms in the hotel that the British delegates always frequented.

My first duty was the meeting with Laval on the following day. September 10, therefore, was devoted to a long discussion with him, first, in his hotel, and next, in mine. From the start it was clear that our Ambassadors in Rome had given us very different advice. Chambrun had reported that Mussolini was impressed by the Paris Conference between Eden, Laval and Cerutti, whilst Perth had just telegraphed to me that " in their present mood both Mussolini and the Italian people are capable of committing suicide if this seems the only alternative to climbing down." Both by instinct and habit Laval adopted the more hopeful view. His whole career had been founded on what the Italians call *combinazioni*, and he now saw the chance of playing the hand that Talleyrand had so successfully played for much higher stakes in 1814 and 1815. It was the first time that I had met him personally. Whilst his greasy hair, dirty white tie and shifty look did not prepossess me, I could not help admiring the quickness of his versatile mind. More than once, and particularly during the 1931 crisis, when on his own responsibility he had sent to London three billion francs in gold from the Bank of France to steady the value of the pound, he had been most helpful to Great Britain. Everyone knew him to be a cunning intriguer, but at the time there seemed a good chance of his wits once again being useful to us. Not only was he head of the French Government whose co-operation was essential to us, but he was a personal friend of Mussolini, and seemed to have considerable influence in Rome. I described at the time the impression that he made on me: "the kind of gipsy who would be doing a deal with Jaspar Petulengro at Barnet Horse Fair."

Our long talks on September 10 and 11, although they produced no new proposals for Abyssinia, were valuable in fixing the importance of the crisis upon the central point that mattered, the growing threat of German rearmament. From the start I insisted that it was with this point always pressing upon us that we had to make our plans for dealing with Mussolini. A double line of approach was essential. On the one hand, a most patient and cautious negotiation that would keep him on the Allied side; on the other, the creation of a united front in Geneva as a necessary deterrent against German aggression. Within this framework we needed French support in our efforts to make an Air Pact with Germany that would lessen the risk of a knock-out blow against France and Great Britain, and Eastern and Danubian Pacts that would give confidence to our allies in Eastern and Central Europe. As to land armaments, the possibility of any agreement with Germany looked more difficult. On that account I suggested that the wise course was to begin with the air negotiations as the line of least resistance.

Laval agreed with my conclusions. Up to a point he was ready to co-operate, but only on condition that we avoided war. Not only was he determined to preserve the Franco-Italian Pact that he regarded as the greatest achievement of his career, but he was convinced that French public opinion would repudiate a breach in the Latin front against the Germans. We both therefore excluded the idea of war with Italy as too dangerous and double-edged for the future of Europe. We also agreed that as we must, if possible, avoid provoking Mussolini into open hostility, any economic pressure upon which the League collectively decided should be applied cautiously and in stages, and with full account of the unescapable fact that the United States, Japan and Germany were not Member States of the League. In Laval's words, we had " to prevent Mussolini being driven into the German camp. Since the murder of Dolfüss, Mussolini has turned to France. It is all a question of fact, the reconciliation of prudence with principles." The long talks, lasting many hours, eventually came to an end with a better understanding of our respective positions. Whilst, however, we seemed outwardly to have reached complete agreement, I never lost the feeling when I was talking to Laval that, though our words sounded the same, the minds behind them were making reservations. Laval, whatever he might say to the contrary, thought me irritatingly obstinate in my attitude towards Mussolini, and I had the uneasy feeling that he really wished to give the Duce a completely free hand.

We were now ready for the meeting of the Assembly on the following day, September 12. Nothing had been said by Laval to make me change my carefully prepared speech. As he did not wish to start the debate, it was arranged that I should be the first speaker. Accordingly, after a few opening words by Benes, the President of the Assembly, I hobbled up to the tribune, limping on one leg and supported by a stick. From it, I surveyed the great hall, the very sophisticated audience of official delegates below me, and in the galleries, the grim-looking crowd of the hot-gospellers of Geneva. Around me were crowded an array of secretaries, interpreters and microphones. As I proceeded with my speech, I became conscious of the fact that I was interesting my hearers. Perhaps it was the new turn of a new actor in the Assembly, perhaps it was my precise manner, that often displeased the House of Commons, but was in contrast to the rhetoric of most of the Geneva speeches. In any case, by the time that I had finished I was convinced that I had made a definite impression. What kind of impression, I was not sure. One of the British delegates took the view that what I had said would be resented by the Assembly as it criticised the League's weakness and let Mussolini off too lightly. An exactly opposite opinion was taken by most of the journalists, who regarded it as a resounding call for rallying the League ranks. I myself was amazed at the universal acclamation with which they received it. Wondering what it was that had so greatly excited them, I read it through again and again later in the day, and could find nothing in it, except the passages about the free access to raw materials, that I had not said time after time in the House of Commons without creating any notable reaction.

> " The League is what its members make it. . . . The League is at present weak because it is incomplete. No progress has been made with disarmament, nor has any attempt been tried for modifying the *status quo* to meet new needs or unsatisfied demands. . . . If the burden is to be borne, it must be borne collectively. If risks for peace are to be run, they must be run by all. The security of the many cannot be ensured solely by the efforts of the few, however powerful they may be. On behalf of His Majesty's Government in the United Kingdom I can say that in spite of these difficulties they will be second to none to fulfil, within the measure of their capacity and the obligations which the Covenant lays upon them. . . . Something must be done to remove the causes of war. Better means must be found to make it possible for all countries to obtain the raw materials that they require for their existence. . . . It is to the principles of the League, and not to any particular manifestation, that the British nation has demonstrated its adherence. . . . In conformity with its precise and explicit obligations, the League stands, and my country stands with it, for the collective maintenance of the Covenant " (and at this point I paused and repeated the word ' collective ') " in its entirety, and particularly for steady and collective resistance to all acts of unprovoked aggression."

Collective security must be really comprehensive, if it is to be effective. That was the text of my speech, and it certainly implied criticism of a system under which it had been little more than a phrase that meant nothing, or a mask behind which the Great Powers had carried out their own plans. All this I had already said over and over again, and no one had become particularly excited. Was there ever a better example of the fact that in nine cases out of ten it is the occasion that makes the speech and not the speech the occasion? Time after time in my political career I had made what I thought was a good speech, and it had fallen absolutely flat. Then I had made what I was sure was a bad speech, and everyone else had thought it a good one. It is the moment and the audience that make the difference. When I spoke to a tired House of Commons at the end of the session, my words about real collective security made no great impression. When I repeated them at Geneva before a cosmopolitan audience faced with an international crisis, they reverberated over the whole world. Even so, only Simon amongst my colleagues seemed to realise the impression that they had made. His telegram of congratulation and approval was the only comment that I received from Whitehall.

The speech had certainly rallied the League forces. So far, I had been successful. The much more difficult task remained of using the new enthusiasm for maintaining the provisions of the Covenant without endangering the peace of Europe. The hotheads were already clamouring for the closing of the Suez Canal. Besides amounting in practice to a declaration of war against Italy, the closing of a great international waterway would have been strongly resented by the United States. The French were not prepared even to discuss the proposal. When Aloisi, Mussolini's representative in Geneva, saw Laval on September 16, he was explicitly told that the French Government would on no account agree to the closing of the canal. The economic blockade, Laval declared, was a different matter; the League States were fully entitled to refuse to buy Italian goods. " After all, you cannot make the British buy Gorgonzola and Chianti if they do not want to," was his very typical aside. He went on to say that if the Italians made threatening demonstrations, the French and we were perfectly entitled to take military precautions. What, however, he did not disclose to Aloisi was his fixed intention to take no military action. We had strengthened the fleet and air force in the Mediterranean. He, on the other hand, did not move a ship or an aeroplane or sanction even preliminary preparations for Anglo-French air bases. His general assurance, therefore, that the French would stand by us if we were attacked had no substance behind it.

The Committee of Five appointed by the League to find a *modus vivendi* for Italy and Abyssinia reported on September 18. After eleven meetings, it produced a most impressive report based on the need of a comprehensive system of League supervision and control in Abyssinia. League advisers centrally directed were to reorganise the administration of Finance, Justice, Education and Public Health, and foreign specialists were to create a corps of police and gendarmerie capable of suppressing slavery, the illicit traffic in arms and frontier raids. Economic development was to be aided by foreign co-operation and better communications. In short, the League was recommended to undertake what amounted in practice to a mandate for the whole country, provided that the Abyssinian Government agreed. We and the French supplemented this proposal by declaring our readiness to transfer to Italy any rights that we possessed under the 1906 Treaty apart from our respective interests in Lake Tsana and the Djibouti Railway.

The Abyssinian Government accepted the Committee's Report, whilst the Italian Council of Ministers made use of such conciliatory language in rejecting it as to amount to an invitation to the League to continue negotiations on its general lines. Eden and I at once realised the importance of a Report that insisted upon the maintenance of Abyssinian sovereignty, but unreservedly admitted the need for great changes, and provided a wide opening for the recognition of Italian special interests. The two facts, first, that the Abyssinian Government accepted it, and secondly, that the Italian Council of Ministers seemed impressed by its recommendations, encouraged us to persist with our efforts. We were nearer to a compromise at this moment than at any other. We afterwards heard that Mussolini, who had not yet started his war, had been inclined to accept the Report. Unfortunately, however, once again, as in the case of Zeila, a premature disclosure in the Press turned him against a proposal that might have been a basis of compromise. A London paper published it before he received it, and what was worse, suggested that he could not possibly accept it. Being terribly sensitive when his *amour propre* was concerned, he felt that it would be humiliating to accept proposals that the London Press expected him to reject and on this account he finally came out against them. None the less, we remained convinced that the Report was not only sound, but capable of becoming the framework of an eventual settlement.

The Committee had ended their Report with an important paragraph emphasising the part that France and Great Britain were expected by the League to play in any agreement.

" The representatives of France and the United Kingdom have informed the Committee of Five that, with a view to contributing to the peaceful settlement of the Italo-Ethiopian dispute, their respective Governments are ready to facilitate territorial adjustments between Italy and Ethiopia by offering Ethiopia, if necessary, certain sacrifices in the region of the Somaliland coast.

" In negotiating on this subject, the Governments of the French Republic and of the United Kingdom will take care to obtain from the Ethiopian Government guarantees regarding the execution, in the territories to be acquired by it, of the obligations by which Ethiopia is bound in regard to slavery and to traffic in arms.

" The representatives of France and of the United Kingdom have further informed the Committee of Five that their respective Governments, without wishing to impair the existing régime in regard to the treatment of foreigners and in regard to external trade, are prepared to recognise a special Italian interest in the economic development of Ethiopia. Consequently, these governments will look with favour on the conclusion of economic agreements between Italy and Ethiopia, on condition that the existing rights of French and British nationals and protected persons are respected by the two parties, and that the recognised interests of France and the United Kingdom under all agreements already in force are safe-guarded."[1]

In the weeks that followed the publication of the Report, this special Franco-British responsibility was several times reaffirmed at the League. Van Zeeland, for instance, speaking on November 5 in the Conciliation Committee that continued the work of the Committee of Five, proposed, with the general approval of more than fifty States represented in the League, that the French and British Governments should be requested to elaborate the general plan into a more detailed scheme.

This, then, was the state of affairs when Mussolini started the invasion of Abyssinia on October 3. The Report of the Committee of Five had received very general support, and the British and French Governments had been specially instructed to follow up the line of advance that had been marked out in it. The Anglo-French front was still unbroken, though upon the clear under-standing that France would not go to war with Italy. In Italy, though Mussolini had rejected the chance of a compromise, there were unmistakable signs that his Council of Ministers was anxious to avoid a European conflagration.

The question now arose as to whether Mussolini's flagrant

[1] Documents relating to the Dispute between Ethiopia and Italy. Ethiopia No. 1 (1935), page 6.

challenge to the League, and the gas attacks on Adowa that followed the invasion, should put an end to all further negotiations. The answer was a unanimous " No " from Geneva. A compromise had obviously become much more difficult, but it had also become more than ever necessary, both for preserving European peace and saving Abyssinia from total destruction. We therefore intensified our efforts for finding some kind of compromise that would end the war before it became a universal calamity. We accordingly accepted a French invitation to send our principal Abyssinian expert, Maurice Peterson, to Paris for discussions with St. Quentin, the chief of the African Department at the Quai d'Orsay. The two experts were to take the Report of the Committee of Five as their text, and to fit into it a detailed scheme that both sides might conceivably accept. It was clearly understood that the two Governments were acting with the League's approval and on behalf of the League, and that any plan that emerged from the discussions would be *ad referendum* to the Conciliation Committee in Geneva, and submitted for approval to both parties in the controversy. When Peterson arrived in Paris, he found that Laval was putting the Italian demands even higher than Mussolini. Peterson at once insisted that we were only prepared to continue negotiations on the basis, first of a definite exchange of territory that gave Abyssinia a port, and secondly, of a formula that, whilst accepting Italian development and settlement in the southern provinces, maintained Abyssinian sovereignty under League supervision. There then followed a series of meetings between the experts that eventually produced a plan that gave Italy an extensive zone for exclusive economic development in the south, a share in the economic development of the rest of the country, but both under League supervision, and an exchange of territory that was to include for Italy parts of the Tigre province that the Italian armies had already occupied, in return for an Abyssinian port, preferably situated on territory ceded by the Italians at Assab in Eritrea.

Laval considered the plan insufficient to satisfy Mussolini, and continually harked back to an alternative proposal that would have ceded the British territory of Zeila to Abyssinia, and prohibited the building of any railway likely to compete with the French-owned Djibouti Railway. Having failed in the previous June to settle with Mussolini over the original Zeila proposal, we now

insisted that Italian and not British territory must be used to
satisfy Abyssinia, and that any exchange must be substantial,
giving the Abyssinians space and scope to build a railway if they
wished. Although we eventually succeeded in persuading the
French to accept this proposal, it was clear that they regarded the
general plan as inadequate for the purpose of any compromise.

Laval then wished to come to London for the purpose of persuading me to be less rigid. For several reasons I did not want a
London meeting. It was certain to excite rumour and agitation
at a moment when the negotiations were in a very delicate state,
whilst my own health had become so bad that I was under urgent
doctor's orders to take a short period of leave in Switzerland. To
explain, however, this background, I must describe some of the
developments in London during October and November.

CHAPTER XIII

The Paris Meeting

A GENERAL ELECTION was inevitable in the next few months, and the only question to be decided was whether it should be held in the winter or in the January of the new year. Baldwin decided for November.[1] The result was that during October and November electioneering greatly complicated and hindered any detailed discussion of the Abyssinian negotiation. Peterson's telegrams describing in detail the concessions to Italy that we were prepared to accept, and in particular, the territories that we were ready to see either exchanged, or regarded as zones of special Italian interest, were very technical, and especially difficult for busy Ministers to follow at a time when they were engaged on speaking tours in the country. Perhaps, therefore, their full scope was never understood.

So far as I was concerned, I stayed in London, and restricted myself to one or two speeches in my constituency of Chelsea in which I tried to meet the attacks of an Opposition that at one and the same time declared that we were abandoning the League and pushing the country into war. In the meanwhile, the League, having declared Italy an aggressor, had set in motion the machinery of economic sanctions by stages. A cautious beginning was made with a restriction upon Italian credits and exports and imports of arms. Opinions differed as to how far these tentative measures were likely to have a restraining effect on Mussolini. Perth held the view that they were more likely to consolidate Italian opinion behind him than to embarrass his war plans. However, there was general agreement both in Geneva and London that we should try out the various processes of the

[1] See Appendix, p. 193.

176

Covenant, provided that they did not lead to war. Behind, however, the apparent unanimity of the League States, there persisted many doubts and hesitations that came to a head when the Canadian representative proposed to extend the comparatively mild embargoes to include oil. It is true that a new Government in Canada soon afterwards repudiated this move, but the proposal, once made, forced the issue into the forefront of the League discussions. Just at the time, therefore, that the General Election was in full blast, a new and grave question demanded a definite decision by the British Government as to the attitude to be taken by our representative when an answer would be expected on December 11 at the League Committee called the Committee of Eighteen dealing with sanctions. Between the start of the new Government and the meeting there was therefore little or no time for full ministerial discussions in the Cabinet at what proved to be the turning point of the crisis. It was clear, however, from the occasional Cabinets that took place, that there was strong opposition both to military sanctions and an oil embargo that might lead to war. The Chiefs of Staff were particularly insistent that we were in no position to risk a war, and their opinion at this moment carried all the greater weight when it was supplemented by the fresh reports that we had just received about German rearmament. Much the same service view reached us from Paris, General Gamelin had told our military attaché that the French could not take precautionary measures for fear of compromising a settlement with Italy, and General Georges had added that he foresaw " serious difficulties " if any kind of mobilisation was attempted at short notice.

At this most awkward moment I once again became ill. Although my foot was better, my general health was very precarious. The doctors took a serious view, and ordered an immediate rest. Accordingly, with Baldwin's approval I arranged to go for two or three weeks to Switzerland, as soon as I had again explained to the House of Commons on December 5 our double policy of negotiation with Italy and loyalty to the League. My departure was fixed for Saturday, December 7. It was only a day or two before that Laval had asked to come to London to discuss the situation with me. When I told him of my difficulties in agreeing to his request, he returned to the charge with an urgent suggestion that I should stop in Paris for a few hours and meet him on my way to Switzerland. It may be that I was so pulled down by overwork that my judgment was out of gear. In any case, I weakly agreed to the invitation, not realising that it would in every way have been better if I had either let Laval come to London, where I should have had my colleagues around me, or dropped altogether out of the negotiation during the short period of my leave. Baldwin, who was fully occupied with the many details connected with the new Government, had little time for discussing with me the implications of my Paris visit. His advice was very simple: " Have a good leave, and get your health back. That is the most important thing. By all means stop in Paris, and push Laval as far as you can, but on no account get this country into war." Looking back, I am certain that I should have insisted upon the summoning of a special Cabinet, and a clear agreement as to how far I could go with Laval. This precaution, that has since seemed so elementary, I failed to take. I did not then think it necessary, as I had no intention of committing the Government to any final plan. Even if Laval and I were able to agree, we were only, at the request of the League, and in continuation of the recommendations of a League Committee, making a purely provisional scheme for bringing together the two disputants that would be referred to Geneva for final approval or rejection. It seemed also that my personal intervention was needed to prevent a rupture between the French and ourselves over the oil embargo that was to be discussed in the Committee of Eighteen that was dealing with sanctions on the following Thursday, December 12.

This was the confused background of my Paris visit *en route* for Switzerland, where my wife was waiting for me. I was to spend a few hours with Laval and Vansittart would join me in the interview. He was already in Paris, partly on leave, and partly engaged in an attempt to counter the virulence of the anti-British articles in the French Press, against which the French Government had taken no action. There had never been such bitterness in the French Press, since the days of Fashoda. There would also be available in Paris George Clerk, our Ambassador, who had been closely concerned with the controversy from the start, and had himself served in the British Mission in Addis Ababa. Lastly, there would be Peterson, our expert who for weeks past had been discussing the territorial complexities with St. Quentin, and whose telegrams had kept the Cabinet informed of the points under negotiation.

All three met me on my arrival, and took me at once to the Quai d'Orsay. I had imagined that my meeting would be a comparatively quiet affair. In view of the general interest in the crisis, there was certain to be some measure of publicity. For this I was prepared, but not for the crowd of reporters and photographers who jostled us round Laval's very door with a barrage of flashlights and staring faces. The mob, that seemed to have taken possession of the Quai d'Orsay as if it had been Versailles in 1789, remained near by during the whole of my interviews, and it was not surprising that there was no secrecy about what happened within Laval's room.

We began at five-thirty in the afternoon and went on late into the evening. Laval sat in the middle with a telephone within his reach that he used several times during the talks, some said in order to impress us, ostensibly at least, to clear up doubtful points with his officials. More than once he rang up Mussolini with whom he seemed to have a direct and secret line. On his right were Léger, St. Quentin and Massigli, on his left, myself, Vansittart, Clerk and Peterson. After the usual compliments, Laval reaffirmed his conviction that an oil embargo would drive Mussolini to a desperate act, and that he was not prepared to agree to it until we had made a further effort for compromise. He insisted that, as France had no intention of going to war, it was more than ever necessary to proceed cautiously and by conciliation. This opening statement made me very doubtful of French co-operation if Mussolini attacked us in the Mediterranean. I therefore asked Laval categorically whether in the event of an attack we could depend upon French help. His answer, though it was in general terms satisfactory, avoided any undertaking to make military preparations, and obviously assumed that French co-operation would depend upon Anglo-French agreement as to our immediate policy. He did, however, agree for the first time to the opening of staff talks, that were subsequently begun, but very soon reached a dead end.

Laval and I then plunged into the details of the joint plan that we were preparing for the League. Laval, who had evidently given Mussolini some idea of its contents, declared that we must extend its scope if there was to be any chance of Italian acceptance. Mussolini had already occupied a considerable part of the northern Province of Tigre, and it was inconceivable that he would surrender his conquests, particularly as they included Adowa, the sensitive spot in every Italian heart. The situation, therefore, had changed since Peterson and St. Quentin had agreed upon a provisional plan. I felt that there was some force in Laval's argument, particularly as I had been informed that the Emperor would find serious opposition from the Rases who had gone over to the Italian side in the occupied districts, if their territory was restored to Abyssinia. My answer, therefore, was that, provided that the rest of the terms were reasonable, I was ready to agree to include some further parts of the Tigre territory in the exchange for a port, but insisted that any such extension must be compensated by the lowering of Italian demands in the rest of the country.

What kind of port, then, should it be, and where should it be situated? Before we could give our answers to these two questions, we realised that as it was already late, it would be impossible to finish our discussions before the next day. From both sides, therefore, I was pressed to agree to stop over the Sunday and continue them for another day. Very reluctantly I accepted what appeared to be the inevitable, and agreed.

The next morning we resumed the discussion of the port. I made it clear that as an outlet to the sea was the compensation that Abyssinia was receiving for the Tigre districts, Italy should provide the territory and the facilities at Assab, and that only if the Emperor preferred Zeila in British Somaliland, would we be prepared to make any cession of British territory in the interests of peace. Laval agreed, and next proceeded to the proposals for frontier rectification and territorial changes in the north and east. These Vansittart and I were able substantially to reduce on the ground that Italy was receiving more than had been originally contemplated in the occupied districts of Tigre.

The third question concerned the form and scope of the economic monopoly that was envisaged for Italy in the non-Amharic provinces of the south. Such a zone had in theory been guaranteed to Italy in the Three-Power Treaties of 1891 and 1906. It now had to be redefined in the changed atmosphere created by the opening of hostilities and the Italian occupation of Abyssinian territory. Vansittart and I took the view that it was wiser to agree

to an extension of the non-Amharic zone of influence, provided
that we were able to restrict the cession of Abyssinian territory in
the Amharic districts. The Province of Ogaden, the main centre
of the Italian zone of economic influence, had never been under the
effective control of Addis Ababa, the slave trade and banditry
had ravaged it for generations, and it was mostly a sandy desert.
In the words of Lord Salisbury, when in the nineties he was
defending in the House of Lords the cession of wide tracts of
Central Africa to France: " This land is what agriculturists call
very light." Even so, I insisted that any Italian economic monopoly in the province should be subject to League supervision.
Laval, who was perfectly ready to give Mussolini complete
freedom, agreed with reluctance to my condition of League
supervision, but insisted, evidently with a view to tilting the
balance back in Mussolini's favour, that our plan should be sent
first to Rome before going to Addis Ababa and Geneva. He
argued that Mussolini would be more likely to accept it if it went
first to him, and that when once he had accepted it, and it went
to Geneva as an Anglo-French plan, no one at the League would
oppose it. Whilst I agreed at the time to this proposed procedure,
I was neither surprised nor concerned when the Cabinet later
insisted upon the plan being sent simultaneously both to Addis
Ababa and Rome. What principally mattered at the time was
Anglo-French agreement on the actual plan.

By the evening of Sunday, December 8, agreement had been
reached between us on a threefold basis. First, an effective outlet
to the sea with full sovereign rights for Abyssinia. Secondly, in
exchange for this outlet, the cession of some, but not all, of the
territory in Tigre occupied by Italy, and a frontier rectification in
the east and south-east. Thirdly, a large zone in the south and
south-west in which Italy, acting under the League, would have
the monopoly of economic development. Fourthly, the maintenance of Abyssinian sovereignty over all but the districts actually
ceded to Italy. Fifthly, the reference of the plan to the League for
approval or rejection as the kind of compromise that we considered
practicable.

The proposals were in striking contrast with Mussolini's earlier
demands. His minimum terms had been the cession to Italy of all
the non-Amharic districts, and an Italian mandate for the rest of
Abyssinia, and he had threatened, if these were not accepted, that

he would wipe Abyssinia off the map. The war had since started with a series of Italian victories, and it seemed certain that unless we could end it in the immediate future, incalculable suffering would be inflicted on the population, and the whole country annexed, the Emperor deposed, Mussolini inevitably driven into Hitler's arms, the League hopelessly disrupted, and German aggression everywhere encouraged.

It was these considerations that on that Sunday evening made me recommend to the Cabinet the acceptance of the joint plan for submission to the League.

The Paris meeting finished in the evening with a declaration from Laval that a new chapter had opened in Anglo-French co-operation. As I drove away, Vansittart and Clerk congratulated me on having re-established the Anglo-French front. When I returned to the British Embassy, I found Charles Mendl, the Press Secretary, waiting for me with several correspondents who wished for an interview. I saw them for a few minutes and gave them a very general idea of what we had been attempting, but made it clear that our plan was only provisional, and needed to be referred first to the two Governments, and secondly, to the League. I asked them, therefore, not to comment upon it in any detail until the two Governments released the actual terms. The correspondents appeared ready to fall in with my request.

CHAPTER XIV

The Storm

IN THE meanwhile, a copy of the whole document that we had initialled had found its way into the offices of certain opposition papers, particularly the *Œuvre* and the *Echo de Paris*, that were bent, for different reasons, upon destroying Laval. Whether the leak from the Quai d'Orsay was intentional or due to carelessness, I could not know. The result the next morning was a premature and partisan disclosure of many of the details in a most hostile light, and before the British and French Cabinets had been able to consider the whole plan in its proper setting. To make things worse, I left Paris for Switzerland soon after seeing the correspondents, and had no idea of the leakages in the Press until I arrived at Zuoz the next afternoon. The harm was then done. The London papers were no less critical than the French, and it was obvious to me that a very awkward political situation had been suddenly created. I at once offered to return to London. Baldwin's answer was slow in coming, but when it came, was reassuring. The gist of it was that I need not worry, as he had complete control of the situation, and did not wish to interrupt my leave in Switzerland. I then heard nothing more from him, though it was clear to me from telephone talks with the Foreign Office that, so far from being in control, the situation was getting completely out of hand. In spite, therefore, of his reassuring words, I decided to go back and face the storm. It was at this point that a cynical providence turned the scene into a medley of farce and tragedy. For months past I had been looking forward to my skating holiday in Switzerland. The sport that I loved above all others was to set me up after a long period of overwork. I had arranged for one of the best rinks in the Engadine to be ready for me before the usual time of opening, and everything was prepared for a few weeks of Swiss paradise. The day after my arrival at Zuoz was one of those perfect days of blue sky, white snow and black ice. I hurried on to the rink, feeling that there was no turn or step that I could not accomplish. There followed a complete black-out, even blacker than those that I had had several times in the previous months, and when I came to myself, it was clear that something serious was wrong with my face. Having tottered back to the hotel and summoned the doctor, I learnt that my nose was badly broken in two places. The doctor added that for weeks past he had been expecting an accident. Indeed, when he had first heard of my projected visit to Zuoz, he had been so certain that something untoward would happen that he had pressed the local authorities to warn me against coming. As this gift of foresight had more than once prepared him for sudden emergencies, he was already expecting to have me as his patient. Here indeed was a complication, a silly one from one point of view, for Foreign Secretaries should not break their noses; a serious one from another, for at this moment it was essential that I should return to London at once, and the doctor declared that on no account could I travel for two or three days, owing to the danger of infecting the two fractures. I had therefore to quiet my mental and physical pains as best I could and count the hours until I could leave for London.

Whilst I was detained in Switzerland, two damaging debates took place in the House of Commons. Baldwin, instead of insisting that the plan had been prepared at the request of the League as the basis of a compromise to stop the war, talked mysteriously of facts that, if they were fully known, would convince the whole House of the wisdom of what had happened. " My lips are not yet unsealed. Were the troubles over, I would make my case and I guarantee that not a man would go into the lobby against me." He had also annoyed his supporters in the Press by refusing to see them. It was not therefore surprising that my private secretary had a very long face when he met me at Croydon aerodrome. As soon as I arrived home, I went to bed under doctor's orders on no account to go out or to see more than a very few visitors. This was the situation when Chamberlain arrived the next morning with a mission from the Cabinet to discuss the position with me. At the meeting held soon after the arrival of my report from Paris, the Cabinet had agreed to accept the plan. In a subsequent

meeting, however, they doubted whether it could be upheld in face
of the outcry against it. Chamberlain came to ask my view in
face of these fears. I told him that I was fully alive to the many
objectionable features in the proposals, but that I was convinced
that they were a great improvement both on the Italian demands
and Laval's first attempts at a compromise, and that they did not
depart substantially from the conclusions of the Peterson-St.
Quentin meetings, all of which had been reported to the Cabinet
without exciting opposition or criticism. In these circumstances
I felt sure that the right course was for me to make a full explanation to the House as to why we had made and accepted them,
and to say very definitely that as we were acting on behalf of the
League, it was for the League to accept or reject a plan that
seemed to the French and ourselves to contain the minimum
proposals for stopping Mussolini short of the risk of going to war
with him. Chamberlain entirely agreed with me, and I accordingly started to make up a speech on these lines.

Baldwin also came to see me, and although he was uncom-
municative, gave me the impression that he also agreed with me.
His last words were: "We all stand together." Later in the day,
however, Chamberlain returned after another Cabinet with a very
different story. He had been asked to tell me that my proposed
statement did not go far enough, and that it was necessary for
me to say that the plan was bad, that I had been mistaken in
accepting it, and that in view of the general opposition I withdrew
my support of it. I told him at once that I was not prepared to
make any such recantation. I was convinced that nothing short
of the proposals would save Abyssinia and prevent Mussolini from
joining the Hitler front. This being so, resignation, not recantation, was the only course open to me. Chamberlain took my
message back to Downing Street. When Baldwin came again to
see me some hours afterwards, he found me determined to defend
the plan, and in consequence to resign. He himself never suggested resignation to me. In fact, he would much have preferred
that I should have fallen in with the Cabinet's wish for a recantation and have remained in the Government. My decision was,
however, final.

The formalities were quickly completed. My resignation was
submitted to the King; I obtained His Majesty's approval to
explain my reasons for it, and a representative of the Privy Council

Office collected my seal of office. My statement in the House of Commons was arranged for the Thursday afternoon, December 19. It only remained for me to prepare my speech, take leave of my more immediate helpers in the Foreign Office, and see two or three intimate friends. One of these friends, Beaverbrook, had never deserted me at any critical moment. Months and perhaps years would pass without our meeting, and then some alarm or excursion would bring us together on the same intimate footing as when we had last seen each other. In these black hours just as he had visited me after the Prague *coup*, he came to me with words of encouragement and advice. Vansittart, also, unshaken by the public clamour, never ceased to hold up my hands while the storm was raging.

I also had a visit from Geoffrey Dawson, who came like one of Job's comforters to mourn over my sins and misfortunes. He had wished to see me Foreign Secretary, chiefly, I think, because he believed that I would assist his policy of Anglo-German appeasement. My efforts to maintain the Stresa front and keep Mussolini on the Allied side had cut across his Anglo-German plans. His reaction, therefore, against the Paris proposals had been particularly savage. It was he who turned the provision of a port for Abyssinia in Italian Eritrea into an offer of " a camel track " to Zeila. At the time that I saw him he was all the more hostile as his intimate friend, Baldwin, in refusing to see the Press, had not made an exception for the Editor of *The Times*. My interview with him was embarrassing to both of us. However, we had been good friends for so long that neither he nor I was prepared to let an exceptional difference of opinion end in a permanent breach.

All this time I was kept by my doctor either in the house or in the garden that adjoined it. When I wished to go to the Cabinet and tell my whole story, he pointed to the two fractures in my nose. " If you go," were his words of warning, " you may very well pick up a serious infection, and be prevented from making your speech in the House of Commons on Thursday afternoon." I therefore stayed at home, a prisoner confined to barracks, when I should have been around and about, fit and free to meet the growing criticism. From time to time the news was brought to me of the storm that was raging outside. I remember in particular hearing of Austen Chamberlain's intervention in the Foreign

Affairs Committee of the Conservative members in the House of Commons. He had gone to it, so Neville Chamberlain told me, with the intention of supporting the agreement as the least bad of several bad alternatives, and had made a speech to this effect. The feeling in the Committee had then been so strong against him that he changed his mind, and made a second speech condemning it. His revised verdict was immediately reported to an adjoining meeting of the National Liberals, and carried the day with little opposition from either side of the Government coalition.

The fateful Thursday arrived, and with my wife, I went to the House of Commons for my speech. I had insisted with Baldwin that my resignation should be announced before I spoke, as I wished to be able to speak unreservedly and as a private member. If, however, I was to make an effective defence of my action, my explanation would inevitably be longer than the conventional resignation speeches to which the House was accustomed. Should I try the House too high if I made a full explanation? Many, perhaps most, of the members were critical of what I had done, not a few were actively hostile to me. I knew from past experience how easy it was to overstep the limits of patience and tolerance even in a friendly House. In the atmosphere of that December afternoon there was no unlimited fund of sympathy upon which I could draw.

When I took my corner seat on the same back bench that I had left to take office many years before, the bandage on my broken nose made me feel very self-conscious. As soon, however, as I started to speak, I lost my nervousness, and as at Geneva two months before, I felt that I was receiving not only a fair but even a friendly hearing. The danger of a European conflagration, the need to maintain the Stresa front, the risk to Anglo-French friendship, the critical plight of Abyssinia and the failure of any League State except Great Britain to take military precautions against a mad dog act by Mussolini—these were the points that I tried to bring out. More than once, also, I insisted that my action had never been influenced by any fear or doubt as to our ability to defeat Italy. If there was to be collective action against Mussolini, we were perfectly ready to take our part, but we did not intend to enter a unilateral war and to call it collective action. Towards the end of my detailed argument I began to feel exhausted. I lasted out, however, until I sat down, when I felt a sudden shoot of pain in my broken nose. Instinctively I put up my hand to stop it. This trivial action started the story that I had broken down in tears at the end of my speech. I never felt less like tears. I was certain that I had done my best for European peace, and that the circumstances had been too strong for me. Recantation, regret, recrimination had no place in my mind.

It only remained for me to take leave of the King. I had not seen him for a fortnight, and I was greatly shocked by his appearance. He looked very ill, and spoke as if he was weighed down with anxiety. His voice sounded weaker and less confident that I had ever known it. I was indeed sad that my resignation should have added to his worries. Having said that he was sorry to lose me as his Foreign Minister, he then very tactfully turned the conversation to the tastes that we shared in Norfolk. " Now you are free, you will have more time for shooting. Go and shoot a lot of woodcocks in Norfolk." These were his last words to me, for I did not see him again before his death a few weeks later.

I believed, and I still believe, that the plan was the best possible, or should I say, the least bad, in the circumstances. What neither I nor anyone directly connected with it expected, was the extent of the opposition that it excited. The general public was ignorant of the past history and had not been able to follow the complicated details of the negotiation, nor was our military weakness taken into account. Perhaps even the Cabinet had not fully grasped the implications of any plan that had a chance of being accepted by Mussolini. To the world at large, the controversy seemed to be a battle between right and wrong in which there must be unconditional surrender and no compromise. What would happen in a fight to the death, most people refused even to consider. Some seemed to think that if the League shouted loud enough, the Italian walls would collapse. Others continued to believe that the League front was unshakable, whereas the cracks in it were painfully obvious whenever it was tested. Very few realised that the real danger to Europe was a Germany with Italy as an ally. The result was an overwhelming outcry that swept away the plan, and with it, a good chance, probably the last chance, of maintaining the Stresa front against Hitler.

If it had not been for the hostile reaction in London against the plan, Mussolini would have accepted it. The telegrams from

Rome showed that he was definitely moving towards acceptance
when my resignation tipped the scales against it. Guariglia, the
Secretary-General of the Italian Ministry of Foreign Affairs, has
given a full account of Mussolini's attitude.[1] The proposals were
communicated to him on December 11. Whilst they fell very
definitely short of his demands, for instance, by restricting the
cession of Abyssinian territory, omitting any facilities for joining
the two Italian colonies by a railway, and maintaining Abyssinian
sovereignty over much the greater part of the country, he considered them a basis for agreement. He accordingly summoned
the Grand Council of the Party for December 18, and had ready
for it a resolution that welcomed the plan. To Guariglia's astonishment nothing appeared in the Press on the following day, although
preparations had been made for the full publication of the
Council's proceedings. When he asked the reason, he was told
that Mussolini, after hearing of my resignation, had at once
cancelled the meeting.

The Emperor of Abyssinia, seeing at the same time the
opposition in England to the proposals, very naturally refused
them. His attitude, however, might well have been different if
they could have been debated in detail by the League, and their
exact scope and possibilities accurately explained.

It was in Germany, however, that the reactions were most
significant. Lipski, the Polish Ambassador in Berlin, subsequently
gave me a detailed account of the effect that the proposals and
their rejection had on Hitler and his entourage. Up till June,
German relations with Italy had been extremely bad. When
Lipski was staying with Goering in the previous April, he had
heard nothing but abuse of Mussolini. With the summer had
come a marked change in the German attitude. The German
Press ceased to attack Italy, whilst Hitler was obviously turning
against the various Pacts that we had urged upon him. In July,
when a breach between the League and Mussolini seemed inevitable, Hitler started the first serious trouble in Danzig. Soon
afterwards the Italian Ambassador, Cerutti, was moved from
Berlin at Hitler's suggestion, and replaced by Attolico for the
express purpose of improving relations between the two dictators.
As the autumn passed, there were other unmistakable signs of a

[1] *Ricordi*, by Rafaele Guariglia, page 294 and following (*Edizioni Scientifiche Italiane.*
Napoli).

rapprochement between the Nazi and Fascist régimes. The agreement in Paris, therefore, came to Hitler as a most unwelcome surprise. On December 18 Lipski had a long conversation with him.

> " Hitler was obviously uneasy over the situation which had resulted. . . ." I quote Lipski's words. " I gained the impression that Hitler was alarmed over the fact that, in the event of a liquidation of the Abyssinian conflict by compromise between Great Britain and France on the one hand and Italy on the other, a united front of the Powers, strengthened by the recent Pact between Paris and Moscow, would reappear."

Hitler's resentment against the agreement was reflected in the obvious anxiety of the Wilhelmstrasse.

> " The nervousness of Berlin official circles "—this was Lipski's conclusion—" can best be explained by the fact that the suppression, by means of the Hoare-Laval agreement, of the conflict of Italy with Great Britain and France was the means of depriving the German Government of an exceptionally convenient position arising for Germany when a high state of tension occurred over the Abyssinian conflict."

The relief therefore was great in Berlin when the news arrived that the agreement had been repudiated.

The agreement was certainly dead, and with it the hope of ending a cruel and hateful war. My wife and I returned to Switzerland, and my successor had the grim task of agreeing a few months later to the total withdrawal of sanctions, the extinction of Abyssinia as a sovereign power, and the annexation of the whole country under an Italian Emperor. Worse than that, he was to see within a few weeks Hitler, freed from any fear of the Italian Army on the Brenner, take military possession of the Rhineland and win a strategic position from which he was only to be dislodged after five years of world war.

So ended my six months of hard labour in the Foreign Office. I emerged into a world that had turned against me. The applause that I had received in September at Geneva had changed to the abuse that rained upon me at the end of the year. I do not argue whether either was deserved. In the following weeks I had ample opportunity for meditating on these vicissitudes and for considering as dispassionately as I could the rights and wrongs of a controversy in which all the alternatives were bad.

My broad conclusion remained unshaken. The so-called Hoare-Laval plan was the only practicable basis for a compromise to end the war that had already begun, and for the re-establishment of the Stresa front. The alternatives were either to do nothing or to face the possibility of war with Italy. Public opinion was equally opposed to either. The intensification of sanctions would not have been supported by the French unless it had been preceded by a further joint attempt to reach a settlement. Even then, there were many who believed that increased sanctions would only consolidate Italian resistance. Month by month, the truth had been forced on me that if governments were not prepared to go to war, they must negotiate. So far as I could judge, there was not a single government in the League that was prepared to go to war, least of all the French. That being so, it was essential to negotiate for a compromise. We ourselves could, of course, have easily defeated Italy. Sir William Fisher, the Commander-in-Chief in the Mediterranean, was rightly confident that he could drive the Italian Fleet from the sea. But what he did not realise was our fixed resolve to avoid unilateral action against a potential ally in a war with Germany. The Naval Staff, considering the crisis from a wider angle, could not have been more insistent with their warnings against diminishing or dissipating our limited strength.

It was considerations such as these that confirmed me in the view that negotiation was the only wise course, and that if it were to succeed, substantial concessions to Italy were inevitable. To this extent, therefore, I felt that there was no cause for blaming myself.

There was, however, another side of the controversy, upon which I was certainly open to criticism. As the weeks passed I became more and more impatient, and impatience is the unforgivable sin that all Foreign Secretaries must avoid. Perhaps it was the strain on my nerves during my four years at the India Office that had made them over-sensitive. I had then shown so much patience that my stock of it was probably exhausted. Perhaps, also, the climbing of a very Everest of Parliamentary mountains had made me feel oversure of my ability to surmount new peaks. In any case, I rushed the attempt before I was ready for it, and I did not take sufficient account of what other people were saying and thinking. It seemed to me so obviously right to keep Italy on our front that I did not take enough trouble to explain to my colleagues in the Government and the country outside the exact details of the controversy and the concrete dangers of failure. Perhaps, too, I shrank from showing my weak hand to the world when I believed that I could still win with it, if I was left to play it myself. Had not Sir Edward Grey kept his intentions to himself and away from colleagues who might have embarrassed him?

In my case, the result was the sudden shock felt by the country when the terms of the only possible compromise became public. If I had been in closer touch with public opinion, I should have realised the need of a long chapter of preparation before I could expect approval of the plan. The details of the actual position should have been stated and re-stated for weeks on end—how we and the French were only making recommendations at the express request of the League and for submission to the League, how much of the territory involved in the proposed change was unadministered and unpopulated desert, and finally how formidable were the risks to Europe of a complete break with Italy. The facts of a grim situation needed to be faced in concrete form. The trouble was that there was little or no time for this full explanation, and my impatience for a settlement suppressed my natural instinct for caution.

It may well be that the story that I have told will change no one's opinion. Some will continue to believe that Mussolini was certain to join Hitler, that no compromise was possible with him, and that if we had persisted with the full rigour of sanctions, we could have brought him to his knees. Others who do not accept the view that the world is irrevocably divided between black and white, and who prefer negotiation to unconditional surrender, will continue to think that we were bound to try for a compromise. Others will agree with Vansittart and me that as the real danger was Germany, the overriding consideration was to keep Mussolini out of Hitler's arms. Only the future historian, removed from the heat of contemporary controversy, will be able to form a dispassionate judgment on these conflicting views. I have given my account. In the nature of things, it cannot claim to be impartial, yet it will have been worth while, if it has provided some further evidence for the historian's verdict.

APPENDIX

"Telling the Truth to the People"

IN THE *Cambridge Journal*, pages 84-95, November, 1948, Mr. R. Bassett has clearly explained what happened.

" Baldwin has been charged with shirking the rearmament issue in the 1935 Election for fear of being defeated on it. The accusation has been based on what he said in answer to Churchill on November 12, 1936. His words have been erroneously taken to apply to the actual Election of 1935, whereas he was dealing with the question of a hypothetical Election in 1933 or 1934. What he actually said in the middle of a long speech on a Liberal resolution dealing with the private sale of arms was as follows:

' I put before the whole House my own views with an appalling frankness. From 1933, I and my friends were all very worried about what was happening in Europe. You will remember at the time the Disarmament Conference was sitting in Geneva. You will remember at the time there was probably a stronger pacifist feeling running through this country than at any time since the War. I am speaking of 1933 and 1934. You will remember the election at Fulham in the autumn of 1933, when a seat which the National Government held was lost by about 7,000 votes on no issue but the pacifist. You will remember perhaps that the National Government candidate who made a most guarded reference to the question of defence was mobbed for it.

' That was the feeling in the country in 1933. My position as the leader of a great party was not altogether a comfortable one. I asked myself what chance was there—when that feeling that was given expression to in Fulham was common throughout the country—what chance was there within the next year or two of that feeling being so changed that the country would give a mandate for rearmament? Supposing I had gone to the country and said that Germany was rearming and that we must rearm, does anybody think that this pacific democracy would have rallied to that cry at that moment? I cannot think of anything that would have made the loss of the Election from my point of view more certain. . . .

' I think the country itself learned by certain events that took place during the winter of 1934-35 what the perils might be to it. All I did was to take a moment perhaps less unfortunate than another might have been, and we won the Election with a large majority; but frankly I could conceive that we should at that time, by advocating certain courses, have been a great deal less successful. We got from the country—with a large majority— a mandate for doing a thing that no one, 12 months before, would have believed possible. It is my firm conviction that had the Government, with this great majority, used that majority to do anything that might be described as arming without a mandate—and they did not do anything, except the slightly increased air programme for which they gave their reasons— had I taken such action as my right hon. Friend desired me to take, it would have defeated entirely the end I had in view. I may be wrong, but I put that to the House as an explanation of my action in that respect.' "

At the time, Baldwin's remarks failed to stir up any notable reaction in the House of Commons. They were accepted for what they were—his explanation of his attitude in 1933 and 1934, and not of the 1935 Election. The debate ended with a normal party vote, in which the Conservatives, including Churchill, voted solidly against the Liberal resolution.

By taking certain sentences out of their context, however, and omitting others, it has been made to appear that Baldwin cunningly suppressed the issue of rearmament in the 1935 Election, and obtained a majority by false pretences. He did nothing of the kind. When he spoke of " going to the country," he was referring not to the Election that took place in October, 1935, but to a problematical Election that might have taken place in 1933 or 1934. Until the Election of 1935, the Government's only mandate was economic recovery. After the 1935 Election, Baldwin's hands were free for a definite programme of rearmament. Both Baldwin and his colleagues, in fact, insisted that rearmament was one of the principal issues in the

Election. As Foreign Secretary at the time, I was in close touch with him throughout the Election. The international situation could not have been more delicate. On the one hand, we were doing our utmost to create a united League front against Mussolini; on the other, we were profoundly conscious of our own military weakness and the urgent need for time to repair it. If, however, we had weighted the scales too heavily on the side of rearmament, we should have given the impression that the negotiations in Geneva were bound to fail. If, on the other hand, we had lost the chance of making rearmament a definite issue in the Election, our hands would have remained tied as they had been in 1933 and 1934. This double policy of negotiation and rearmament inevitably laid us open to attack from two sides. The Opposition concentrated on the rearmament side, and turned the campaign into a movement of resistance against militarism. Chamberlain, the Chancellor of the Exchequer, was particularly selected to be pilloried as a militarist, and the possibility of Churchill becoming the First Lord of the Admiralty was widely exploited to frighten the anti-militarist voters.

In spite, however, of noisy meetings and bitter attacks, the Election gave Baldwin a great majority for the double programme of negotiation and rearmament. The electors fully understood the two issues, not least the issue of rearmament. They had not been deceived, and Baldwin had taken the first available moment for obtaining their verdict. There is therefore no basis for the charge that he concealed the truth in order to obtain a party advantage.

The real case against him is very different. It is that after 1935, and having obtained a mandate for rearmament, he did not make better use of his opportunity. These were the two years during which public opinion was better prepared for a more vigorous policy. Was it that Baldwin was growing old and tired and already thinking of retirement? Or that he was out of his depth in questions of defence and foreign affairs?

As one of his colleagues I could not be blind to the fact that he was a tired man. He was constantly talking of his impending retirement, and particularly after the death of King George V, he seemed to have lost much of his interest in current politics. Foreign affairs worried him. Like Asquith and Grey, he did not understand foreigners; he felt that he could not influence them as he influenced his fellow-countrymen in the House of Commons and on the wireless. These personal considerations certainly strengthened his natural dislike of drastic action. An answer, however, that took account of them and nothing more would be gravely incomplete. The inescapable fact that should never be forgotten was that in spite of Hitler's growing power, the country as a whole remained indifferent to the threat of danger. Up to the time of the Abyssinian crisis I shared the general feeling of complacency.

Part Three

RETURN BY SEA TO WHITEHALL

CHAPTER XV

Return to Office

I was now able to resume my broken holiday in Switzerland. But how entirely the conditions had changed since I started it! The Secretary of State who had gone to the Swiss mountains to gain strength for the next chapter of his work at the Foreign Office had returned, a private member, discredited by failure and benumbed by the blows that had fallen upon him. Should I ever have the chance of returning to office, and if I had the chance, should I wish to take it? Baldwin had told me that he wanted me back, but I knew only too well how quickly the river of politics flowed, and how difficult it was for anyone who had left it to catch again the tide.

As there was nothing to be gained by meditating on answers to hypothetical and depressing questions, I transferred the energy that I had been devoting to the Foreign Office to two objectives. The first was getting well. The second was getting a gold medal for skating. With the first, I succeeded after a few weeks of sun and snow. For the second, I never had sufficient time, and even at the end of the four years that remained before the outbreak of war, I was still practising for a distinction that I never obtained. For the time being, however, the intense concentration that is needed for advanced skating dispelled from my mind any mournful or morbid regrets that I might be nursing over my resignation. Except for a correspondence with Chamberlain and Baldwin, I avoided political contacts. When Hitler invited me to the winter Olympic sports at Partenkirchen, I at once refused. When Titulesco and Benes suggested visits to me, I made excuse on the ground of my health. As the spring approached, the sun became stronger and the ice unfit for skating. The thaw, the only disagreeable season in Switzerland, was beginning, and it was obviously time to return to England. The nearer came the day of my departure, the more reluctant I felt at the idea of starting again on a very broken road, around which were waiting many threatening groups of critics. However, Chamberlain overcame my hesitations, and towards the end of February my wife and I went back to London. Encouragement at once came to me from two very different directions.

McKenna, the Chairman of the Midland Bank, pressed me to leave politics and allow my name to be proposed for his Board, hinting that he would soon be retiring, and that I might be in the running to succeed him. I greatly appreciated his suggestion, but told him that my answer must depend on Baldwin's intentions towards me. If I was wanted back in the Cabinet, I should have to refuse the chance of returning to my family's trade of banking. Baldwin lost no time in making my refusal inevitable. I had several interviews with him immediately after my return, and in all of them he told me that he wished me to rejoin the Cabinet as soon as there was a suitable vacancy. It was at this time that his hand was being forced to appoint a Minister of Defence. The argument in favour of the Minister was the slowness of rearmament. The argument against it was that the heavy coach was beginning to move, and that a fifth wheel would only delay it. Like many questions in Whitehall and Westminster the controversy ended in a compromise. The three Service Ministers were to retain their sovereign powers, but a new Minister was to be appointed to harmonise their plans. Baldwin's first idea was to give me the new post. Indeed, he went so far as to commission Chamberlain to make me the offer. I said that I would accept it, and it was agreed that the announcement should be made immediately after a debate on defence that was taking place in the House of Commons the following week. Chamberlain was strongly in favour of my speaking in the debate in order to establish the fact that I had returned to active politics. I accordingly intervened early in the debate and sketched the kind of problems that a co-ordinating Minister would have to solve. The speech seemed to go well in the House, but the Press, the next morning, particularly *The Times*, bitterly attacked it as a clumsy bid for office. The effect of the criticism was to make Baldwin hesitate, and after two or three days of vacillation, to appoint

Inskip, the Attorney General. His change of mind was a relief rather than a disappointment to me. The post was ill-defined, and its holder was being given an impossible task. Instead, Baldwin offered me the Admiralty, which was falling vacant in the early summer owing to Eyres-Monsell's acceptance of a peerage, and the need for the First Lord to be in the House of Commons. This alternative was in every way more attractive to me, and I gratefully accepted it.

In the meanwhile, Hitler's challenge in the Rhineland in February, 1936, had been ignored. I was not yet a member of the Government, and had no means of following the confidential discussions between the French and ourselves. I do, however, remember the general attitude both of the Government and the British public at the time. There was no vigorous reaction to Hitler's move. " What justification could there be for a European war to uphold an out-of-date clause of the Versailles Treaty, and why should not the Germans have full sovereign rights in some of the most German territories of the Reich? " These were the questions that three people out of four were asking themselves. In view of this almost universal feeling, the Government would have had little or no support for pressing the reluctant French into war. If reports were correct, the French Government was nervous of the political effect of mobilisation, whilst the French people were overwhelmingly opposed to any move that might involve them in war. None the less, I am now certain that if we and our ally had intervened, we could certainly have driven Hitler back, and inflicted a crushing blow on his growing prestige. It was then that he convinced himself that the road was open, and that the Allies would not interfere with his march. Thereafter the story is of a series of rearguard actions that never stopped his advance until years of war had devastated the world.

By June I was back in office after six months in the wilderness. My happiness at being once more a Minister was the measure of my unhappiness when I was deprived of the enthralling interest of administering a great department. The life of a private member had no attraction for me, except as a step on the stairway to the front bench. Having already, as a Cabinet Minister of many years' standing, been given the chance of working in the inner circles of government, I could never have reconciled myself to political life without office. Rightly or wrongly, I believed that any qualities that I possessed were much better fitted for the making of policy and the management of a department than for the many useful activities that fill the life of a private member. I had no wish, therefore, to conceal the fact that I was delighted to descend once more from a corner seat at the back of the House to my old place on the front bench.

Whilst I received a friendly welcome from my old colleagues, I was conscious of a feeling amongst some of them that my return was premature. There were others who feared that it might embarrass Eden, my successor at the Foreign Office. It was obvious to me that I must pick my steps very delicately, and on no account point to the way in which all my prophecies of the previous December, the conquest of Abyssinia, the consolidation of the Axis, and the occupation of the Rhineland, had unfortunately come true. The last thing that I wished was to be drawn back into the eddies of foreign politics. I accordingly tried my best to avoid past controversies, and concentrate my mind upon the needs of my new department.

A very important chapter had just opened for the Admiralty. The White Paper of the previous March and the Defence Loan of £400 millions had made it possible to begin to restore some of the Navy's lost strength. Eyres-Monsell, my predecessor, had already started the recovery; my paramount duty was to expand it. The Estimates would be the test of my success. I therefore lost no time in discussing the programme from every possible angle, not only with the Board of Admiralty, but also with Chamberlain as Chancellor of the Exchequer. I had so often seen battles between the Service Departments and the Treasury that on this occasion I determined to forestall a clash by giving the Chancellor an outline of my plans several months before the usual time for inter-departmental discussions. Chamberlain was as anxious as I was to strengthen the navy, and as I shall show later, the result was a programme of unprecedented size in peace time, and an expenditure of £105,065,000, and all of it agreed between us without any of the usual wrangling in Whitehall.

At the Admiralty, my surroundings reminded me not a little of the pleasant atmosphere of the India Office. It is true that my room in the ugly Victorian wing had none of the charm of my home on the other side of the Horse Guards Parade. The Board

Room, however, more than compensated for the commonplace room of the First Lord. The Board Room was to the Admiralty what St. Edward's Chapel is to Westminster Abbey, the central shrine of tradition, the scene of momentous decisions, the repository of historic relics. When I sat for the first time in the First Lord's chair and looked at the Grinling Gibbons carvings, the oldest wind dial in the country, and the picture of Nelson painted immediately after the Battle of the Nile on the walls, and around the table at the company of well-known admirals, my fellow members of the Board, I felt deeply moved by the *genius loci*. I remembered Herbert Fisher's judgment that the sea and the Bible were the two greatest forces in British history, and there, was I in the full current of the sea. The influence of tradition extended far beyond the Board Room. At the end of the passage was Admiralty House, built like the Horse Guards in the style of some great magnate's residence in country or town. Like the navy, Admiralty House had fallen on evil days. The First World War had taken many rooms from the First Lord and given them to the office; the house itself had fallen into disrepair, and when peace came, First Lords no longer regarded it as a coveted perquisite of office worth the £500 a year that they were asked to pay for it.

Almost the first decision that I had to take after my appointment was whether or not we would leave our comfortable home in Chelsea and move to an official residence that was lacking in many modern requirements. When I discussed the question with the Chancellor of the Exchequer and the First Commissioner of Works, I found them both not only anxious that we should live in Whitehall, but determined to make Admiralty House both comfortable and worthy of its traditions. Fortunately for me, Philip Sassoon was First Commissioner, and already enthralled by the duties of his department. His sensitive taste and vivid imagination, after adding colour and beauty to his own houses at Trent, Lympne and in Park Lane, were already felt in the Houses of Parliament and the offices of Whitehall. Together with him, my wife and I set ourselves to rebuild the glories of a historic house. It was the last of the official residences of the Board that had at one time occupied most of the space now filled by the Department. It had remained as an official house and been enlarged for the member who came to be known as the First Lord from the fact that his name was the first to be mentioned in the Board's Commission, and who because of his political position became the acknowledged chairman at its meetings. The officials and workmen of the Office of Works entered heart and soul into the task of restoration, whilst on our side, we took several of our pictures, a cut-glass chandelier, and a suite of Aubusson chairs and carpets to add dignity to the state rooms. In the course of the work we discovered that a former First Lord had put a pitch-pine shelter over the front door for an evening party, and that as it had never been removed, it still obscured and defaced the entrance. We had it removed. We also found that under the very dirty linoleum that covered the hall floor, were solid blocks of eighteenth-century stone that only needed to be cleaned to transform the effect upon coming into the house. My wife took the keenest interest in these various arrangements, and when the work was completed, gave a large evening party that included the officials and workmen who had carried it out. She and I were delighted to find that the house was rated as one of His Majesty's ships, so that the linen and household stores came from the victualling yard at Deptford. A famous admiral greatly approved of our efforts to improve the house. " The Admiralty have done you thundering well," was his comment after he had had a good look at the rooms.

The house, apart from the interest that its restoration had given us, exercised a continuous influence over me. Its naval traditions, its Fish furniture, its pictures of Captain Cook's voyages, its pikes and grappling-irons in the entrance hall created the right background for my dealings with the Sea Lords. They, and, indeed, the whole staff, were very different from my former advisers in other offices. The world of the Admiralty was still in many ways a world apart. The constitution of the office was peculiar to itself, the habits and methods of the sea dominated its activities, the story of the great admirals and the splendid record of the fleet inspired as a religion the two hundred and fifty naval officers who were working in it. Even more than in the India Office, I found tradition enthroned in every room. Their Lord-ships of the Board kept alive the memories of Pepys and his Commissions. The Patent of 1832 under the Great Seal that gave them their responsible powers was couched in the solemn language of a Biblical injunction. It is true that subsequent Orders in Council had exalted the political member into the First Lord and given him an authority over his colleagues. But in spite of the efforts of Erskine Childers in 1869 to suppress all idea of joint responsibility, and to make the First Lord solely responsible to Parliament for all the business of the Admiralty, the Board continued to exercise its great power as a corporate body capable of collective action. A First Lord would be extremely reluctant to override the views of the naval advisers entrenched in so traditional a stronghold, and a Cabinet would try very hard to avoid a clash with an institution that had so much popular support behind it. It was clear to me from my first day in the office that the conditions were very different from the Air Ministry, where Trenchard, a Commander-in-Chief *de facto* if not *de jure*, and I had been able, whilst carrying the individual members with us, to ignore the Air Council as a collective body. I quickly noticed another difference. With a combative First Sea Lord, a Fisher or a Beatty, for example, the Board could still become powerful enough to challenge the political decisions of the Government. I had seen an example of its belligerent powers in the battle over the Fleet Air Arm in 1923. No such crisis fortunately arose during my period. The Service members of the Board were not only men of exceptional ability like Chatfield, sailor and statesman, and Reginald Henderson, the Sea Lord responsible for naval construction, but were one and all determined to work in harmony with the Cabinet and the other departments.

Two questions overshadowed our meetings, the Fleet Air Arm and the programme of new construction. The controversy over the control of naval aviation had been endemic in Whitehall since the end of the First World War. It had provided the dramatic battleground for the champions of the two armies, Beatty and Trenchard. From 1922, when I first became Secretary of State for Air, until the fall of the second Baldwin Government, I was in the thick of the fight, and some time I will tell the story in detail. It is sufficient in this book to deal with it only in so far as it concerned me as First Lord.

Neither side had lowered, much less abandoned, its claim—for the air force, that the air, being one and indivisible, should not be partitioned between different Services, for the navy, that the sea being one and indivisible, with everything above it, should be the exclusive domain of the fleet. Trenchard and I had fought the naval claim in 1923 and won the case for the Air Ministry. The air force was then so small that any partition would have meant

its virtual extinction. The problem as I saw it in 1936, though
fundamentally the same, had changed in the important respect
that during the intervening years the air force had been firmly
established as a great and growing Service. There was no longer
any risk of a concession to the navy leading to the disruption of
an independent air force and the end of the Trenchard conception
of air strategy. There was also undeniable advantage to be
gained by stopping or at least mitigating the bitter inter-departmental controversy that had for years been devastating Whitehall. It was these considerations that made me tell Chatfield that
I was prepared to support the Admiralty case so far as it concerned carrier-borne aircraft, but that I could not agree to the
separation of the coastal air command and land based aircraft
from the Air Ministry. Inskip was at this time engaged in an
arbitration between the two sides. I gave evidence at it in
accordance with my undertaking to Chatfield, and it was on
these lines that the Minister of Co-ordination made his recommendations to the Cabinet. The Cabinet approved them, with
the result that only the faintest echoes of a past controversy
subsequently disturbed the newly established peace between the
two Departments.

The second urgent problem concerned the naval programme.
The fleet had never recovered from the economies made at the
end of the First World War and in the years between 1925 and
1930. The Washington Treaty of 1921 had destroyed many more
British ships of war than the German Fleet. The reductions were,
however, made with discrimination. The Treaty stopped competition between the naval powers by limiting the size and
number of capital ships and aircraft carriers, and left us free to
build as many cruisers and destroyers as we wished. Besides, there
was added an escape clause providing for amending the Treaty
in the event of " any change of circumstances affecting national
security." These were concrete advantages for which it was
worth making sacrifices. It was very different with the unilateral
disarmament and the crippling restrictions on our naval developments that followed in the ensuing years. I am afraid that the
Governments of which I was a member were as much responsible
as the Labour Governments. The fact remains that year by year
the old ships became obsolete and the new ships were not built.
Our cruiser strength, for instance, fell from 51 in 1922 to 47 in

1926, and 48 in 1927, although the Naval Staff insisted that the minimum standard of safety was 70. In spite of the recommendation of a strong Cabinet Committee under the chairmanship of Birkenhead in 1925 that five a year should be built, the Chancellor of the Exchequer, Churchill, had the number reduced to eight in four years, and further diminished by a later cut to three. It was not surprising in this atmosphere of unilateral disarmament that the Labour Government of 1929 agreed to anticipate the scrapping of five valuable ships, all completed in 1914 and with many years' service before them, to postpone until 1937 the replacement of our older battleships, and to limit our cruisers and destroyers to a number that suited American prestige rather than our own needs. This was the *damnosa hereditas* from which the navy was suffering until the White Paper proposals for rearmament in the previous March 1935. As a former Foreign Secretary, I felt a special responsibility for strengthening the fleet. The Abyssinian crisis had thrown a spotlight on its many deficiencies. The Naval Staff had then pointed out the extreme danger of tying up the Fleet in the Mediterranean at a time when the Japanese were threatening British interests in the Pacific, and of losing ships that we could not spare from our limited number. With the memory of my experience at the Foreign Office deeply engraved on my mind, I set about doing what I could to prevent the events of 1935 ever happening again. The result was a programme unprecedented in peace time of three battleships, two aircraft carriers, seven cruisers, sixteen destroyers, seven submarines, three escort vessels, four minesweepers, and about forty miscellaneous vessels. In addition to this programe of new construction, my Estimates included two other important proposals. Nearly £4 millions[1] were set aside for grants to firms for plant and equipment. The protracted period of disarmament had involved so much deterioration and scrapping of plant in the armour and gun factories that, without this aid, the armament firms could not have undertaken the programme.

Another of my proposals raised a different issue. It had been decided in the previous year, for economy reasons, to scrap five cruisers of the C class. I felt that not only did we need every ship that we could put or keep on the sea, but that the political effect of scrapping serviceable ships at a time when our policy

[1] £3,762,000.

was based on the urgent need for more ships, would be very damaging. The ships were due to be scrapped under the Naval Treaty of 1930 that restricted our cruiser tonnage to 339,000 in 1936. The Sea Lords were rightly anxious to carry out loyally and scrupulously our part of the Treaty, and held the view that as the tonnage must be brought down to 339,000, it was wisest to scrap ships that were becoming obsolete. I felt bound to put them another aspect of the question. It seemed to me illogical in face of their demand for seventy cruisers as a minimum of safety to reduce the number from fifty-two to forty-seven at the very moment when, mainly because of the international situation, we were starting to build a new and bigger fleet. It was to their credit that, much as they wanted the cruisers, their feeling for the sanctity of naval treaties made it difficult for me to convince them. Fortunately there was a clause in the Treaty that gave us the right to exceed the limits in the event of unforeseen dangers. This provision enabled me to raise the question with the American and Japanese Governments on the ground of the developments in Germany and Russia. Neither objected to our retaining the ships. The controversy that at one time became bitter, ended in general agreement, with Churchill throwing bouquets to me in the House of Commons, and the Sea Lords doubly satisfied in having kept both the Treaty and the ships. The cruisers subsequently became escort vessels, and fully justified their retention in the early years of the war.

Chamberlain, breaking with the traditions of the Treasury, supported me in all these proposals. Indeed, I do not suppose that any Chancellor of the Exchequer in peace time had ever been so helpful to a First Lord engaged upon a programme that involved a very heavy demand on the national finances.

My Estimates were well received apart from the conventional criticism of the front Opposition bench. The only real trouble that I had in the House of Commons during the whole of my time at the Admiralty was over the question of the dismissal of five men from the Royal Dockyards. There had for some time past been suspicion of sabotage in the dockyards, and in the course of the autumn five cases of serious damage to ships had been reported to me. The reports, both from secret sources and reliable fellow workers, pointed unmistakably to premeditated sabotage. My advisers pressed for the immediate dismissal of five men whom they were convinced were responsible for the criminal acts. As the men could neither be put on trial nor informed of the secret sources that led to the accusations, I referred the whole of the evidence to three senior Civil Servants whose opinion was likely, if anything, to be biased against the dismissal of government servants who had not been given the chance of replying to the accusations against them. The three Civil Servants reported unanimously in favour of dismissal. My colleagues in the Cabinet took the same view. I had, therefore, no other course open to me than to authorise the dismissals. The Opposition at once tabled a motion of censure aimed at the Government in general and the First Lord in particular. Arthur Greenwood moved it in a speech of resounding generalities about the elementary rights of accused persons. As I could not divulge the full details of my case without compromising the sources of my information, it was impossible to make a convincing reply. The motion was none the less defeated by 330 to 145. I was, however, conscious of the strong feeling in the House that, whilst the men had been rightly dismissed, it would have been more satisfactory if they could have been given the chance of answering the charges against them. In order, therefore, to remove as far as possible any suggestion of unfair victimisation, I arranged to meet a number of Trade Union leaders for the purpose of finding a way round the dilemma that was worrying all of us. I found the trade unionists as anxious as I was to prevent and punish sabotage, whilst from my side I was able to tell them that in all but very exceptional cases, the Admiralty would in future take into their confidence representatives of the Union of which the accused men were members. Ernest Bevin was particularly helpful at the meeting. His natural common sense at once grasped the issues of a question that concerned national security. The meeting put an end to the agitation, and resulted in a procedure that so far as I know has worked successfully to the present time.

As the spring approached, I began to make my plans for the Conference of Dominion Prime Ministers arranged for May, 1937. The question of defence was certain to take a foremost place in the discussions, and the new chapter of naval rearmament, illustrated by the Naval Estimates, was likely to be of particular interest to the delegates. I prepared the ground for my case in several speeches that I made in the provinces. One of them, at

Bradford on February 5, excited some criticism in Canada. I had emphasised the magnitude of the burden that the Mother Country was bearing for the defence of the Commonwealth, and the need for a common defence policy. Whilst I had been careful to say that we had no thought of imposing our views on the Commonwealth Governments, I had insisted that we could not blind ourselves in modern conditions to the inadequacy of local defence. My cautious remarks were caught up into the controversies of Canadian internal politics, and made to look like a threat to Canadian independence. By May, however, when these troubled waters had subsided, the representatives of the Dominions, including Canada, were very ready to listen to my more detailed argument. As my speech followed a general survey of defence by Inskip, I kept it as concrete as I could. My theme was the need of a two-ocean fleet. Without a fleet in the Far East, the local defence of Australia, New Zealand and Canada would be useless against Japanese aggression, and without the help of the French Fleet in the Channel and the Mediterranean, we could not with our existing strength find the necessary ships. Our policy was to build new and modernise old ships in sufficient numbers for both the West and the Far East. The result, which could only be obtained at immense cost, was placing on the taxpayer of the United Kingdom an almost intolerable burden. Could a small island continue to bear the financial strain involved in maintaining at so great a strength the necessary standard of naval power? The safety of the whole British Commonwealth might well depend on increased naval support from the Dominions. Whilst we were grateful for the increasing help that we were receiving from them, we asked their representatives carefully to consider the situation that I had described. The Prime Ministers, so far from resenting what I said, seemed impressed by my argument, and the subsequent meetings of the Conference marked the beginning of the campaign for a navy capable of operating both in the East and the West. I still have a sheaf of notes that were pushed across the table to me at the end of my speech; a half-sheet, for instance, from Baldwin approving what I said, another from Chamberlain showing the Chancellor of the Exchequer's keen interest in rearmament. " V. good. The most interesting and impressive review of defence that we have had. It should be v. useful."

If the final objective of the two fleets was not achieved, the reason was not failure on our side, but the loss of the French Fleet in 1940. When the defence of the Mediterranean sea-way fell entirely upon us, it was no longer possible to maintain an adequate fleet in the Pacific.

So much for the high politics of the navy. There were, however, other activities to which I must refer in any account of my year at the Admiralty.

CHAPTER XVI

Ark Royal and Enchantress

FIRST, THERE were many pleasant social gatherings in Admiralty House and in *Enchantress*, the Admiralty yacht. A great house and a superb yacht provided unique opportunities for official entertainment. Admiralty House, newly decorated, became the scene of many official parties. One dinner I remember in particular, when Queen Mary emerged for the first time from her mourning for King George V and dined with us to meet the Dominion Prime Ministers. The historic silver plate was brought up for the occasion under very careful escort from Greenwich. Particular care was taken with a set of Stuart salt-cellars. No one was allowed to touch them except the petty officer whose special duty it was to bring them, arrange them, take them off the table and return them to Greenwich. Queen Mary, with her memory that never failed her, remembered their history and recognised the principal pieces as old friends.

Enchantress enabled us to extend our official hospitality outside London. The yacht had been laid up since the First World War, and the question at once arose when I went to the Admiralty, whether it was worth making use of her again. I argued that she was more than ever needed to show the flag at a time when we were starting to build a new fleet. Chamberlain agreed with me, and accordingly she was once again put into commission. When she was ready, we used her in foreign waters for the inspection of the naval bases in the Mediterranean and in home waters for great occasions such as the launching of *Ark Royal* and the Coronation Naval Review. She was admirably suited for ceremonial visits, with a saloon capable of holding twenty or thirty guests, and a service of silver plate that would have done credit to a palace. The silver had come from various sources, the *Herald*, built as a sixth-rate sloop in 1820 and used for "transporting Ambassadors and Governors," the royal sailing yachts *Royal Sovereign* and *William and Mary*, the paddle steamer *Firebrand*, and the first *Enchantress*, launched in 1862. Its effect at a dinner in honour of some great personage was dazzling. When, for instance, we took the yacht to Birkenhead for the launching of *Ark Royal*, we were able to make the dinner that we gave to the Lord Lieutenant of Lancashire, the Lord Mayor of Liverpool and the neighbouring Mayors, an occasion that would long be remembered in the north of England. The launching itself created the greatest excitement. As the first launching of a big ship since the end of the First World War, and the first ship ever specially built as an aircraft-carrier, it not only marked a milestone in the history of the fleet, but it brought new hope to the shipyards of Birkenhead that had lain almost idle for many years. My wife was honoured and delighted when the King said that he wished her to launch the historic ship. While she performed the traditional ceremony, a roar of cheers went up from the crowd of twenty thousand who had come to celebrate the great event. The launching she regarded as one of the most thrilling incidents in her life. The great ship became a member of the family. Before being commissioned, she visited her at Portsmouth and wished her well with a gift of silver plate. Her achievements seemed to be family triumphs. When we both arrived in Spain, and *Ark Royal* came to Gibraltar in June, 1940, we were close to each other, and all the better able to follow the changes and chances of her career. More than once we visited her, and heard at first hand the story of her charmed life. Convinced of her immortality, we scoffed alike at Lord Haw Haw and Mussolini when they claimed to have sunk her. When, after many brilliant actions and hair's breadth escapes, her end came in November, 1941, we felt that we had suffered not only a national calamity, but also a very poignant personal loss.

The inspection of the Mediterranean bases created in its own way the same kind of interest that the launching had excited at Birkenhead. Our visits were the outward and visible sign of a new chapter of reviving naval prestige. More than once I pointed the moral to inquiring Press correspondents at the ports where we stopped. It was very necessary to disabuse Mussolini of any idea that we were leaving the Mediterranean.

Amongst the many lessons that I learnt from the tour was one, of the extreme importance of Malta as a strategic centre, and another, of the possibilities of Cyprus as a military and civil base. Visits by Ministers to overseas centres were then much rarer than they are to-day. Our tour, therefore, made all the greater impression on places and people when there had been no official visits for many years.

CHAPTER XVII

The King's Abdication

I FIND it difficult to leave these pleasant memories of delightful visits and enthralling scenes. I must, however, pass on to events of a very different kind in which I was deeply involved. As First Lord, I was brought into frequent contact with King Edward VIII. He had known me for many years, and at the time of the Abyssinian crisis had shown his sympathy with my efforts for a settlement. We had often met in London, and he had dined with us in Chelsea, and we with him at York House. As a mark of his friendship, he had appointed me an Elder Brother of Trinity House when I became First Lord, an honour that I have valued as greatly as any that I have ever received. My work gave me many opportunities of seeing him. Naval affairs seemed to interest him more than any other public questions. The navy had been his first love, and it still retained an unshakable hold upon him. He was keenly interested in the new programme of construction. Even the smaller details of naval administration he liked to discuss with me, and his knowledge of the fleet's personnel was altogether exceptional.

Knowing that I often saw him, Baldwin, in the hope that I might have some influence with him, took me into his confidence over the question of the Royal marriage. The trouble had been brewing since King George V's death. Two of the new King's intimate advisers had told Baldwin after the funeral that the King had made up his mind to marry Mrs. Simpson. Partly because he hesitated to put pressure upon a young King within a few days of his father's death, partly because he felt that his intervention might be resented by the public when so little was generally known of the attachment, partly because his natural

instinct was to wait until the last possible moment before committing himself, Baldwin refrained from raising the question at
the time. For the next six months, therefore, the ground was left
open to rumour that, beginning in London society, spread quickly
to the provinces, the Dominions and the United States.

Until the Prince of Wales succeeded to the throne, I only knew
by hearsay of his friendship with Mrs. Simpson. Her name had
appeared in the Court Circular when she was presented at
Buckingham Palace, and she and her husband had been welcomed
in London society. My first meeting with her was in the spring
of 1936. Not living in her gay world, I wondered how we should
get on when we talked to each other. She may well have thought
me very dull—if so, she did not show it, and could not have been
more agreeable. I well remember not only her sparkling talk, but
also her sparkling jewels in very up-to-date Cartier settings. In
the notes that I made at the time I described her as very attractive
and intelligent, very American and with little or no knowledge
of English life. This was the lady who was to cause us so much
anxiety in the autumn of 1936. Until the end of the summer,
whilst every gossip had something to say about the friendship,
there was nothing in the nature of a political crisis. Parliament
adjourned as usual before August Bank Holiday, and Baldwin,
as regular in his habits as King George V, went off to Aix for his
annual cure. The holidays, so far from quieting the rumours, gave
them new life. The King had chartered a private yacht, the
Nahlin, for a voyage in the Mediterranean, and Mrs. Simpson was
known to be one of the guests on board. I also had planned a
Mediterranean tour in the Admiralty yacht, with the object of
personally inspecting the naval bases at Gibraltar and Malta. At
one point, the yachts passed each other. The curiosity displayed
by my most discreet ship's company showed me how widely the
interest in the King's affairs had spread in recent weeks. Public
disquiet was further increased after the King's return when the
Court Circular announced that Mrs. Simpson was staying at
Balmoral. In the meanwhile, letters of protest were pouring into
No. 10 Downing Street, so many, in fact, that the miraculous
happened, and Baldwin decided to cut short his stay at Aix. This
was the situation when, towards the end of the summer recess, the
weekly Cabinets started again.

Baldwin, who had told me in general terms of his anxiety, did not raise the question at the early meetings, nor did he discuss it in detail with any of his colleagues. He still hoped that somehow or other the crisis would blow over, and that, to use his own words, " the young man would see sense." It was only in the first weeks of October that he realised that there was no chance of its subsiding, particularly when, on October 12, Mrs. Simpson's husband announced to the American Press his intention of starting proceedings for divorce. In the meanwhile Mrs. Simpson had herself started proceedings against her husband, and the case was to be heard at Ipswich at the end of the month. The danger, therefore, stared Baldwin in the face. If Mrs. Simpson won her case, she would be free to marry the King. If the King married Mrs. Simpson, she would be Queen, and both would be crowned by the Archbishop of Canterbury in Westminster Abbey in a solemn service of Holy Communion and with the rites of a Church that disapproved of the marriage of divorced persons. These were the facts that forced Baldwin to move. No question of Mrs. Simpson's American nationality or of her non-royal birth ever entered his mind. English sovereigns had always been free to marry commoners, and had frequently married foreigners. It was solely the fact of the two divorces that convinced him that the peoples of Great Britain and the Dominions would never accept her as Queen.

This was the situation when I was invited by the King to stay at Sandringham from October 19 to October 23 for partridge shooting. I naturally felt both pleased and honoured by an invitation to the King's first, and as it proved, only shooting party in Norfolk.

There was, however, a serious difficulty in the way of my accepting it. The weekly Cabinets had only just re-started, and social engagements were rarely, if ever, allowed to interfere with Ministers' attendance at them. I thought, however, that before asking to be excused, I had better consult Baldwin. When I saw him, instead of approving of my intention to refuse, he said at once: " You must certainly accept the invitation. Your visit may be very helpful. Do what you can to convince the King that the divorce proceedings that are due at Ipswich at the end of the month must be dropped, and try to persuade him to give up the idea of marriage altogether."

He then confided to me in detail his own anxieties. Until then I had not fully realised the imminence of the crisis. Nor had I grasped the fact that the turning point was the divorce case at Ipswich. While describing his fears, he gave me the impression that the King might still be deflected from the course upon which he was set. In any case, he wished me to go to Sandringham and try my hand at a forlorn hope. Accordingly I accepted, but with the uneasy feeling that the lady's divorce case and the King's marriage were very unsuitable subjects for conversation at a friendly shooting party. None the less, my stay was very enjoyable. The King, as usual, was an excellent host, and though it was not a good season for game, there were more partridges at Sandringham than anywhere else. What, however, I did not understand at the time was the King's sudden return to London by car on the first night of my visit. It was only afterwards that I learnt that it was for his first interview with Baldwin at Fort Belvedere on the subject of the marriage. What with long days shooting and pleasant company, it was difficult for me even to hint at grave affairs of State. I heard enough, however, during my visit to convince me that the King had finally made up his mind. The news, therefore, that I brought back to London only added to Baldwin's worries.

Within a fortnight I once again stayed with the King, this time in the royal yacht, *Victoria and Albert*, as First Lord and Minister in Attendance during the royal inspection of the Home Fleet. Whilst I had little chance of discussing the marriage with the King in the continuous rush of naval visits and ceremonies, I had a unique opportunity of seeing the most attractive side of his personality. If on the one hand he was, as many thought, wayward and irresponsible, on the other hand, no one could deny his surpassing talent for inspiring enthusiasm and managing great crowds. He seemed to know personally every officer and seaman in the fleet. On one of the evenings there was a smoking concert in the aircraft carrier *Courageous*. No officers except Chatfield, the First Sea Lord, Roger Backhouse, the Commander-in-Chief of the Home Fleet, and Louis Mountbatten were present. The vast underdeck was packed with thousands of seamen. In my long experience of mass meetings I never saw one so completely dominated by a single personality. At one point he turned to me and said: " I am going to see what is happening at the other end." Elbowing his way through the crowd, he walked to the end of the hall and started community singing to the accompaniment of a seaman's mouth-organ. When he came back to the platform, he made an impromptu speech that brought the house down. Then, a seaman in the crowd proposed three cheers for him, and there followed an unforgettable scene of the wildest and most spontaneous enthusiasm. Here, indeed, was the Prince Charming, who could win the hearts of all sorts and conditions of men and women and send a thrill through great crowds.

The whole visit had been one long series of personal triumphs for the King. When I travelled back with him, I was amazed at his liveliness after two days of continuous inspections in the worst possible weather. As we sat together in the very shaky and noisy royal saloon on the return journey to London, his bright and vivacious conversation never flagged. Outwardly, he showed no sign of weariness; inwardly, as he has since disclosed in *A King's Story*, he was, in fact, both tired and worried.

The political storm broke when he arrived at Buckingham Palace and found waiting for him a letter from Alec Hardinge, his Private Secretary, warning him in very formal language of " the serious situation which is developing," of an impending outburst in the Press, and the urgent need for Mrs. Simpson to leave the country. The letter came as a great shock both to the King and Mrs. Simpson. It also caused a permanent breach between the King and Hardinge, his principal personal adviser, with the result that Walter Monckton, an old Oxford friend, became his intermediary with Baldwin.

This was the background when the King sent for Baldwin on November 16. The atmosphere, as the Duke of Windsor has told us, though outwardly friendly, with Baldwin smoking his inseparable pipe, was very strained. As Baldwin described it to me, the King had been more definite than ever before in stating that he would abdicate rather than give up the marriage. At the end of the interview, the King, who was sensitive to the obligations of his constitutional position, asked Baldwin to let him seek the advice of two members of the Cabinet, Duff Cooper and myself. Baldwin agreed, and accordingly I spent a morning with the King in the small room on the ground floor at Buckingham Palace that he always preferred to his father's room on the first floor.

I own that I was more nervous of the meeting than I had been even of my first encounter with Gandhi. It was very easy once again to give a wrong impression that might do serious harm.

On the one hand, I greatly admired many of the King's qualities. He had been very kind to me, and the thought of a tragic end to his brilliant career made me very sad. On the other hand, I was convinced that the world of Great Britain and the Dominions would never accept Mrs. Simpson as Queen. My personal feeling for him, therefore, must not give him the impression that I sympathised with his determination to marry, or that I thought that public opinion was narrow-minded and antiquated in condemning it. According to his own account of the interview, I succeeded in making my position clear.

I quote his description of the interview in his own words:

" Sam Hoare I saw first. The First Lord of the Admiralty's temperament was not such as to encourage the belief that I might convert him into a champion of my cause. The most that I hoped from our meeting was that, after hearing my story, he would understand the compulsions working upon me, and might be moved, when the matter came up for formal discussion in the Cabinet, as soon it must, to speak up in my defence to marry. But I failed to win him as an advocate. He was sympathetic, but he also was acutely conscious of the political realities. Mr. Baldwin, he warned me, was in command of the situation; the senior Ministers were solidly with him on this issue. If I were to press my marriage project upon the Cabinet, I should meet a stone wall of opposition.

" I saw Mr. Duff Cooper at the Palace later the same day. Because of our closer association the facts that I had to tell him came as no surprise to him. He was as optimistic and encouraging as Sam Hoare had been pessimistic and discouraging. His advice was that I should be patient, that I should ignore the furore, go ahead with the Coronation, and in due time, after the people had become accustomed to me as King, raise the question of my right to marry whom I pleased. This was the counsel of a sophisticated man of the world." [1]

His desire to obtain the independent advice of two Ministers had ended in a clash of conflicting advice. He seems to have disagreed with both of us. He ignored my warning, and he equally rejected Duff Cooper's plea for delay.

The final act of the drama proceeded with lightning speed to its inevitable end. The last-minute proposal of a morganatic marriage was made, only to be turned down by the Dominion

[1] *A King's Story*, pp. 339-340, by the Duke of Windsor. Cassell & Co.

Governments. Nor was the Cabinet able to accede to his wish to broadcast his case to the world. As soon as it was pointed out to him that a constitutional King could only take such public action on the advice of his Ministers, he withdrew his request. When there remained no possibility of avoiding the abdication, a proposal to pass a Bill that would avoid the delays and uncertainties inherent in the divorce proceedings was also rejected as certain to be unacceptable to Parliament. The attempt to raise a King's Party ignominiously failed. Mrs. Simpson went off to the South of France, and I well remember a visit that I had in the House of Commons from two of the King's entourage in connection with the arrangements for her journey. In the meanwhile, Baldwin had his final interviews with the King in the confused and restless atmosphere of Fort Belvedere in Windsor Great Park.

Throughout these anxious days the King remained resolute, and, indeed, seemingly indifferent to the consequences of abdication. When he signed the fifteen documents that were needed for ending his reign, he showed not the least emotion. His farewell broadcast, excellently worded and well delivered, after the abdication had taken effect, seemed to me to betray no deep regret. All the evidence showed that he had made up his mind, and that having made it up, he was at peace with himself, and anxious to begin the new chapter of his life as quickly as possible.

The scene in Parliament I need not describe at any length. The King's message of Abdication and Baldwin's speech in the House of Commons can be read in Hansard and the Press. The speech was probably the most impressive and persuasive that Baldwin ever made. Having had little time to prepare it, he kept to a clear narrative of what had actually happened. In the clear and intimate English that always made his broadcasts so effective, he gave the account of his interviews with the King and his fruitless efforts to save the situation. The House listened spellbound, and in silence, as the moment demanded.

One curious incident is worth recording. On the day's Order Paper, two Bills were set down for first reading: the first, ' The Edinburgh Maternity and Simpson Charity Bill '; the second, ' The Family Inheritance Bill, Mr. Windsor.' A freak of chance had mingled comedy with tragedy. Were members to laugh at this strange coincidence or to cry? Laughter and tears are often so near to each other that the one quickly overflows into the other. If, on December 10, it was laughter that preponderated, it was not due to any lack of human feeling for the departing King. It was the almost inevitable breaking of the emotional strain that weeks of anxious waiting had made no longer bearable.

The Deed of Abdication did not end my obligations as First Lord to the Duke of Windsor. He wished to leave England in a destroyer on the night of his abdication. The First Sea Lord and I, who had to make the arrangements, pressed him in vain to let us provide a more fitting departure, but he was determined to go alone, and would not accept our offer to accompany him. He was determined also to go in the middle of the night, and to be out of the country before the new King was proclaimed on the following day.

When I read again the report that Admiral Fisher, the Commander-in-Chief, Portsmouth, made to me on the morning after his departure, I still feel a lump in my throat:

" Shortly after midnight four cars containing staff and luggage arrived at the Unicorn Gate and were piloted to Fury. There was no sign of His Late Majesty at 0130, but shortly after, the police at the Main Gate reported that a large car had passed through. I proceeded in my car to intercept His Late Majesty, and was fortunate in doing so when his driver had just realised that he did not know which way to turn. His Late Majesty explained that he knew that he should have come in by the Unicorn Gate, but had misdirected his chauffeur. I was able to tell him that I had listened to his broadcast, and felt that he would like to know what a great impression it must have made upon all who heard it. I think this pleased His Late Majesty.

" On board Fury to receive him were the commander of the ship, Admiral Sir Roger Backhouse, and Vice Admiral Sir Dudley North. His Late Majesty went below to his cabin immediately, asking the flag officers to come down. We all replied that he must be terribly tired, and suggested that he might sooner we said good-bye without a delay, but he preferred that we should come down, if only for a minute, and this we did, and bade him farewell. . . .

" Fury sailed shortly before 0200 in clear, calm weather, and proceeded to St. Helen's Roads, where she anchored for the night in company with Wolfhound. Both ships sailed at 0630 to-day for Boulogne.

" The secrecy of the departure seems to have been well kept.

. . . His Late Majesty looked, as might be expected, as if he had passed through a very trying experience, but his manner betrayed no weariness, his voice had animation, and my general feeling was one of relief that he was so normal.

" The reason for his late arrival at Portsmouth was, I was informed, that it was decided at the last moment, that instead of seeing Queen Mary before his broadcast, he went to say good-bye to her after it. It had apparently been felt that the trying nature of his visit to his mother might affect the broadcast."

And so, late at night, ended the reign of Prince Charming, whose fatal weakness, more serious than his personal affections, was that he did not like being King. The ritual and tradition of a historic office made no appeal to him. He had never changed his mind since as a boy he wrote in his diary:

" What rot and waste of time, money and energy all these State visits are! This is my only remark on all this unreal show and ceremony."

How often I had noticed his irritation with the established habits of a court. " You are out of date," he once said to me, " you know nothing of the modern world." If I thought too much of the past, he seemed to me to think too little of it. Even without the affair of the marriage, whilst I hoped against hope that the interests of a King's life would gradually reconcile him to kingship, I doubted whether he would ever like the part sufficiently to make a success of it. As it was, I gave him no cause for misunderstanding, and if I failed, like many others, to dissuade him from his fixed intention, I can certainly say that it was not for want of trying.

The abdication was more than the end of a short reign; it was the beginning of a long and new chapter. Although the world seemed to have settled back into its normal place, the shock of the crisis had left its unmistakable mark. In the political world, Baldwin, although he had emerged from it with a great personal triumph, was obviously shaken, and only waiting for the Coronation of the new King to resign the Premiership. Chamberlain, his acknowledged successor, with his quick mind, resolute character and passion for efficiency, was certain to transform the atmosphere of Whitehall and Westminster as soon as he became Prime Minister. In my own case, the formation of a new Government was likely also to have a considerable influence on my political life.

When the change came in the following June, I had only been a year at the Admiralty, and it was generally thought that I would not be moved. I was myself in two minds over what was best in the circumstances. Simon was leaving the Home Office for the Exchequer, and having had twelve years in Service and Overseas Departments, I was anxious to have the experience of a great domestic office. The Home Office particularly interested me from its connection with penal questions. Penal Reform had been a tradition in my family since the days of Samuel Hoare, my great-great-grandfather, and my great-grandmother's sister, Elizabeth Fry, who together had formed the first committees for supporting it. The thought of carrying on this tradition made a very strong appeal to me. As to the Admiralty, I hated the idea of leaving it. I had, however, in twelve months accomplished the task that I had set myself. The controversy over the Fleet Air Arm was settled. The building of a new fleet strong enough to operate in both the East and West was already settled. The Board of Admiralty was so firmly established under the First Sea Lord that it could be fully trusted to make the most of the approved programme. In the full assurance, therefore, that my departure would not injure the navy, but not without much personal regret, I exchanged *Enchantress* for a police car, and accepted the post of Home Secretary left vacant by Simon. It was after dining in *Victoria and Albert* at the Coronation Review that the new King discussed the change with me. Both he and the Queen were kind enough to say that they were glad to have an old friend as the Minister who was most closely in touch with the Court.

CHAPTER XVIII

Criminal Justice

Y LOVE of history and reverence for tradition were once
again stimulated when, as Home Secretary, I became the
senior of the seven Secretaries of State. I came at the end
of a long line that had started under the rule of the Normans.
Not being men of letters, the early kings had needed a confidant
to carry out their purposes. At first, they had found their man of
trust in the Chancellor, but as he tended to live in London, they
had kept with them a clerk known as the Secretary, the keeper
of the King's secrets. The clerk, who was always at hand, steadily
increased his influence until, under the Tudors, a Thomas
Cromwell or a Robert Cecil, now called Secretary of State,
became in practice the Prime Minister of the country. When the
work was too great for one man, it was divided between two and
sometimes three secretaries, and eventually, in 1782, was formally
delimited between a Secretary of State who was responsible for
Home Affairs, and a Secretary of State who was responsible for
Foreign Affairs. Shelburne, the first Home Secretary, being a
peer, took precedence of Fox, the first Foreign Secretary, and ever
since, the Home Secretary has always retained his precedence in
the Government hierarchy. The family of twins has now grown to
a family of seven, but the office is still in theory one and indivisible.
Each Secretary of State is competent to carry out the duties of
every other Secretary of State. I myself, for example, twice acted
for the Home Secretary when he was abroad and I was Secretary
of State for Air, the most junior of the Secretaries of State.

These details provided me with a series of coloured illustra-
tions for the great volume of British history. They showed me in
miniature the gradual change from personal to parliamentary

government, the steady increase, usually expedited by war, in the Government's responsibilities, and the growing need to re-allocate departmental duties in a modern state.

The first batch of papers that I found in my tray was typical of these developments—a veritable treasury of historic relics and modern needs—warrants for my signature authorising the Lord Chancellor to issue patents under the Great Seal, approval of the pay of the bedesmen of Ely Cathedral, the appointment of a Recorder, a circular for magistrates, a question of prison dis-cipline, the rules of an industrial school, the report of a factory inspector, the draft of a royal speech, the homage of a Bishop, the privileges of a County Borough. When I looked at a collection that would have done credit to Sir Thomas Browne's cabinet of curiosities, I could well understand why the Home Secretary had been described as the residuary legatee of the Government. Nor were my first files in any way exceptional. Day after day the same kind of miscellany would arrive—great documents on superb paper, swelling with monumental English, humbler sheets from the Stationery Office filled with the jargon of Whitehall, the old and the new, the picturesque and the prosaic, and when from time to time there was included the red file of a capital case, the solemn and the grim. There was certainly no monotony about an office of this kind.

The Secretary of State's room filled me with gloom. Why am I so susceptible to my *cabinet de travail*? Some of my friends can work equally well anywhere in any conditions. I looked with admiration at the officers in the two wars who could produce superb reports in noisy barrack rooms. I could not follow their example. Like Buffon, who could only write his books in a classical summer-house amidst flowers and avenues, and Glück, who could only compose music in the open air with a bottle of champagne at his side, I needed congenial surroundings for any good work. Such sensibility has often been a nuisance not only to myself, but also to my wife, my friends and secretaries. Good or bad habit, I have never been able to rid myself of it; and the room in the Home Office had all the sombre heaviness left by Palmerston's attempt to graft Italian Renaissance on Victorian convention. It was essentially the bureau of the Minister who, on the Continent, is euphemistically called the Minister of the Interior, but who in actual practice is the Minister of the Police. The Home Office, although there have been disturbed periods when the maintenance of internal order has become almost the sole pre-occupation of the Secretary of State, was much more than a department of coercion. Even though several of its social services had in recent years been transferred to new offices, it had already been expanded into one of the great departments of the future Welfare State. The Secretary of State's room took no account of the change. In particular, the most prominent feature in it was a vast Victorian writing-table upon which was placed a card with the line from Juvenal: *Nulla unquam de morte hominis cunctatio longa est*—" No delay is ever long when it is a question of death."—and a calendar in which certain days were marked with red. The quotation was a sententious reminder of the three weeks of life that a murderer was allowed before his execution. The second was a notification of the date for which the execution had been fixed. These mementoes of the scaffold repelled me. I was well aware of my responsibility for the exercise of the prerogative of life and death, and I did not need to be reminded of it. I knew also that my excellent advisers would keep me informed of the proper processes of the law without my having to follow them hour by hour. The Latin quotation seemed to me altogether objectionable. Hangings are grim enough in themselves, and any Home Secretary is bound to think about them. They do not, however, need moralising quotations to underline their blackness and to keep them morbidly in his mind. I remembered Madame de Staël's protest against her friends who applied their wit to the grim events of the French Revolution. The guillotine was bad enough, " *Mais montrer l'esprit faire des phrases, quelle persistence de la vanité dans une telle scène!* " At all events, I could not bring myself to sit at a writing-table with these dismal souvenirs, and I had them at once removed. So far as I was concerned, I thought the more and not the less of my duties when they had gone, and started upon two years of hard labour in which I set myself to humanize and rationalize rather than to sentimentalize our penal methods. Philip Sassoon, ready as always to give his advice, agreed with my view of the room, and together we gave it a new look that obliterated the hindrances to my daily work.

Before I had time to leave Admiralty House, I already found myself plunged in the deep waters of the Home Office pool. The

Prison vote was on the Order Paper of the House of Commons for the Friday after I became Home Secretary, and the report stage of a new Factory Act of three hundred clauses, for which I was now responsible, was already under consideration by a Standing Committee that was meeting twice a week.

With the Prison vote, I had an unexpected gift of good luck. My advisers had ready an excellent story for me to tell, and the time had just arrived for it to be told. The penal reformers in the Howard League and the Prison Commissioners in the Home Office had for some time past been insisting on the need of a fundamental change in prison methods. The old idea was to think only of prison treatment as a deterrent and to make it as severe and terrifying as possible. The gulf between prison and ordinary life was deep and almost unbridgeable. As soon as the gates closed on an offender, the full rigours of prison discipline were inflicted upon him, and only slowly and precariously could he gain the small privileges that brought him nearer to normal life. The reformers claimed that the treatment was based on a misconception of human nature. If a man starts at the bottom and knows that only after a long and uncertain period of trial he will be able to better his condition, he will have only the slightest possible incentive for improving his behaviour, and feel that he has nothing to lose and little to gain. The better course, the reformers urged, was to let him start in possession of certain privileges, with the knowledge that he would lose them if he behaved badly. They illustrated their argument by the effect that the chance of earning wages would have on a prisoner's conduct. If a prisoner could earn, even though it was only a few cigarettes a week, he would have something to lose, and would not wish to lose it, and besides the good effect on his self-respect, would be less likely to become unmanageable and desperate. The experiment was tried on a very limited scale, but with such undeniably good results on individual prisoners and prison discipline, that the time had come to extend it. The speech, therefore, that the officials wished me to make, took the form of a description of the excellent results that had already been obtained, and an announcement that the system was to be considerably extended.

I could not have had a brief better suited to stir my hereditary interest in prison questions. It may be that I spoke all the better for being fresh to the post and free from over-preparation. In any case, I made what I believe to have been my most successful speech in the House of Commons. Although it was a Friday afternoon and a small House, I was able to feel from the debate the strength of the public interest in penal questions. Then and there, I was given unmistakable encouragement to proceed with a plan that I had hitherto only sketched in my imagination for gathering together into a single Act the lessons of a generation of experience and experiment that were ready to hand, and were only waiting to be used for bringing up to date our methods of penal treatment.

My first flush of enthusiasm gained warmth and colour from my surroundings. My advisers, seeing my interest in penal questions, entered heart and soul into the project of a comprehensive Criminal Justice Bill that was long overdue.

Alexander Maxwell in particular helped me with wise and stimulating advice. How lucky I was to have him! His predecessor, Russell Scott, a former Treasury official, was on the point of retiring as Permanent Secretary, and within a few hours of my entering my new office, I had to recommend a successor to the Prime Minister. Knowing the strength of the *esprit de corps* of a great department, I felt sure that it would be most unwise to select someone from outside the Home Office. Fortunately, in the Deputy Secretary, Maxwell, there were to be found the various qualities that the post required. Unruffled amidst all the alarms and excursions that periodically shake a Ministry of public order, he possessed the imperturbable assurance essential to a department of historic traditions. He had also a sensitive sympathy with many new ideas that made itself felt in his attitude towards crime and punishment. As a former Chairman of the Prison Commission, he had carried on the good work of Ruggles Brise, and had seen the need for many further changes in our system of criminal justice. This personal contact with men and women of all sorts turned his minutes into human documents, and his advice into practical proposals. The Prime Minister, by agreeing to his appointment, opened the way for him to become one of the leading figures in Whitehall.

Other members of the staff transmitted to me much of their crusading fervour. For instance, Alexander Paterson, nervous, assertive, transparently sincere, essentially the new man with the new ideas of prison treatment; and Lilian Barker, short haired and short skirted, usually in a tweed suit that, when she was sitting beside me, made her look like a prosperous farmer, but none the less, an alert woman of the new world whose opinion on lipstick and cigarettes in women's prisons was as up to date as it was sensible. For instance also, several of the Prison Governors whom I visited in their prisons. Visits to prisons, particularly visits by a Secretary of State, were at that time uncommon. I did my best to start a new precedent. I had unearthed in the archives of the Home Office a correspondence between Addington, most complacent of Home Secretaries, and my great-great-aunt, most persistent of penal reformers. Elizabeth Fry was determined that the Home Secretary should see for himself the horrors of Newgate. Addington was equally determined not to see them, and politely but very definitely refused the invitation. To have visited Newgate or any prison would have shocked his sensitive susceptibilities and might have shaken his rooted convictions as to the advantages of severe punishment. Elizabeth Fry, whose faith removed many mountains, had on this occasion to admit defeat at the hands of an agreeable but elusive Home Secretary. I now had the chance of atoning for my predecessor's sin of omission. I needed no pressing, and at once arranged a programme of personal visits to prisons all over the country.

One of my first journeys was to Dartmoor. I went there from Norfolk on a very stormy day in a small fighter aeroplane. The pilot was frequently driven off his course by the bad weather. When I eventually arrived, after one of the most bumpy flights that I have ever had, I told the excellent Governor, Captain Pannell, the hero who quelled the Dartmoor mutiny, that what I chiefly wanted was a long talk with him and a good look at the prisoners' records, rather than any formal inspection of the prison. The talk let me into the secrets of managing a great prison, and the records showed me how the worst offenders had often begun their careers of crime with some silly childish offence that had led to an equally stupid sentence of short imprisonment, and had ended with Dartmoor and penal servitude. One of the pages of the book set out the eighteen sentences of a man of fifty-four for offences involving thirty-four years of prison and penal servitude, that rose in a steep crescendo from a boy's mischief to attempted murder. Here, indeed, in the records kept in the porter's lodge was the human evidence against short sentences of imprisonment, particularly for the young. Here was the case for probation, approved schools and long periods of corrective training. Here, also, was the proof that repeated sentences of penal servitude were no deterrent to the comparatively small number of desperate criminals, and that only by longer terms of preventive detention could the community be protected from their ravages. The visit to Dartmoor was one of many that I made to penal institutions of all kinds; in every case it was the talks with the men and women on the spot that influenced my line of thought.

These personal contacts I supplemented with a careful study of the reports of the many committees that had investigated practically every aspect of crime. I have always been a quick reader, sometimes, in fact, too quick, for I have often exceeded any reasonable speed limit in rushing through books and reports. In reading the penal textbooks, however, I did not need to put on the brake. I was working against time if the Criminal Justice Bill, as I contemplated it, was to be passed during my time at the Home Office. Beginning, therefore, with the most remarkable Reports of Sir James Mackintosh's Committee on the State of the Criminal Law in 1819, continuing with the equally remarkable Report of the Duke of Richmond's Royal Commission on Capital Punishment in 1864, and ending with the more recent inquiries into probation, approved schools, Borstal treatment, preventive detention, corporal punishment and mental responsibility, I did my best to absorb the countless recommendations that had emerged from scores of official inquiries. As at the India Office, so now in the Home Office, I was a gatherer rather than a sower. The harvest was ready, drilled and cultivated by skilled men and women, and needing only to be cut and winnowed in a combine machine.

I very soon had to make an important decision upon the best way of dealing with it. There were two ways of carrying out the recommendations of the experts and their committees. The first was to proceed with several small bills, each dealing with a limited aspect of penal reform; the second, to collect all the proposals into a comprehensive Criminal Justice Bill. It was urged in favour of the first that as the small bills could be handed over to private members, there would be little or no demand on the Government's timetable. The objection against it was the loss of an impressive picture that would strike the imagination of the general public. I chose the second method, and began to work at the preparation of a Bill that would cover the whole field of criminal justice.

By November I was able to circulate to the Cabinet a memorandum containing an outline of my proposals. The Cabinet approved the general lines, and gave me authority to draft a Bill. The following six months were fully occupied with the drafting of the complicated clauses, and with what was perhaps even more important, the checking of the plan by many practical penal workers. I can imagine that few Ministers have ever had more interviews about a single measure than I had in connection with the Criminal Justice Bill. The notes that I have kept of these talks are amongst the most vivid and interesting of my papers. When I read them again after several years, I see once more the great company of devoted men and women with a vocation, social workers with their feet firmly on the ground, and students teaching the lessons of history, whom I met and consulted.

When I needed further inspiration, I found it in the lives of the great penal reformers that for human interest were second only to the lives of the Admirals that I had read when I was First Lord, the life for instance of John Howard, making the Grand Tour of Europe not to collect pictures and statues, but details about the misgovernment of prisons, of Elizabeth Fry, the first woman to enter British public life, of Jeremy Bentham, doctrinaire like many Liberals, and like Beccaria in Italy, helping to create a philosophy of penal treatment, and most of all, Robert Peel, greatest of Home Secretaries, whose career in the Home Office established once and for all the wisdom of attacking crime on the widest possible front and with a combined operation of the Statute law, efficient administration and a well-organised police. History, experience, experiment, each had its essential place in the background of the Bill. Theory only entered into it so long as it was supported by practice; sentiment, only so far as human sympathy was needed for dealing with human troubles.

Aided by Maxwell and his excellent staff, I had the Bill ready for the new session, and was able to obtain a Second Reading for it on November 29, 1938, eighteen months after my going to the Home Office. The speed, however, with which the first stage had been passed did not blind me to the length and difficulty of the road to be traversed before it could reach the Statute Book.

The Bill, with its 83 clauses and 10 schedules, covered a very wide field. Even the non-controversial parts involved long discussions. There was, for instance, the question of alternative punishments, if the imprisonment of the young and corporal punishment were abolished. Everyone liked the idea of alternative punishments in theory, but any that were actually proposed were immediately attacked from one quarter or another. The proposal, for instance, of compulsory centres for naughty children who would lose a few half-holidays by their attendance at first excited ridicule. The Detention Centres, intended to give an unpleasant lesson to older and more serious offenders, were criticised as little prisons for the young. Until the final passage of the Bill ten years later, these criticisms persisted. None the less, the Bill as it was originally drafted, remained substantially intact, and subsequent experience has so far justified the experiments that we introduced in it.

Another part of the Bill that was certain to lead to long debates concerned the treatment of persistent offenders. Here again, while there was general agreement that the existing Prevention of Crimes Act was ineffective, there were differences of opinion as to any alternative. On the one hand, there was a widespread feeling against the indeterminate sentences of other countries; on the other, the obvious fact that short sentences did not protect the community from hardened criminals. The proposals in the Bill were a compromise. Whilst the sentence was to depend on the offender's whole record rather than the last offence, the period of detention was fixed within certain limits. A general agreement on the reasonableness of the clauses dealing with the question did not save me from a long discussion on a question that, though it was urgent, had been ignored for many years.

Of the really controversial parts of the Bill, the most trouble-some was the clause that prohibited judicial flogging. The question of flogging had never failed to raise furious passions. Sensible men and women became almost demented when they talked about it. Any newspaper that started a campaign about it could be sure of a hysterical response. I must have annoyed both sides in the controversy. I could not regard corporal punish-ment as morally wrong, but neither could I find any evidence to show that it was an effective deterrent as a judicial punishment. I treated the question as I treated the other questions dealt with in the Bill, and as the available evidence was all against this particular kind of punishment, I came down in favour of abolishing it. Why did I ask for trouble in putting it into the Bill at all? asked many of my Conservative friends. " Leave it out and you will get your Bill through with little or no opposition." My answer was the same that I gave to many other criticisms of the Bill. " The Bill is not based on theory or sentiment, but upon the considered opinions of social workers, penal administrators and impartial investigators. One of the many inquiries that has produced it is the Cadogan Committee on Corporal Punishment. Nine completely impartial men and women of wide experience have unanimously recommended the abolition of judicial corporal punishment, on the ground that it is a survival of a discredited penal system and ineffective as a deterrent. How can I make a single exception of this recommendation when I am drafting my Bill on the findings of half a dozen similar inquiries? "

The clause at first excited less opposition than I had expected. It was, however, only the quiet before the storm. By the time that the Bill had reached the Committee Stage, a raging agitation against abolition had been started by my old diehard opponents of Indian days, and by large sections of the Press. The front-line troops of the Party passed many resolutions in favour of flogging in the meetings of the National Union of Conservative Associations. The chief Whip told me that nine-tenths of the Conservative members were against me in the House of Commons. None the less I persisted and carried the abolition clause in the Standing Committee by a substantial majority.

When war came in September, 1939, the Bill was almost on the Statute Book. All that was then needed was a week or two for the report stage and its passage through the House of Lords. There then followed two new developments that made the last lap take nine years instead of nine days. Chamberlain asked me to join the War Cabinet on the understanding that I freed myself from the departmental work of the Home Office and became Lord Privy Seal, and Maxwell, on behalf of the staff of the Home Office and the Government draftsmen who were working on the amendments to the Bill, told me that duties connected with the war would occupy all their time, and that, this being so, it was impossible either to complete the last stages of the Bill or to bring it into operation when it had been passed. Knowing this to be the view of my most sympathetic advisers, I sadly and very reluctantly accepted the inevitable, and left the Bill in cold storage in the Home Office when I crossed the road to the office of the Lord Privy Seal.

Would it have made a difference if I had deleted the controversial flogging clause? I do not think so. The insuperable obstacle created by the war would have remained. In the new conditions there was no chance for the kind of social reform contained in the Bill. Air Raid Precautions, and all that went with them, made a complete black-out of the brighter world to which I had been groping. If, therefore, I had broken the solid front of the Bill by a surrender at one point, I should have gained nothing. By holding to it, I made as sure as I could that when the Bill was eventually introduced by another Home Secretary, the prohibition would stand, and an antiquated anomaly be finally removed from the Statute Book. The important point was to keep intact a comprehensive and coherent scheme and begin a new and up-to-date chapter in our penal methods. Whilst I deeply regretted the delay of nine years, I at least had the satisfaction in the House of Lords of eventually helping another Home Secretary to pass an almost identical Bill, and to succeed where I had been checked.

CHAPTER XIX
A.R.P. and W.V.S.

SIMULTANEOUSLY WITH the Criminal Justice Bill, I was heavily engaged on the first Air Raids Protection Bill. The subject was new and universally unpopular. No one in 1937 could even approximately assess the risks to civil life and property in the event of war, and everyone grudged the spending of millions for turning civilised men and women into grotesquely masked troglodytes. When I discussed the question with Inskip, the Minister for the Co-ordination of Defence, I found him not unnaturally reluctant to see defence funds dispersed over an uncharted and limitless field, and a new service pushed on to him for co-ordination. Chamberlain was hesitant for another reason. His resolute and active mind had little faith in passive defence. None the less, all the many awkward questions raised by A.R.P. had to be faced, and authority to deal with them obtained by Acts of Parliament.

Most important of all, public opinion, still apathetic and often hostile, needed to be mobilised behind any Government proposals. How could I convince people of the reality of the danger and of the possibility of resisting it? This was by no means an easy question to answer in the pre-Munich days. It was at this point that I was helped by Wilfred Eady, an adviser who had recently joined the Home Office staff for A.R.P. duties. Before his arrival, there had been the barest skeleton of any A.R.P. organisation in the Department. The emphasis had then been almost exclusively on the danger from gas attacks, and the programme restricted to little more than the provision of gas-masks. The small band of officials who were working in the office had most creditably succeeded with their limited objective, and by the time of the Munich crisis, had the masks ready for distribution. Their activities, however, covered only one small corner of a vast field, and I saw at once that if I was to make any effective impression on it, I must have a fully organised staff for the purpose. Warren Fisher agreed with me, and suggested that in the new organisation, Eady, who had made a considerable reputation in Whitehall, should leave the Unemployment Assistance Board and join the A.R.P. staff in the Home Office. I readily agreed. Eady appeared, and almost immediately and quite innocently created one of those incidents that often lead to political crises. Speaking at what he thought was a private dinner, he made no secret of the many deficiencies in the A.R.P. services. Unknown to him, reporters had been admitted, with the result that the next morning the papers were black with scare headlines and filled with what were described as the startling disclosures of a high official in the Home Office. Chamberlain and Warren Fisher took the affair very seriously. Here, they said to me, was a senior Civil Servant making a very controversial speech in public about his own Department; so flagrant a breach of the conventions and rules of the Civil Service could not be ignored. I had seen enough of Eady to know that he was as loyal to the traditions of the Civil Service as he was to me. Besides, I particularly needed his quick mind and wide knowledge of the world for the new service. Accordingly, I argued with Chamberlain and Fisher that the fault, if any, was not his, but that of the organisers of the dinner, who, without telling him, had invited the reporters. Chamberlain eventually accepted my defence, and Eady remained as my adviser.

He and I at once started upon a campaign to stir public interest in the unpopular service. As his work on the Unemployment Assistance Board had given him many contacts with representatives of Labour, he was able to help me in directions that might otherwise have been closed to me.

The first evidence of our new campaign was a broadcast that I made on March 14 on Air Raids and the Citizen, in which I asked for a million voluntary helpers. The broadcast had all the greater effect as it coincided with Hitler's *coup* in Vienna. For the first time the country awoke to the danger, and during the following three months thousands of volunteers joined the A.R.P. services. On June 2 I followed it with a second broadcast, and again was helped by the thunder of an international storm. Whilst

I was able to report substantial progress, there were still many gaps to be filled. Hitler's pressure on Czechoslovakia helped me to raise the number of recruits to four hundred thousand.

Simultaneously with the recruitment of volunteers, we were issuing instructions, providing training, making technical experiments and planning a national fire service to supplement the efforts of the local authorities. The ball had started rolling, but it needed a very powerful kick to take it even near the goal. I had obtained four hundred thousand volunteers in three months, but I still needed six hundred thousand for the million for which I had asked. Judged by my post-bag, the women were showing a particular interest in the appeal. It was to them, therefore, that I made my next approach. Out of my talks with Eady, there emerged the idea of a new women's organisation, free of rigid articles of association, as little bureaucratic as possible, and sufficiently elastic to face any of the unexpected difficulties that had or might come into the field of civil defence. If the idea was to succeed, the new organisation must have a very new look, with original minds and receptive imaginations to direct it; Eady at once produced an excellent woman Civil Servant for the Whitehall side of the work, and I had one of the best ideas of my life in thinking of Stella Lady Reading for the chairmanship of the new organisation. Stella Reading, being very hard-headed, needed not a little persuading before she accepted the post. My talks with her in her house in Chesterfield Gardens eventually convinced her that the work would give her great scope for truly useful and practical service. The sixteen years that have followed since she became the head, have proved not only the need for the new organisation, but the value of her superb leadership. The record of the Women's Voluntary Services is the monument of both the one and the other, whether at home or overseas, in war time or in peace.

I do not suggest that even with the growing army of recruits and the W.V.S. the A.R.P. services were in a satisfactory state. We were trying to prepare in peace time against risks that we could not estimate, and were depending on the one hand upon voluntary recruits whose numbers varied from place to place, and on local authorities that, particularly in London, were unwilling to undertake any new burden. For all my journeys round the country, and my discussions with local councils over the amount

of the Treasury Grants, I was painfully conscious of the many
weak points in the A.R.P. front. As I shall show in a later
chapter, the Munich crisis disclosed the gaps to the general public.
The disclosure, that should have surprised no one, had the
excellent effect of stimulating public interest. The number of
volunteers jumped to the million mark, and when, some months
later, I was able to transfer the whole field of A.R.P. to John
Anderson, the Minister's powers had been duly confirmed by
two Acts of Parliament, the services were beginning to work, and
the volunteers were coming forward in increasingly great numbers.

Having dealt with the two principal chapters in my Home
Office miscellany, I must say something about the column that
I have described in my notes as ' sundries.' I will pick out two or
three examples of the most interesting of these *varia*.

My first comes from the days of Hitler's persecution of the
Jews. Heartrending appeals poured in upon me from refugees
who, particularly after the Nazi occupation of Austria, sought
political asylum in Great Britain. All my sympathies were with
them on humanitarian grounds. There was the further utilitarian
argument in favour of the open door, that this country had often
profited from the immigration of political outcasts. I had always
taken a special and personal interest in the fate of exiles since I
went as Nansen's Deputy Commissioner to the Balkans in 1921-22
to organise relief for the White Russians who had arrived in
Constantinople and the neighbouring countries. The hapless state
of those thousands of men, women and children of all ages, classes
and characters, thrown together by an overwhelming calamity,
had left an impression on my mind that could never be effaced.
Generals of the Imperial Army, Bishops of the Orthodox Church,
professors of the universities, ladies of the court, peasants up-
rooted from the land, the flotsam and jetsam of a tidal wave that
had swept away much more than human beings—there they
were, drab and desolate, in urgent need of food and clothing, but
most of all, of new homes and the chance of making new lives.
One of them, a Buddhist priest from Central Asia, was mourning
the loss of his sacred books, without which, as he told me, he
could not live. Some of these poor people I saw again in Czechoslovakia, where Masaryk, with a far-seeing wisdom, was forming
a centre for Slav intellectuals in the University of Prague. For
him it was more than an act of Czech humanity for fellow Slavs,

it was a chance of attracting to the new State scholars and scientists who would enrich its national life. With these memories deeply engraved on my mind, I was not likely to forget the needs of the exiles from the new tyrannies.

As the Hitler persecution became more savage, the number demanding asylum became very great. Questions in the House of Commons began to show a growing anxiety over the immigrants. Was I not letting in German spies? Was I not endangering professional and Trade Union standards by admitting cheap labour? More than once I received an unpleasant shock to my humanitarian sentiments. When, for instance, I attempted to open the door to Austrian doctors and surgeons, I was met by the obstinate resistance of the medical profession. Unmoved by the world-wide reputation of the doctors of Vienna, its representatives, adhering to the strict doctrine of the more rigid trade unionists, assured me that British medicine had nothing to gain from new blood, and much to lose from foreign dilution. It was only after long discussions that I was able to circumvent the opposition and arrange for a strictly limited number of doctors and surgeons to enter the country and practise their profession. I would gladly have admitted the Austrian medical schools *en bloc*. The help that many of these doctors subsequently gave to our war effort, whether in the treatment of wounds, nervous troubles and paralysis, or in the production of penicillin, was soon to prove how great was the country's gain from the new *diaspora*, and how much greater it might have been if professional interests had not restricted its scope. As it was, I pushed what powers I possessed to the utmost limit, and never lost a chance of saying publicly that England ought to welcome foreign brains, and so become the free market for the intellectual gold of the whole world. It is at least comforting to remember that in these months we gave a home to Freud in his old age, and that Einstein, who had once paid me a visit in Norfolk, was so much impressed by the possibilities for meditation and research in Great Britain that he suggested that some of the younger refugees should be permitted to live in British lightships, where they would be undisturbed in their study of basic problems. This imaginative proposal, although we could not carry it out in practice, showed that the intellectuals of the world were looking to Great Britain for the opportunity to carry on their life's work. In spite of the clamour to keep them out of the country, we managed to absorb a notable company of foreign scholars and scientists, very few of whom failed to repay their welcome. It was left to a later Home Secretary to reverse this traditional British policy by interning all the refugees, intellectuals as well as others, as enemy aliens. As a result, the scholars and scientists were torn from their work and deported to the Isle of Man, or Canada and Australia. Never was there a more obscurantist act. Fortunately, a flood of protest soon swept away the new regulations, and the internees went back to their laboratories and universities to the great gain of the country.

The next examples of these varied experiences illustrate the suddenness with which storms can burst upon the Home Secretary's head. On January 31, 1931, a demonstration in favour of arms for Republican Spain led to considerable disorder outside the Houses of Parliament. The police had some difficulty in dispersing it, and in the course of a general scrimmage had recourse to their truncheons.

The extreme Left, inspired by the Communists, turned the affair into a bitter attack on the police for what was alleged to be their violent brutality. Stafford Cripps at once leapt into the arena, and took the side of the accusers. There followed a very heated debate between us in the House of Commons, he accepting as completely accurate the many charges against the police, I repudiating them unless and until actual evidence was produced to substantiate them. In the end, I agreed to make a personal investigation of the charges, and to interview certain of the complainants if I thought it necessary after reading their evidence, but that only in the event of my being satisfied as to the evidence, was I ready to agree to a public inquiry. This pledge I carried out. I advertised in vain in the Press for specific complaints, and as I received no genuine evidence, and only vague letters abusing the police, I did not think it necessary to interview the writers, but I offered the fullest possible facilities for testing any concrete charges in court. Cripps regarded this refusal as a breach of my promise. He and I exchanged many words on the subject both in the House and in the Press. Eventually, the heat subsided. I continued to regard him as the most formidable, and sometimes the most bitter and fanatical critic on the Labour benches, while he declared that my word could not be trusted.

The same kind of sudden trouble looked like blowing up over

the Official Secrets Act. A journalist in Manchester had published a memorandum marked ' Confidential ' that had been widely circulated to the local police, and when challenged as to how he obtained it, refused to disclose the source of the leakage. He was then convicted under a clause of the Official Secrets Act of 1920. In an appeal the conviction was confirmed by Hewart, the Lord Chief Justice, although as Attorney General in 1920 he had expressly stated that the Act only applied to espionage. The decision meant that a journalist could be prosecuted for refusing to say how he obtained any document marked ' Confidential ' by any Government department. I saw at once that the freedom of the Press was genuinely in danger, and that it was absolutely necessary to return to the original conception of the 1911 Act, which only contemplated a very special procedure in cases of espionage. I tried at first a compromise that would have made the demand for information under the Act depend on the explicit direction of the Attorney General or Home Secretary, and then only in cases of serious public importance. When I realised that the proposal would not remove public suspicion, I adopted the clearer course of an amendment of the Act that definitely restricted its operation to espionage. Parliament, Press and the general public were satisfied, and the storm that looked at one time very threatening immediately subsided.

Another group of questions that affected individual liberty concerned Fascist and Nazi agitators and Irish Republican terrorists. The English Fascists I regarded as a troublesome nuisance rather than a political danger. They and the Communists were in the habit of holding rival demonstrations in East and Central London, and of putting the police to intolerable trouble in stopping their internecine battles. Much to Mosley's fury, I prohibited all processions in certain districts, and he and his Black Shirts were deprived of the opportunity of posing as heroes in smart black suits.

The case of the German Nazis in England was not so simple. Hitler had undoubtedly many agents in the country, and our various services were active in investigating cases of alleged espionage. In the case of Nazi propaganda, however, the Home Secretary could only intervene if some British interest was definitely endangered. I was at the time most anxious to show Ribbentrop and the German Embassy that we knew all about their activities, and that we intended to intervene as soon as they went beyond the recognised limits. When my reports clearly proved that two men and one woman, operating from the old Austrian Embassy in Belgrave Square and an office in Cleveland Place, were exceeding the bounds of British tolerance, I had them deported. Ribbentrop in London and Hitler in Berlin violently protested against the expulsion, particularly as the deportees were three leading members of the German community in London. I of course ignored the protest, and for a time at least, the Nazi agents became less active in London.

The Nazi deportations affected foreigners who had always been liable to expulsion by administrative action. A more difficult question arose over the activities of Irish terrorists, who, being citizens of Eire, were entitled to the legal safeguards possessed by British subjects. In January, 1939, the Foreign Office received an extraordinary document in the form of an ultimatum from the Irish Republican Army to the effect that if British forces did not leave Ireland within four months, war would be declared by Eire against Great Britain. Shortly afterwards, the police seized a copy of a plan of campaign known as Plan S in which the most minute and technical instructions were given for bringing the normal life of Great Britain to a standstill by outrages of all kinds. The instructions were much more than a propaganda leaflet. They were operation orders worked out in great detail. No less than 127 outrages followed in the next six months on the exact lines marked out in the plan. Many of them were planned with diabolical ingenuity. Centres like Piccadilly when the theatres were emptying, and tube stations in the rush hour were carefully selected for well-timed explosions. Lives were lost and damage done, but owing to a combination of extraordinary luck and police efficiency, only on a limited scale. The attempts, although they fortunately failed in their full effect, clearly showed that the power of the police to search and arrest suspects was so restricted as often to be ineffective against such dangerous conspirators. Worse still, there was no way of deporting an Irish terrorist. The risks became all the greater with the worsening of the inter-national situation. The Republican Army was evidently working on the old watchword of England's difficulty being Ireland's opportunity. If war broke out, the carefully considered pro-gramme of outrage and destruction would be dangerous in the extreme to the national effort. These urgent considerations impelled me to take emergency action before the end of the session of 1939. Accordingly, within a week of the adjournment, on July 24, I introduced a Bill for the Prevention of Violence that gave the police wider powers of search and arrest, and enabled suspects to be deported. Valuing as keenly as anyone the civil rights of the subject, I made it a temporary measure for two years restricted to a particular emergency, and arranged for Walter Monckton to advise me upon specific cases where deportation was ordered. Parliament seemed satisfied that I had held the balance between public security and individual liberty, and passed the Bill with almost universal approval. About a hundred Irish men and women were deported to Eire. De Valera, contrary to the warnings that we received, agreed to take them back, and the fact that only two of them appealed against their deportation showed that the police had thrown their net over the real culprits. It is also significant that nothing more was heard of Plan S, and that not even at the worst moments of the war were the Irish fanatics able to endanger the country's security.

When war was on the point of breaking out, I had to ask Parliament to pass other security measures that went far beyond the limited scope of the Prevention of Violence Act. Once again, however, I was able to obtain the necessary authority without delay and with little or no opposition. Members on all sides responded at once to the grave call of public danger, and the unpopular D.O.R.A. was welcomed back with open arms. I had learnt the lesson that in dealing with the House of Commons, particularly on questions that involve civil liberties, the only safe course is to bring the whole case into the open without any concealment of facts, or any mental reservation on the part of the Minister.

I have given some description of the alarms and excursions that disturb the life of a Home Secretary. Remembering the story of many of my predecessors, I was always expecting sudden trouble. Had not Spencer Walpole collapsed with the railings of Hyde Park? Would not Henry Mathews have been driven from office if the murderer, Lipski, had not saved him at the last moment by a deathbed confession? Had not the arrest of a lady of easy virtue more than once involved the adjournment of the

House of Commons and a sudden attack upon the Home Secretary?
These warnings from the past kept me constantly on the alert.

None the less, I had time and opportunity for satisfying some
of my most cherished personal tastes. I had, for instance, the
pleasant duty of planting a tree in Windsor Forest to comme-
morate the Coronation of King George VI. A glade was designed
on the lines of a map of the British Empire. Representatives from
overseas, and the Home Secretary on behalf of the United
Kingdom each planted a tree in its appropriate place. Trees of
all kinds, and landscape planting have always been one of the
passions of my life. The ceremony, therefore, meant more to me
than a formal act. I kept it in the same corner of my memory
as the planting of a double avenue of limes at Cranwell that I
had arranged when I was Secretary of State for Air.

So, also, with another of my tastes—my love of birds. Living
in North Norfolk, where rare birds and game abound, I would
indeed be a Philistine if I did not take a keen interest in the
residents that live in my woods and fields, and the migrant
visitors that join them. It was, therefore, an unexpected pleasure
when I discovered that the Home Office was responsible for the
protection of wild birds, and that there was an immediate opportunity for improving the very inadequate measures that existed
for the purpose. The growing company of bird enthusiasts,
students, sportsmen and amateurs were at the time pressing for
action in two directions. They pointed to the duck population
that was diminishing to a disturbing extent, and the restaurants
in London and Paris that, by making quail their most popular
dish in the season, were likely to destroy the smallest and most
delightful of game birds. It was clear that both species urgently
needed better protection. Conferences with the experts led to the
drafting of two Bills by my department, the first, to extend the
close time for ducks, and to prohibit their sale during the spring
and summer months; the second, to prohibit the sale of quail. I
then found a private member to introduce them in the House of
Commons, and as they both received very general support, they
successfully reached the Statute Book. They were admittedly of
limited scope, but were none the less of immediate interest to bird
lovers, whilst their subsequent effect proved very important. They
started, in fact, a strong demand for comprehensive legislation
covering all wild birds, and set an example that has already been

followed by several foreign countries. I am glad to find a place in memories that are concerned with great Bills of hundreds of clauses, and legislation that stirred political controversy to the depths, for these two little measures that helped to preserve a delightful part of our natural treasures, and started a campaign that has gathered irresistible volume for their wider and fuller protection.

So much for what I have described as the ' sundries ' in the Home Office miscellany.

CHAPTER XX

The Prerogative of Mercy

IF, HOWEVER, this description of my two years as Home Secretary
is to be complete, I must add some account of my duties as the
guardian of the Royal Prerogative, and as the Minister chiefly
in contact with the Court. Home Secretaries have written so often
of their constitutional responsibilities in advising the King on the
exercise of the Prerogative of Mercy that I will keep my comments
to my own personal experience.

Before I went to the Home Office, I had taken capital punishment for granted, and had given no thought to the case for or
against it. It was during my preparation of the Criminal Justice
Bill that I came to ask myself questions about its justification. For
the time being I put my doubts aside. The task of passing a Bill
that already contained scores of difficult clauses and abolished
judicial corporal punishment was hard enough without adding to
it a clause about the death penalty. I therefore took the line that
as capital punishment had always been given a unique place in
the administration of justice, its abolition should be the subject of
specific and not general legislation. The Committee on the Bill
accepted this view, and the question of legislation on the subject
was consequently postponed.

The existing law had to be administered, and scarcely a week
passed without the need for the Home Secretary to decide whether
he should or should not recommend to the sovereign the exercise
of the Prerogative of Mercy. During my period of office there were
397 murders of all kinds known to the police. In 133 of these cases,
the offender committed suicide, 26 were acquitted, and 71 declared
insane by the courts. Of the cases specially referred to me for the
exercise of the Prerogative, 24 of the offenders were reprieved and
four found insane upon further inquiry. Altogether there were
in the end only nineteen executions. The number was so small

that it was often urged that there was no reason for abolishing a punishment that was so carefully safeguarded, so rarely used, and so generally accepted by the public as an effective deterrent against murder. I drew from the figures a different conclusion, and asked myself whether it was worth retaining a punishment that was a survival of an antiquated penal system, and all the grim machinery of the black cap and the gallows for the execution of a handful of murderers who, judged by the available evidence, did not appear to be specially deterred by the penalty of death.

As to the exercise of the Prerogative, I could not from my experience suggest a better method, though I was profoundly conscious of the weakness in the procedure. The Home Secretary's decision is made without the calling of witnesses, without seeing the accused, and without any of the publicity that is one of the chief safeguards of British justice. Inevitably, it depends upon the mentality of the individual Home Secretary. Whilst there is no startling divergence between the recommendations of one Home Secretary and another, past history certainly shows that a difference of outlook upon penal questions undoubtedly shows itself in the matter of reprieves.

Looking back at my own experience, I ask myself whether I am satisfied that I made the right recommendations in the cases upon which I had to recommend or refuse the use of the Prerogative of Mercy.

I must divide my answer into two to cover the cases upon which I advised when I was acting for the Home Secretary, and the cases when I myself was Home Secretary. As to the first, I am convinced that in questions of life or death for which the Home Secretary is responsible, there should be no delegation of his powers to any of his fellow Secretaries of State even in the exceptional cases in which it has been delegated in the past. When cases were referred to me at the time that I was Secretary of State for Air and Secretary of State for India, I possessed none of the Home Secretary's experience or special information. I had, in fact, to accept the recommendation made to me by the Home Office. The most that I could do was to ask one or two questions, but that was all. It was clear that what was required of me was a signature without which an execution could not take place, and I was in no position to refuse it. When, therefore, I am asked whether I made the right recommendations in the cases upon which I had only a delegated authority, I can only answer, " I do not know."

As to the second class of case upon which I acted as Home Secretary, I can give an answer that, whilst it is more satisfactory, is none the less hesitant and incomplete. I put to myself the question in its most concrete form. Am I certain that, during my two years at the Home Office, twenty-four murderers were rightly reprieved, four rightly sent to Broadmoor, and nineteen rightly executed? I cannot honestly say " Yes." All that I can claim is that I took every possible step to reach a right decision. As to being infallible in this more than in any other question that has faced me during my public life, the claim is too foolish for anyone to suggest. The difference, however, between fallibility in this and every other question that I have had to decide, is that upon a question of death my decision was irrevocable. If I made a mistake and refused to recommend a reprieve, there was no remedy. More than once, I had two capital cases to decide at the same time. They were brought to me in the midst of Cabinet and departmental work. There were dozens of other urgent questions that were claiming my attention. Yet I had to say the fateful " yes " or " no " within a few hours, or at most, a few days. As I had not been present at the trial, I could have only a very inadequate impression of the murderer's personality and character. My information, whilst it was given to me in good faith, and by the most reliable judges and departmental experts, inevitably came to me at second hand. My decision was bound to be based on the advice of others, though I would not say that my own views might not occasionally modify theirs. Whilst some of the cases were comparatively simple, others were obscured by the baffling fog that enshrouds the maze of mental abnormality in human beings. Upon the issue of mental responsibility, I had no other course than to accept the medical opinion that was available to me. Was this advice complete and conclusive? I frankly do not know. I own that my belief in medical infallibility as to the mental condition of murderers has since been gravely shaken by the disclosure in the evidence to Sir Ernest Gowers' Royal Commission, that in prisons such as Cardiff and Swansea, where executions regularly take place, there has been no whole time medical officer, and that nowhere do prison medical officers have to qualify themselves specially for dealing with mental cases. Yet it is upon reports from the medical officers of prisons that the Home Secretary depends to a considerable extent for the essential information about a prisoner's mental state.

Each case that came before me impressed me more strongly with the inevitable danger of making a mistake. Since then, my general anxieties have been increased. I have studied some of the past cases where, in the face of every probability and a mass of convincing evidence, there have undoubtedly been miscarriages of justice. It was possible in the majority to reinstate and compensate the sufferer. If, however, the convicted men had been hanged, they would have died a murderer's death, and nothing would have been heard of their innocence.

I am not citing these cases for the purpose of disparaging the Home Secretary's part in the exercise of the Prerogative of Mercy. As long as there is a death penalty, his is probably the best court of final appeal, however deficient it may be. It is rather because this or any other human tribunal can make mistakes that I object to any system under which a mistake is irrevocable. So long as death is the rigid penalty for murder, and there is a consequent need for commuting it in particular cases and a Minister or a court responsible for recommending the mitigation, so long will there be the possibility of error. If, instead of death, the punishment is long-term imprisonment, there is always left an opportunity to remedy a mistake.

The war came before I was able to crystallise my doubts into any concrete proposals. I ceased to be Home Secretary when I entered the War Cabinet in September, 1939. The Criminal Justice Bill did not become law until 1948, and the attempt failed to include in it a provision for abolishing capital punishment. The violent agitation that inflamed the discussions on the death penalty, whilst they confirmed the wisdom of my decision to exclude the question from the 1938 Bill, greatly strengthened the trend of my own mind in favour of total abolition.

Although it might be supposed that the Home Secretary's recommendation for the exercise of the Royal Prerogative of Mercy would bring him into personal contact with the Sovereign, this is not the case. So far as I know, no Home Secretary in modern times has ever raised in an Audience the question of a death sentence. The Sovereign always leaves the decision to the Secretary of State, and I imagine that if ever he felt it necessary

to intervene in a doubtful case, he would send the Private
Secretary to discuss it with the Home Secretary or the Permanent
Under-Secretary. Certainly in my own experience there was
never any suggestion of intervention.

The Home Secretary's personal dealings with the King are
of a different kind. In the ministerial hierarchy he is our equiva-
lent of a Minister of the Court. Whilst there have been British
Ministers who have been Court favourites, we have never had
Ministers of the Court in the Continental sense. In the Hapsburg,
Romanov and Hohenzollern Courts the Minister of the Court
often exercised very important political influence. I knew the last
Minister of the Imperial Court in Russia, Count Friedrichs. His
tall and venerable figure was set off by a splendid uniform and a
blaze of stars and *grands cordons*. Although he might have seemed
only an impressive social personage, his close relations with the
Emperor Nicholas made him one of the most influential Ministers.
In his relations with the Court the British Home Secretary was
altogether unlike this great officer of state. His contacts with the
Palace gave him no exceptional influence in politics. Although
there was a small ceremonial department in the Home Office,
he did not control the Court's ceremonial. The greater number of
his official actions in connection with the Prerogative were carried
out as formalities that did not need any personal influence or
discussion.

None the less, there were many occasions when the Home
Secretary was required to take part either officially or unofficially
in the affairs of the King and the Royal Family. In my case, the
most notable of these occasions was when from time to time I
accompanied the King and Queen on royal visits to different
parts of the country. Three of these visits I vividly remember.
The first was to open the new civic buildings in Norwich, the
capital of my native East Anglia, and the city that my father had
represented in Parliament for a generation. The King, himself a
Norfolk man, particularly wished me, as another Norfolk man, to
be the Minister in Attendance, and to combine my duties with
some very good shooting at Sandringham. We drove into Norwich
from Sandringham on a radiant autumn day. From the terrace
of the new building we looked down on a scene that would have
delighted Cotman. Below was the Flower Market, one of the most
delightful still left in England, and in front, the Norman castle,

dominating the whole city. When I handed the King his speech, I felt the same kind of thrill that had inspired George Borrow's moving tribute to the " old city."

The second royal visit that I attended was a tour of the West Riding of Yorkshire and Lancashire. We stayed first at Harewood, and would have ended the tour at Knowsley if the King had not been called back to London in connection with the appointment of Kingsley Wood to the Air Ministry. Derby, as Lord Lieutenant of Lancashire, arranged the Lancashire programme with the skill of a supreme stage manager. As he met us in every town that we visited, and saw us off when the visit was over, he was in a state of perpetual motion, hurrying on before us to greet us on our arrival, and looking anxiously at his watch to see that we were up to time. The weather was warm, and as the day advanced, his collar collapsed round his ample neck, and his face assumed the colour of vintage port. The uncrowned king of Lancashire, he was everywhere acclaimed with rousing cheers that were scarcely less enthusiastic than those that greeted the Sovereign.

Lastly, there was the royal visit to Northern Ireland. This was a very imposing affair. We went from Stranraer in *Victoria and Albert*, and when we arrived at Belfast, appeared in full-dress uniform. My main duty was to hand the King his various speeches and receive in return the formal addresses of welcome. For two whole days the King and Queen were in the midst of spontaneous and deafening demonstrations of loyalty. My head reeled with the cheers as we drove practically unescorted through the narrow streets of Belfast. Yet, the King and Queen in Northern Ireland, no less than in Yorkshire and Lancashire, seemed completely untired at the end of these exacting visits. While the staff and I could scarcely stand at the end of the day for weariness, they would remain gracious and alert until late in the evening, talking to the local magnates, asking about the local industries, remembering the names and the faces of any former acquaintances. How glad I was of these chances to see the superb display of royal technique! No King and Queen ever carried out their royal duties better. When I asked myself the reason, I found it in their natural instinct for doing the right thing, combined with the obvious enjoyment that the visits gave them. Their work was all the better done because they liked doing it.

Part Four

MUNICH, PRAGUE AND WAR

CHAPTER XXI

Chamberlain and Eden

WHEN I returned to the Cabinet in June, 1936, I looked forward to a period of comparative calm from controversial questions. The Admiralty worked so smoothly and majestically that it scarcely needed a First Lord to control it, whilst my five years at the Air Ministry had given me sufficient experience for dealing with a Service Department without undue trouble. What, therefore, I hoped and expected was a chapter of the kind of departmental administration that seemed to suit me.

It was the Spanish Civil War that upset my calculations. Franco's attempted blockade of the Spanish coast and his bombing of British ships brought British naval policy into the very centre of international affairs. Scarcely a day passed in the autumn of 1936 and throughout 1937 that did not involve discussions with the Foreign Office over the many problems raised by incidents in Spanish waters and our policy of Non-Intervention. The Cabinet was unanimously agreed upon doing everything possible to localise the Spanish conflict. When, however, non-intervention led to interference with British shipping, complicated questions arose over belligerent rights and specific breaches of international law. Should we, for instance, escort British merchant ships into Spanish harbours and retaliate at once against Spanish attacks? Should we sink unidentified submarines as soon as they were sighted? These were the kind of questions that were constantly arising. I remember in particular the excitement in the House of Commons over one of several small tramps that plied between South Wales and the Bay of Biscay. The skipper, known to his friends as ' Potato ' Jones, was determined to carry on his lucrative trade with the north of Spain, whatever either side might say or do.

In Lloyd George's eyes the obstinate Welshman was a national hero engaged upon a crusade against a threatening tyrant. The unprintable language with which ' Potato ' Jones abused the Republicans no less than the Nationalists for interfering with his ship did not suggest that Spanish politics affected his attitude. Our difficult task was to prevent the ships of the Welsh skipper and his friends from embroiling us and possibly the whole of Europe in a conflagration. Whilst the Board of Admiralty was inclined to Palmerstonian methods, the Foreign Office insisted upon the risks of war. Eventually, an international agreement was reached at Nyon, under which submarines could be instantly attacked in certain specified zones. The result was the disappearance of the submarines and the removal of one of the chief causes of danger. Soon afterwards, Franco's successes brought within sight the end of the civil war, and with it, the risk of our being involved in the fighting.

Throughout these months I was inevitably dragged back into the vortex of foreign affairs. For more than personal reasons the consequences were unfortunate. I had a great respect for Eden, my successor at the Foreign Office, and the last thing in the world that I wished was to embarrass his conduct of foreign policy. From the day when I had listened to his maiden speech from the back benches, I had always admired his easy grasp of international questions and his readiness and courage in debate. As his influence increased, he had not only come to represent the Canning tradition in the Conservative Party, but also to express the emotions and aspirations of many men and women of the Centre and the Left. I had, however, been gradually forced to the conclusion that whilst our personal relations were never impaired, our outlooks differed. If I described this difference in a sentence, I would say that I was more inclined than he to move step by step in the international field, and more ready to negotiate with the dictators until we were militarily stronger. Perhaps this divergence was not so fundamental as it sometimes appeared, or as our respective camp-followers often assumed. In any case, it would have been better if, after I became First Lord in 1936, I had not been pushed back into the Foreign Office orbit. A Foreign Secretary should be given the freest possible liberty of manoeuvre, and it is unfortunate when the impression is created that he is being intentionally or unintentionally impeded by doubting colleagues and former Foreign Ministers. Eden's sensitive temperament was bound to react to any appearance of disagreement. Whilst I cannot point to any specific difference of opinion between us over British policy during the Spanish Civil War, I formed the impression, when I was First Lord, that he regarded the conflict as one between absolute right and absolute wrong in which the dictator should at all costs be totally defeated and democracy totally defended. This almost passionate feeling, which was fully shared by his intimate friends, differed from my own view. I was convinced that both sides in the Civil War were to blame, but that probably the Right, being less divided than the Left, would ultimately win.

When Chamberlain became Prime Minister in May, 1937, this underlying divergence of outlook undoubtedly became more definite. Chamberlain seemed at once to crystallise all the fluid forces in the Cabinet. His clear-cut mind and concrete outlook had an astringent effect upon opinions and preferences that had hitherto been only sentiments and impressions. As soon as he succeeded Baldwin, I became increasingly conscious of two distinct points of view in the Cabinet. For the time being, the general relief at the advent of a very efficient and vigorous Prime Minister preserved its outward unity. Eden in particular seemed delighted with a change that gave him the support of a more active chief, who was always ready to help him in the Cabinet discussions.

As for myself, both by instinct and training I was bound to find myself in accord with Chamberlain's ideas. Not only did we approach public questions in much the same way, but our habits of life brought us continually together. During the Parliamentary session, for instance, we made a practice of walking round the lake in St. James's Park and discussing Government affairs before going to our offices. This daily procession would consist of three couples, each following the other, Chamberlain and myself, our two wives and the two detectives. In the recess, we regularly met at various country houses. It was in intimate meetings of this kind that I succeeded to some extent in penetrating behind his outward reserve. Minds so akin in domestic affairs were certain to keep together in the field of foreign politics.

I suppose it was the sense of agreement both in outlook and method that made him take me into his confidence on foreign questions over and above those in which the First Lord was directly concerned. It was the same when I became Home Secretary in June, 1937, and he often discussed with me his hopes and fears for international peace. These talks have left on my mind a clear picture of his intentions. Just as between 1924 and 1929, when he was Minister of Health, he had set before himself a five-year programme of social security, with each stage clearly marked at the appointed time, so in 1937, when he became Prime Minister, he had in his mind an equally concrete programme of international security based on definite action, and concentrated, stage by stage, upon carefully selected points in the foreign front. It was typical of his mentality that in November, 1925, he was ready within a few days of becoming Minister of Health with a programme of no less than twenty-five Bills of social reform, and that by 1929 he had successfully carried them all to the Statute Book. In 1937, he was equally determined to concentrate his analytical and methodical mind upon the crucial points in the foreign front. A period of drift in Europe had made more urgent than ever the need of a concrete and concerted programme for preventing a catastrophe. When he came to consider the stages of the plan, he reached the conclusion that had already been forced upon me two years before when I was Foreign Secretary. To both of us, the first stage seemed to be an attempt to separate the two western dictators. It was notorious that Mussolini not only resented Hitler's patronage, but personified the Italian dislike of the German people. If the worst happened and Hitler went to war, it was of supreme importance to us to avoid an unfriendly Italy across our communications in the Mediterranean. The re-establishment, therefore, of friendly relations with Italy was, with very good reason, Chamberlain's first objective. Eden fully accepted the programme, and until the beginning of 1938 actively worked for it. It was in accordance with Chamberlain's timetable that one of his first acts as Prime Minister was to write on July 27, 1939, a letter to Mussolini in which he expressed the hope of a return to the atmosphere of the Anglo-Italian 'Gentlemen's Agreement '[1] of the previous January. The move was generally approved both here and in the Commonwealth as well as in Italy. Talks on the possibility of further negotiations began soon afterwards in London with Grandi, the Italian Ambassador.

[1] Anglo-Italian declaration of peaceful intentions. 2nd January, 1937.

It was at this point that Chamberlain showed the faults of his great qualities. He was so sure that his plan was right, and so deeply convinced that he must carry it through without a moment's delay, that his singleness of urgent purpose made him impatient of obstacles and indifferent to incidental risks. The old-established machine of the Foreign Office did not seem to him to move quickly enough for the crisis that threatened Europe. A Foreign Secretary left to himself always appeared to be entangled in the web of an intricate Department. The classical methods of diplomacy under which ambassadors interviewed Foreign Ministers and leisurely dispatches passed between distant capitals, seemed out of date in the new world of dictators, wireless and aeroplanes. Had not the time come, he asked himself, when the British Prime Minister should deal direct with the man who really controlled Italian foreign policy, rather than through intermediaries who had no power of their own? Being so completely concentrated upon his plan of action, he did not fully realise some of its implications, the danger, for instance, of side-tracking the Foreign Secretary, and dealing with advisers who were not always the accredited experts on foreign affairs. If he was not very careful, his direct approach was bound to create an atmosphere of resentment amongst those whom he left on one side. Suspicion was sure to exaggerate any supposed differences between the Foreign Office and No. 10 Downing Street.

The position was not made easier by the visit that his sister-in-law, Lady Chamberlain, paid to Rome in the autumn of 1937. Austen Chamberlain had formed a friendship with Mussolini whilst visiting Italy during a yachting holiday. Lady Chamberlain, therefore, was assured of a friendly welcome by the Duce when she went to Rome for the winter. Whether it was Mussolini's astuteness in playing upon her susceptibilities, or her own excessive zeal in pressing her brother-in-law's policy of better Anglo-Italian relations, the result was unfortunate. Mussolini assumed that we were ready for negotiations with little or no preliminary discussion, and that Chamberlain's move disclosed a policy of weakness rather than a carefully considered plan of general peace. In the meanwhile the Foreign Office very naturally resented an unofficial intervention at a moment when the delicate question of the withdrawal of the Italian troops from Spain was still unsettled. Chamberlain, when once he realised that the personal letters that he was receiving from his sister-in-law were increasing rather than lessening his difficulties, tactfully suggested to her that her talks with Mussolini should be discontinued.

This incident, although apparently unimportant, left behind it an atmosphere of suspicion and irritation. It was too much like the happenings during the Lloyd George régime, when the Prime Minister preferred the gossip of his own friends to the official dispatches. If it had been suggested to Chamberlain that he was unconsciously following Lloyd George's bad example, he would have been horrified. The fact is that anyone who is heart and soul set upon a single purpose is apt to ignore the feelings of others, and to depend more and more upon the circle of friends and advisers who entirely agree with him. As Simon and I, the two ex-Foreign Secretaries in the Cabinet, and Halifax, the Lord President of the Council, did agree with him, it almost inevitably happened that he regularly took us into his confidence. Ours was therefore a particularly joint responsibility with his.

This was not the case with his principal official adviser, Horace Wilson. Horace Wilson was in every respect the orthodox, conscientious and efficient Civil Servant. The partisan attacks upon him, on the ground that he was Chamberlain's *éminence grise*, who intrigued himself into a position of great political influence, are totally untrue. Left to himself, Wilson would have preferred to devote himself to his normal duties in the Treasury. As an administrator, he was of outstanding reputation in Whitehall. In contrast to Warren Fisher, his brilliant but erratic predecessor, he had worked amicably with his Civil Service colleagues, and had kept clear of inter-departmental battles. Two Prime Ministers found him indispensable. For both Baldwin and Chamberlain he was a past master in preparing difficult questions for ministerial decision. Indeed, it was he more than any Minister or Civil Servant who developed the new technique started by Warren Fisher under which the heads of the principal departments jointly sorted out the data of the more important problems before they went to the Cabinet. Chamberlain had found this kind of official help particularly useful in the Ministry of Health and the Treasury, where the orderly sifting of detail was essential. When he became Prime Minister and found himself overwhelmed with domestic and foreign problems, most of them overdue for decision, he very naturally had recourse to the same methods that had already proved so valuable, and to the trusted adviser whose help had so often been useful to him in the past. To suggest that Wilson pushed his way into Downing Street is the exact opposite of the truth. It was Chamberlain who insisted upon taking him into the new field of foreign affairs. Prime Ministers and, indeed, all the more important Ministers of the Crown, have always been entitled to choose their own more intimate advisers. Churchill, for instance, has never hesitated to take with him from one department to another a small and faithful personal staff. If Chamberlain made a mistake, it was in the method rather than the principle. When he installed Wilson in the room adjoining the Cabinet Room where Prime Ministers habitually worked, the world at large assumed that a rival Foreign Office was being formed at No. 10 Downing Street. Could this unfortunate impression have been avoided with a little more tact and patience? I believe that it would have been possible to dissipate the atmosphere of suspicion, but at the cost of some delay and many explanations. It may be that a heart-to-heart talk with Eden would have cleared the air. It must, however, be remembered that Chamberlain was working against time and in an atmosphere of urgent crisis. He was thinking so completely of the threat that was overhanging Europe that in his anxiety for action he was apt to underrate the need for discussion and explanation. The result was certainly unfortunate. Within six months of the start of the Government, the Foreign Secretary resigned, and a deep rift was opened in the one field of public affairs in which unity was essential.

CHAPTER XXII

Chamberlain and Roosevelt

T
HE SERIOUS trouble began in January, 1938. The Foreign
Secretary had left England for a short holiday in France, and
in accordance with traditional procedure, the Prime Minister
had in his absence taken over the control of the Foreign Office.
On January 11, while Eden was away, President Roosevelt, in a
personal message to Chamberlain, declared his intention to
summon an international Peace Conference in Washington, but
only if his suggestion " met with the cordial approval and whole-
hearted support of the British Government." The message was
transmitted by the American Under-Secretary of State, Sumner
Welles, to Lindsay, the British Ambassador, for direct and very
secret communication to the Prime Minister. Chamberlain, who
had good reason to be sceptical of grandiose proposals of this
kind, and was convinced that the best chance for European
peace was by direct negotiation with Mussolini, feared that his
own carefully considered plan would be side-tracked by generalities that would lead to nothing. Accordingly, without waiting
to consult Eden, or to call Ministers back from the Christmas
recess, he telegraphed to Washington, thanking Roosevelt for his
initiative, and suggesting that a general conference might not be
opportune at the moment in view of the discussions that were
already starting between London and Rome. Eden, on his return,
felt that the answer should have been delayed until he had seen it.

Whilst Chamberlain's telegram did not lead to an immediate
rupture with the Foreign Secretary, it was, I feel sure, the underlying reason for Eden's resignation a month later. Without it, I
doubt whether the question of the actual date on which the
Italian negotiations were to begin would have been a sufficient

justification for his leaving the Foreign Office. Whether this was the case or not, so many attacks[1] have been made on Chamberlain's alleged failure to welcome Roosevelt's offer that it is necessary to examine the incident in some detail, and in particular, to consider it in the framework of the circumstances at the time.

Rightly or wrongly, we were deeply suspicious not indeed of American good intentions, but of American readiness to follow up inspiring words with any practical action. I, like the rest of my colleagues, had closely followed for several years the diplomatic correspondence between London and Washington, and had come to the only possible conclusion that, whatever the President might wish, Congress would never approve of any resolute intervention in European affairs. Was this conviction the result of any anti-American prejudice? So far as I was concerned, I am sure that it was not. I sincerely regarded Anglo-American friendship as the very basis of our foreign policy, and it was only with the greatest reluctance and disappointment that I was forced to agree with Chamberlain and admit that in view of the strength of American isolationism, we must for the time being rely chiefly upon ourselves in the immediate crisis that was facing Europe.

What, then, was the evidence upon which Chamberlain and those like myself who agreed with him, came to this conclusion? To answer this question it is necessary to recall certain chapters of Anglo-American history since the end of the First World War. As the years passed, the divergence of British and American policy had become more and more conspicuous. On their side, Americans felt that we had not sufficiently supported them in the Far East, and that we had failed to take any effective action against aggression in the West. On our side, we were convinced that in no circumstances, short of a direct attack upon American security, would Congress approve of any coercive action against the dictators. In support of our view there was certainly a

[1] " That Mr. Chamberlain, with his limited outlook and inexperience of the European scene, should have possessed the self-sufficiency to wave away the proffered hand stretched out across the Atlantic leaves one, even at this date, breathless with amazement."
" No event could have been more likely to stave off, or even prevent, war than the arrival of the United States in the circle of European hates and fears. To Britain it was a matter almost of life and death. No one can measure in retrospect its effect upon the course of events in Austria and later at Munich. We must regard its rejection —and such it was—as the loss of the last frail chance to save the world from tyranny otherwise than by war." (Winston Churchill: *The Gathering Storm*, page 254.)

voluminous cloud of witness. We had not to go back as far as the American refusal to join the League of Nations and ratify the Security Pact with France, or, indeed, to the years of extreme isolationism that followed under the Harding and Hoover régimes. The evidence that was chiefly in our minds in January, 1938, was to be found in the years that had started with Hitler's rise to power in the early thirties, when we had hoped in vain for American co-operation in the face of the difficulties with which a weakened England and France were confronted.

I take two or three examples that explain our doubts about American help. In 1933 we had set great store upon the World Economic Conference in London. We believed that American co-operation would make possible an effective recovery from the economic crash of 1931, and in particular, result in the lowering of American tariffs on European goods. Our hopes were raised by the arrival in London of Cordell Hull, the American Secretary of State and a lifelong advocate of freer trade. I remember very well the opening days of the Conference. As Secretary of State I was representing the Government of India. A vast, white and cold hall in South Kensington, shortly to become the Geological Museum, was filled with delegates from every part of the world. Speech after speech of high hope resounded through its gaunt spaces. Before, however, the discussions had made any headway, Roosevelt telegraphed to his Secretary of State that domestic politics made American co-operation impossible, and that higher rather than lower tariffs were to be the American policy. The shock of this sudden change of front not only confirmed the doubts of the many Europeans who disbelieved in any effective American help, but inevitably, by exposing the differences in the democratic front, strengthened the growing power of the dictators.

I find my second example in the attitude of Congress during the succeeding years. In 1934, there had been passed the Johnson Act prohibiting the raising of loans in the United States by any foreign governments that were not paying the full interest on the American loans of the First World War. We and the French were consequently debarred from borrowing in the States for the purchase of munitions, either before or during another war. When our Ambassador protested, and pointed out the effect of the Act upon the democracies, he was curtly informed by Cordell Hull that " Congress is a co-ordinate and independent branch of the government, and has an equal right to express its attitude on this Act." In other words, it was no business of ours to criticise or protest.

Worse still, there followed the so-called Nye Committee of the Senate to investigate the manufacture and sale of arms and munitions. To quote again Cordell Hull:[1]

"It is doubtful that any congressional committee has ever had a more unfortunate effect on our foreign relations, unless it be the Senate Foreign Relations Committee considering the Treaty of Versailles submitted by President Wilson."

For many months on end the Committee, through its chief investigator, Stephen Raushenbush, directed its efforts to unearthing alleged scandals, with the object of proving that unscrupulous profiteers, particularly British, had been responsible for the 1914 war. Most of the evidence was worthless—for example, the amazing story that King George V had engaged in munition speculations. Some of it outraged the most fundamental canons of international conduct—for instance, the disclosure without the consent of the British Government of a confidential memorandum given by Balfour, then Foreign Secretary, to Lansing, the American Secretary of State, dealing with British secret agreements with other Allied Governments.

The effect of these groundless and sensational charges was not only to shake our confidence in American co-operation, but to increase the American prejudice against any move that might involve the United States in European commitments. The atmosphere indeed became so poisoned that Cordell Hull, asked Roosevelt to summon the members of the Nye Committee and advise them to be more discreet. The President agreed, but when the Committee actually came to see him, instead of mentioning Hull's request, started them off upon the scarcely less dangerous line of the Neutrality Legislation that was to embroil our relations and cripple our efforts so disastrously during the next three years.

The tangled history of the successive Neutrality Acts demonstrated the overwhelming strength of the isolationists. It showed also how ill-considered legislation could have boomerang effects that the promoters could not have expected. The three Neutrality

[1] *The Memoirs of Cordell Hull*, Vol I, page 398 (Hodder and Stoughton).

Acts were intended to isolate American interests from any international conflicts, justified or unjustified. With this object in view, the United States prohibited all aid to both sides when once a war had started. This plan of complete isolation seemed at first sight to be a simple policy for avoiding embroilment. From the very first, however, anomalies and complications of every kind gathered around it. When, for instance, was a war not a war? The old clear-cut distinction between peace and war had been obliterated by the dictators. Then again, as if there was to be no distinction between the treatment of the aggressor and the victim, the victim was debarred from obtaining American aid in a war such as Mussolini's in Abyssinia. In the Spanish Civil War, the Republican Government was equally excluded from American help. Worse still, in the Far East, China was left at the mercy of Japan. The only possible mitigation of this anomalous state of affairs was based upon the assumption that, although both sides were fighting to the death, no formal war had been declared.

In spite of the obvious need of a flexible policy that took account of the differences between the combatants, the President's efforts to retain some measure of discretion in his own hands was time after time frustrated by the isolationists. Indeed, his single success, when he obtained what came to be known as the ' cash-and-carry ' provision, under which belligerent countries were allowed to obtain supplies if they sent their own ships to the United States and paid in cash for their purchases, made it possible for Japan, with its navy, to gain a further advantage over a country like China, which had no ships to send. Even this attempt at partial co-operation with the democracies lapsed in the summer of 1939, when the temporary Act that made it possible, came to an end.

The climax was reached in the reaction against what was known as the President's ' Quarantine ' speech on October 5, 1937, in which Roosevelt, struggling against the isolationist wave, proposed a general boycott of all aggressors, " a quarantine, in fact, to protect the health of the community against the spread of the disease." He hoped by this means to differentiate between the aggressor and the victim. The result was the very opposite of what he intended. The immediate reaction against a more active policy, that distinguished between belligerents was overwhelming, and the isolationists became more powerful than ever. Even after Japanese planes had bombed and sunk the American gunboat *Panay*, so far from modifying their attitude, they succeeded in bringing out of cold storage the so-called Ludlow Resolution, which had been pigeon-holed in a committee of the House of Representatives since February, 1937, with its proposal that the constitutional power of Congress to declare war should not take effect until the issue of peace or war had been decided by a national referendum. It was only by the narrow majority of 209 to 188 that this revolutionary proposal was eventually defeated. In Cordell Hull's words:[1]

" This episode was a striking indication of the strength of isolationist sentiment in the United States, since the Administration had to exert its whole force to prevent—barely to prevent—approval of a proposal designed to take one of the most vital elements of foreign policy, the authority to declare war, out of the hands of the Government."

In the meanwhile, the Secretary of State continued to assert with the eloquence of a Lincoln or a Gladstone the fundamental principles of international good conduct. In the summer of 1936, he had set out his international creed in Buenos Aires, in a speech entitled " The Eight Pillars of Peace." To all of us who shared the same ideas about right behaviour, his propositions seemed not only admirable, but incontrovertible. Indeed, they were described as the Sermon on the Mount applied to international affairs. But what sanction was there behind them? And how were they to be applied in specific instances? It was certainly disquieting that both Hitler and Mussolini felt able immediately to accept them, and that the Secretary of State pointedly refrained from any suggestion of American action if they failed to carry them out.

In the meantime the President made no secret either of his hatred of dictatorships and his determination to keep the United States out of war. All the available evidence, moreover, pointed to the fact that, whilst Roosevelt sympathised with the democracies, he neither would nor could risk a conflict with his own isolationists. His policy throughout, as it seemed to us, was not to lead the American people step by step into war with the dictators, but rather to modify the extremer forms of American

[1] *The Memoirs of Cordell Hull*, Vol. I, page 563.

isolationism, and within the limits allowed him by public opinion, cautiously to weight the scales in favour of the democracies. Faced as we were with the threat of an imminent conflagration, it seemed dangerous in the extreme to postpone action that we believed at the time to be the most likely to prevent the fire, in the hope that eventually America would join us in salvaging the ruins of Europe.

I have stated these facts in no censorious spirit. Americans, like ourselves, could not easily bring themselves to abandon the belief that, after a century of freedom from world war, the war of 1914 was an act of unique madness that would never be repeated. Indeed, they had been sedulously educated to believe that the war was not only a failure, but a fraud, that only profited un-scrupulous Europeans. They had a further reason for turning away from the European turmoil. Europe, the continent that they and their ancestors had left with the definite intention of living their lives aloof from their former troubles, had little to attract them, particularly after their financial losses in Germany during the economic crash of 1931, and the failure of collective security in the subsequent years. When, therefore, I emphasise these evidences of isolationism, it is not because I wish to shift the blame from British to American shoulders, or to suggest that there were not many reasons for the American attitude. It is not for us who, throughout the nineteenth century, gloried in our policy of splendid isolation, to blame the Americans for being isolationists in the twentieth. Indeed, the pacifism that was so general in England during the years between the wars was in many ways the counterpart of the isolationism that was so persistent in America. If, however, there were good reasons for the American attitude, there were equally strong reasons for British doubts. In January, 1938, Chamberlain was convinced that American isolationism made effective American action impossible. It was this conviction more than any other reason that not only made him impatient of American lectures on international conduct, and American re-iteration of moral principles, but more than ever forced his mind in the only direction that then seemed likely to avert war, the negotiation of specific, and probably limited, agreements, first with Mussolini, and secondly with Hitler.

Roosevelt was aware of Chamberlain's intentions, and judging from his later statement upon the Anglo-Italian Agreement in the following April, did not disapprove of them. Chamberlain's policy was in fact clear and definite. If, however, it was to succeed, it was necessary to pursue it consistently, and to avoid deviations that would shift it into a contrary direction. As ecumenical conferences and general statements of moral principles had constantly failed to stop the dictators, the time had come to try a different approach to peace. Only the future would show whether it could succeed. If, however, it was to have a fair trial, it was essential to avoid confusing it with the discarded alternative. The two methods were not suddenly interchangeable. Chamberlain was bent upon trying out to the full his programme of gradual and specific agreements upon each of the chief questions that were endangering peace. An abrupt turn to a different path not only delayed the journey, but made it very unlikely that he would ever reach his destination.

This was the background of the correspondence between Chamberlain and Roosevelt in the early weeks of 1938. I deal with it in some detail as it brings out the difference between the two lines of approach to peace, and at the same time, meets the charge that Chamberlain lightly and irresponsibly rejected a valuable offer. The correspondence shows, in fact, the care and patience with which both he and Roosevelt discussed their respective attitudes, and the eventual success of their efforts in removing mutual misunderstandings.

The first telegram, as I have already stated, arrived from Lindsay on January 11. It was marked " very secret and immediate," and conveyed a personal message from the President to the Prime Minister. The President asked for the Prime Minister's approval within a week of a proposal that he wished to make to the representatives of all the diplomatic missions in Washington on January 22. The Heads of Missions were to be summoned to the White House to hear a speech in which he would first describe the horrors of modern warfare and the growing burden of expenditure upon armaments. He would then appeal to all governments to agree upon the essential and fundamental principles which should be observed in international relations, the most effective methods of achieving the limitation and reduction of armaments, and the means by which all peoples might obtain the right of access upon equal and effective terms to raw materials and other elements necessary for their economic life.

He would next proceed to say that:

" In the unhappy event of war," there should be agreement on " rights and obligations of governments, both on land and sea, except in so far as, in the case of certain nations, they may be determined by existing international agreements and laws and customs of warfare whose observance neutrals may be entitled to require."

Then came the specific proposal for carrying the plan into effect.

" Should it be found, as I hope it may be, that other governments of the world are favourably disposed to this suggestion, and should they so desire, the U.S. Government will be prepared to request a number of other governments to join it immediately in the formulation of tentative proposals in elaboration of the points above enunciated for subsequent submission to all nations for such disposal as they may in their wisdom determine."

The governments that the President had in mind for this purpose were the Netherlands, Belgium, Switzerland, Yugoslavia, and five from South America, about ten in number, and all of them to a greater or less degree detached from the chief centres of international trouble.

Lastly, the President added a very significant paragraph.

" The traditional policy of freedom from political involvement, which the U.S. Government has maintained, and will maintain, is well known. In the determination of political frontiers the U:S. Government can play no part."

The message came, in Chamberlain's own words, as " a bolt from the blue." Only some weeks before, the President's cautious attempt to outflank the isolationist front had ended in the fierce reaction against his ' Quarantine ' speech. Still more recently, Norman Davis had, under instructions from Washington, made it clear at the Brussels Conference on the Japanese invasion of Manchuria that the United States would not undertake any obligation that might lead to intervention against Japan. Was there not, therefore, some justification for Chamberlain's doubts about the usefulness of Roosevelt's proposal, particularly at the moment when, with Roosevelt's knowledge, he had just begun his specific negotiation with Mussolini? Chamberlain's first reaction was not unnaturally one of considerable perturbation. The delays and dangers of an ill-prepared international conference seemed likely to destroy his hope of concrete agreements upon specific points.

None the less, he soon realised that, however dangerously the President's plan might cut across his own, it would be both unwise and wrong to give a curt refusal to any suggestion of American co-operation, even though it was vague and inconvenient. Lindsay had underlined the President's interest in the plan, and the danger to Anglo-American relations if we refused to give it " a quick and cordial reception." Accordingly there followed a series of telegrams with the object of clarifying any differences between Washington and London, and ending with what practically amounted to a reversal of our respective positions. It was, in fact, we who finally agreed to support the proposal, and Roosevelt who decided that the moment was no longer suitable for pressing it.

Throughout, we were acting under great pressure. Chamberlain was expected to give an urgent answer in less than a week although the proposed programme involved the discussion of all the most intractable questions that had failed to find an answer since the First World War. Disarmament, raw materials, belligerent and neutral rights, the essential principles of international conduct—these were the very problems that had baffled the world for nearly twenty years and that he now wished to be discussed in a Conference without any preparatory agreement. Was a committee of ten of the lesser Powers, we asked ourselves, likely to find an agreed agenda on these almost insoluble problems? In any case, could there be swift action on any ambitious plan? Doubts like these were made the more disturbing by the declaration at the end of the message, that the U.S. Government would on no account change its " traditional policy of freedom from political involvement."

Chamberlain was so sure that the proposal was ill-considered that he did not wait to summon the Foreign Policy Committee. It would have been difficult to arrange a meeting at short notice during the recess, and there was no time for delay. Besides, he knew that the members of the committee supported him in his approach to Mussolini, and that they would disapprove of any plan that cut across it. He therefore sent the interm answer on

January 13 thanking the President for his "courageous initiative," and suggesting that as we were engaged upon specific negotiations with Italy and Germany, the President might wish to consider whether " there was not a risk of his proposal cutting across our efforts," and if this were so, whether it would not be better to reconsider the timing of his plan and of any public announcement.

The President replied without any delay on January 16 that he agreed to postpone the announcement. Eden had now returned to London, and thinking that our telegram had been too negative and abrupt, recommended a further explanation of our position in which it should be made clear that in our negotiations with Mussolini we were only considering the recognition of the Italian claim to Abyssinia as part of a general settlement of Anglo-Italian differences. A second telegram was, therefore, sent to Roosevelt which, judging from his reply on January 18, fully satisfied him:

> " I greatly appreciate the very frank and friendly spirit in which the Prime Minister has replied. The full and detailed information which the Prime Minister has been good enough to send me as to the steps already taken and at present contemplated by H.M.G. has been particularly helpful to me. . . . I am willing to defer making the proposal. But keep me informed."

A change had clearly taken place in the President's mind. There had also been a change in Chamberlain's. Realising more fully the importance that Roosevelt attached to his plan, Chamberlain became more than ever anxious not to disappoint him. He therefore telegraphed on January 21 that there was no longer any need to defer the President's statement, and that if the President took the initiative, the British Government would support it. Roosevelt expressed his " deep gratification " at this message, but nothing further happened until February 10, when we were told that the President had decided to postpone the plan " for the time being." Once again, on February 12, we informed him that, so far from opposing it, we would willingly co-operate in carrying it into execution. The reply came that, as the President was leaving Washington on February 16, he would not launch the plan until his return on February 23. In the meanwhile, Chamberlain's statements of foreign policy in the House of

Commons met with the President's full approval. According to Sumner Welles, the Under-Secretary of State:

" The opinion of the President and of every responsible minister of the Administration was that the intended procedure of H.M.G. as described in the Prime Minister's statements to Parliament was entirely right and that present prospects were favourable."

A fortnight afterwards, on March 13, the President again expressed " warm appreciation of the Prime Minister's messages," but, adding that as his plan was indefinitely postponed, " the opportunity would not recur."

So ended in friendly understanding an incident that has been magnified into a critical breach between Washington and London. What neither Chamberlain nor any of us knew at the time was the inner history at the back of Roosevelt's proposal. Both Cordell Hull, the Secretary of State, and Sumner Welles, the Under-Secretary, have since published the details of the battle that went on behind the scenes in the State Department.[1] The story that they have told completes my own memories of the Roosevelt-Chamberlain telegrams, and confirms my conclusions that we were justified in treating the Roosevelt proposal with caution. It also disposes of the charge that our hesitations at a critical turning point compromised Anglo-American relations.

It was Sumner Welles who put the idea of an international conference into Roosevelt's mind. His plan was that on Armistice Day, 1937, the President should summon to the White House the Heads of Missions in Washington, and, in a highly dramatic atmosphere, confront them suddenly with his proposals. Whilst Roosevelt was evidently attracted by this spectacular programme, Cordell Hull was strongly opposed to it. Having experienced at the World Economic Conference the difficulties and dangers inherent in international proposals that had not been fully thought out, and having, in his " Eight Pillars of Peace " speech, formulated without any result the right principles of international conduct, Cordell Hull regarded the plan as both futile and dangerous. To quote his own words:[2]

" When I found that the President was all for going ahead with

[1] The Memoirs of Cordell Hull (Hodder and Stoughton). Seven Major Decisions, Sumner Welles (Hamish Hamilton).
[2] The Memoirs of Cordell Hull, Vol. I, page 547.

the Armistice Day drama in the White House, I earnestly argued against the project as being illogical and impossible. I outlined the situation to Mr. Roosevelt as I saw it. At this late stage in 1937, Germany, Japan and Italy had pushed their rearmament so far that there could be no doubt that it was intended for offence, not defence, for conquest, not for peace. It would be fatal to lull the democracies into a feeling of tranquillity through a peace congress, at the very moment when their utmost efforts should actually be directed toward arming themselves for self-defence.

" Welles' somewhat pyrotechnical plan was to be ' sprung on Armistice Day,' without any advance consultation or sounding out of the other nations. Not to ascertain in advance the opinion of Britain and France, at least, seemed unwise and unfair. They were at that moment engaged in delicate negotiations with Germany and Italy; they were trying to keep alive and functioning the Non-intervention Committee for Spain; and to ' spring ' so ambitious a project on them without warning might seriously embarrass them."

In face of the Secretary of State's opposition, the programme for Armistice Day was dropped. The substance of the plan was, however, revived some weeks later, when Cordell Hull reluctantly agreed to it, but only on the condition that the comments of the British Government were first obtained. Our comments neither surprised nor disappointed him, and it is clear from his memoirs that he was even more sceptical than we were of any good results from an international conference. We in London knew nothing of the controversy between the Secretary of State and the Under-Secretary. All that we observed was the President's readiness to heed Chamberlain's words of caution.

So far as we could judge, no feelings of resentment remained after the exchange of telegrams. Indeed, as the result of Chamberlain's explanations, there was afterwards in Washington a better understanding of British intentions. The result was shown two months later when the President issued the following statement on the Anglo-Italian Agreement, the direct result of Chamberlain's policy:

" Whilst the United States Government does not attempt to pass judgment upon the political features of accords such as that recently reached between Great Britain and Italy, it has seen the conclusion of an agreement with sympathetic interest because it is a proof of the value of peaceful negotiations."

Chamberlain, after a first impulse of annoyance at what seemed to be the crossing of his political wires, became more sympathetic to the President's attitude after the interchange of the messages between London and Washington, Roosevelt seemed completely satisfied, and Cordell Hull has left on record a tribute to the good relations that existed between the State Department and London. To quote once more the Secretary of State's own words:

" I had become very well acquainted with the new Prime Minister at the London Economic Conference in 1933, where we worked together almost daily for six weeks. He was unassuming, agreeable, and frank, and I enjoyed the conversation and conferences in which he took part. I learned quite a little of his personality, political leanings, and record. This knowledge stood me well in hand in dealing with the British Government when Chamberlain became Prime Minister. The Chamberlain Government was always accessible to us and was disposed to consider seriously any matters we presented to it and to give us frank replies."[1]

Each side in fact, had come to appreciate the other's point of view. As the result of the mutual explanations, Roosevelt realised more clearly than before the importance of an Anglo-Italian agreement, whilst Chamberlain, convinced of the value of American interest in the affairs of Europe, withdrew his opposition to a proposal that in its first form seemed to endanger his efforts for peace. If Roosevelt was disappointed at finding obstacles in the path of his ambitious and spectacular programme, he none the less recognised the strength of our arguments, and felt no resentment at Chamberlain's hesitations. Indeed, in the months that followed, Anglo-American relations became increasingly intimate, and culminated in the parallel efforts that Washington and London made throughout the Czechoslovak crisis.

[1] *The Memoirs of Cordell Hull*, Vol. 1, page 531.

CHAPTER XXIII

Eden's Resignation

AT HOME the episode, however it had ended, had struck a discordant note in what appeared to be the general harmony of the Cabinet. Eden, although he approved of the later communications to Roosevelt, continued to feel that he ought to have been more fully consulted about the original telegram, and that our immediate response should have been more friendly. It was certainly unfortunate that he was in the South of France at the time that the first telegram was sent, and that Roosevelt's request for an immediate reply made it very difficult to delay it until his return. Whilst I doubt whether our answer would have been substantially altered if he had been in London, or whether indeed he would not have himself agreed with it, he had some reason for feeling that the Foreign Secretary had not been sufficiently consulted upon an important issue of foreign policy. This was particularly regrettable, as he and Chamberlain, though they had hitherto worked well together, undoubtedly approached foreign affairs from different angles. Chamberlain regarded them pragmatically in the same way as he regarded domestic questions. General principles were much less important to him than what he himself called ' piecemeal ' modifications. Eden, whose reputation had been made in the League of Nations, was much nearer to the Roosevelt position of international action based on broad legal and moral principles. The events of January accentuated this difference of outlook, although it was not for another two or three weeks that it was publicly exposed. Indeed, on February 13, after the further interchange of telegrams with Roosevelt, Chamberlain was writing to his sister:

" I saw Anthony on Friday morning and we were in complete agreement, more complete perhaps than we have sometimes been in the past."

Yet, within a week of this letter, the Foreign Secretary had resigned, the apparent reason being a difference between him and the Prime Minister over the timing of the Italian negotiations. Eden, whilst anxious for an Anglo-Italian agreement, was opposed to the opening of any negotiations before Italian troops in substantial numbers had actually been withdrawn from Spain. Chamberlain, obsessed with the need for speed and the imminent danger of another German *coup* after the occupation of Vienna, wished to profit immediately by Mussolini's anxiety to begin the talks. He insisted, however, on the condition that no agreement would be ratified until the withdrawal of troops had begun. The ostensible difference, therefore, was not one of principle, but of the timing of the start of the negotiations. Both were equally determined to withhold the ratification of any agreement until Mussolini had shown his good faith by actually withdrawing Italian troops from Spain. Chamberlain, who had already begun direct conversations with Grandi in London, was bent upon keeping the initiative. I remember hearing him press the case for speed at one of Philip Sassoon's luncheon parties of Ministers on February 11, when Eden and Cadogan were both in favour of great caution. The following day, Chamberlain and Eden met Grandi, and the two different points of view at once emerged in the strongest possible relief.

Eden wished to discover Mussolini's reactions to Hitler's Austrian *coup*, and to postpone the start of the negotiations until the position was clarified. Chamberlain, on the other hand, felt that any delay would destroy the goodwill between the two countries that he had created since he became Prime Minister, and that, once lost, might be very difficult to recover. Grandi was even more anxious than Chamberlain to avoid the Austrian issue and restrict any discussion to the question of Anglo-Italian relations. When, therefore, Eden asked him to come to the Foreign Office, the Ambassador made the excuse of a golf engagement for not accepting the invitation. Chamberlain, at the same time, urgently wished to see Grandi about the Italian negotiations, and Grandi, guessing what was in Chamberlain's mind, was ready to go

to Downing Street, as he rightly assumed that the talk would not
be about Mussolini's reactions to Hitler's Austrian *coup*, but about
Mussolini's relations with Great Britain. Whilst this was the
position in London, Ciano in Rome was pressing Perth for direct
talks between the Prime Minister and Grandi. It was to break
the deadlock between the Foreign Office and the Italian Embassy
that Chamberlain stepped outside the channel of regular communication, and used as a go-between an official in the Conservative Party Office, who had worked with him for many years,
to propose to Grandi a meeting in Downing Street. The background of this unconventional approach was found in a long-
standing contact between Chamberlain's messenger and a sub-
ordinate member of the Italian Embassy. Whilst the Foreign
Office knew of the association and attached little importance to
it, it had occasionally provided Chamberlain with scraps of
information that had helped him to assess Mussolini's attitude
towards the negotiations, and in particular, towards the question
of the withdrawal of Italian troops from Spain. When, therefore,
an *impasse* had been reached between the Foreign Office and the
Italian Embassy, he turned to his old confidant, and authorised
him to make it known to the Ambassador, through the intermediary at the Embassy, that he would welcome a visit to Downing
Street.

There followed the long discussion between Grandi, Chamberlain and Eden in Downing Street on February 12. Grandi,
delighted with the importance that the interview gave him, and
the chance of painting the kind of picture that Mussolini wished
to see, immediately described in a lengthy dispatch to Ciano his
version of the story.[1] The picture that he produced could not have
been more vivid and dramatic. Chamberlain's secret intrigues to
circumvent the Foreign Office, the meetings with the intermediary, the battle between Chamberlain and Eden before
Grandi's eyes—what a subject for an ambassador with Grandi's
lively imagination! Certainly the Ambassador made the most of
his subject, and produced as good a story as was ever put into a
diplomatic dispatch. Indeed, it was one of those pictures that
had every quality except a resemblance to the original. Grandi's
claim that he had " almost daily contacts " with Chamberlain's

[1] *L'Europa verso la catastrophe*, by Galeazzo, Ciano, p. 249 and following (*Mondadori
editore*).

messenger greatly exaggerated what had actually happened. In point of fact, he himself seldom saw the messenger, and the later story that has been circulated, that they met in a taxi, is entirely untrue. The two intermediaries exchanged information from time to time on a much lower level. Unofficial contacts of this kind have not been uncommon in Whitehall. In this case, the Foreign Office regarded them as unnecessary rather than objectionable or dangerous. There was no mystery about the meeting. Chamberlain's determination to short-circuit delays was as well known to the Foreign Office as it was to Grandi. It was Grandi's own action in exaggerating the incident, and still more in prematurely divulging a suggested communiqué, that not only gave the meeting a sinister aspect, but gravely compromised the chances of an Anglo-Italian agreement.

The interview ended with a promise that Chamberlain would definitely inform the Italian Government on the following Monday as to whether or not we were prepared to begin the negotiations. It was agreed that in the meanwhile there would be no public statement of any kind. The Italian Embassy, however, immediately divulged the story, and by doing so, undoubtedly widened the breach between the Foreign Secretary and the Prime Minister. The next day, Eden went to his constituency. When he returned to London, he had already made up his mind to resign. What had seemed to be a difference of opinion over method, had become a more fundamental difference of principle as to whether negotiations should ever begin with a dictator. The issue was no longer the date at which the negotiations should start, but whether there should be any negotiations at all.

" I have gradually arrived at the conclusion "—these are Chamberlain's own words in a letter to his sister—" that at bottom Anthony did not want to talk either with Hitler or Mussolini, and as I did, he was right to go."

Eden's resignation came as a surprise and shock to his Cabinet colleagues, to Duff Cooper and his more intimate friends as much as to any. Halifax and several others did everything in their power to persuade him to withdraw it. We had continued to hope that his differences with Chamberlain were over details of method. We had eventually to admit that they went far deeper. It may be

that the not unnatural resentment of a younger man against an
older man's interference entered into them. It may also be that
Eden's personal supporters were anxious to force an issue between
the Prime Minister and the Foreign Secretary. In any case, it
became clear that Chamberlain and the Cabinet were in favour
of an early start of the Italian negotiations, and that Eden was
not. The result was the loss of a Foreign Secretary who, if he
could have continued to work with Chamberlain, would have
greatly helped and influenced the subsequent negotiations with
his wide experience and exceptional qualities. As it was, his
departure left a serious gap in the ranks of the Cabinet. At the
moment when we most needed an unbroken front in face of the
dictators, a division appeared that was certain to be exploited by
our enemies abroad and by party politicians at home.

It was hoped at the time that Eden's resignation would
facilitate Chamberlain's policy, and that the new Foreign
Secretary would close any breach that existed between the Foreign
Office and Downing Street. Halifax was Eden's obvious successor.
Universally respected, and possessing many of the qualities that
had established the reputations of his ancestor, Lord Grey, and
his kinsman, Sir Edward Grey, he was pre-eminent among the
Conservative Ministers for character and judgment. In India he
had shown his wisdom in reconciling bitter differences. Communal troubles had become less acute under his mediating
influence, Gandhi had become his personal friend. Might he not
have the same success in Europe that he had won in Asia? In any
case, his qualities were exactly those that Chamberlain needed for
his considered and concentrated programme of appeasement. The
two men would obviously work well together and never get out of
step. Any internal differences within the Foreign Office would
become less serious under the man who had kept the Indian Civil
Service stable and loyal in a period of great tension. The result
justified the hopes placed on the new combination. The conduct
of foreign affairs was no longer subject to internal strains, not,
indeed, because the Prime Minister dominated the Foreign
Secretary, but because the Prime Minister and the Foreign
Secretary were fundamentally agreed upon British policy. The
suggestion that Halifax merely said " Yes " to Chamberlain's
ideas is altogether baseless. Chamberlain always listened with
sympathy and respect to Halifax's views, and frequently, as the

result of hearing them, modified his own. Halifax's influence in the Cabinet was great and persistent.

The appointment, however excellent in itself, had one unfortunate result. It still further involved the Prime Minister in the day-to-day details of foreign affairs in the House of Commons. With a Foreign Secretary in the House of Lords, Chamberlain was forced to answer scores of questions in the House of Commons about the Civil War in Spain and the Japanese in China, whilst in the frequent debates upon foreign policy, it was the Prime Minister who had to bear the brunt of the Opposition attacks. The effect of these responsibilities in the House of Commons was to stimulate his remarkable aptitude for combative debate, and to underline the differences between his own ideas and those of his opponents. If Halifax had still been a member of the House of Commons, although the policy would have remained the same, the Prime Minister would have been shielded from the daily wrangles that then embittered almost every discussion of foreign affairs.

Chamberlain had frequently consulted Halifax upon questions of foreign policy before he became Foreign Secretary, and on one well-known occasion, had made use of his services in an attempt to improve Anglo-German relations.

This was in the winter of 1937, when Halifax visited Goering and Hitler. As the episode occasioned much criticism and not a little ridicule, it is worth recording what actually happened. With the full approval of the Foreign Secretary, and, indeed, of the whole Cabinet, Chamberlain had just begun his systematic efforts for lowering the political temperature of Europe and the Far East. It seemed at the time that direct approaches to the dictators afforded the best chance of progress. At this moment Halifax, as Master of the Middleton Foxhounds, received an invitation from Goering in his capacity as Chief Huntsman of the Reich to attend a Hunting Exhibition in Berlin. Goering, whose *manie de la chasse* was already notorious, wished no doubt to advertise himself as the patron saint of German sport. At first, Halifax laughed at the invitation, and all the more so, as it proposed a *battue* of foxes as one of the principal attractions. His immediate impulse, therefore, was to throw it into the wastepaper basket, but before he did so, he mentioned it to Eden, who thought that it was worth considering. The result was a talk with both Chamberlain and Eden in which it was agreed that an informal contact with Goering, and possibly afterwards with Hitler, might be helpful to the cause of peace.

He therefore accepted the invitation, and spent the time that had been set aside for shooting foxes, in talks with Goering and Hitler. Whilst I shall revert later to the results of personal talks of this kind, I have alluded to the hunting visit at this point for two reasons. It was evidence both of the Government's determination to seize every opportunity to remove dangerous misunderstandings, and of Halifax's active share in foreign affairs before he actually became Foreign Secretary. The visit was part of Chamberlain's governing plan from which he could not be deflected either by criticism or ridicule.

The visit failed to produce any good result. There was nothing in common between Halifax and Hitler. The fact that Hitler completely underrated Halifax's qualities exposed the narrow limits of the Führer's outlook. If anything emerged from the talks, it was the bleak sight of the wide gulf that had to be bridged if peace was to be assured.

The immediate sequel could scarcely have been worse. Within a few weeks Hitler occupied Vienna. Although we had been warned that his next objective would be Austria, we did not contemplate a sudden military occupation. Indeed, the *coup* seems to have taken even Ribbentrop by surprise. On the day when the German tanks entered Vienna, Ribbentrop was in London, for the purpose of taking leave of the British Government at the end of his very unsuccessful mission as German Ambassador.

I was at the farewell luncheon given for him in Downing Street. In view of the Ambassador's admitted failure at the Court of St. James, it was certain to be a grim affair, but to make it even grimmer, a messenger arrived towards the end of it with an urgent telegram announcing the seizure of Vienna. Cadogan, after reading it, handed it to Halifax, who at once showed it to Chamberlain. The three then left the dining-room, taking with them Ribbentrop. When they told him the news in another room, he seemed completely taken aback. Halifax was convinced that either he knew nothing of the *coup*, or that, if he did, he was a most successful and barefaced liar in concealing his knowledge of it. Whichever was the case, we were left to finish the luncheon in an atmosphere of icy coldness. The shock that we suffered immediately made itself felt throughout Great Britain and France. It was, however, evident that, deeply as both countries resented Hitler's brutal action, neither the British nor the French people were prepared to go to war to prevent German Austria from becoming a part of the German Reich. Indeed, there were many who believed that Austria, in the truncated form to which it had been reduced by the Treaty of Versailles, could not exist as an independent state. Walford Selby, our Minister in Vienna, had done his best to impress upon us the contrary view. On the other hand, Neville Henderson in Berlin was convinced that the Reich was certain to absorb it, and that the only possible course was to accept the inevitable. So long as there was a comparatively quiescent Germany, and Mussolini was not committed to Hitler, it had been possible to maintain a precarious state of affairs. In February and March of 1938, however, there was no chance of stopping Hitler except by war or a threat of war, and neither we nor the French were prepared to fight against what was claimed to be the unification of the German people. The result as far as Hitler was concerned, was the winning of a strategic position in readiness for a move against Czechoslovakia.

Confronted with this failure in Central Europe, Chamberlain turned his eyes nearer home. The forces of peace needed to be strengthened in the British Isles as well as on the Continent. Breaches in the Home Front compromised and might even endanger his whole campaign for peace. Good relations with Eire, therefore, were an essential factor in his general policy. So far from their being satisfactory, he found them embittered by the refusal of the Government of Eire to carry out its financial obligations under the Irish Treaty of 1921. Our reply had been the imposition of penal duties on Irish imports into the United Kingdom. A complete deadlock had been created, and with it, an opportunity for stirring up the old animosities against Great Britain that were very near the surface both in Eire and the United States. It required courage as well as foresight to set aside our legitimate grievances and make an agreement that waived almost all our financial claims, and abandoned the rights that we retained under the Irish Treaty of 1921 in three ports that were regarded as strategically important. As Home Secretary, the Minister who was responsible in London for our relations with Ulster, I was one of his colleagues at the Conference. The discussions were long and often tedious. It was a conflict of patient argument between the two Prime Ministers, Chamberlain on the one hand, concrete and very practical, de Valera on the other, romantic and diffuse, ready to go back to Strongbow and Cromwell upon the slightest provocation, and not to be deflected from his historical lectures by any limit of time, but each in his own way prepared to continue the discussions until they reached the agreement that was signed on April 25. My part was to keep in contact with Craigavon, the wise statesman who was Prime Minister of Northern Ireland, and who, to his great credit, placed no obstacle in the way of the negotiations.

In the midst of the crisis over Austria, the importance of the Irish agreement was not fully realised, and since the war, it has been violently criticised for the surrender of the Treaty Ports. In point of fact, the Chiefs of Staff regarded our rights in the three ports as a liability rather than an asset. One of them afterwards went so far as to declare that if we had the use of the French ports we did not want the Irish ports, and if the French ports were lost, the Irish would be of no use to us. In any case, Chamberlain was fully prepared to face criticism in an effort to remove the causes of friction between the two countries, and to take a definite step forward in the campaign for European peace. Over and above the improved relations between Britain and Eire, there was the great gain of a more friendly atmosphere in the United States, where hostile Irish opinion had so persistent and dangerous an influence.

CHAPTER XXIV

The Road to Munich

HITLER LOST no time in making his next move. With Austria in his possession, the Czech southern frontier was wide open to the enemy. The Czech defences had been turned, and the army left powerless to withstand an invasion, whilst on all sides the Republic was surrounded by potential foes. The chance had been given him to destroy the chief bastion of the Little Entente, and to eliminate a formidable obstacle to German aggression in Central Europe.

To make his task easier, providence had provided him with the grievances of the Sudeten Germans. So much has been written of them that I will assume as accepted the story of the agitation before and during 1938, and will only describe my personal reactions during the protracted crisis that led up to Munich.

Since the First World War I had taken a very close interest in the Czechoslovak movement that led to the recognition of the Republic, and I had followed with sincere admiration the fortunes of the new State. When I was head of military missions in Russia and Italy between 1916 and 1919, I had been brought into intimate contact with Masaryk, Benes and Stefanek, the three great leaders who had, almost unaided, created Czechoslovakia.

Masaryk and Benes I met before I went to Russia in 1916. They were then in London, and Seton Watson brought us together. He and I helped to prevent their internment by the British Government as enemy aliens. We were also able to introduce them to several Ministers who hitherto knew nothing of Czechoslovak aspirations. I remember in particular a luncheon that I gave at the Marlborough Club in order that Milner should make

Benes's acquaintance. Throughout luncheon, Milner maintained
a stiff and sceptical reserve to all Benes's powers of persuasion. It
was typical of the general attitude. Scarcely anyone at that time
took serious account of the Czech movement. None the less, thanks
almost entirely to the united efforts of the three leaders, the
Czechoslovak cause prospered, and the National Committee in
Paris steadily developed into the Provisional Government of the
Czechoslovak State. Unlike the leaders of the other national
movements, the three men were always agreed amongst themselves. They formed, in fact, a superb trio in which each played
his part in perfect harmony with the others. When their help was
needed for breaking the Austrian front, Masaryk went to Russia
to organise the Czech prisoners in Tsarist hands, and Benes to
Italy to start propaganda amongst the Slav prisoners and the
Slav units of the Austrian Army on the Italian front. I helped
them both. In particular, I was able to obtain permission for
Benes to visit the Italian front, and I also arranged for him an
interview with Sonnino, the very anti-Slav Foreign Minister. It
was then also that I fell under the spell of the third of the trio—
the brilliant Stefanek, the Slovak who had started the war as a
cook in a French regiment, and whose overriding anxiety was lest
his routine cooking should spoil his mathematical and astro-
nomical studies. One night in Rome, where he was helping Benes
with his Slav propaganda, we dined together and afterwards
visited the Colosseum by moonlight. Being a poet and an artist,
he immediately reacted to the surroundings, and before the night
was out, proposed marriage to the beautiful lady who afterwards
became his devoted wife. As Masaryk was the hero of the Czechs,
so was Stefanek the hero of the Slovaks. When the war ended, a
triumphant return to Slovakia was prepared for him. It was to
be by air, as he refused to set foot on the hated territory of Austria
and Hungary. When the aeroplane was over his native village it
crashed, and he was killed. So ended the life of this Slovak Icarus
and my friendship with a man who might have been of priceless
help to his Slovak countrymen in the difficult days to come.

With Masaryk my association continued until his death.
More than once I had the privilege of staying with him in Prague,
and of listening to the conversation of one who seemed to me the
wisest man that I ever met. One of my pleasantest memories is of
a visit to his country house at Lani, where, at the end of a day that

started with a ride on his favourite grey horse and continued with
the intensive study of every detail of government in the new State,
he sat in an upright chair after supper in the evening, and in his
quiet, dry voice, made what diplomats call a *tour d'horizon* of the
world. With what broad wisdom and unique wealth of detailed
knowledge he discoursed upon England and America, France and
Germany, Slav and Teuton:

When he finished, two impressions remained in my mind.
The first was of his irreconcilable opposition to any attempt to
re-create Vienna as the capital of Central Europe. Although the
most liberal-minded of men, his toleration stopped short when it
became a question of modifying the peace settlement that had
created the Succession States. The hatred of Austrian domination
had entered into his soul; the suspicion of Vienna and the
memory of its German bureaucracy had never left him. It was
not so much that the Hapsburg system had been violently tyran-
nical or cruel, as that it had been ignorant and patronising. When
the Czechs were preserving their national identity by their passion
for education and their cult of physical fitness, it had been
especially galling for brilliant intellectuals like himself to see easy-
going and obscurantist Austrians in control of the country's daily
life. Western Europe liked the Austrians, and could never understand the bitterness of the feelings that the dual monarchy had
excited amongst the Czechs. The brilliance of Vienna made the
bourgeois life of Prague seem drab and unattractive. Masaryk,
who looked beneath the surface, regarded the Austrian domination
as an evil and corrupting influence. I particularly emphasise this
anti-German feeling in the most tolerant of Czechs, as it had a
very direct bearing upon the Sudeten crisis.

The second impression was of his belief in a federal system for
Czechoslovakia. Federations appealed to him, as to most liberals.
In the case of Czechoslovakia, he outlined to me the kind of
federal régime that he hoped to create, and, incidentally, told me
that he had never asked for the inclusion of the Sudeten Germans
in the Czech State. His words have since convinced me that, had
he been ten years younger, he would have achieved his purpose
and prevented the nationalist crisis that gave Hitler his pretext
and opportunity for intervention.

Benes, left to himself after Masaryk's death, and deprived of
the massive support that only the philosopher president could give

him, was not the man to change a highly centralised Czech administration into a federation of nationalities. He was essentially a very able and active Czech politician. His whole career had been founded on the organisation of the Czech political forces of resistance. With the Czech party machine behind him, and a meticulously drawn centralised constitution to control him, it was certain from the start of the Sudeten crisis that he would move reluctantly and painfully towards any fundamental change in the accepted policy of his party. He has since been blamed for want of flexibility. In point of fact, he was naturally very flexible, as his diplomatic successes had proved during the First World War. I have never criticised him for obstinacy. To have adjusted his mind, however, to a change that was diametrically opposed to his party's policy needed so abrupt a turn that without Masaryk's powerful support, it was almost impossible for him to make it. A brilliant politician and true Czech patriot, his narrower mind could never have embraced the wide horizons of Masaryk's spacious outlook.

I have felt it well to make this preface to my account of the crisis that has come to be known as the Munich crisis for three reasons. First, I wish to make it clear that I tried my best to understand the Czech position. Secondly, I do not desire to shift the responsibility or the blame from the British and French Governments to Czech shoulders. The Czechoslovak Republic was better governed than any central European state. Both agriculture and industry made notable progress during the short period of its existence. Opinions of all kinds could be freely expressed in its press and daily life. In Masaryk and Benes it produced two of the outstanding figures in the First World War, and in Stefanek, the Chevalier Bayard of Central Europe.

Thirdly, at the outset of my comments, I must insist that, after the fall of Austria, Czechoslovakia was militarily indefensible against a swift act of aggression. The trouble was not so much Czech policy as Czech geography. If it had not been for the country's geographical position, its future might have been assured. Not, however, for the first time in history, the hard facts of geography destroyed the carefully arranged plans of statesmen and peoples. When military protection is lacking in support of a weak geographical position, the temptation to aggression is not only almost inevitable but often irresistible.

Throughout the critical days of 1938 there was never absent from our minds the vital question of British military strength. My long years at the Air Ministry had particularly made me conscious of the gaps in our air defences and the need for time to repair them. None the less, it would not be correct to say that our military weakness was the principal cause of the Munich Agreement. The over-riding consideration with Chamberlain and his colleagues was that the very complicated problem of Czechoslovakia ought not to lead to a world war, and must at almost any price be settled by peaceful means. No doubt, if we had been stronger in 1938, we should have found Hitler more ready to accept a reasonable settlement. Force was the only argument that had any permanent influence on him. To what extent, however, an increase in our military strength would have affected his set purpose, it is impossible to say. In any case, Chamberlain was not prepared to go beyond an agreement to transfer the Sudeten Germans to the German Reich, even though he knew that militarily we were in a vulnerable condition. Where the question of defence decisively influenced the course of the controversy was not so much because we were militarily weak, as because it was geographically impossible for us to stop a German occupation of Czechoslovakia. For some time past we had been forced to the conclusion that after Hitler's absorption of Austria, nothing short of a world war could prevent the annihilation of the Czech military forces if Hitler attacked them. This was not the cowardly opinion of weak politicians. It was the considered and consistent verdict of the Committee of Imperial Defence and the Chiefs of Staff. It was supported by the Prime Ministers of Canada and South Africa, and re-examined month after month by the British Cabinet, and always with the same conclusion. Indeed, I can remember no conclusion in the field of defence and foreign affairs that within my own experience received such constant and unanimous support. To suggest that the Cabinet's action was dictated by the Prime Minister, and that it was his personal policy of surrender at Munich, is a travesty of the facts. During 1938, Chamberlain and Halifax worked in full harmony. It would, therefore, be quite wrong to imagine that the foreign policy of the Cabinet was solely directed by the Prime Minister himself, or by the Prime Minister and the Foreign Secretary to the exclusion of their colleagues. In actual fact, no

Prime Minister ever before consulted his colleagues as fully or continuously upon questions of foreign policy. When he succeeded Baldwin, he found in existence a Foreign Policy Committee of the Cabinet that included most of the principal Ministers. Baldwin had used it intermittently for questions connected with the future of Germany and the Disarmament Conference. Chamberlain brought it into much closer contact with the Chiefs of Staff, and summoned it for advice on every one of the urgent international problems of 1938 and 1939. Between 1937 and 1939 there were over fifty meetings of the Committee. Austria, Spain, Czechoslovakia, Russia, Poland, Roumania, Greece, Turkey—the problems of each and all led to long meetings of the Committee in which the reports of the Chiefs of Staff were most carefully considered. Throughout all these discussions Chamberlain, so far from dictating a line of his own, showed himself most receptive both to the views of his colleagues and the conclusions of the experts.

To understand the course of events, it is necessary to say something of this Committee's proceedings. Like everything that concerned Chamberlain, the meetings were regular and methodical. If any criticism could be made of them, it would be that they tended to short circuit the full Cabinet. This result was inevitable. Foreign affairs were moving too quickly and dangerously for a weekly meeting of twenty Ministers to deal with them. Decisions had often to be taken very quickly. The full Cabinet, however, had always the last word upon the more important questions after hearing the explanations and recommendations of the Foreign Secretary and the Prime Minister.

Whenever a difficult international question came to the fore, the Committee, which was composed of nine or ten of the principal Ministers, was summoned. Halifax would explain the position, and Chamberlain would almost invariably be ready with suggestions for dealing with it. If it was necessary to send instructions to a foreign mission, the Committee would discuss the draft telegrams that were proposed by the Foreign Secretary. Very often, as the result of the discussion, considerable alterations would be made in the original drafts. Although Chamberlain was an excellent draftsman, he was too good a colleague to insist upon the verbal inspiration of his own words. The final form, therefore, was the result of joint discussion and not of any Prime Minister's *diktat*. His great influence in the Committee came from his convinced belief in the wisdom of the policy that he had set before himself for many months, and from his skill in explaining it. It was no secret to any of us that, long before he became Prime Minister, he had fretted under the easy-going methods of Baldwin. Baldwin was not really interested in foreign affairs. Never having given them any close study, he regarded them either as a mystery to be handled apart by some Levitical caste in the Chanceries of the world, or as a disturbing diversion from the domestic questions that he understood. The result was that during the last two years of his Premiership, he never seemed to have any clear-cut idea as to what our foreign policy should be. Chamberlain, on the other hand, had the most definite views as to what was needed. Even before he succeeded Baldwin, and when he was still Chancellor of the Exchequer, he had taken the unusual course of sending a detailed memorandum to Morgenthau, the American Secretary of the Treasury, in which he had set out proposals for improving Anglo-American relations. He had followed the same line of personal approach in the letter to Mussolini that I have already mentioned, and that Henderson in Berlin was instructed to follow up with suggestions to Hitler for a general *modus vivendi*. Each of these moves was a part of his plans for peace.

There was, however, another side of his policy that has never been fully appreciated. Intent as he was upon peace, he was keenly alive to the need for British rearmament. From the first, he realised that his peace plans were most likely to succeed if we were militarily strong, and that if they failed, we were very vulnerable. Side by side, therefore, with his efforts for peace, he was continually insisting on expediting and enlarging the programme of rearmament that Baldwin had started in 1934. The fact that the programme moved slowly was not due to any want of support on his part, but to the prevailing conditions that I shall try later to describe.

It was in the late summer of 1938 that the Inner Cabinet of Chamberlain, Halifax, Simon and myself tended to take the place of the Foreign Policy Committee. The critical situation was then changing so constantly that the summoning of a large committee became practically impossible. When Daladier and Bonnet had come to London on April 28 to discuss Hitler's Austrian *coup*, the Committee had been kept fully informed of the proceedings, but only Chamberlain and Halifax had been present at the conference. In the later conferences with the French at the end of the summer, both Simon and I took part and the Committee had then practically ceased to exist.

Shortly before the first conference, I had been exchanging letters with the Czech Minister in London, Jan Masaryk, who, like his father, was an old friend, and a man for whom I had both respect and affection. The correspondence was started at the time of Chamberlain's speech in the House of Commons on March 14[1] after Hitler's Austrian *coup*.

[1] " The House may desire me to repeat what our position in regard to Austria was. We were under no commitment to take action *vis-à-vis* Austria, but we were pledged to consultation with the French and Italian Governments in the event of action being taken which affected Austrian independence and integrity, for which provision was made by the relevant articles of the Peace Treaties. This pledge arises from agreements reached between the French, Italian and United Kingdom Governments, first in February, 1934, then in September of the same year, and finally at the Stresa Conference in April, 1935, in which the position was reaffirmed, to consult together in any measures to be taken in the case of threats to the integrity and independence of Austria. We have fully discharged the pledge of consultation with both the French Government and the Italian Government, to whom we made an immediate approach when Austrian independence seemed to be threatened by recent events. As a result of that consultation with the French Government, His Majesty's Government and the French Government addressed similar protests to the German Government on the action that had been taken. From the Italian Government we received no full exposition of their views, but their attitude has been defined with great precision in the statement issued on behalf of the Italian Government which appears in the Press to-day.

" It is quite untrue to suggest that we have ever given Germany our assent or our encouragement to the effective absorption of Austria into the German Reich. We had, indeed, never refused to recognise the special interest that Germany had in the development of relations between Austria and herself, having regard to the close affinities existing between the two countries. But on every occasion on which any representative of His Majesty's Government has had opportunities to discuss these matters with representatives of the German Government, it has always been made plain that His Majesty's Government would strongly disapprove of the application to the solution of these problems of violent methods. It must have, as I have constantly pointed out to the House, a damaging influence upon general confidence in Europe.

" In appraising recent events it is necessary to face facts, however we may judge them, however we may anticipate that they will react upon the international position as it exists to-day. The hard fact is—and of its truth every hon. Member can judge for himself—that nothing could have arrested this action by Germany unless we and others with us had been prepared to use force to prevent it. I imagine that according to the temperament of the individual the events which are in our minds to-day will be the cause of regret, of sorrow, perhaps of indignation. They cannot be regarded by His Majesty's Government with indifference or equanimity. They are bound to have effects which cannot yet be measured. The immediate result must be to intensify the sense of uncertainty and insecurity in Europe. Unfortunately, while the policy of appeasement would lead to a relaxation of the economic pressure under which many countries are suffering to-day, what has just occurred must inevitably retard economic recovery, and, indeed, increased care will be required to ensure that marked deterioration does not set in."

It began with the following letter sent me on the same day as the speech. It is perhaps worth quoting, as it shows the closeness with which I was following the crisis in the early days of the spring, and Jan Masaryk's eagerness to find a peaceful solution.

" *March 14th*

" MY DEAR SIR SAMUEL,

" It is not easy for me to write this note.

" You know how my father valued your friendship and how my sisters and I humbly follow in his footsteps in our devotion to Lady Maud and you.

" I did not approach you while the P.M.'s speech was being discussed and drafted. I remained meticulously neutral wondering at certain indications of your Government's opinions and regretting the Opposition's attitude of using Czechoslovakia as a stick to beat the Government with.

" To-day the statement is prepared and I feel I am free to write to you. I hope you will not feel it is outside my place or trespassing upon our friendship when I tell you that I am sure that whatever mistakes my Government has made in their treatment of the Germans, I think their good will is evident, to come to a lasting and satisfactory settlement. It is interesting to note how the Henlein movement followed closely on Hitler's attaining power and how the tremendous German propaganda machine has been put at the service of the Sudeten grievances. I repeat, we made mistakes (it is a prerogative of a democracy to make them and to acknowledge them), but when I see the treatment of minorities in many other countries and not a word is said, I cannot help feeling that picturing Czechoslovakia as the bad boy of Europe is unjust.

" I have tried to influence my Government in the direction of concessions and conciliation not altogether without results and I am anxious to continue to do so. But I am asking myself what is to be done now? What will satisfy Hitler? Is he only interested in the welfare of the souls of 3 million Germans or equally so in Skoda and the natural and agricultural resources of Central and South-Eastern Europe? If we make all concessions compatible with fundamental self-respect, will it be the end or the beginning of our troubles? These and similar questions are hounding me day and night. I need not tell you that I have never asked for or expected any specific guarantees or commitments from your Government— I am not so naïve.

" But what I do ask and need is advice, direct, blunt, concrete advice—not vague admonitions of the advisability of ' doing something.' My influence with Prague is not quite worn out and I would like to use it in the right direction. Maybe some day you will spare me a little time to discuss my worries with me.

" I may go to Prague for a day or two to see for myself how matters stand and when I return I will make bold and ask you to receive me. Naturally if you would like to send a message to Benes or Hodja I would delay my trip—but *please* don't think you have to.

" Excuse this long letter but you are one of the people who knows Europe and who has looked at the maps since its reshuffling —and I am trying to carry with dignity a name which in itself is a great responsibility.

" Sincerely,
" JAN MASARYK "

This very moving letter made a deep impression on me, and shortly afterwards I had a long talk with him that I later described in the following letter to Halifax.

" *25th March, 1938*

" Jan Masaryk, a very old friend of mine, asked to see me this morning before he left for Prague. I do not imagine he said anything to me that he had not already said to you. In case, however, he did, I send you the following note of the conversation.

" He told me that he had never expected that we should make a new commitment about Czechoslovakia. He himself had been urged from many quarters to ask us for a commitment, but he had steadily refused to do anything in the matter. As to the future, he was not as pessimistic as I had imagined. He admits, of course, that in any bilateral war Czechoslovakia would be quickly destroyed. None the less, the Czech Army is in his view good, nor does he believe that a majority of the Germans really desire annexation. Henlein himself would probably prefer to remain a great man in Czechoslovakia rather than a small man in Germany.

" As to the economic position he said that Czechoslovakia had satisfactory trading relations with Poland and through Gdynia with the outer world, and that their trade relations with Germany were not bad.

" What he seemed chiefly to fear was some move by us that might weaken the moral resistance of the Czech Government against the annexation of the German districts. If we and the French continued to take an interest in the integrity of the country and made it constantly clear to the German Government that this was our position, he felt that most of the South Germans would be prepared to accept concessions from Benes, but that if it looked as if annexation was only a question of time, then it would be impossible to get the South Germans to accept even the most generous arrangement.

" To my question about the possibility of a federal solution to the problem he replied that his father had originally supported the idea of a federation on the lines of Switzerland, and that he himself had not excluded the possibility of a confederation of Germans, Slovaks and Czechs. But here again it was useless to attempt such a solution if Hitler had a free hand with his propaganda and his threats.

" More than once he asked me what advice in these circumstances he ought to give his Government. I told him that I was merely speaking as an old friend and as an individual and that I had had no discussion with you upon the details of the position. My own view, however, for what it was worth, was that if I were in the position of Benes I should ask the French and British Governments to give me their good offices in helping to make a really satisfactory arrangement for the Sudeten Germans. It was much better that Benes himself should take the initiative in a matter of this kind and that there should be no suggestion of any dictation from outside as to what he ought to do with his own fellow subjects. Masaryk said that he had come to very much the same conclusion.

" He finally told me that he had been on the whole encouraged by Neville's speech. It had gone further than he expected in support of the Czechoslovak position and it was likely to have a deterrent influence upon the Germans.

" Hoping that nothing that I said was in any way an embarrassment to you."

Halifax answered on March 28:

" I am greatly interested to read your account of your conversation with Masaryk. I am very far from thinking that what you said was in any way an embarrassment to me. Far from it, for I think you gave him admirable advice."

Masaryk shortly afterwards went to Prague, and told Benes what I had said. Benes in reply sent me a friendly and optimistic answer that omitted any mention of my suggestion of Anglo-French intervention. It was clear from it that he felt that he could deal successfully with the crisis without the help of other governments. Life in Czechoslovakia was proceeding peacefully when, a few days later, I received another message from him asking me to go to Prague for the Sokol celebrations. I have always regretted that as I could not miss Cabinet meetings, I had to refuse the invitation.

This was the position as I saw it at the time of the first conference in London on April 18 with the French Ministers. Three urgent questions came up at the first session—the need for staff talks between the British and French naval, army and air staffs, the reactions of the Austrian *coup* on Central and Eastern Europe, and the policy to be adopted towards Czechoslovakia. The French, as always, were pressing for more definite British commitments, and Chamberlain, in this respect expressing the British public opinion of the time, was opposed to undertaking them. Whilst he was ready to agree with the proposal to start air staff talks, he was reluctant, I suppose owing to his fear of further commitments and possible reactions in Italy, to start talks between the naval and army staffs.

The main discussion was centred on Czechoslovakia. Agreement was quickly reached upon the need for wide concessions to the Sudeten Germans. The differences appeared on the question of what was to happen if Benes made reasonable proposals, and the Germans refused them and had recourse to force. The French were bound to the Czechs by their Treaty of 1935 to come to their aid against aggression. Would the British Government, the French Ministers asked, be definitely committed to military intervention in this event? Chamberlain and Halifax answered the question by re-stating the position that Chamberlain had defined in the House of Commons a month before, on March 24.[1] In the

---

[1] " The question now arises, whether we should go further. Should we forthwith give an assurance to France that, in the event of her being called upon by reason of German aggression in Czechoslovakia to implement her obligations under the Franco-Czechoslovak Treaty, we would immediately employ our full military force on her behalf? Or, alternatively, should we at once declare our readiness to take military action in resistance to any forcible interference with the independence and integrity of Czechoslovakia, and invite any other nations, which might so desire, to associate themselves with us in such a declaration?

" From a consideration of these two alternatives, it clearly emerges that under either of them the decision as to whether or not this country would find itself involved in war would be automatically removed from the discretion of His Majesty's Government, and the suggested guarantee would apply irrespective of the circumstances by which it was brought into operation, and over which His Majesty's Government might not have been able to exercise any control. This position is not one that His Majesty's Government could see their way to accept, in relation to an area where their vital interests are not concerned in the same degree as they are in the case of France and Belgium; it is certainly not the position that results from the Covenant. For these reasons His Majesty's Government feel themselves unable to give the prior guarantee suggested.

circumstances of the moment, British and Dominion public opinion was not prepared to go further than Chamberlain's warning to Hitler. Besides, a more definite commitment in April would have been likely to stiffen Benes just when it was necessary to induce him to be conciliatory and to move quickly.

The conference, therefore, ended without any further British commitment, but with the decision to make a joint *démarche* both in Prague and Berlin in support of a settlement, and to supplement it in Berlin with a reminder of Chamberlain's solemn warning to Hitler on March 24.

I now pass to my own part in the crisis. Throughout the spring I was actively working at the Home Office upon two very exacting programmes, the Criminal Justice Bill, which covered almost every phase of our criminal law and practice, and the organisation of Civil Defence, a new, uncharted and unpopular service that raised every kind of central and local controversy. The strain upon me in combining this Home Office work with the Cabinet and the Foreign Policy Committee was therefore very great.

Outside the Cabinet and the Committee, Chamberlain and I continued to meet most mornings in St. James's Park. Even in these intimate conversations he never let himself go. The spring of his mind was too tensely wound to allow of even a momentary loosening. He was overwhelmingly convinced that a world war would be an appalling disaster, and that it was his responsibility to try to prevent it. Although fundamentally modest, he was well aware of his own qualities, particularly his power of concentrated action, and he believed that the kind of intensive effort that he had decided to make on the double line of negotiation and re-armament had a fair chance of success. This belief in his mission underlay the whole of his talks to me in the spring and summer of 1938. When he told me of any new project for furthering his objects, it was not so much to ask for my comments, although he

---

" But while plainly stating that decision I would add this. Where peace and war are concerned, legal obligations are not alone involved, and, if war broke out, it would be unlikely to be confined to those who have assumed such obligations. It would be quite impossible to say where it would end and what governments might become involved. The inexorable pressure of facts might well prove more powerful than formal pronouncements, and in that event it would be well within the bounds of probability that other countries, besides those which were parties to the original dispute, would almost immediately become involved. This is especially true in the case of two countries like Great Britain and France, with long associations of friendship, with interests closely interwoven, devoted to the same ideals of democratic liberty, and determined to uphold them."

was a good listener and certainly took account of what was said to him, as to explain to me the reasons why this or that step was necessary. The idea of the Runciman Mission, for instance, came out in one of our talks, not as a debatable possibility, but as a logical incident in his plan for taking every possible step towards avoiding war, and creating an atmosphere in which a working arrangement could be reached between the Czechs and Hitler. It did not strike him that a highly respected English Liberal, who had never been confronted with the passions of continental nationalism, might have little influence upon a controversy that had already burst into flames. As a matter of fact, the Mission, which was immediately approved by both the British and French Governments, and subsequently welcomed by Benes, very nearly succeeded. Both Benes and the majority of the Sudeten Germans were ready to accept the main lines of Runciman's proposals. It was Hitler who at the last moment destroyed an imminent agreement. Was, therefore, the whole attempt futile? Chamberlain was convinced that it had been worth trying, if only to explode the charge of obstruction that Hitler was making against the Czech Government, and to prove to the British Commonwealth that every impediment to a reasonable compromise had been removed. Perhaps none of us fully realised at the time that the Mission, however much we insisted that its purpose was mediation and not negotiation, inevitably dragged us more deeply into the forefront of the struggle between Germans and Slavs. The fact was that in July, 1938, it still seemed possible upon the evidence that we then 'possessed to avoid final conflict. This being so, our mediation might be invaluable to the cause of peace.

When August came and the Parliamentary recess suspended our walks in St. James's Park, the position did not appear entirely hopeless. Runciman had made very definite progress with his mission. Ably helped by Ashton Gwatkin, a very astute and hardheaded Foreign Office Secretary, he had brought Benes and the Sudeten Germans within reach of a possible compromise. Although Hitler was continuing to rage and threaten, he had not yet declared for the separation of the Sudetenland or ordered Henlein, his Sudeten agent, to torpedo the negotiations in Prague.

It was not until the end of the month that the Nazis began to stir up the kind of incidents that were likely to make any agreement impossible. It was then that Nevile Henderson came to London to report on the German aspects of the crisis. As several Ministers were away, no formal Cabinet was summoned, but those of us who were within reach met to hear his report. It was one of the rare occasions when I had the opportunity of seeing the Ambassador for more than a few minutes. As the discussion lasted most of the day, and I sat next to him at luncheon, I was given the chance of forming some impression of the man whom the Foreign Office had recommended to me in 1935 as the coming young diplomat in the Foreign Service. What impression did I form of him? Fortunately, the notes that I kept at the time prevent my basing my opinion of to-day on what I have subsequently read in his *Failure of a Mission*. I described him to myself as very alert, sensitive and agreeable. In his own way he was as profoundly intent upon preventing war as was Chamberlain. Unlike Chamberlain, however, he was governed by his nerves. So anxious was he that war should be averted that, no doubt unconsciously, he quite obviously took sides against anyone who seemed to be obstructing the way of peace. As in the case of the Austrians, so in the case of the Czechs, he was undoubtedly convinced that, if international peace was to be maintained, their small countries must accept virtual absorption in the Reich. What is more, being by nature emotional and expansive, he did not disguise his feelings in his interviews and dispatches. I believe that I can understand his attitude. It is very difficult to keep one's nerves steady in a dictator's country, as I know from my own experiences in Spain. In Henderson's case, his sensitive nerves had been stretched almost to breaking point by Ribbentrop's provocations. It was not surprising, therefore, that he seemed to me on August 28 to be overwrought. How different, I noted at the time, from Horace Rumbold, one of his predecessors in Berlin, whose imperturbable manner and appearance gave all the greater weight to his solid advice. I remembered the judgment of a foreign diplomat on this great Ambassador: " Malgré sa mine idiote, c'est un homme très intelligent." No one could have said that Henderson's appearance gave any impression of stupidity. He was obviously very intelligent. What he lacked was a very necessary measure of British phlegm.

The result of Henderson's visit was to confirm us in the view that, to avoid war, the Czechs would have to make very formidable concessions, but that Hitler had not yet decided upon military action.

It was almost immediately after the visit that I went as Minister in Attendance to Balmoral. Both King George V and King George VI annually invited me to take my turn as Minister in Attendance when they went to Scotland in August. I always welcomed the Royal Command. There were no days in the year that I enjoyed more than those at Balmoral, or that were more useful to me in the chance that they gave me not only of discussing public affairs at leisure and informally with the King, but also of renewing a valuable contact with one of the most important of British officials, the King's Private Secretary. I was therefore glad when Chamberlain told me that the Czech crisis must not be allowed to interfere with my visit. Accordingly, in spite of disturbing telegrams, I spent from September 5 to September 9 at the Castle. Except for Archbishop Lang and myself it was a family party, and there were many opportunities for intimate talks that helped me to understand the reactions of the crisis upon the King and Queen. As the King wished me to shoot on September 9, I stayed on for an extra day which ended in a long and beautiful evening drive to Perth to catch the night train.

As soon as I arrived back in London on the morning of September 10, I went straight to Downing Street to hear the latest news, and to report to Chamberlain on my talks at Balmoral. I found him alone in the Cabinet Room. He at once told me that the situation had become exceedingly critical, that Hitler might very well start a general conflagration when he spoke at the Nuremberg party rally in two days' time, and that some dramatic intervention was needed to stop an appalling calamity. He then disclosed to me his idea of a personal visit to Hitler. It had been in his mind for some days, but he had kept it to himself in order to ensure its full effect at the final moment. The time had now come to try it out. What did I think of it? I told him that he was taking a great political risk by personally intervening in a way that was quite likely to fail. His answer was that he would never forgive himself if war broke out and he had not tried every expedient for averting it. Having warned him of the danger, I told him how much I admired his courage, and how profoundly I wished him success.

CHAPTER XXV

"The Big Four"

I T WAS at this moment that Halifax and Simon entered the room. Seeing at once that they had come to confer with the Prime Minister, I got up to go. Chamberlain stopped me, and told me to join the conference. This was the typically English beginning of what has since been known as the Big Four The casual start involved me in almost incessant conferences for the next three weeks. Having been kept for the talk on September 10, Chamberlain wished me to attend all the subsequent meetings of what actually developed into a small committee of himself, Halifax, Simon and myself, with Alec Cadogan, Horace Wilson and Vansittart as our official advisers. Once again, therefore, without any wish on my part I was deeply involved in foreign politics.

The immediate question to decide on September 10 was whether we should send a further warning to Hitler before he spoke at Nuremberg on September 12. The arguments for and against were about equal. After weighing them carefully, we came to the conclusion that another warning, after the many that he had received, was more likely than not to excite him and push him into war. Ever since May, when the Allied Press had triumphed over what seemed at the time to have been a check to German mobilisation, he had been like a bear with a sore head, and any suggestion of a threat now made him growl and rage.

Chamberlain then raised the question of his personal visit. The Ministers present were all agreed that it should be made, and that the Cabinet should be asked to approve of it.

When the talk ended and we left the Cabinet Room, we found Churchill waiting in the hall. He had come to demand an immediate ultimatum to Hitler. He was convinced that it was our last chance of stopping a landslide, and according to his information, which was directly contrary to our own, both the French and the Russians were ready for an offensive against Germany.

There then followed a continuous series of meetings of the Cabinet and our smaller circle of the four Ministers. Almost hourly, rumours and incidents clouded and interrupted our discussions. In the meanwhile, Maisky, the Soviet Ambassador, was very active behind the scenes, stimulating criticism against the Government, and implying that it was only our hesitations and the cold-shouldering of Russia that were endangering peace. The critics of the Government were quick in rising to Maisky's fly. His story that the Soviet was only waiting for our invitation to help, was no more than the stock Communist propaganda for making mischief. Stalin had at the time no intention of involving Russia in a quarrel between Germany and the Allies that seemed all to his own interest, nor, after the great purge of the Russian Army, was he in any position to join in coercive action against Hitler, even if he had wished to intervene. The troubled waters were giving the Ambassador the best possible fishing conditions.

The French Government, faced with the terrible dilemma of abandoning the Czech alliance or going to war unprepared, welcomed Chamberlain's proposal of the visit to Hitler. Unofficial leaders of French opinion like Herriot equally approved it. In the meanwhile, Hitler's speech on September 12, for all its sound and fury, did not entirely close the door to a peaceful settlement. There was, therefore, no reason to postpone or reject Chamberlain's plan of personal contact, and the Cabinet readily agreed on September 14 to the proposal being telegraphed to Hitler. Would Hitler accept? Would he refuse? Or, still more likely, would he delay his answer until he had struck some crushing blow? To the general relief, the answer came back within a few hours that he agreed, and as he added to his acceptance an invitation to Mrs. Chamberlain to accompany her husband, it looked as if the Prime Minister's unconventional move had improved the atmosphere.

This was the situation when Chamberlain flew on September 15 to Berchtesgaden, leaving Halifax, Simon and myself to continue our meetings in almost continuous session. As soon as he returned on the 16th, he gave us a full account of his interview with the Führer. Schmidt, the German interpreter, has since confirmed his description in every substantial detail. Chamberlain had evidently formed a poor opinion of Hitler. The Führer, with his little moustache, his khaki tunic, evening trousers and patent-leather shoes, had looked like Charlie Chaplin. As I heard Chamberlain's description of his reception, I pictured to myself the contrast between the very reserved English Prime Minister in his neat dark suit, armed with his bourgeois umbrella, and the hysterical spellbinder in clothes that equally flouted all the civil and military standards of the old world. It was when Hitler began to talk that the Charlie Chaplin effect disappeared, and the rôle of the fanatic Führer began. Within a few minutes of the start of the discussion, Hitler made it clear that any solution on the basis of local autonomy for the Sudetenland within a federal Czech state was no longer possible, and that the principle of self-determination must be categorically accepted if the discussion with Chamberlain was to prevent immediate military action. Chamberlain, who saw at once that the only chance for peaceful negotiation was the application of a principle that had been fundamental to the Versailles Treaty, answered that whilst he himself might be prepared to see it applied to the Sudetenland, he must first be satisfied as to the methods to be used, and in any case consult his colleagues in the Cabinet before he could accept it. It was necessary, therefore, for him to return to London. The meeting ended, and Chamberlain flew back to London.

When we heard his report and came to assess the value of the interview, we were convinced that the Prime Minister had certainly stopped the immediate invasion of Czechoslovakia. It was clear, however, that the crisis was even more dangerous than we had imagined, and that the German Army was on the point of marching. The acceptance of the principle of self-determination with its certain implication that it would mean the separation of the Sudetenland from Czechoslovakia, seemed to us to be inevitable if war was to be prevented. Public opinion had already been veering towards self-determination as the solution. Indeed, *The Times* had, a week before, come out in favour of it in a most inopportune article that completely torpedoed Runciman's proposals for Sudeten autonomy. Whilst it cannot be known to what extent the article had influenced Hitler, it was evident that the choice lay between the acceptance of a principle that was widely admitted and the practical certainty of war. It is not surprising that in these circumstances the Cabinet unreservedly authorised the Prime Minister to continue the negotiations on the only basis that made them possible. This was the turning point in the crisis. Self-determination, once admitted, and however carried into effect, meant the separation of the Sudetenland, and the transformation of the Czechoslovak state.

Chamberlain's visit had certain other results. He had undoubtedly impressed Hitler by his directness and sincerity. He had also obtained from Hitler the statement that he had no further territorial ambitions when once the Sudeten question had been settled. When, therefore, he returned to Germany and resumed the negotiations at Godesberg, there seemed a somewhat better chance of a peaceful end to the crisis.

Before Chamberlain's departure, Corbin expressed his Government's full support of the course that the negotiation was taking. In order, however, that French Ministers should know exactly what had happened at Berchtesgaden, and what was likely to emerge at the Prime Minister's next meeting, the French Premier and Foreign Minister were invited to a conference in Downing Street on September 18. As Chamberlain had made provisional arrangements to resume his discussions with Hitler on the following Wednesday, it was necessary to establish a united Anglo-French front with the least possible delay.

The meeting lasted the whole of Friday, the 18th. It began at eleven o'clock in the morning, and ended after eleven o'clock at night. The British Ministers were Chamberlain, Halifax, Simon and myself, and our official advisers, Vansittart, Horace Wilson, Cadogan, Bridges the Secretary of the Cabinet, William Strang and F. K. Roberts from the Central Department of the Foreign Office. The French Delegation consisted of Daladier and Bonnet, with their advisers, Corbin, Alexis Léger, Rochat, Jules Henry and de Margerie. We met in the Cabinet Room, the British sitting beside and behind the Prime Minister, with the French opposite to us.

Reading again the notes that I made after the meetings, and sorting my memories of what actually happened, I have again experienced the deep depression that possessed me throughout the many hours of these dismal talks. It was not only that I felt frustrated on our own account, but that I could see, and indeed feel, the emotional strain through which the French were passing. In front of me sat Daladier, square and squat, his face flushed redder than ever, the man who, as an artilleryman, had stubbornly fought through the First World War, and as a Minister, had faced the Paris mob. By his side was Bonnet, as white as Daladier was red, sensitive, and apparently on the verge of a *crise de nerfs*, with a mind that moved like quicksilver, made especially sensitive since he had discovered that there were no gas-masks in France. Behind them sat Léger, the very embodiment of the conservative traditions of the Quai d'Orsay, yellow-complexioned, silent, imperturbable and sphinx-like. Their faces, each in its own way, showed that they were confronted with questions to which all the answers were bad. As for ourselves, it was at least some comfort that, although we were under no treaty obligation to the Czechs, we had already acted, and Chamberlain's bold stroke had permitted us to retain a certain measure of hope.

The French decisions were much more difficult than ours; they had let things drift, and lost the initiative for stopping a great calamity, and yet were still bound by a treaty that depended on military strength that they no longer possessed.

It was a relief when Chamberlain, in his peculiarly incisive and matter-of-fact manner, began the conference with a detailed description of his three hours' talk with Hitler. It is always helpful to start a difficult discussion with the sedative of a long narrative. In this case, the full story was necessary to bring out the two overriding factors in the crisis—Hitler's set purpose to march at once, if no agreement was reached, and the separation of the Sudetenland from the Czechoslovak Republic as the one indispensable condition of any accommodation. As was only to be expected, the main burden of the discussion fell upon the two Premiers.

The first session turned upon the danger of admitting the far-reaching principle of self-determination. Where would it stop in Hitler's hands? If plebiscites were accepted as the method of applying it, what of the Magyars and Slovaks in Czechoslovakia? What, nearer home, would be the reactions in Alsace? As I listened to Daladier's French logic, admirably expressed and accurately documented, I could not help wondering what the nineteenth-century Liberals and President Wilson would have thought of the Frankenstein monster of self-determination that they had so optimistically created at Versailles. Daladier soon convinced us that it was much too dangerous to base our attitude on any general proposition, and that in particular, plebiscites would put into Hitler's hands an irresistible lever for future revolutions. We therefore agreed to restrict any negotiation to the narrow point of the Sudetenland, and to consult the Cabinet upon the question of substituting the direct transfer of territory for Hitler's proposal of plebiscites.

The discussion of these points brought us to the central issue. Should we or should we not press Benes to accept the loss of the Sudetenland? It was at this stage that we adjourned in order that the French Ministers should discuss between themselves the implications of this very grave question, and that we should obtain the Cabinet's approval of our provisional decisions.

When we resumed the conference, Daladier informed us, as the prelude to further discussions, that he agreed with our proposal that the Czech Government should be advised to postpone mobilisation pending Chamberlain's further meeting with Hitler. He then reverted to his objections to a plebiscite, with the result that Chamberlain reluctantly, but with the authority of the Cabinet, accepted the alternative of a direct transfer of territory. There then arose the question of the future of the Czech Republic, when once it had lost the Moravian frontier and the line of fortifications that had been built along it. If Czechoslovakia was to continue at all, and equally, if France was to be compensated for the loss of a bastion against Germany in Central Europe, it was essential in Daladier's view for the British Government to join in an international guarantee of the weakened and attenuated state.

It had always been a tradition of British Governments to refuse to undertake guarantees on the Continent that left the final decision of peace or war in hands other than our own. With the growth of the Dominions and their extreme reluctance to be involved in Continental commitments, the need for caution in undertaking European obligations had in recent years become increasingly important. When, therefore, Daladier pressed for a British guarantee, we had to consider very carefully the reaction on Dominion as well as British opinion, and it was only after a long meeting between ourselves that we were able to tell the French that we accepted their proposal.

The ground was then cleared for the final act, the drafting of

the telegram to Benes announcing our considered view that only
the cession of the Sudetenland could avoid war, that we strongly
pressed him to agree to it at once, and that if he agreed, we would
join in an international guarantee of Czechoslovakia against
unprovoked aggression.

Daladier, in approving the draft, was obviously under an
almost intolerable strain. He was sacrificing an ally, and weakening a strategic outpost of France in Central Europe. None the
less, it seemed to be the only choice open to him. If war broke
out, France was grievously unprepared, and would be forced to
choose between the undisguised repudiation of the Franco-Czech
Treaty and fighting in conditions that made the immediate defence
of Czechoslovakia impossible. In these circumstances he felt bound
to agree to the telegram that was sent to Prague on September 19
asking categorically for the Czech acceptance of self-determination
for the Sudeten Germans.

One question still remained unanswered. What was to happen
if Benes refused to cede the Sudetenland? Daladier brushed it
aside on the ground that a refusal was unthinkable. I thought on
the contrary that Benes was sure to refuse, if only to make it clear
that he was acting under duress. I was also convinced that the
French Ministers, having once accepted the separation of the
Sudetenland, would sooner or later be forced to make it plain that
the French would not go to war, if their advice was rejected.

It was at this point that the conference ended. Between its
termination and Chamberlain's second meeting with Hitler at
Godesberg there were only three days. In this short time it was
necessary to obtain Benes's agreement to the cession to Germany
of the Sudetenland. The increasing gravity of Nazi incidents, and
the news of German troop concentrations on the Czech frontier
made any postponement of the Godesberg meeting very dangerous.
Hour by hour, we awaited with deep anxiety the news of Benes's
reply. Only if it was an acceptance of the Anglo-French proposals
would it be possible for Chamberlain to resume his talks with
Hitler and stop the German march with all its consequences into
Czech territory. Telegrams from Prague, Paris and Berlin began
immediately to arrive in quick succession. One of Henderson's
from Berlin, in which he informed us that Ribbentrop had refused
to let the Prime Minister have the shorthand note of the Berchtesgaden conversation, was anything but reassuring as to the prospects

of the next meeting. From Paris came further evidence of Bonnet's desire to obtain Benes's agreement. From Prague Newton, the British Minister, a convinced and sympathetic friend of Benes and his country, described in short but poignant language the steps that he and his French colleagues took to obtain the Czech Government's reluctant assent. Indeed, it was only after Lacroix, the French Minister, had definitely told Benes that if he refused, the French would disinterest themselves in the consequences, and Newton had said that the British Government agreed with the French declaration, that Krofta, the Czech Minister of Foreign Affairs, handed to the British and French Ministers the Czech acceptance. The final telegram from Prague only arrived so near the time that had been planned for Chamberlain's flight to Godesberg that he had most reluctantly to postpone his meeting with Hitler until 11 a.m., an hour after the time originally arranged on the morning of the 22nd. Its short staccato sentences described one of the most painful interviews in British diplomatic history. I quote it in full:

" *Mr. Newton (Prague) to Viscount Halifax* "[1] *Received September 21, 6.45 p.m.*

"My French colleague and I were summoned to Ministry of Foreign Affairs shortly before 5 p.m. where Dr. Krofta handed to each of us together a note dated September 21 of which following is a summary:

' Under pressure of urgent insistence culminating in British communications of September 21 (see my telegram No. 672, paragraph 5) Czechoslovak Government sadly accept French and British proposals on supposition (translate following into French ' in supposing ') that the two Governments will do everything in carrying them out to safeguard vital interests of Czechoslovak state.

' Czechoslovak Government accept them as a whole emphasising principle of guarantee as formulated and on supposition that the two Governments will not tolerate a German invasion of Czechoslovak territory which will remain Czechoslovakian until its transfer has been effected after fixing of new frontier by international court.

' They are of opinion that details for execution of proposal will be settled in agreement with Czechoslovak Government.' "

[1] *Documents on British Foreign Policy*, Vol. II, Third Series, page 444.

It was in this nightmare of hopes and fears, and after three days of continuous meetings and discussions, that Chamberlain began his second talk with Hitler. It seemed that as Benes's acceptance enabled him to agree to the cession of the Sudetenland, his further discussions would not be as difficult and explosive as they had been at Berchtesgaden. It was a shock, therefore, to us when, late in the evening of the 22nd, Halifax received a personal message from Chamberlain: "First meeting unsatisfactory."[1]

Whilst we had little or no further news from Godesberg, Halifax, Simon and I were faced with a very urgent question from Prague. Should the Anglo-French embargo on the Czech mobilisation now be withdrawn in view of the growing evidence of German mobilisation and of a premeditated plan to stir up frontier incidents? We in London were strongly in favour of instructing Newton in Prague to say categorically that we could no longer advise the Czech Government to postpone mobilisation. Fragmentary messages from Godesberg seemed to suggest that the wiser course was to wait a little longer. A difference of opinion of this kind was inevitable in the circumstances. Chamberlain was in the throes of a critical negotiation upon which the peace of the world might depend. The news of the Czech mobilisation might destroy the last chance of success. Our feeling, however, that we could no longer tie the hands of a country that seemed to be on the eve of invasion, overrode our fear of the reactions in Godesberg, and Newton was authorised to make the announcement. We afterwards learnt that Ribbentrop had done his best to compromise the talk between Hitler and Chamberlain by bursting in upon them with the news of the mobilisation. I doubt, however, whether the Czech action made a settlement any more difficult.

It was the apparent difference of outlook between London and Godesberg that made Halifax at this moment send Chamberlain an appreciation of British opinion:

" *Viscount Halifax to British Delegation (Godesberg).*[2] *Foreign Office, September 23, 1938, 10.0 p.m.*

" It may help you if we give you some indication of what seems predominant public opinion as expressed in press and elsewhere. While mistrustful of our plan but prepared perhaps to accept it with reluctance as alternative to war, great mass of public opinion seems to be hardening in sense of feeling that we have gone to limit

[1] Page 473. [2] *Documents on British Foreign Policy*, Vol. II, Third Series, page 490.

of concession and that it is up to the Chancellor to make some contribution. We, of course, can imagine immense difficulties with which you are confronted but from point of view of your own position, that of Government, and of the country, it seems to your colleagues of vital importance that you should not leave without making it plain to Chancellor if possible by special interview that, after great concessions made by Czechoslovak Government, for him to reject opportunity of peaceful solution in favour of one that must involve war would be an unpardonable crime against humanity."

Of the telegrams that we received during these days, the two that most disturbed us came from Paris. The first enclosed a memorandum by our military attaché describing a conversation with the French General, Dentz. The General, who was evidently well informed, declared that Hitler was already extending his demands far beyond the Sudetenland, and that if there was war, French cities would be laid in ruins, and had no means of defence. " He left me with the impression that the French did not intend to fight."

This pessimistic view was confirmed by a telegram from the Ambassador in Paris on September 24. Phipps, who in the past had always supported a policy of resistance to German aggression, and might, therefore, have been expected to state the case for strong measures, declared categorically that " all that is best in France is against war."

These were his words:

" *Sir E. Phipps (Paris) to Viscount Halifax.*[1] (*Received September 24, 5.45 p.m.*)

" *Paris, September 24, 1938.*

" I wish to submit to His Majesty's Government my purely personal impressions, which are the following:

" Unless German aggression were so brutal, bloody and prolonged (through gallantry of Czechoslovak resistance) as to infuriate French public opinion to the extent of making it lose its reason, war would be most unpopular in France.

" I think therefore that His Majesty's Government should realise extreme danger of even appearing to encourage small, but noisy and corrupt war group here.

" All that is best in France is against war, *almost* at any price

[1] *Documents on British Foreign Policy*, Vol. II, Third Series, page 510.

(hence the really deep and pathetic gratitude shown to our Prime Minister). Unless we are sure of considerable initial successes we shall find all that is best in France, as well as all that is worst, turn against us and accuse us of egging French on to fight what must have seemed from the outset a losing battle.

" To embark upon what will presumably be the biggest conflict in history with our ally, who will fight, if fight she must, without eyes (Air Force) and without real heart must surely give us furiously to think.

" It may be asked why I have not reported sooner in the above sense. The answer is that up to the last hour the French had hypnotised themselves into believing that peace depended upon Great Britain, and not upon Herr Hitler. They were convinced, that is to say, that if Great Britain spoke with sufficient firmness Herr Hitler would collapse. Only now do they realise that Herr Hitler may well be meaning to take on both our countries."

It was against this depressing background that we eventually received the account of Chamberlain's meetings with Hitler on September 23 and 24. Chamberlain gave several descriptions of what happened, first to the Cabinet, then to the French Ministers, and finally, to the House of Commons, and it is only necessary for me to add to them my personal impressions that I noted at the time. Like him, and, I imagine, like my Cabinet colleagues, I had been caught up in the toils of a critical negotiation. The longer it went on and the more serious the issue became, the more anxious I grew to see it succeed. This is almost always the course of negotiations. As they proceed, the parties concerned in them become increasingly obsessed with the need to prevent their final failure. If they are to continue, it is necessary to make concessions, and one concession almost invariably leads to another. The time comes when the question has to be faced: Is the substance being sacrificed to the negotiation, and is it not better to admit failure rather then make further proposals and concessions? Throughout the Munich discussions, I often asked myself whether the slide into surrender had not started. Following closely what actually happened, I was and still am convinced that this was not the case. Halifax and Simon took the same view. Whilst, however, the officials who advised us never overstepped their constitutional position, it was clear to us that Vansittart was convinced that we had drifted too fast and too far. I could well understand the reaction of his chivalrous nature against Hitler's brutality. When, however, we looked for alternatives that he or anyone else might suggest, we could not find them. The position seemed clear to us. We and the French had agreed to the principle of self-determination for the Sudetenland. The next step was to set in motion what Chamberlain described as ' orderly methods ' for carrying out the transfer of territory. Chamberlain held firmly to this position. Hitler, who had seen the efficient working of his mobilisation plan, and had been tempted into further demands by Ribbentrop and the German minority in Czechoslovakia, had completely shifted his ground since the Berchtesgaden meeting. He now demanded a military triumph, a Sadowa, in fact, without a war, and the immediate occupation by German troops of a great tract of Czechoslovak territory. Chamberlain made it plain that he could take no responsibility for an ultimatum of this kind. As a mediator, the most that he would undertake would be to transmit it to the Czech Government, and he never imagined that it would be accepted. The two meetings between him and Hitler, the letters that passed between them across the Rhine, and the subsequent messages that Horace Wilson took from London made only a single modification in Hitler's time-table. The march into Slovakia that had been ordered for September 24 was postponed until October 1.

When Chamberlain returned to London, the issue, therefore, was stark and rigid. The meeting of the four Ministers at once decided that Hitler's new demands were unacceptable. Our view was strongly confirmed by the Cabinet. This was the situation when the French delegation arrived on September 25 to hear from Chamberlain himself the account of his second interview with Hitler, and to discuss with us the steps to be taken in face of the darkening crisis.

The same Anglo-French conference met in Downing Street, exactly a week after the meeting of September 18. If the first meeting had been embarrassing, the second was painful in the extreme. Once again, Chamberlain started with a narrative of what had happened. There followed a complicated discussion upon the differences between the Red and Green Zones that had been proposed in the German memorandum for the transfer of Czech territory. This was only a preliminary to the discussion of

Hitler's demand for the immediate military occupation of the Sudeten districts.

"What then would follow," asked Chamberlain, "if German troops marched in and seized Czech territory?" Daladier's first answer was: "Return to the Anglo-French proposals agreed to last Sunday." Chamberlain's next question followed at once. "What should be done if Hitler refused?" "Each of us," answered Daladier, "would have to do his duty." There then followed a tense examination of what Daladier meant by this broad assertion. Chamberlain's mind always reacted against generalities, and in this case he was supported by Simon's un-rivalled skill at cross-examination. It may be that our inquiries were pushed too hard. We were, however, faced with so tremendous an issue that it did not seem possible to leave the answer to this fundamental question in any doubt. Daladier once again was confronted with the dilemma that had faced him the week before. He could not repudiate the French Treaty with Czechoslovakia, but he knew that France was powerless to make it effective. I quote some of the dialogue that passed between him and Chamberlain.[1]

"M. Daladier said that the matter was very clear. The French Government had always said, and he had himself repeated three days ago, that, in the event of unprovoked aggression against Czechoslovakia, France would fulfil her obligations. It was because the news from Germany had been bad that he had asked 1,000,000 Frenchmen to go to the frontier. They had gone calmly and with dignity, conscious of the justice of their cause.

"Mr. Chamberlain said that no doubt M. Daladier had considered what the next step should be after that. It would be of great assistance to His Majesty's Government to hear from M. Daladier whether the French General Staff had got some plan, and, if so, what that plan was. He assumed that it was impossible to give direct assistance to the Czechoslovak people if aggression took place. He presumed, therefore, that it must be the intention of the French Government to carry on hostilities against Germany in some other area.

"M. Daladier said he would certainly reply to this question, which had been put to him five or six months ago, and to which he had already replied then. It was not possible for France to send help directly to Czechoslovakia by land, but France could

[1] *Documents on British Foreign Policy*, Vol. II, Third Series, pages 520 and following.

materially assist Czechoslovakia by drawing the greater part of the German Army against France.

" Mr. Chamberlain hoped M. Daladier would not think he was bringing pressure to bear unduly upon M. Daladier in these questions. One could not, however, go into so great a conflict with one's eyes and ears closed. It was essential to know the conditions before taking any decision. He would, therefore, like further information and would ask Sir John Simon to put certain points to M. Daladier which had troubled the British Ministers a great deal for some time past."

It was at this point that Simon took up the examination. There then followed a series of questions and answers that did little to clear up many of the obscurities and uncertainties with which the answer to Chamberlain's leading question was surrounded. It did, however, emerge that all that the French could do whilst Czechoslovakia was being overrun in the east, would be to hold the Maginot Line with a limited number of divisions after the army had been concentrated in the west, possibly attempt a probing offensive against the Siegfried Line, and make a small demonstration in the air that would not involve the bombing of German cities.

Daladier was obviously growing restive under the inquiry when Chamberlain passed me a note in which he asked me to intervene when Simon had finished. I therefore tried to develop a proposal that Daladier had made in answer to one of Simon's questions. He had been emphasising his opposition to any unilateral action on Hitler's part, and had declared himself in favour of an international commission for supervising the transfer of Sudeten territory. Whilst I felt that it was most unlikely that Hitler would accept any international intervention, the proposal not only merited further discussion, but provided an escape from a cross-examination that was becoming acrimonious. The official report describes my intervention.[1] I quote the account of what followed.

" Sir Samuel Hoare fully understood M. Daladier's feelings and hoped he would not think that anyone present liked the German proposals. He wished to know a little more about the suggestion M. Daladier had just made. Did he mean that, even if the Germans did not accept it, we should nevertheless at once send out an

[1] *Documents on British Foreign Policy*, Vol. II, Third Series, page 531

international commission to make inquiries quickly, and so enable
Herr Hitler and the German Army to take possession of many
areas in the near future? If he had understood the suggestion
aright, it seemed worthy of consideration, particularly as it kept the
initiative in our hands. It would show Herr Hitler that it was not
in our mind to make further delays, and, even if he disliked the
suggestion, it would be very difficult for him to refuse it, when it
would be clear that in two or three days the international commission would be ceding to him the territory in question. M.
Daladier said Sir Samuel Hoare had correctly interpreted his
proposal.

" Mr. Chamberlain felt he must say that, although this proposal
sounded extremely reasonable, he had just returned from his
conversation with Herr Hitler and was clear in his own mind that
the proposal would not be acceptable to the Chancellor. Mr.
Chamberlain doubted whether it would in practice be possible to
get an international commission together, to send it to the territory
concerned and carry out the cession of these areas within a few
days. He must remind the French Ministers insistently that, in
Herr Hitler's view, this question had gone on far too long (he had
mentioned having had no satisfaction for twenty years) and that
he was determined to reach a solution at once. If Mr. Chamberlain
had not gone to Germany, he was convinced that Herr Hitler
would have already attempted a military invasion. As a result of
Mr. Chamberlain's efforts, Herr Hitler had postponed such action,
but only for a few days. Mr. Chamberlain did not believe that
Herr Hitler would accept such a proposal if it were put to him."

Although Chamberlain's answer did not satisfy Daladier, my
intervention seemed to have relieved the growing tension. I
accordingly pushed a note to Chamberlain suggesting that he and
Daladier should meet alone after the meeting, and try to clear
up any differences between the two delegations. Chamberlain
accepted my suggestion, and the personal meeting took place with
no one else present.

When the full conference was resumed, the sultry atmosphere
had been dissipated, and I rightly assumed that Chamberlain
had given Daladier the specific pledge of a British expeditionary
force to France if France went to war with Germany. It was
late in the evening, and at 11.40 p.m. we asked for a short
adjournment to consult the Cabinet. When we returned at
12.35 a.m., it was to decide upon a further adjournment until the

next morning. By that time Chamberlain and Daladier had
succeeded in reaching complete agreement. The final meeting
on September 26 was only needed for registering our conclusions
and approving the proposal to send Horace Wilson with a letter
of final appeal to Hitler.

I do not think that anyone believed that Wilson's mission
would deflect Hitler from his set purpose. Once again, however,
we were determined to leave nothing undone that might avert a
catastrophe, and save France from the terrible dilemma of breaking a solemn treaty, or fighting without adequate strength and
with the majority of the French people opposed to war. As a
matter of fact, Chamberlain's letter and the two very heated
interviews that Hitler had with Wilson, imposed a definite delay
upon the start of the planned invasion. When Wilson left London,
the German troops were on the point of marching. A short
breathing space was at least gained by the time needed for Wilson's
visit and for Hitler's written answer to reach Chamberlain. It
was a rejection of Chamberlain's appeal, but it looked at one
time in the first of Wilson's interviews, as if he would not answer
it at all.

In London there was no light in the surrounding darkness.
Gamelin had come over as the result of the ministerial conference, and given a very depressing account of the value of
Czech resistance. In the meanwhile, the Poles were preparing to
seize their share of the Czech spoils, and the British public were
becoming restive under the strain of the crisis. The time, in fact,
seemed to have arrived when war was inevitable, and the only
course open to us was to set in motion the security measures that
had been in readiness for several months. As Home Secretary, I
was responsible for Civil Defence, with the result that in addition
to the many meetings at the Foreign Office and in Downing Street,
I had to start up the complicated machinery that dealt with gas-
masks, decontamination, shelters, gas attacks, blast destruction,
fire fighting and evacuation. It was now necessary to bring into
action the untried plans upon which I had been working incessantly for more than a year. As it required a Royal Proclamation to confirm the Regulations, a Privy Council was held on
September 28 to declare a State of Emergency and give the
Government the appropriate powers.

Every possible step had been foreseen and defined in the War

Book prepared for the Committee of Imperial Defence by Maurice Hankey and his staff. In this veritable encyclopædia of British Defence were set out in detail all the war duties of Ministers and their departments, and the dates and stages at which each action was to be carried out. On September 28 the great machine that had been so carefully designed began to work with a remarkable precision. The first stage of the precautionary measures did not involve full mobilisation. While there was still the faintest chance of a peaceful settlement, it had been agreed to postpone the mobilisation of the fleet. When, however, we heard of Wilson's hostile reception by Hitler, we felt that we could not run the risk of waiting any longer. Chamberlain himself gave the order to the First Sea Lord at the end of one of the meetings of the four Ministers.[1] Even so, we did not abandon all hope. In one last attempt we prepared a detailed plan guaranteed by ourselves and the French for the Czech evacuation of the German districts by October 18, and added to it a proposal of an international commission for delimiting doubtful areas. The French approved the plan, and the Czech Government, after some hesitation, agreed to accept it.

In the meanwhile, Roosevelt was renewing his pressure upon Hitler. Mussolini was also, according to our reports, definitely trying to avert war. Events had pushed the Duce into the centre of the stage. If war came, he was convinced that he was indispensable to Hitler. If war was to be avoided, he was equally convinced that it was his influence more than anyone's that would weight the scales on the side of peace. The part that he had been given in the play seemed exactly to suit the qualities that he claimed for himself.

[1] Duff Cooper, the First Lord, was subsequently informed of the decision.

CHAPTER XXVI

The Balance Sheet

IT was at this point that the work of the Inner Cabinet of the Big Four became less important. As events were moving too swiftly for the summoning of several Ministers, Chamberlain and Halifax took charge of the final act, the details of which have become matters of general history.

The country was in a state of tense excitement, and war seemed certain within a few hours. It was then that Chamberlain asked me to meet regularly the leaders of the Press, and to keep them informed of hour-to-hour developments. A contact of this kind seemed to be urgently needed. There had already been some trouble over a communiqué from the Press Department of the Foreign Office on September 26 stating that Russia was ready to join us and the French in resistance to an attack on Czechoslovakia. As we had no authority to speak for Russia, and all our evidence pointed against the likelihood of Russian help for the Allies, we immediately issued a repudiation of the statement. The incident warned us of the need for improving the relations with the Press, and it was for this purpose that I held daily meetings with the representatives of the leading papers. *The Times History* has described one of my meetings with the Editor, and has published the notes that he took at the time.

As the crisis developed, Chamberlain became more than ever alive to the importance of an Italian intervention on the side of peace. The personal appeals that he made to Mussolini, particularly the telegram that he himself drafted in the small hours of September 28, undoubtedly had a considerable effect. When we heard that in response to Mussolini's intervention, Hitler had postponed mobilisation for twenty-four hours, I became more hopeful, though some of my colleagues did not attach any importance to the delay.

When the House of Commons met on September 28, the general feeling was that the respite made little difference, and that war was inevitable within the next few days. In the incredible debate that followed, Chamberlain sat between Simon and the Chief Whip, and I next to Simon. When Dunglass, the Prime Minister's Parliamentary Private Secretary, passed along the bench the slip of paper that was Hitler's answer to Chamberlain's last appeal, I handed it on without looking at it, and imagined that the officials under the Gallery were correcting some detail in Chamberlain's speech. The disclosure of the postponement of German action and the invitation to the Four Power-Conference in Munich were as dramatic a surprise to me as to the rest of the House. When Chamberlain sat down almost immediately after reading Hitler's message, and said that he accepted the invitation, the Chamber was swept by a wave of emotion. Speeches of congratulation came from every side, and when they were finished, members of all parties crowded past the Front Bench to shake Chamberlain's hand. All the party leaders joined in the *Te Deum* of praise. When the chorus of thanksgiving was over, I went off to the Home Office to supervise the details of Civil Defence.

The Munich Conference took place the next day, September 29, at 3 p.m., and was followed by the meeting between Chamberlain and Hitler on September 30. Chamberlain took with him Wilson, and was joined by Henderson and Kirkpatrick from Berlin. We now know that Mussolini prepared in the train a memorandum on the general lines of the Anglo-French proposals of September 27, and had it ready as the basis of discussion when the conference opened. Hitler was obviously in a more reasonable mood, and agreement was reached without much difficulty after Chamberlain had obtained the acceptance of certain amendments that were intended to strengthen the international supervision and prevent the complete dissolution of the Czech state.

These breathless events took place in an atmosphere of great confusion. For once at least the German power of organisation failed. Papers were lost, drafts were badly edited, and the final document was left with ragged ends. Confusion became worse confounded, and when the time came to sign, there was no ink in the pretentious inkpot that had been produced for the purpose.

After the signature of the agreement, Chamberlain quite un-expectedly arranged a private meeting with Hitler for the following morning. The two then went over most of the out-standing questions of controversy between Great Britain and Germany, and at the end signed a joint declaration that Chamber-lain had drafted on the importance of better Anglo-German relations, and the desire of the two peoples " never to go to war with one another again."[1] The declaration was not only loosely worded, but could also be criticised on the ground that it created a sense of false security. Yet, with all its imperfections, it was welcomed at the time as evidence of a victory in the cause of peace, and it was amidst general acclamation that Chamberlain and Daladier returned to their capitals. Daladier has told us how he imagined that the crowds on the Paris aerodrome had come to mob him for having sacrificed an ally and endangered France, and how great was his astonishment when he landed, to find that they had come to applaud him as the saviour of his country.

I went with other Ministers to Heston to meet Chamberlain on his return. The streets were filled with cheering crowds. As he drove from the aerodrome to Downing Street, he said to Halifax, pointing to the people who lined the streets, and remem-bering the fickleness of public emotion: " This will all be over in three months." When he arrived home, he was very near a physical collapse. The strain of the last few days had been almost unbearable. Words that had been used at tea in Downing Street just before his final flight to Munich were still ringing in his ears. " Go and bring back peace with honour like Disraeli," his friends had said to him. The crowds outside were clamouring to see him. The words of the day before came back as a kind of refrain that everyone in Downing Street was humming. " What can I say? "

---

[1] " We, the German Führer and Chancellor and the British Prime Minister, have had a further meeting to-day and are agreed in recognising that the question of Anglo-German relations is of the first importance for the two countries and for Europe.

" We regard the agreement signed last night and the Anglo-German Naval Agreement as symbolic of the desire of our two peoples never to go to war with one another again.

" We are resolved that the method of consultation shall be the method adopted to deal with any other questions that may concern our two countries, and we are determined to continue our efforts to remove possible sources of difference and thus to contribute to assure the peace of Europe."

(Signed) ' A. Hitler.' (Signed) ' Neville Chamberlain.' "

he asked. " Say that you have come back with peace with honour, and go on to the balcony where Dizzy said it before," answered one of his staff. With these words running in his tired mind, he was almost pushed on to the balcony, and without weighing their full meaning, made the claim that has so often been brought up against him.

> " This is the second time in our history that there has come back from Germany to Downing Street peace with honour. I believe it is peace for our time."

He had forgotten in the turmoil of the moment that Disraeli's boast had ended in disappointment and disillusionment. If the sudden loosening of the strain brought Ministers like myself very near to the point of collapse, I could well understand how near to breaking point was the man who had taken the foremost part in the three weeks of breathless crisis.[1]

As for myself, I hurried off for a few hours in Norfolk, where I almost immediately received a telephone message from Herbert Morrison who, in order to test the machinery, wanted to continue the evacuation of children from London, although the crisis was over and everyone else was anxious to return to normal life.

The reaction that Chamberlain had foreseen on his way back from Heston showed itself almost immediately. It was focused on two questions. The first, to what extent did the terms that he accepted at Munich differ from the terms that he had rejected at Godesberg? The second, would it not have been better to resist Hitler before Czechoslovakia had been made militarily impotent?

The four days' debate in the House of Commons constantly reverted to these two issues. The prelude was Duff Cooper's

---

[1] Chamberlain himself explained these words in the House of Commons debate of October 5th:

" I hope hon. Members will not be disposed to read words used in a moment of some emotion, after a long and exhausting day, after I had driven through miles of excited, enthusiastic cheering people—I hope they will not read into those words more than they were intended to mean. I never meant to suggest that we should do that by disarmament. Our past experience has shown us only too clearly that weakness in armed strength means weakness in diplomacy. One good thing at any rate has come out of this emergency through which we have passed. It has thrown a vivid light upon our preparations for defence, on their strength and on their weakness. I should not think that we were doing our duty if we had not already ordered that a prompt and thorough enquiry should be made to cover the whole of our preparations, military and civil, in order to see in the light of what has happened during these hectic days what further steps may be necessary to make good our deficiencies in the shortest possible time."

resignation speech. As a *tour de force* it was fully up to his high standard of easy eloquence and incisive argument. As, however, he had already accepted as inevitable the cession of the Sudetenland and admitted the considerable differences between the Godesberg ultimatum and the Munich agreement, it failed to make more than a personal impression on the House. Throughout August, while the crisis was reaching a climax, he had been yachting in the Baltic and absent from the Cabinet discussions in which each of Chamberlain's moves had been approved, but he had unreservedly agreed on his return to the demand for self-determination.

Chamberlain asked me to speak on the first day. He gave me very short notice, and it was only in the evening that he told me that I was to wind up the day's debate at ten o'clock. I did not at all wish to speak. Unlike some of my friends, I was profoundly depressed. I felt great sympathy for the Czechs. Their leaders had been my personal friends, and their country I had admired for many years.

This being so, I felt that if I had to speak, the only ground for me to take was the simplest and most personal. I accordingly insisted that we were not celebrating a triumph. We had made our choice, not because it was good, but because it was less bad than the alternative. Under an international guarantee, it should at least be possible for the Czech state to survive. We had prevented a European war, and a war postponed might never happen. I did not pretend to myself that it was a good speech. The following day, however, the *Manchester Guardian*, whose comments I have always valued, seemed to prefer my simple approach to any complicated defence of the details of the agreement.

Deeply as I deplored the crushing blow to a loyal ally, I was satisfied that the Munich terms were definitely better than the conditions of the Godesberg *diktat*. They at least provided an orderly transfer of a limited amount of territory by stages instead of an immediate military occupation. The critics were, of course, sure to say that cold-blooded murder by instalment was no better and perhaps worse than a sudden act of homicidal violence. This line of argument assumed that Hitler would upset any orderly arrangement by some future *coup*. The next six months were to prove the critics right. In September, 1938, however, it was not possible for us to foresee the occupation of Prague in the following March. Hitler had publicly stated that after the cession of the Sudetenland he had no further ambitions, and that he did not want Czechs in the Reich. There was no justification for starting any negotiations at Munich, unless we believed that an agreement would have some substance behind it. In September, 1938, the conditions agreed by Chamberlain and Hitler, supplemented by the Anglo-German Declaration, gave some hope not only of the peaceful and orderly transfer of territory that had already been accepted in principle by the British, French and Czech Governments, but also of more permanent security.

To Chamberlain, the difference between the Godesberg and Munich terms, a difference that was freely admitted in the debate by Duff Cooper, one of the keenest critics of the Agreement, was all-important. During the whole of the three weeks of the negotiations Chamberlain had been haunted by the horror of the personal tragedies that war and an uncontrolled military occupation would bring to the lives of countless simple men and women. National sentiment made little appeal to him. The satisfaction of German or Czech aspirations seemed altogether less important than the security of the peaceful families that were living and working in their own homes. It may be argued that he carried too far this sentiment for the small man and woman, and that he did not take sufficient account of the disastrous consequences to the Czech state. Yet was it not to his credit that he tried to save the simple people from the catastrophe of war and the devastating effects of an immediate invasion?

Whether this be so or not, the fact remains that the Commonwealth Governments were unwilling to go to war on the issue of Czechoslovakia. Dominion opinion was at the time overwhelmingly against a world war. This opposition was continually in our minds. Time after time we were reminded of it, either by the High Commissioners in London, or by Malcolm MacDonald, the Secretary of State for the Dominions. As early as March 18, 1938 we had been told that South Africa and Canada would not join us in a war to prevent certain Germans from rejoining their Fatherland. This was no doubt an overstatement, as Canada and South Africa almost certainly would not in the last resort have stood by inactive when once the Mother Country was at war. None the less, in 1938 they certainly did not consider war to be justifiable. They agreed with the verdict of Newton, who for all his sympathy for the Czechs and his hatred of Hitler, had told us bluntly on March 15 that[1]

> " Having regard to her geographical situation, her history and the recent divisions of her population, Czechoslovakia's position is not permanently tenable. " H.M.G. are entitled to decline the risk of involving Great Britain in a fresh war to shore up the present position if it is one which seems to us fundamentally unsound."

What Newton telegraphed from Prague, the Dominion Ministers were saying in their capitals and transmitting to their spokesmen in London. When, therefore, they heard the news of the Munich settlement, they acclaimed Chamberlain as the leader who had saved the world from an unnecessary catastrophe.

> " A great champion has appeared in the lists, God bless him! " (in the words of Smuts) . . . " The path of the peacemaker was difficult and dangerous, but he gave no thought for himself or his future. He risked all, and I trust he has won all."

Mackenzie King, the other outstanding Dominion statesman, was as enthusiastic as Smuts. The great relief with which Canada heard the news of the Munich settlement conclusively showed how strong in 1938 was the Canadian opposition to war. Mackenzie King's letter to Chamberlain on September 30 vividly expressed the Canadian feeling.

> " *Office of the Prime Minister,*
> " *Canada, Ottawa*
> " *September 30, 1938*

" DEAR MR. CHAMBERLAIN,

" I wish to send you in my own hand the message which I sent by cable last night.

" The heart of Canada is rejoicing to-night at the success which crowned your unremitting efforts for peace. May I convey to you the warm congratulations of the Canadian people, and with them, an expression of their gratitude which is felt from one end of the Dominion to the other.

" My colleagues in the government join with me in unbounded admiration of the service that you have rendered mankind.

" Your achievements in the past month alone will ensure you an abiding and illustrious place among the great conciliators whom

[1] *Documents on British Foreign Policy*, Vol. I, Third Series, p. 56.

the United Kingdom, the British Commonwealth of Nations, and the whole world will continue to honour.

" On the very brink of chaos, with passions flaming, and armies marching, the voice of reason has found a way out of the conflict which no people in their hearts desired, but none seemed able to avert. A turning point in the world's history will be reached if, as we hope, to-night's agreement means a halt in the mad race of arms, and a new start in building the partnership of all peoples. May you have health and strength to carry your great work to its completion.

" Yours very sincerely,

" W. L. MACKENZIE KING "

Nor was it only to Chamberlain that Mackenzie King expressed his relief. Immediately after the Munich Agreement he and Roosevelt exchanged letters of mutual congratulation.

" To me," wrote Roosevelt to him on October 11, " the most heartening aspect of the situation is the fact that this feeling of relief has been so spontaneous and has been expressed with such obvious sincerity throughout the world. I can assure you that we in the United States rejoice with you and the world at large that the outbreak of war has been averted."

Roosevelt had been following the crisis as closely and sympathetically as the Prime Minister of Canada. Indeed, of all the expressions of support that Chamberlain received during those dark days, there was none that encouraged him so much as the two words that he had been telegraphed by the President on September 23rd, on the eve of his journey to Munich. As the President's message was conveyed in a personal and confidential telegram to Kennedy, the American Ambassador, it was never published in London. Now, however, that it has been included in the second volume of Roosevelt's " Personal Letters," it is possible to quote both the exact words and the paragraph with which they were prefaced.

[1] " Prime Minister Chamberlain was interrupted during his House of Commons speech about the impasse with Hitler by the arrival of a despatch informing him that a meeting at Munich had been arranged. Immediately the news was flashed to the

[1] *F.D.R. His Personal Letters*, Vol. II, p. 826c. Duell, Sloan and Pearce.

United States, F. D. R. sent the congratulatory cable to Cham-
lain through Ambassador Kennedy in London.

" *Courtesy F.D.R.L.*

" *Wed. Sept. 22. 12 noon.*

" Kennedy.

" Personal for Prime Minister Chamberlain (quote) Good Man
signed Roosevelt (unquote). Telephoned to S. Wells to send at
once (file confidential).''

" Good man "—what could be more typical of the President's
very personal style, and what two words could better show
his full approval of Chamberlain's efforts? Were these words of
encouragement of no account? And if they were, could we have
ignored the unmistakable views of the Dominions?

From 1914 onwards, I had watched in particular the gathering strength of Dominion influence upon British policy. The
world at large never fully grasped the magnitude of the change
that, starting with the Dominion participation in the conduct
of the First World War, had been completed by the Statute of
Westminster. The new partnership often delayed and complicated
our decisions in Downing Street. The need for consultation took
valuable time at critical moments when agreement upon many
awkward questions was sometimes urgent but difficult to reach.
The outstanding fact, however, was that a co-equal partnership
had been created, and that no major decision involving the
Commonwealth could thenceforth be taken unilaterally in
London. Supposing that Chamberlain and the British Government had decided upon war in September, 1938, we should have
been ignoring the terms of partnership, and might well have
irrevocably broken the unity of the whole front.[1]

[1] Cp. Mackenzie King's statement in the House of Commons at Ottawa
on January 25, 1937, that " Canada will not necessarily become involved in any
war in which other parts of the British Empire may enter simply because we are part
of the British Empire.''

CHAPTER XXVII

The Pace and Scope of Rearmament after Munich

IN THE five months that followed Munich, hope and fear alternated in a cloudy atmosphere of relief and frustration. Sometimes it seemed that the chances of peace had improved, at other times that Hitler's appetite had only been whetted by the check that had been given to his plans for a military triumph. On the one hand, a Pact was signed in Paris by Bonnet and Ribbentrop on the lines of the agreement between Chamberlain and Hitler, and soon afterwards, Chamberlain and Halifax visited Rome, where, in spite of Mussolini's reserve and Ciano's sneers, they made a marked impression upon the Italian public. On the other hand, Hitler in his public speeches raged against British rearmament, and in his private talks scoffed at " the man with the umbrella " who had baulked him of his *blitzkrieg*, whilst Kirkpatrick, the British Counsellor in Berlin, reported that according to a German General's secret report, a sudden bombing raid was being planned against London.

Here, most people regarded the Munich settlement as inevitable, but none the less wished that it could have been avoided, although they could not say in what way. Whilst they tried to believe Hitler's promise of no further aggression, at the back of their minds they instinctively doubted its sincerity. Towards the German people they felt no great resentment, but an uncomfortable suspicion that Germans were always incorrigible. In face of these uncertainties, war was not yet regarded as inevitable. Neither the Government nor the people were ready to abandon the hope of peace, and with it many of the peace-time habits of the country. It seemed only common sense, whatever the future might bring, to give the agreement a chance of producing results.

Hope was rudely dashed by Hitler's sudden occupation of Prague on the following March 15. I suppose that we ought to have been better informed of the Führer's intrigues with the Slovak Government. The Slovaks were, in fact, proving as useful to him in disrupting the Czech State as the Sudeten Germans had been in the previous summer. So far, however, as I remember, we had no warning of the Prague *coup*. Chamberlain was away for the week-end fishing, when the news arrived. Not only had the Nazi system created a barrier between the totalitarian states and the democracies almost as insurmountable as the Iron Curtain that to-day isolates us from the Communist world, but Hitler's changing moods and sudden decisions were often as little foreseen by his intimates as they were by us. Indeed, the German Generals, although they knew that the occupation of Czechoslovakia was Hitler's next plan, were completely taken aback by the suddenness of the blow.

I remember very vividly the days before the storm. I was about to make my annual speech to my constituents in Chelsea on March 10, and as I wished to allude to foreign affairs, I consulted Chamberlain on the line that I had better take. His comment was that I should discourage the view that war was inevitable, and insist upon the great possibilities of peace. When I spoke, I followed his advice, and claimed that if the four leading statesmen in Europe, Chamberlain, Daladier, Hitler and Stalin, found it possible to work together in peace and amity, the world could look forward to a golden age of prosperity. The speech at the time met with wide approval. I was, in fact, saying what was in many minds. Later, my words were misrepresented as an unconditional prophecy of a golden age on the eve of a world war. They were no more a prophecy, still less an unconditional prophecy, than subsequent forecasts of the peace and prosperity that would follow the removal of the Iron Curtain between the Communists and the Western world.

The events of March 15 pushed any such hopes into a future that was out of sight. Like Chamberlain, I had regarded European peace as the supreme aim of our policy. It now seemed clear to me—our critics would say, better late than never—that only force counted with Hitler. The first chapter, in which we had tried negotiation, had ended, and a new page had begun in which rearmament would push into the background many, perhaps all, of the peaceful projects upon which I had been chiefly engaged. I had approved of every stage of the Munich negotiations, and had since supported Chamberlain with a hope as strong as his own that, in spite of sinister evidences to the contrary, Hitler would keep his word. I felt that my part in the Government was finished, and that I had better retire from public life. A sudden attack of influenza made my depression even blacker. Beaverbrook, once again a faithful friend as in the days of the Abyssinian crisis, came to see me. He, like me, had set his heart on peace. None the less, his advice was against my leaving the Government, although he fully realised the magnitude of the change that had come over the political scene. After all, war had not started, and there was still a chance of preventing it. It might well be that when we had become militarily stronger, we should be able to resume our efforts for a peaceful settlement with a better chance of success.

I accepted his advice, and as soon as I was well enough, went back to the Cabinet, the Committee of Imperial Defence, and the Foreign Policy Committee. There, a striking change had come over the proceedings. It was not that the hope of peace had been finally abandoned, or that our policy had been completely reversed. It was rather that Hitler's challenge had forced an immediate increase in the *tempo* and scope of the rearmament programme. Thenceforth, periodical reviews of our defences by the Committee of Imperial Defence became more than ever frequent and important.

These examinations had regularly taken place since Chamberlain became Prime Minister in 1937. They embraced the whole field of national defence, civil and industrial, as well as military. Chamberlain always took the closest interest in them, and unlike Baldwin, kept a close grip on the discussions. Under the new Prime Minister's chairmanship the Committee had become the clearing house for all the many plans of rearmament upon which the principal departments of Whitehall were engaged. In the days of Baldwin, the Prime Minister had attended the meetings intermittently, and then chiefly for the purpose of giving final approval to some proposal that had already been accepted by the experts.

Chamberlain took a different view of his functions. Not only did he interest himself in the technical details of defence, but he often intervened to give a lead to the experts. Whilst, therefore, Inskip or Chatfield, as Minister for the Co-ordination of Defence, took the chair at the routine meetings, the Prime Minister was always ready to give his advice when the more important questions were on the agenda. His personal interest was greatly needed. The complicated machinery that Hankey had most efficiently developed, had become so intricate that it was often difficult to obtain a quick or clear decision upon a specific question. Rearmament had ceased to be the sole concern of the Service Departments and almost every Minister, service and civil, had come to have an interest in it. The result was the creation of innumerable committees for dealing with every kind of defence question, and an inevitable tendency to defer decisions until most of them had been consulted. Chamberlain's grasp of detail enabled him to remove some at least of the causes of delay.

The change of atmosphere had become evident soon after he became Prime Minister. It was on March 24, 1938, that he had announced in the House of Commons a decisive break with the conventions of the past. Rearmament was for the first time to be given preference over peace-time habits and requirements, and the needs of the air force were to have precedence over the needs of the army and navy. These were his words at the opening of the debate on the Consolidated Fund Bill:

> " We have now come to the conclusion that in the present circumstances acceleration of existing plans has become essential" (Opposition cries of " Why? "), " and moreover there must be an increase in some parts of the programme, especially in that of the Royal Air Force and the anti-aircraft defences. In order to bring about the progress that we feel to be necessary, men and materials will be required and rearmament work must have first priority in the nation's effort. . . . This priority will enable us to expedite the programme of air-raid precautions."

From the point of view of Whitehall, the statement meant the beginning of a new chapter in which the Defence Departments would be able to make their plans without always having to subject them to the prior demands of civil life. It meant also that the ceiling was removed from the air force programme, and that the estimates of aircraft production were to be based not on a target number of machines, but on the total capacity of the aircraft industry. If Chamberlain had been able to profit immediately from these decisions, the state of our defences would have been very different at the time of Prague, if not at the time of Munich. The trouble, however, was the peace-time psychology of the country that persisted right up to the evacuation of Dunkirk, and the shortage of skilled labour and machine tools that was the inevitable result of many years of defence economies.

These were the obstacles that blocked better progress after the March statement. It may be said that the Prime Minister and the Government ought not to have accepted this atmosphere of " business as usual." Yet what could they have done in the circumstances? To have created the kind of atmosphere that would have frightened the country into immediate war measures, might, in the autumn of 1938, have destroyed the hope of any result from the Munich agreement. A possible alternative was a Dissolution, with a demand for complete liberty of action. Chamberlain would undoubtedly have obtained an overwhelming majority in the weeks that followed Munich. Some of his supporters, particularly his friend and admirer, Kingsley Wood, pressed him to seize what appeared to be a golden opportunity for confirming his position. It was greatly to the Prime Minister's credit that he firmly and even angrily rejected the proposal. He was on no account prepared to exploit in his own or his party's interest the emotional wave of support that his action had let loose. Unable, therefore, to reverse the methods and habits of peace as long as there was a chance of Hitler keeping his word, and debarred by his own feelings of what was right and patriotic from appealing to the country, he was forced, whether he wished it or not, to accept the prevailing conditions.

This was the obscure and disturbing state of affairs in the late summer, of 1938, when the Chiefs of Staff reported to the Committee of Imperial Defence on the overriding need to gain time for the completion of the defence programme.

Their conclusions were set out in a series of fundamental propositions. The first was that we were not ready for war; the second, that we could not fight a war on three fronts, German, Italian and Japanese, without powerful allies; next, that the Czech frontier of two thousand five hundred miles, bordered by unfriendly neighbours and isolated from supplies, could not be protected from a German attack, and that the Czech forces could only hold out for a few weeks; fourthly, that the French could hold the western front with their eighty-six divisions and the Maginot Line, the strongest fixed defences in existence, but were not willing or able to undertake an offensive against Germany either by air or land; and lastly, that if we were not willing to face a world war of attrition on the Czech issue, we must play for time.

The inescapable fact was only too obvious, that we had started rearmament too late. If, in 1933, we had realized the complete change that had come over Europe after Hitler's advent to power, and had at once embarked upon a bigger and quicker programme, and in particular, upon an intensified expansion of the Air Force, the Chiefs of Staff would have had a very different story to tell at the time of Munich. A single year would have made a vast difference to the actual results that they reported to us. New types of aeroplanes, for instance, were taking up to six or seven years before they came into service, and in the meanwhile we were passing through a critical period of transition in which the fighters and bombers were either obsolescent or obsolete, and a great part of our efforts was being devoted to training and ground establishments for the general expansion of the Force, rather than to the immediate formation of first-line units. Until the new machines arrived and the foundations of the expansion were firmly laid, we were in a very vulnerable position. We had, it is true, telescoped the normal stages of development, and taken the new fighter types direct from the drawing-board into production. Yet even so, at the time of Munich we had in service only five squadrons of Hurricanes and one of Spitfires, and as the Hurricanes were without heating for their guns, they could not fight above 15,000 feet, even in summer. In other words, we had less than a hundred eight-gun fighters against more than a thousand German bombers.

The new types of bombers were estimated to take longer than the fighters to reach the squadrons, and two years were needed for the change over from the Hampdens, Battles, Blenheims and Whitleys. The Halifaxes, Stirlings and Manchesters, when they came into service from early 1941 until 1942, would, however, be decisively better than the corresponding German machines.

When the sum was added up, it appeared that, excluding overseas units and Fleet Air Arm machines, we had in October, 1938 1606 first-line fighters and bombers against the German figure of 3200. The French strength of 1454 did little to compensate this disparity, as the French machines were almost entirely obsolete. A more comforting fact was that our reserves and standards of training gave us a very definite advantage in quality over the Luftwaffe.

Our ground defence against aircraft scarcely existed. None of the 3.7-inch and 4.5-inch guns, the only effective military artillery against aeroplanes, had yet come into production. There were only 1430 searchlights out of the 4128 required, and 140 balloons out of 450. More important still, radar protection only covered the Thames Estuary.

For Civil Defence, the need for more time was no less urgent. The new service had started in very unfavourable conditions. Most people, but by no means all, thought that it was necessary, but no one liked it. The fighting services, particularly the Air Force, had little faith in passive defence of any kind; the scientific experts were sceptical of the value of gas-masks and shelters; the local authorities objected to any charge on the rates, while the Treasury refused to undertake the full burden of the expense. It was not surprising in view of these doubts and difficulties that progress had been slow. Indeed, the only section of this part of the report that told a satisfactory story, dealt with gas-masks, of which there was an adequate supply for the young as well as the old, but for which, as I shall show later, there was little or no use. From the point of view of recruitment, however, the position had steadily improved since the two appeals that I had made on the radio. The number of recruits had reached the million for which I had asked, and their training was already beginning.

It was shortly after the Staff review that I had to meet a vote of censure in the House of Commons on the deficiencies that the Munich crisis had disclosed. As I was keenly conscious of the many gaps, I was not surprised at the Opposition's attack. It did, however, seem somewhat incongruous that it should have been led by Herbert Morrison, whose supporters on several London Councils had made better progress almost impossible.

It will be seen from the description that I have given of our air and civil defences at the time of Munich that we were militarily unready for war. There had been no time or opportunity since

Chamberlain's statement in the previous March to make any substantial progress. What had happened in the interval had been an extension of the plans, and an attempt, not always successful owing to peace-time psychology, to speed them up. The result had been to leave our first-line strength much as it was in the spring, but to give it a power of expansion that would gradually gather very great volume. It was estimated that, provided that we had a further twelve months without war, we should in the autumn of 1939 have a radar chain from the Orkneys to Land's End, sufficient 3.7-inch and 4.5-inch anti-aircraft guns to cover London and the chief industrial centres, enough searchlights and balloon barrages for all the main strategic points, ten squadrons of Spitfires and twenty-five of Hurricanes, all of them with improved equipment, and the first of our new types of bombers within sight.

In the meanwhile, thanks to Swinton's foresight, the shadow factories would be producing more than twice as many machines and engines, and the Empire Training Scheme would be organized for producing large numbers of pilots.

The disturbing factor in the estimates for the future was the undoubted capacity of the Luftwaffe to increase its lead during the next few months. This was a risk that had to be faced. The Air Staff, however, had no doubt as to the necessity of taking it in view of the fact that at the end of twelve months our production of machines would exceed the German figure, rise in 1942 to 2500 a month, and shortly afterwards make it possible for us to win the command of the air.[1] We were also encouraged in the view that time was on our side by the reports that began to come to us from France of a new spirit in the aircraft industry. Daladier was speaking confidently of rising production, the French Government was buying American machines, and a better chapter seemed to be opening for the French Air Force. What, therefore, our programme seemed to need, was time, rather than any fundamental change.

As to the Army, we accepted the fact that the Reichswehr

[1] This estimate has since been confirmed by the official figures of German production. The following are the relative production figures for 1940:—

	Bombers	Fighters	All Operational Aircraft
Britain	3,710	4,283	9,924
Germany	3,954	2,424	8,070

(From the files of the German Ministry of Armaments and War Production.)

would become stronger with every month that was given it for expansion and organization. Our relative position was, therefore, certain in this respect to become worse. At the same time, we should, as some compensation, have the chance of improving our anti-aircraft defences, and of organizing the expeditionary force for the Continent. The consideration, however, that chiefly influenced us in Army policy was our reliance on the French Army to hold the line until we had mobilized and trained our manpower. Every Staff appreciation that we received was based on this assumption. None of the military experts either in London or Paris ever expressed a doubt as to the French ability to resist. Churchill, most experienced of observers, and close friend of General Georges, the most active of the French Generals, never questioned this joint opinion of the French and British Staffs, either before or after he joined the Government.

Reliance on the French also affected our naval policy. We depended on the French fleet of three battleships, two battle cruisers, fourteen cruisers, and the French ports in the Channel and Western Mediterranean for giving our own fleet liberty of movement. It was true that Hitler, apart from exceeding certain agreed limits in the case of the pocket battleships, was not only carrying out the main provisions of the Anglo-German Naval Agreement, but had not built up to the strengths to which he was entitled. Yet, even so, we needed the French fleet for reinsuring our communications in the Mediterranean, and for freeing us to meet a Japanese threat in the Far East. Feeling sure of this support in the autumn of 1938, we rightly attached more importance to the expansion of the Air Force than to our programmes for the Army and Navy.

It was the Prague *coup* that made us reconsider in a new light the needs of the two older Services, and at the same time make one important change in the air programme. This change concerned the priority to be given to bombers over fighters. Hitherto, the emphasis in the programme had been on the bomber force. The threat of Prague had, however, made the danger of German raids much more formidable. When, therefore, Air Marshal Dowding pressed for a substantial increase of the fighter squadrons, the priority was changed in favour of fighter defence. I doubt whether we then realized the full importance of the new decision. Dowding saw dangers at hand that many thought to be still distant. It was due to his foresight that the programme was changed, and new fighter squadrons added to it over and above the existing plans. The result was an expansion of fighter strength between the autumn of 1938 and the summer of 1940 that eventually made possible the victory of the Battle of Britain.

For the Navy and the Army, Prague necessitated several decisions of great importance. Naval policy was still based upon the conception of a naval war in the Far East, and a holding operation in western waters. The Admiralty, however, had been pressing for a formal recognition of the fact that a naval war, if it came, would need to be actively fought on two fronts. The March crisis brought the question to the only issue that was possible, and the Naval Staff was instructed to plan for active operations in the Mediterranean and Atlantic as well as in the Pacific. This new direction, however, could not have any conspicuous or immediate effect on the naval programme. The naval yards had already on hand as much work as they could undertake, and until more skilled labour was available, particularly for gun mountings, the possibilities of expansion were closely circumscribed. None the less, the decision marked a definite change in the Government's attitude towards the threat of war.

The change in Army policy was even more significant. Within a fortnight of March 15, we agreed to a bigger and more definite programme for the Expeditionary Force to the Continent. Two corps, each of two divisions, and an Air component were to be in France within thirty days of the outbreak of war. Secondly, staff talks with the French, that had hitherto been desultory and inconclusive, were to start at once on a methodical plan. Thirdly, the Territorial Army was to be doubled. In some ways this last decision was the most important, for, although it seemed to the critics little more than a paper expedient, its inevitable result was sooner or later the introduction for the first time of compulsory military service in a period of peace.

This intensification of the programme immediately exposed the difficulties that faced the Government. On the one hand, the danger of war had become more formidable, on the other, the country was still living in the conditions of peace. Hitler's occupation of Prague had shown that he was no longer concerned with the liberation of Germans, but was bent on the domination of Europe. Rumours were everywhere current that he was about to attack Poland and Roumania. British rearmament, therefore, was now a preparation for war, instead of being merely a safeguard of peace. The immediate need was to show our determination to resist further aggression.

It was in this confused and critical atmosphere that the strongest possible pressure was put on Chamberlain by many of his Conservative supporters, and by the French Government, to introduce at once compulsory military service. Chamberlain, who was always well informed upon industrial questions, at first resisted the immediate demand, on the ground that the munitions industry, and particularly the aircraft firms, were working well, and that it was dangerous to disturb the good relations between employers and employed. Nor could he forget that when he had become Prime Minister, he had endorsed Baldwin's pledge not to introduce conscription in peace time, and had repeated it immediately after the Prague *coup*. The international outlook had, however, become so black and threatening that he was very soon forced to review the position, and consider a plan of limited and temporary military training for young men of 20 and 21 for a period of six months. Before, however, reaching the final decision, he made a further attempt to obtain the co-operation of organised labour for the relaxation of restrictive practices in the production of munitions. On March 23 and March 26, therefore, within ten days of the Prague *coup*, he and the Minister for the Co-ordination of Defence met the representatives of the Trade Union Congress to discuss possible methods of accelerating the rearmament programme. The reaction of the Labour leaders was most unsympathetic. Rebuffed on the industrial line, Chamberlain was forced back upon the military issue of compulsory national service. The French were desperately insistent that only our introduction of conscription would steady French morale, and the great majority of the Conservative Party backed the French demand. In this twilight that was neither peace nor war, Chamberlain, having failed with his proposals for the modification of labour restrictions, set aside his doubts and hesitations over national service.

Having made up his mind, he again met the representatives of the T.U.C. to inform them of his changed attitude before the Bill for carrying it into effect was actually introduced. I was one of half a dozen Ministers who were present at the meeting in

Downing Street on April 25 with the Labour leaders. Chamberlain began with a full statement of the critical position, in which he particularly insisted on the need of better protection against a lightning blow. Our existing preparations were too slow for the new conditions of modern warfare. It was no longer safe to leave the anti-aircraft defence of London and the great cities in the hands of part-time Territorials. The traditional procedure of a Royal Proclamation ordering the embodiment of Territorials and Reservists was too deliberate for a sudden emergency. It was therefore necessary to have regular personnel permanently available, and as things were, we were short of men. He therefore felt bound to introduce immediately a measure of compulsory military training. As to the pledge that he had given against conscription in peace time, his conscience was clear. After the occupation of Prague and the threats to Roumania and Poland, it was no longer peace time in the accepted sense of the term, and in any case, there was no question of adopting conscription as a permanent part of the life of the country. The Bill would be temporary, and at the end of three years, would need affirmative resolutions of both Houses of Parliament for its renewal. In order that it should not be said that Labour alone was called upon to make sacrifices, there would be a limitation of profits and a rise in income and super tax.

As he developed his argument, I looked across the table at the glum and angry faces of the Trade Union leaders. Bevin in particular was obviously restraining his resentment with considerable difficulty. Citrine followed Chamberlain, and spoke of Labour's deep and unyielding feeling against conscription. Bevin spoke with undisguised anger. The Government was violating its pledge. The Trade Union Congress would have to reconsider their promise to co-operate in the voluntary national service scheme that had already been started. The proposed Bill would lead to full-blooded conscription and divide the country from top to bottom. Until I listened to Bevin's attack, I had never realised the extent of the personal bitterness felt by the Labour leaders against the Prime Minister.

The debates in the House of Commons on April 26 and 27 were equally hostile. When the Prime Minister gave notice of the Bill, Attlee retorted:

" Is the Prime Minister aware that this decision will break the pledge solemnly given to this country and reaffirmed only four weeks ago that compulsory service would not be introduced in peace-time, that it will increase the already widespread distrust of the Prime Minister, that so far from strengthening this country, it will be sowing divisions in the ranks of this country, and will gravely imperil the national effort, and that this departure from the voluntary principle will meet with strenuous opposition? "

When the Bill was actually introduced on the following day, it was met by a Labour amendment of no confidence in the Government.

" We are opposed to conscription," declared the Leader of the Opposition. " It will weaken the country. If there is to be a gesture, it should be the conscription of wealth. . . . There is no need for conscription so far as men are concerned. The Navy and the Air Force are up to strength, and there are no arms for more men."

Cripps reinforced Attlee's attack. The right course, he declared, was to drop any idea of compulsory military service, agree with Russia, have a capital levy, and democratise the fighting services. At the end of this heated debate the full strength of the Opposition was thrown into the lobby against the second reading of the Bill.

The debate and the two conferences in Downing Street clearly showed how impracticable it was in 1938 and 1939 fully to mobilise the country's manpower and resources. The truth was thrust upon us that until the people were faced with the stark dangers of actual war, it was impossible to introduce war methods of production and organisation, and to form a National Government for a single purpose. Up to September, 1939, there was still a chance, no doubt diminishing, but none the less a chance, that war would be prevented. As long as the doubt remained, the peace-time psychology persisted. While it was possible for the Government to expand the rearmament programme and, as the risk of war increased, to expedite the date for its completion, neither the Prime Minister nor anyone else could undertake the responsibility of saying that war was inevitable and that therefore the habits and methods of peace must be compulsorily ended. It was therefore necessary to proceed by conciliation and persuasion. Even after the National Service Bill had passed, there were the difficult problems still to be solved of attracting skilled labour into munitions work, of upgrading and dilution, of more women, and of the transfer of workers to new districts. Although the aircraft firms were clamouring for more skilled workers, there were still a million and a half unemployed men and women registered at the Employment Exchanges, most of whom could not be moved without compulsion, and who in any case needed training and houses that were not then available. There was no chance of this state of affairs coming to an end until the Labour leaders were prepared to agree to drastic changes in peace-time conditions, and to these changes they were opposed until they were faced with a direct and clear challenge to our national existence. I doubt whether even Churchill, if he had been a member of the Government, could have roused the country in the spring and summer of 1939 to an all-out war effort. Certainly amongst Chamberlain's Ministers there was no spellbinder to make the attempt. Even if we had possessed a great popular leader, I do not believe that the country would have accepted war conditions in the months before war started.

Prague, although it shook the national complacency, did not remove it. Indeed, even the actual outbreak of war in the following September failed to make the deep impression that might have been expected. With the slow motion of the campaign, and the land fighting far removed from our shores, the country still hesitated to throw aside the peace-time habits and practices of many years. It needed the explosions of Dunkirk and the Battle of Britain to dissipate once and for all the misty atmosphere of peace, and to give the nation a clear view of the needs and dangers that faced it.

CHAPTER XXVIII
Russia and Poland, 1939

I N THE last chapter I gave some account of our efforts for rearmament in face of the peace psychology that still possessed the country. Looking back, I freely admit that none of us, from Chamberlain downwards, was likely to excite a crusading spirit in a world that was set on peace. We were essentially a peace-time Ministry, the successors of the first National Government that had been created to meet an economic crisis, and as I have shown, both industry and labour were opposed to any drastic changes in the national economy. None the less, within these obvious limitations we succeeded in making definite progress with rearmament in the months after Munich, and in strengthening the sound foundations of a plan of defence that was never substantially changed during the war.

I come now to the story of our negotiations with the Soviet, in which the difficulties were so great and the details so confused that I need the evidence that has become available since the war to explain our action. The German official documents that have since been published and the proceedings of the Nuremberg trials throw a vivid light on the many dark corners that have hitherto seemed impenetrable. Without them, the description of our repeated attempts to make an agreement with Stalin is so complicated as to be almost unintelligible. With them, we can see exposed the ruthless intrigue that was proceeding behind the Iron Curtain while we were negotiating in London. I am therefore supplementing my day-to-day account of our London activities with the parallel story of what was happening in Berlin and Moscow. Only in this way, can the failure of our efforts be fairly understood.

After the fall of Prague it was clear to everyone that Danzig was the next point of immediate danger. Hitler had for some months been testing the ground for an attack on the Polish Corridor, but until March 15, he had given Beck, the Polish Foreign Minister, the impression that he was still prepared for a reasonable settlement. The Prague *coup* smashed the chance of any successful negotiation, and unmistakably threatened an imminent offensive against Poland. What, we asked ourselves, could we do to check the next aggression? Was it possible for us to make alliances in Eastern Europe that would give substance to our warnings or guarantees? These were the questions that at once faced us in the Foreign Policy Committee, and for which we tried our best to find answers in the following months.

Throughout the long and tedious discussions that followed, we were influenced first by British and French military opinion, and secondly by the deep-rooted suspicion that we felt towards the Soviet. These two influences must constantly be kept in mind in any impartial review of the Anglo-Russian negotiations. The details, therefore, must be followed against a background of disbelief in Russian military strength and suspicion of Russian political motives.

I begin with the question of our disbelief in Russian military strength. The Great Purge of the years 1936 and 1937 seemed to have left the Soviet incapable of any military action. Our military attaché in Moscow had described to us its devastating effect on the fighting services, and particularly on the corps of senior officers. Gamelin and the French General Staff confirmed his reports.

The revolutionary change in Russian policy had started in 1934 with Stalin's savage reaction to the murder of Kirov, the secretary of the Communist Party in Leningrad. A dark and terrible chapter of wholesale denunciations, arrests and executions followed. The victims were no longer the men and women identified with the past, but many of the new leaders who had gained power under the Stalin régime. Between 1937 and 1939 the former national hero, Tukhachevsky, was shot, and almost all the senior officers in the army arrested. When I was First Lord of the Admiralty I had a vivid glimpse of what was happening. Admiral Orlov, representing Stalin at the Coronation of King George VI, was suddenly ordered back to Russia to stand his trial.

On the evening of the Coronation Review at Spithead, I gave a dinner in the Admiralty yacht, *Enchantress*, to the chiefs of the foreign naval missions. The Russian, being the senior admiral, sat on my right. In the middle of dinner he was handed a telephone message on a slip of paper and immediately asked to be excused. The message was his sudden recall to Russia. I afterwards heard that upon his return he was arrested and executed. His was the fate of hundreds of other naval and military officers. Whilst we noticed at the time how name after name disappeared from Russian life, we now know the facts in greater detail. Three out of the five marshals, thirteen out of the fifteen army commanders, thirty out of the fifty-eight corps commanders, one hundred and ten out of the one hundred and ninety-five divisional commanders, and sixty to seventy per cent of all the field officers were arrested, imprisoned, and, in many cases, executed. The technical and training establishments of the army were denuded of their skilled personnel. The transport system was brought almost to a standstill by wholesale arrests. The foreign technicians, upon whom it greatly depended, were tried as spies and expelled or imprisoned. In short, Russian military and economic life was thrown into complete confusion.

There was ample justification in face of this upheaval, for our doubts about the efficacy of any Russian assistance. They were further strengthened by the absence of any sign of Russian mobilisation at the time of the Polish seizure of Czech territory after Munich. We drew the conclusion that Stalin did not consider it safe to mobilise the army while the effects of the Great Purge were still shaking the country. Indeed, he appeared to be by no means unfavourable to Fascist aggression. If Hitler and Mussolini could be diverted to the West, and France and Great Britain weakened or destroyed by war, he would at the worst be given time to fill the gaps in Soviet defences, and at the best, profit in Eastern Europe by the opportunities offered him in Poland, the Baltic States and the Balkans. From the crisis of 1938 until the end of the war, his purpose, in fact, never changed. Waiting on events, and ready to seize any chance of carrying out an entirely ruthless policy, he was able in 1939, without striking a blow, to exploit the collapse of Poland, and in 1945, to satisfy Russian ambitions in the Far East by entering the war against Japan, when there was no longer any risk, and the fighting had finished.

If it is asked how our estimate of Russian weakness in 1938 and 1939 can be reconciled with the amazing Russian victories in 1943, there are several answers. In the first place, there was the heavy strain upon German resources caused by Allied pressure, particularly by Allied air raids; secondly, the arrival of Allied munitions from the United States and Great Britain; thirdly, the wave of Russian patriotism that was stirred to fever point by German brutalities on the sacred soil of Russia; but most important of all, the effect of the Russian winter upon Hitler's bad strategy and inadequate preparations. In 1938 and 1939, we could only judge the military position of the Soviet as we saw it at the time. It was not humanly possible to foresee the change that was to come about after four years of world war, and a winter that equalled in severity the cold of 1812. At the time, we had to depend for our estimate upon the unanimous verdict of the British and French General Staffs that the Russian Army was completely demoralised.

Their second conclusion followed that Poland was a more valuable ally than Russia. Not only did they hold a high opinion of the Polish Army, but they regarded the wide spaces of Poland as excellent *terrain* for Polish defence. As the crisis developed, it was made repeatedly evident that we and the French had to make our first choice between the two. On the one hand there was Russia, militarily impotent for the moment, but with her vast man-power and limitless distances as a bulwark against ultimate defeat; on the other, Poland, in the eyes of the experts militarily strong, but balanced precariously between her two powerful neighbours, and determined to avoid provoking Hitler by joining in any pact of mutual aid with Russia, her historic enemy.

Faced with this dilemma, and fortified at every stage by expert military advice, the British and French Governments came down on the side of Poland as at least the first and most effective choice. The need during the crisis over Danzig was for some definite action that would immediately impress Hitler. The course that seemed to avoid delay and to give the best hope of providing a deterrent pointed to co-operation with Poland, and an agreement with Roumania, Greece and Turkey, the countries that, according to our reports, were the most likely to be immediately attacked. All the Baltic States, particularly Poland, were opposed to any arrangement that involved the passage of Russian troops across their territories, and even if this objection could be surmounted, the road and railway communications were so bad that any substantial Russian aid was impracticable. Russian participation in a mutual aid pact with her neighbours seemed, therefore, to be not only politically and geographically impossible, but in the face of the immediate threats of Nazi aggression, of little military value. Throughout the discussions of the Foreign Policy Committee in the spring and summer of 1939 these considerations were constantly in our minds.

As soon as we heard of the Prague *coup* on March 15, Chamberlain decided to make a swift counter-move. The first step was to give Hitler a solemn warning in a speech at Birmingham on March 17. The question next to be settled was the best and speediest method of still further marking the gravity of the crisis. As a preliminary move, we turned instinctively to the possibility of either a joint Four-Power Conference with France, Russia and Poland, or a joint Four-Power Declaration of Resistance to any further aggression. While we were still discussing the two alternatives, and were trying to allay the Polish suspicions of Russia, circumstantial and very alarmist reports arrived in London that Hitler was on the point of attacking Poland and Roumania. One of these reports was given to Chamberlain by the Secretary of State for War at the State Banquet in honour of President Lebrun at Buckingham Palace. "Another Brussels Ball" was Hore-Belisha's comment. A second and equally disturbing story came from a newspaper correspondent who had just returned from the Continent and who gave a hair-raising account of Hitler's warlike preparations.

Shortly afterwards, there was another scare to disturb a royal banquet. The Foreign Secretary was entertaining King Carol of Roumania at the Foreign Office. When dinner was over, I was asked to talk to the King. On my way to the corner where he was sitting, I was told in a whisper that the Channel Fleet had been put in readiness to meet a sudden German attack. Whilst the report upon which the Admiralty had based the order, proved to be groundless, the emergency action that was immediately taken upon it, was further evidence of the explosive atmosphere that had overspread Europe. From all sides came rumours and reports of impending *coups*.

In the meanwhile, the Baltic States made it clear that they

would not join in any pact with Russia, not only because they suspected the Soviet of sinister designs, but because they feared that any such joint action would provoke Hitler to attack them.

Beck in particular could not have been more outspoken in his opposition to Litvinov's suggestion of a Four- or Six-Power Conference. As Polish Foreign Minister, he left us in no doubt as to his country's attitude, declaring categorically that there would be an " explosion " if we persisted with the proposal of any joint action that was intended to include Poland and Russia in the same *bloc*. His many critics have seized on his answer as an example not only of Polish intransigence, but of his own personal recklessness. Yet it is difficult to see how, in the early months of 1939, he could have risked endangering the traditional Polish balance between Germany and Russia. It was not so much his policy as his personality that made both the democracies and the dictatorships distrust him. He was undoubtedly very secretive. Although he had for months past been rejecting Hitler's repeated offers of the Ukraine in exchange for Danzig, not only the French and British Governments, but even his own Ambassadors were, throughout the winter, left in doubt as to his final intentions.

The influences of his early life had never weakened. As Foreign Minister, he still retained the habits that he had learnt as one of Pilsudski's fellow conspirators against both Russian and German domination. The German police and the Tcheka had been equally active on his track when he was recruiting Poles for Pilsudski's Legion. Once indeed, he had only escaped by disguising himself as a coachman, and then, driving a priest over the Polish frontier who was carrying the *viaticum* to a dying parishioner. The adventures of the secret agent had left a permanent mark on him. When Pilsudski made him military attaché in Paris, the old habits persisted. During a visit to the Deuxième Bureau, he took a confidential report from the table when the chief of the French secret service had been called for a few minutes from the room. The French Government insisted upon his recall, and neither he nor successive French Ministers ever forgot the incident. The result was that while his rival, Benes, made many friends in London and Paris, and everywhere became a sociable and popular figure, Beck remained aloof, suspected and suspicious, only too ready both to take offence and to assert his claims with little regard for the dangers and susceptibilities of his neighbours. These personal failings undoubtedly damaged his credit. Whenever I met him, I started with a prejudice against him, but after a few minutes' talk I found it difficult to avoid a certain admiration of his self-reliance in the face of appalling dangers. With two such neighbours as Hitler and Stalin, I doubt whether he could have avoided the final catastrophe. In trying to balance between the two, it is true that in the end he brought their united weight upon his country. Yet not even the wisest of Ministers would have prevented Germany and Russia from making another partition of Poland as soon as the opportunity was given them. The fate of his unhappy country was settled when once Hitler and Stalin had made a compact of partition.

When it became evident that multilateral action that included both Poland and Russia was impracticable, we had to consider other alternatives for convincing Hitler that further aggression would mean war. There were two choices open to us. We could ignore the Polish opposition and embark upon a negotiation for a Three-Power Pact with the Soviet that was certain to take time and was unlikely to succeed. Or we could abandon the idea of a multilateral front and fall back upon unilateral declarations that did not bring Russia and Poland together into a joint agreement.

To the first alternative, there was the unanimous objection of the British and French military staffs. Poland, we were told, was the key to the situation. Halifax in London and Bonnet in Paris supported the military view and agreed that the essential point was to manage matters so as to secure Polish support. In the face of this weight of opinion, we refused to sacrifice the help of the Polish Army, and turned to the second alternative of unilateral declarations, although we never completely discarded the subsequent possibility of a mutual aid treaty with the Soviet, in which Poland would not take part. It seemed essential to act at once, and Beck agreed with us that, provided that Poland was not involved in a multilateral pact, the risk of provoking Hitler by unilateral declarations was less than the risk of doing nothing.

This was the history of the British guarantee to Poland that Chamberlain announced in the House of Commons on March 31. The decision to make it was taken very quickly. To the world at large, the Prime Minister's action of March 31 appeared almost as sudden as Hitler's *coup* of March 15. Chamberlain's swift reaction was typical of his obstinate character. Far from stunning him, the Prague *coup* made him hit back as hard and as soon as he could. He at once saw the leaders of the Opposition and told them that, as it was impossible to bring Russia and Poland into a joint agreement, the only immediate course open to us was a unilateral declaration that an attack on Poland would mean war with Great Britain. While they certainly would have preferred a pact that included the Soviet, they were not opposed to the Government's proposal. There followed on March 31, little more than a fortnight after Prague, the Prime Minister's statement in the House of Commons, in which he not only declared our determination to resist further aggression, but announced a change in our traditional policy so great and grave that his exact words need to be quoted in full:

> " The right hon. Gentleman the Leader of the Opposition asked me this morning ,whether I could make a statement as to the European situation. As I said this morning, His Majesty's Government have no official confirmation of the rumours of any projected attack on Poland and they must not, therefore, be taken as accepting them as true.
>
> " I am glad to take this opportunity of stating again the general policy of His Majesty's Government. They have constantly advocated the adjustment, by way of free negotiation between the parties concerned, of any differences that may arise between them. They consider that this is the natural and proper course where differences exist. In their opinion there should be no question incapable of solution by peaceful means, and they would see no justification for the substitution of force or threats of force for the method of negotiation.
>
> " As the House is aware, certain consultations are now proceeding with other Governments. In order to make perfectly clear the position of His Majesty's Government in the meantime before those consultations are concluded, I now have to inform the House that during that period, in the event of any action which clearly threatened Polish independence, and which the Polish Government accordingly considered it vital to resist with their national forces, His Majesty's Government would feel themselves bound at once to lend the Polish Government all support in their power. They have given the Polish Government an assurance to this effect."

It will be seen that the guarantee was very carefully worded. We were not giving Poland a blank cheque, and in taking what seemed to us to be the only step immediately practicable, we were not finally excluding the possibility of three- or even four-Power action in the future. The two conditions under which we undertook to intervene were, firstly, a clear threat to Polish independence that we should ourselves define, and secondly, Polish armed resistance to the aggression. The decision as to whether or not we should take part in a war was retained in our own hands. As to co-operation with Russia, we were prepared to make further efforts to obtain it, but it was clear that what was needed at once was action of some kind, and a multilateral agreement would, at the best, take time to complete.

The announcement was well received. The Opposition in the House of Commons approved it, and Churchill gave it his support.

It is only in subsequent years that it has been criticised. Why, it has been asked, were we ready to give a guarantee to a semi-totalitarian government in Poland that had shamelessly exploited the Czech crisis, and had for many years followed a devious foreign policy, when we had refused to uphold the integrity of Czechoslovakia, a democratic country whose friendliness to France and Great Britain had never faltered? How could we give effective military aid to Poland without Russian co-operation? Was not the guarantee, particularly when it became reciprocal in the late summer, likely to provoke rather than deter Hitler? Why did we not have recourse to the only effective deterrent, a military alliance with Russia, even if it estranged Poland and all Russia's neighbours?

Most of the answers that have been given to these questions fail to take into account the facts of the situation in March 1939. Hitler, by his Prague *coup*, had turned a Europe that still hoped for peace at the time of Munich, into a Europe that expected war. Whilst in 1938 the British Commonwealth was reluctant to fight a world war for keeping the Sudeten Germans in Czechoslovakia, in 1939 an unprovoked attack on Poland was clear evidence of Hitler's determination to dominate Europe, and the Commonwealth, true to British tradition, was ready to resist. Whilst also in 1938 it was still possible to believe Hitler's word, in 1939 it had become evident that force and the threat of force would alone prevent him from breaking it.

As to the further criticism that if we could not have given effective military help to Czechoslovakia, still less could we give it to Poland, the answer is that in each case a world war with Great Britain and not local British aid, was the deterrent. In 1938, when Hitler's full intentions were still unknown, we were not willing to start a world war for Czechoslovakia. In 1939, when it was clear that he intended to dominate the Continent, we took up the challenge, just as we had taken it up against Philip II, Louis XIV and Napoleon.

The Polish Government certainly understood the tactical limitations of any British intervention, but none the less welcomed our guarantee, and believed that it would deter rather than provoke Hitler.

In coming to our decision we were undoubtedly influenced by suspicion of the Soviet, whilst we believed that we could rely both upon the Polish will to resist and the Polish Army to hold out until Anglo-French resources were mobilised. Even if our military experts overrated Polish strength, we had solid reasons for distrusting the Soviet. For more than twenty years, successive British Governments had suffered from Russian plots and intrigues. British party politics had been constantly poisoned by Russian propaganda. Russian secret agents were continuously exploiting any chance of stirring up trouble, Russian money was finding its way into the pockets of British agitators. The Zinoviev Letter[1] that created so resounding a sensation in 1924 was not an isolated instance of Russian interference in our affairs. The attempts to incite mutinies in the fighting services and strikes in the ranks of labour went on unabated during the whole period between the two wars, and the Russian Embassy in London never ceased to be a centre of espionage and agitation.

Whilst we fully realised that the prejudices of the past should not deflect our later policy, we should not have been human if we had not been influenced by this long record of Russian duplicity and hostility. On the Russian side, Stalin was equally suspicious. In particular, he had resented his exclusion from the Munich negotiations. I doubt, however, whether his inclusion in them would in any way have deflected him from his set purpose of exploiting for his own ends the differences between Germany and the West. It certainly would have made any agreement impossible.

His irritation had already shown itself in the speech that he

[1] See Appendix, p. 434.

made to the All-Union Communist Party in Moscow on March 10, 1939. His words, though at the time they were open to different interpretations, forecast his future attitude. Our Ambassador, Sir William Seeds, in a long dispatch of March 20, pointed out how, whilst he had attacked Hitler, his chief criticisms had been directed against the Allies for their alleged attempt to embroil Russia with Germany. The Ambassador ended his summary of the speech with the following comments:

". . . In matters of foreign policy, account is taken of the realities of the situation and, above all, of the fact that, in the present state of the Red Army, of the Soviet economic system and of Soviet transport, the Soviet Union should avoid intervention in a conflict of capitalistic Powers. Thus, while M. Stalin and various other speakers at the Congress emphasise Soviet readiness to defend the frontiers of the Soviet Union, should they be attacked, the line taken by all of them is that the chief care of those responsible for Soviet foreign policy must be to prevent the Soviet Union from being dragged into the struggle now in progress between the Fascist States and the so-called democracies. M. Stalin did, of course, say that the Soviet Union would be prepared to support all peoples who had been the victims of aggression and who were fighting for their national independence. This, however, may merely imply that the Soviet Government would be prepared, as in the case of China and Republican Spain, to provide assistance in the form of war material, provisions and technical help, after aggression was in full swing. Those innocents at home who believe that Soviet Russia is only awaiting an invitation to join the Western democracies should be advised to ponder M. Stalin's advice to his party: ' To be cautious and not allow Soviet Russia to be drawn into conflicts by war-mongers who are accustomed to have others pull chestnuts out of the fire.' "

We did not then, realise the full significance of Stalin's words. As events proved, however, they were the text for the Russo-German Pact in the following August, although their exact meaning was obscured in the following weeks by what appeared to be a Russian desire to co-operate with us. When, however, Litvinov shortly afterwards made a proposal for a Four- or a Six-Power Treaty of Mutual Aid, he and his Government knew perfectly well that Poland would refuse to join it.

Our first impression of the speech, was that Stalin had not

yet joined Hitler's camp. Accordingly, we at once started
discussions with the Soviet, to see whether it was possible to
obtain Russian co-operation without losing the support of Poland
and the Baltic States. Throughout the whole summer of 1939
we never ceased these efforts in the hope that Stalin's fear of a
predominant Germany might in the end induce him to work
with us. There was scarcely a day in the months of May, June
and July when we did not hold meetings of Ministers for the
purpose of finding a basis of agreement with him.

Chamberlain began by doubting the possibility of any satisfactory pact with a government whose motives he continually
suspected.

> " I must confess," he wrote to his sister on May 26, " to the
> most profound distrust of Russia. I have no belief whatever in her
> ability to maintain an effective offensive, even if she wanted to.
> And I distrust her motives, which seem to me to have little con-
> nection with our ideas of liberty, and to be concerned only with
> getting everyone else by the ears. Moreover, she is both hated and
> suspected by many of the smaller States, notably by Poland,
> Roumania and Finland."

Halifax, whilst he was also doubtful whether it would ever
be possible to reach an agreement, was determined to go to very
great lengths to obtain one. Chatfield, the Minister for the Co-
ordination of Defence, supported the effort by emphasising on the
one hand, the importance of Russia as a possible deterrent to
Hitler, even though Russian military strength was at a low ebb,
and on the other hand, the danger of pushing the Soviet into the
Axis. So far as my influence counted, I was persistently on the
side of making every effort to bring Stalin over to the Allies, and
if that was impossible, at least to keep him from throwing the
weight of Russian power, whatever it might be, on to the enemy's
side. Our genuine desire in spite of the past was to try to set aside
our suspicions and to supplement our unilateral declarations,
which were intended as the first and immediate line of defence,
with a Tripartite Pact of Mutual Aid based upon three unilateral
declarations of our respective positions.

CHAPTER XXIX

A Hopeless Negotiation

HAVING SUPPLEMENTED the Polish guarantee with further guarantees to Greece and Roumania, the two other countries that seemed most likely to be attacked, we concentrated our efforts on the negotiation with the Soviet. No time was lost. It was on April 11, within three weeks of the Prague *coup*, that Halifax began the discussions with an exploratory talk with Maisky in London. Our object was clearly explained in a telegram to Seeds three days later. We were proposing an agreement, based on unilateral declarations of the French, Russian and British Governments for resisting the invasion of Poland, Roumania and Greece. We did not at the time contemplate any pact that guaranteed Soviet territory, or included the Baltic States. The Governments of the Dominions, particularly the Governments of Canada and South Africa, were strongly opposed to any obligation that might involve us in war with Germany on behalf of Russia, still more to any military alliance that guaranteed Russian territory. A large body of British public opinion supported the Dominion view. Nor did we contemplate any obligation that covered the Baltic States or involved automatic intervention where the Governments concerned did not desire it.

Litvinov, whom Seeds saw on April 17, did not at first reject our suggestion of a unilateral declaration by the Soviet, but demanded further information before committing himself. The next day, however, he handed Seeds a written proposal for a comprehensive Three-Power Pact that involved both an automatic guarantee of Soviet territory and included the Baltic States and Turkey in the guarantee. The Russian alternative directly raised the controversial issues that particularly worried the

Dominions and the Baltic States. There then followed nearly three weeks of continuous discussion between ourselves in the Foreign Policy Committee and the Cabinet, and between the Foreign Office and the various Governments concerned, as to the possibility of some compromise between the Russian and British proposals. Our inquiries only confirmed the strength of the opposition to any extension of our guarantee. The furthest, therefore, that we were able to go was an offer of a new formula that made it completely clear that we were not asking the Russians for any action that we ourselves were not prepared to take, and that they would only be involved when we and the French were actually engaged in hostilities.

Our reply reached Moscow at an unpropitious moment. Litvinov, who understood the complexities of European politics, had just been dismissed, and Molotov, a party leader who had never been out of Russia or studied foreign affairs, had succeeded him. When Seeds met the new Commissar on May 16, he was handed a reply that not only maintained the extreme Russian position, but for the first time added Finland to the list of States to be guaranteed. It was clear throughout the interview that our new formula of full reciprocity had made no impression in Moscow, and that Molotov was only prepared to continue the negotiation on the basis of a wide pact, political and military, covering all the border States whether they wished it or not.

We had therefore reached a complete *impasse*, and were faced with the choice of breaking off the negotiations or extending our limited guarantee to a comprehensive alliance with Russia. Much as the Dominions disliked the idea of any alliance, we hesitated to bring the negotiations to an end. Eventually, after many meetings and searchings of heart, we decided to continue them on the Russian basis. We were not, however, prepared to include the Baltic States in the guarantee unless they asked for it, but we were ready to extend our definition of aggression beyond the scope of physical invasion to cover the violation of a country's political neutrality. Our proposals appeared to us so reasonable that we not unnaturally assumed that, having accepted the principle of a comprehensive pact and an extended definition of aggression, we should find no insuperable difficulties in concluding an agreement. The Prime Minister, in these circumstances, felt justified in making an optimistic statement in the House of Commons on May 24:

" The House is aware that my noble Friend the Secretary of State for Foreign Affairs was able to have conversations with the French Ministers in Paris on his way to Geneva. He was also able to continue in Geneva the conversations which had been conducted with the Soviet Ambassador in London.

" As a result of these conversations all relevant points of view have now been made clear, and I have every reason to hope that as a result of proposals which His Majesty's Government are now in a position to make on the main questions arising, it will be found possible to reach full agreement at an early date.

" There still remain some points to be cleared up, but I do not anticipate that these are likely to give rise to any serious difficulty."

As the main principles of the Pact had been agreed between us, we not unnaturally expected that the details would be satisfactorily settled. We did not sufficiently realise that the only word in Molotov's vocabulary was " No," or, as Seeds meticulously described it, a " phrase that conveyed a negative impression in the dictionary rendering."

Our proposals were presented to Molotov on May 25. They began with a preamble intended to reassure western opinion that they were based on the principles of the Covenant of the League of Nations. They then covered the two contingencies of the violation of the neutrality of the guaranteed States provided that the States wished for help, and aggression against each of the Three Contracting Powers. Two days later Molotov, greatly to our surprise, declared that his " personal reaction was in the negative." He then proceeded to argue that our reference to the principles of the League involved delay in the execution of a pact, and that we were " proposing to safeguard the rights and position of an aggressor State." Once again, our telegrams of explanation had no effect upon him. Seeds then made a personal effort on May 30 to convince him of our reasonableness. Whilst Molotov was in a somewhat better mood over our reference to the League, he made it clear that the automatic guarantee of the Baltic States, whether they wished it or not, was a fundamental condition of any agreement. The effect of accepting this condition was explained to us in the Foreign Policy Committee by a hypothetical, but by no means improbable case taken from the relations between Russia and Esthonia. Suppose, it was said, that the Esthonian Government employed German technicians, and the

Soviet declared that their employment, by altering the political status of the country, justified the entry of Russian troops to turn them out, Hitler would in this event retaliate with a counter-move, and we should automatically be involved in war with Germany in a Russian quarrel. Clearly this was a commitment that we could not accept.

Once again we tried to find a compromise by suggesting that each country should draw up a secret list of the States whose independence was vital to them. We refused, however, to budge from the position that we could not countenance any intervention in a country that objected to it. The Baltic States, without exception, supported our refusal. They realised only too clearly that what Stalin really wanted, was a pretext for re-absorbing into the Russian Empire the provinces between the Baltic and the Black Sea that had been lost in the First World War. The fear of the Russian bear's embrace became all the more terrifying when Molotov seized this moment for sending threatening notes to Esthonia, Latvia and Finland.

We were not prepared to compromise upon this issue, and it looked at the beginning of June as if the negotiations had finally broken down. Before, however, we accepted complete failure, we determined to make a last effort to find an issue out of the impasse. Seeds had been in Moscow since the negotiations had begun, and there had been no personal contact between us and him. The moment seemed to have arrived to bring him back to London for discussions with the Foreign Office and the Foreign Policy Committee. Halifax, therefore, telegraphed on June 6 asking him to return at once " for a thorough discussion of all outstanding points." The answer came on June 7 that he was in bed with a temperature, and could not travel for two or three days.

CHAPTER XXX

The Mission to Moscow

As SEEDS could not come to us, the question arose of sending someone from London to Moscow. Halifax and Malkin, the legal adviser to the Foreign Office, could not be spared at a time when the threat to Danzig was creating a daily crisis. The choice then fell upon William Strang, not as the head of a special mission, but as an assistant to Seeds, who undoubtedly needed further help. Strang, who had been Counsellor in the Moscow Embassy, was well acquainted with Russian questions, and was also in the full confidence of the Foreign Secretary and the Cabinet. Molotov at once misrepresented our action in selecting a high official of the Foreign Office rather than a Cabinet Minister as a slight upon the Russian Government.

When Strang arrived, Molotov repeated his full demands for a political and military alliance and the right of intervention in the Baltic States, and maintained his habit of saying " No " to every alternative proposal that we and the French made to him. Throughout the negotiations he " sat on a throne "—I quote a description that was given us at the time:

" . . . and frequently left the meeting, no doubt to obtain guidance, and whenever the Ambassadors attempted to maintain a sustained argument, he interrupted them by saying that the Soviet Government had given their decision, and demanding that they should pass on to the next item on the agenda."

In spite of this provocation we persisted, and urged again our formula under which we accepted a definition of indirect aggression that did not involve the physical crossing of a frontier by military

357

forces, and that included the Baltic States, provided that the guarantee should only take effect if the threatened state requested intervention. We went even further, and said that we were ready, if our proposal was unacceptable, to agree to an alternative procedure, to allow the guarantee to take effect, if any two of the three guarantors agreed upon intervention. This move seemed at last to make further progress possible. On July 24, Molotov suddenly and quite unexpectedly announced that he was satisfied with our proposals. At the same time, with a cunning that was not at first apparent to us, he stipulated that any political pact must be supplemented by a military agreement. We lost no time in making the most of the better atmosphere, and by July 27 we had agreed with the French to send a joint military Mission to complete the negotiations.

The practical questions that had faced us over Strang's journey confronted us again over the arrangements for the military Mission. As the Chiefs of Staff could not leave London owing to the international situation, the choice of military personnel was limited. Serving officers could not be flown across Germany in peace time by military aeroplanes, the few Sunderland flying boats that we possessed were out of action, and the only civil machines available were the slow Hannibals with a performance so limited that an intermediate landing was necessary on German territory. Whilst transport by air was impracticable, transport by sea also raised difficult questions. A Southampton cruiser passing through the Baltic might suggest some hostile intention on our part, and provoke Hitler into the very action that we wished to prevent. This being so, our choice fell upon a passenger ship, the *Exeter*. Once again, Molotov welcomed the chance of criticising us for selecting what he described as the slowest possible means of transport for the Mission's journey. Almost with the same breath, however, he was letting it be known in Moscow that he did not wish the Mission to arrive for eight or ten days, the reason, which he did not disclose, being the need to postpone the negotiations with the Allies in order to give more time for the development of his negotiations with the Germans.

In spite of Molotov's public criticisms, the Mission was welcomed at the first meeting in a not unfriendly way by Marshal Voroshilov. Before the second meeting, however, the atmosphere had suddenly and completely changed. Voroshilov at once forced the issue over the most intractable of all the military problems, the right of passage for Russian troops across Poland. Molotov, controlling the negotiations in the background, knew very well that the Polish Government had repeatedly refused any such facilities, and that to insist upon them as the primary condition for further negotiation made any agreement impossible. General Doumenc, the head of the Mission, made the only possible reply by stating that the French and British could not give a guarantee on behalf of another sovereign state, and that any such proposal must be negotiated between the Polish and Russian Governments. The Russian answer was that this explanation was unacceptable, because any direct negotiation between Moscow and Warsaw was certain to fail. In spite of the rebuff, the British and French Governments persevered, and made a further effort to avert the break-up of the conference. They accordingly declared themselves ready to continue the negotiations upon the assumption that the Polish Government would in practice agree to the right of passage if war actually broke out. Even this advance did not satisfy Voroshilov, who demanded the immediate and formal agreement of the Polish Government. As the delegation could not give the formal guarantee, the impasse was insurmountable. The meeting ended, and within a few hours Ribbentrop was in Moscow, and the Russo-German Pact announced to the world.

So far, I have told the story as I actually followed it from the table of the Foreign Policy Committee and the telegrams that passed between London and Moscow. There is, however, another side that has only recently come to light. Of all the secret papers that have been discovered among the Nazi archives, there are none more revealing than the reports that describe the relations between Moscow and Berlin during the months in which we were struggling in London with the Russian cross-questions and crooked answers. It is now clear that all this time, Ribbentrop in Berlin, and Schülenberg, the German Ambassador in Moscow, were methodically outbidding us, while Molotov was exploiting our offers as levers for extorting his full terms from Hitler.

To complete, therefore, and clarify my London account of the Russian bargaining, it is necessary to supplement it with the story that has now been divulged of the simultaneous negotiation between the two dictators.

At the time we knew little or nothing of the German moves. Henderson in Berlin did not regard as serious the rumours of any German approach to Stalin. Seeds in Moscow seems to have been kept completely in the dark. The announcement in August of the Russo-German Pact was, therefore, a great shock for all of us. Yet throughout the whole time during which we were negotiating with Moscow, Stalin and Molotov were actively carrying on parallel discussions with Germany. The German negotiations had started immediately after Stalin's speech on March 11. Thenceforth Stalin followed his definite and unchanging objective—the recovery of the lost provinces, Esthonia, Latvia and Finland, and the partition of Poland and Roumania. The spring and summer of 1939 had given him the chance of choosing one of two roads to his destination. If the Allies gave him what he wanted, he would co-operate with them. If they refused, and Hitler was ready to satisfy him, no ideological differences would stand between him and the Nazis. Even if he failed to reach an agreement with either side, he would none the less gain. The more deeply the democracies were involved in their struggle with Hitler, the more time there was for Russia to recover from the Purge, and the better the chance to exploit the crisis. The western struggle was in fact providential for him. His fear had been a Russian war on two fronts against both Japan and Germany. In the spring and summer of 1939, the Japanese Government was still resisting Hitler's advances, and, at least for the present, seemed unlikely to join the Axis. Without Japan as a firm ally in the East, the fear of a war on two fronts was worrying the Germans even more acutely than the Russians. As the date for the invasion of Poland approached, Stalin's co-operation had become more than ever indispensable to Hitler. When, therefore, the German negotiations with Japan seemed likely to fail, Ribbentrop at once began to hint at a reversal of German policy and at an *entente* with Russia.

Events moved quickly, and at the very moment when, in April, we were proposing in Moscow joint action, Ribbentrop in Berlin was breaking the ground for negotiations for a trade agreement that was intended to be the first step to a political treaty. Thenceforth, the German moves corresponded in point of time almost exactly with our own. With completely cynical duplicity, Molotov played off his two suitors against each other.

If one of the negotiations went well, he used it as the means for obtaining better terms from the other. This was the explanation of the sudden changes in his attitude. In the middle of May, for instance, it looked as if our readiness to meet every reasonable Russian demand had removed all the difficulties, and as if an agreement was certain within a few days. Bonnet was talking in Paris as if the agreement had already been signed. Potemkin, Molotov's Under-Secretary, was telling the Balkan Governments that they could expect help from Russia against Germany. Yet suddenly, Molotov extinguished our hopes with one of his brutal and abrupt " Noes." What had happened was that he had realised the full scope of the opportunity that had been given him by the trade talks with Schülenberg. He saw at once that the apparent success of our negotiations would help him to wring better terms from Hitler. The proceedings went as he expected. By making Hitler genuinely nervous of a Russian agreement with the Allies, he succeeded in raising the German offer, and the Allied offer, having served its purpose, was then set aside.

This first failure was not without its effect on us. We also became nervous and raised our bid. Halifax had just come back from Paris, where he had seen for himself the French desire for a Russian Pact. Rather, therefore, than let the negotiations fail, we reluctantly revised our conditions, and declared ourselves ready to include the Baltic States in a guarantee, provided that the Pact was registered at the League of Nations, the list of guaranteed states kept secret, and any military action made dependent upon the request of the state attacked.

The talks between Moscow and Berlin were by this time becoming more serious. The new British offer, arriving at an opportune moment, once more enabled Molotov to add to his German terms the demand for a political agreement as the basis of any trade pact. Hitler then saw that he must raise his bid, and while he was considering it, Molotov held up the Anglo-French negotiations. For the whole of June, therefore, we made no progress, and a final breach seemed to have been reached at the end of the month when an obviously official article was published under Zdhanov's name in *Pravda*, accusing the Allies of using the negotiations for the purpose of embroiling Russia with Germany. A few days afterwards, Molotov intensified the attack in a speech to the Politbureau, and made it clear that even a change of government in the Baltic States, if it was not approved by the Soviet, would involve Soviet intervention. This violent reaction to our latest offer made Chamberlain and several members of the Government doubt the wisdom of continuing the negotiations. At the very moment, however, when we were seriously considering the question of bringing them to an end, Molotov completely reversed his position. He had realised that if he was not to lose his lever for extorting greater concessions from Hitler, he must keep in being the negotiations with the Allies.

The suspicion seems to have entered his mind that we might be playing his own game, and carrying on a simultaneous negotiation with Hitler. It was about this time that a German official, Wohltat by name, was in London, discussing whaling questions with Robert Hudson, the Secretary for Overseas Trade, and rumours were being spread by German propagandists that we were contemplating a loan to Germany. Although there was no truth in the story about the loan, the mere fact that these talks were in progress made Molotov wonder whether we were shifting our advances from Moscow to Berlin. His change of attitude was as sudden as it was unexpected. After ostentatiously announcing on July 22 that the trade talks with Germany, that had been dragging on for months without result, were being resumed, and implying that our negotiations were ended, on July 24 he consented in principle to our definition of indirect aggression, the reference to the League, and the prior consent of the Baltic States to any intervention, provided that we simultaneously supplemented the political with a military agreement. We immediately declared our readiness to discuss a military agreement, and started the various arrangements for sending a military mission to Moscow for the negotiations. Once again, Molotov was given an effective instrument of pressure upon Berlin. Hitler had planned to attack Poland at the end of August, and could on no account risk a long delay that would bog down an offensive in the mud of the Polish autumn. As it was vital to him to ensure a friendly, or at least a neutral Russia during his campaign, he inevitably gave Molotov the chance of extorting even better terms. The announcement of July 24, therefore, that an agreement between Russia, Great Britain and France had been accepted in principle, immediately forced Hitler to raise his bid for Russian co-operation. Molotov, by insisting upon a military agreement

as a necessary preliminary to a political agreement, had cunningly
kept the market open with us. Before the week was out, the auction
was again under way. On July 27 Schülenberg was instructed
by Berlin to tell Molotov that Hitler was ready to agree to Stalin's
demands in connection with Poland and the Baltic States, and on
August 2 Ribbentrop told Astakhov, the Soviet Chargé d'Affaires
in Berlin, that any Polish resistance would be liquidated in a week,
and that Germany would agree with Russia as to Poland's future.
By the end of the week Hitler was ready to give Russia a free hand
in the Baltic States and Finland, and it only remained for Ribbentrop to go to Moscow to sign a detailed agreement.

In the meanwhile, as I have already described, the Allied
Military Mission had arrived in Moscow. At the first session on
August 12, Voroshilov received instructions to appear friendly
disposed to the Allies. The character of the welcome was no doubt
due to the fact that the German negotiation was not yet completed. By August 14, however, Molotov, feeling sure of the
Germans, told Astakhov to encourage Ribbentrop in Berlin, and
at the same time instructed Voroshilov to force a rupture with
the allies in Moscow. The result was that at the second session
Voroshilov pressed the issue of the right of passage for Russian
troops across Poland in such a way as to make a break inevitable.

Even so, Molotov was still determined to keep the Germans
dangling a little longer on the hook. Ribbentrop was frantically
pressing to arrive in Moscow within the next few hours to sign
an agreement. As the attack on Poland was timed to begin
within a fortnight, it was vitally important for Hitler to make
sure at once of Russian neutrality. For Molotov and Stalin,
however, the delay of a few days enabled them to stimulate still
further the German appetite. With a Slav subtlety of which the
Germans were incapable, Stalin suggested that Ribbentrop's visit
should be postponed until the ground for a political pact had been
further explored. The Polish invasion was about to start, and
Hitler was by this time ready to accept any terms that were
demanded of him. It was only when it was clear to Stalin that
Hitler's anxiety had been fully exploited, that he agreed to Ribbentrop's arrival on August 23.

During all this time, the Russians were still maintaining the
outward appearance of a negotiation with the Allies. So long as
the discussions continued, Molotov retained a potential safeguard

against a last-minute breakdown of the German negotiations. The Allied delegates were still doing their best to clear the impasse that blocked the passage of Russian troops through Poland. Indeed they seemed, after consulting London and Paris, to have obtained a formula that would satisfy both Russia and Poland. Voroshilov, who had postponed the meeting of the Conference— no doubt with the object of gaining time for the German negotiations—was informed on August 22 by General Doumenc that the negotiation could continue on the assumption that the Polish Government would grant the right of passage to Russian troops. Voroshilov's answer could not have been more uncompromising. Not only must the Polish Government give its formal and immediate consent, but " the situation must remain the same." He was speaking with his tongue in his cheek, for on August 22 he knew that the situation had completely changed, that the German trade agreement had been concluded on August 19, and that a political pact with Hitler was on the point of being signed.

The next day saw Ribbentrop's arrival and the signature of the political pact at eight o'clock in the evening. The terms of the Pact and the Secret Protocol that was attached to it show that Molotov's double dealing had been completely successful. By encouraging one bidder against the other, he had extricated Russia from the very dangerous threat of a war on two fronts, and had regained without a blow almost all the former territories that had been lost in the First World War. Outwardly and publicly, the agreement was a Pact of Non-Aggression. It differed very seriously, however, from other Pacts of Non-Aggression in the provision that prohibited help to any country or group of countries at war with either of the signatories. In other words, Stalin bound himself to withhold help from any country that was attacked by Germany. Serious, however, as was this change in a Non-Aggression Pact, it was less cynical and brutal than the provisions of the Secret Protocol that gave Russia Esthonia and Latvia, divided the control of Lithuania and Poland between Russia and Germany, and guaranteed a free hand for Russia in Bessarabia.

CHAPTER XXXI

The Boon Companions

ON THE night of the signing of this infamous treaty, August 23, Stalin, Molotov and Ribbentrop met to celebrate the great event. Gaus, the head of the legal department of the German Foreign Ministry, has left so full and candid an account of the meeting that I close this chapter of events with the description in his own words.[1] I give it at length, as it not only discloses in detail the attitude of Stalin and Hitler on the eve of the war, but it explains better than all the telegrams that passed between London, Paris and Moscow the reason for the failure of our long negotiations with the Soviet.

This is Gaus's record of the discussions and the celebrations that followed them:

" The following problems were discussed:

1. Japan: The Reich Foreign Minister stated that the German-Japanese friendship was in no wise directed against the Soviet Union. We were, rather, in a position, owing to our good relations with Japan, to make an effective contribution to an adjustment of the differences between the Soviet Union and Japan. Should Herr Stalin and the Soviet Government desire it, the Reich Foreign Minister was prepared to work in this direction. He would use his influence with the Japanese Government accordingly and keep in touch with the Soviet representative in Berlin in this matter.

Herr Stalin replied that the Soviet Union indeed desired an improvement in its relations with Japan, but that there were limits to its patience with regard to Japanese provocations. If

[1] Nazi Conspiracy and Aggression, Documents from the Military Tribunal at Nuremberg. Supplement B 140-2. Part of Affidavit of Frederick Gaus, dated Nuremberg, March 15, 1946.

Japan desired war, it could have it. The Soviet Union was not afraid of it and was prepared for it. If Japan desired peace—so much the better! Herr Stalin considered the assistance of Germany in bringing about an improvement in Soviet-Japanese relations as useful, but he did not want the Japanese to get the impression that the initiative in this direction had been taken by the Soviet Union.

The Reich Foreign Minister assented to this and stressed the fact that his co-operation would mean merely the continuation of talks that he had for months been holding with the Japanese Ambassador in Berlin in the sense of an improvement in Soviet-Japanese relations. Accordingly, there would be no new initiative on the German side in this matter.

2. Italy: Herr Stalin inquired of the Reich Foreign Minister as to Italian aims. Did not Italy have aspirations beyond the annexation of Albania—perhaps for Greek territory? Small, mountainous, and thinly populated Albania was, in his estimation, of no particular use to Italy.

The Reich Foreign Minister replied that Albania was important to Italy for strategic reasons. Moreover, Mussolini was a strong man who could not be intimidated.

This he had demonstrated in the Abyssinian conflict, in which Italy had asserted its aims by its own strength against a hostile coalition. Even Germany was not yet in a position at that time to give Italy appreciable support.

Mussolini welcomed warmly the restoration of friendly relations between Germany and the Soviet Union. He had expressed himself as gratified with the conclusion of the Non-Aggression Pact.

3. Turkey: Herr Stalin asked the Reich Foreign Minister what Germany thought about Turkey.

The Reich Foreign Minister expressed himself as follows in this matter: he had months ago declared to the Turkish Government that Germany desired friendly relations with Turkey. The Reich Foreign Minister had himself done everything to achieve this goal. The answer had been that Turkey became one of the first countries to join the encirclement pact against Germany and had not even considered it necessary to notify the Reich Government of the fact.

Herren Stalin and Molotov hereupon observed that the Soviet Union had also had a similar experience with the vacillating policy of the Turks.

The Reich Foreign Minister mentioned further that England

had spent five million pounds in Turkey in order to disseminate propaganda against Germany.

Herr Stalin said that according to his information the amount which England had spent in buying Turkish politicians was considerably more than five million pounds.

4. England: Herren Stalin and Molotov commented adversely on the British Military Mission in Moscow, which had never told the Soviet Government what it really wanted.

The Reich Foreign Minister stated in this connection that England had always been trying and was still trying to disrupt the development of good relations between Germany and the Soviet Union. England was weak and wanted to let others fight for its presumptuous claim to world domination.

Herr Stalin eagerly concurred and observed as follows: the British Army was weak; the British Navy no longer deserved its previous reputation. England's air arm was being increased, to be sure, but there was a lack of pilots. If England dominates the world in spite of this, this was due to the stupidity of the other countries that always let themselves be bluffed. It was ridiculous, for example, that a few hundred British should dominate India.

The Reich Foreign Minister concurred and informed Herr Stalin confidentially that England had recently put out a new feeler which was connected with certain allusions to 1914. It was a matter of a typically English, stupid manœuvre. The Reich Foreign Minister had proposed to the Führer to inform the British that every hostile British act, in case of a German-Polish conflict, would be answered by a bombing attack on London.

Herr Stalin remarked that the feeler was evidently Chamberlain's letter to the Führer, which Ambassador Henderson delivered on August 23 at the Obersalzberg. Stalin further expressed the opinion that England, despite its weakness, would wage war craftily and stubbornly.

5. France: Herr Stalin expressed the opinion that France, nevertheless, had an army worthy of consideration.

The Reich Foreign Minister, on his part, pointed out to Herren Stalin and Molotov the numerical inferiority of France. While Germany had available an annual class of more than 300,000 soldiers, France could muster only 150,000 recruits annually. The West Wall was five times as strong as the Maginot Line. If France attempted to wage war with Germany, she would certainly be considered.

6. Anti-Comintern Pact: The Reich Foreign Minister observed that the Anti-Comintern Pact was basically directed not against the Soviet Union but against the Western democracies. He knew, and was able to infer from the tone of the Russian press, that the Soviet Government fully recognised this fact.

Herr Stalin interposed that the Anti-Comintern Pact had in fact frightened principally the City of London and the small British merchants.

The Reich Foreign Minister concurred and remarked jokingly that Herr Stalin was surely less frightened by the Anti-Comintern Pact than the City of London and the small British merchants. What the German people thought of this matter is evident from a joke which had originated with the Berliners, well known for their wit and humour, and which had been going the rounds for several months, namely, ' Stalin will yet join the Anti-Comintern Pact.'

7. Attitude of the German people to the German-Russian Non-Aggression Pact:
The Reich Foreign Minister stated that he had been able to determine that all strata of the German people, and especially the simple people, most warmly welcomed the understanding with the Soviet Union. The people felt instinctively that between Germany and the Soviet Union no natural conflicts of interests existed, and that the development of good relations had hitherto been disturbed only by foreign intrigue, in particular on the part of England.

Herr Stalin replied that he readily believed this. The Germans desired peace and therefore welcomed friendly relations between the Reich and the Soviet Union.

The Reich Foreign Minister interrupted here to say that it was certainly true that the German people desired peace, but, on the other hand, indignation against Poland was so great that every single man was ready to fight. The German people would no longer put up with Polish provocation.

8. Toasts: In the course of the conversation, Herr Stalin spontaneously proposed a toast to the Führer, as follows:
' I know how much the German nation loves its Führer: I should therefore like to drink his health.'
Herr Molotov drank to the health of the Reich Foreign Minister and of the Ambassador, Count von der Schülenberg.

Herr Molotov raised his glass to Stalin, remarking that it had been Stalin who—through his speech of March of this year,

which had been well understood in Germany—had brought
about the reversal in political relations.

Herren Molotov and Stalin drank repeatedly to the Non-
Aggression Pact, the new era of German-Russian relations, and
to the German nation.

The Reich Foreign Minister in turn proposed a toast to
Herr Stalin, toasts to the Soviet Government, and to a favourable
development of relations between Germany and the Soviet
Union.

9. When they took their leave, Herr Stalin addressed to the Reich
Foreign Minister words to this effect:
The Soviet Government takes the new Pact very seriously.
He could guarantee on his word of honour that the Soviet
Union would not betray its partner.

Moscow, August 24, 1939."

So ended the months of negotiations with a complete Soviet
victory. Could our failure have been avoided? Even if the
Russians were playing a double game, could more resolute action
on our side have prevented the final agreement with Hitler?
Could we not from the first have accepted without reservation
the Russian demand for the guarantee of the Baltic States, and
by this means, have kept the Soviet on the anti-German side?
The terms of the Secret Protocol seem to me to be a complete
answer to these questions. Stalin was determined to gain control
of the Baltic States and Poland, and to co-operate with whichever
of the two powerful groups in Western Europe was prepared to
let him have what he wanted. Were we or were we not ready
to satisfy him with the gift of five sovereign States? Our
answer was " No." We were ready to go to the utmost limit in
accepting Russia's special interest in the neighbouring countries,
but we were not prepared to agree to their occupation by Russian
troops upon the flimsy ground that this or that government was
unfriendly to Moscow. Throughout all the weary months of the
negotiations, this was the real dividing issue between us. On our
side, we stood firm on the need for the consent of the Baltic
States to the entry of Russian troops. On their side, the Russians
demanded the right to intervene at their own discretion. Hitler,
faced with the urgent problem of neutralising Russia before the
attack on Poland, saw no difficulty in agreeing to the same kind

of intervention in the east that he had himself undertaken in Czechoslovakia. If we made a mistake, it was that we continued to believe that there was a chance of an agreement when nothing short of his full demand was in the least likely to satisfy Stalin. Our own good faith and intentions blinded us to the fundamental incompatibility of our objectives. We never fully realised the cynical duplicity that was exploiting our efforts to obtain better terms from the Germans. It would not have made the least difference to the result if we had sent to Moscow Halifax, the Prime Minister, or the chiefs of all three fighting services. Stalin was not to be deflected from his prey, and we were not prepared to help him seize it.

Was, then, all the time wasted that we gave to the negotiations? I fear that it was. Perhaps, however, the months of discussion were inevitable. Our French allies clung desperately to the forlorn hope of a Russian alliance, and in spite of all the evidence to the contrary, the parties of the Left both here and in France continued to believe that salvation could come from the Kremlin.

When I look at the notes that I made at the time, I find that Chamberlain was constantly declaring that the Russians could not be trusted. He was proved to be right. I often argued with him, for though I never believed that we could depend upon Stalin as a loyal ally, I felt that there was a chance of preventing him from siding with Hitler. If we could not have a friendly Russia, we might have a genuinely neutral Russia. It was in the hope of Russian neutrality rather than of a Russian alliance—for, in view of Stalin's attitude, an alliance seemed unattainable—that I consistently supported every attempt to keep the negotiations in being. So long as they continued, they were evidence of our goodwill and an answer to Stalin's suspicion that our real policy was an agreement with Hitler and Japan, and the abandonment of Russia to a war on two fronts. The long months of fruitless negotiation showed that while even these modest hopes were groundless, we never gave up the attempt to obtain Russian co-operation. It was Russian duplicity and not British prejudice that made these months of baffling discussion end in failure.

Stalin did not wait long to throw off his double mask. As soon as war started, he seized his share of the Polish booty, and within a few months re-occupied Esthonia and Latvia and made war on

Finland. With Hitler's full support, an aggressive Russian Empire was re-established. The nemesis that was to make trouble between the two dictators over Bessarabia and the Balkans was still only hovering in the background.

CHAPTER XXXII

Chamberlain's Mind

I HAVE now described, as I saw them, the principal phases of the crisis of 1938 and 1939. As a member of the Committees of Imperial Defence and Foreign Policy, I was able to follow the telegrams and dispatches, and as a friend of Chamberlain to discuss them with him in our daily walks. How did he strike me in this trying time? Did he really believe, when he returned from Munich, that Hitler's professions of peace and friendship could be trusted? Was he intolerant of criticism, and did he force his views on his colleagues? Should he have brought both Labour and Churchill into a Coalition Government after the occupation of Prague? Did he show hesitation in the programme of rearmament? Did he throw away the chance of active co-operation with the United States and Russia?

These are the questions that have often been asked, and usually with the object of proving that he was completely deceived by Hitler, and that his policy was blind, weak and cowardly. Whilst no one can fully penetrate into another's mind, least of all into a mind as reserved as Chamberlain's,[1] I can suggest the answers that seem fair to one of his intimate colleagues.

The last of my questions, as to his alleged rejection of American and Russian aid, I have already discussed. The only fair answer, supported by the evidence, is that Roosevelt, whilst ready to show his general sympathy with the democracies, was, during the whole of Chamberlain's Premiership, determined to keep the United States out of a European war, and that Stalin was only prepared to help if we accepted his demand to absorb the Baltic States and partition Poland. I have also dealt with the charge that Chamberlain was dilatory and hesitant over rearmament.

[1] "You can't know Mr. Chamberlain till you have been with him five years," was his chauffeur's comment to me.

In dealing with the remaining questions, it is necessary to remember their setting at the time to which they refer. When Chamberlain became Prime Minister in 1937, Hitler was already entrenched, the German Air Force the greatest in Europe, the German Army a match for the French Army, and Mussolini almost, but not quite, an ally in the German camp. British rearmament, that had started in 1934, was as yet producing insignificant results in first-line strength, and at every stage meeting with bitter opposition from the Labour Party in the House of Commons. Given time, however, the programme gave promise of a system of defence strong enough to provide a formidable deterrent to any aggressor, and likely to ensure a decisive victory in the air as soon as British production overtook the German lead.

On the political side, appeasement, having been universally applauded, was still a term of faint praise rather than violent abuse. Since the time when Eden first used it with general approval during the debates on the German occupation of the Rhineland in 1936, it had been freely accepted into the reputable currency of political discussion. It was a noble word, and at the time seemed to express a wise and humane policy. What finer achievement could there be for a Minister than to bring about peace between France and Germany, and allay the suspicion and fear that were poisoning the life of Europe? It was only after Munich that a sinister and shady meaning was fastened to a splendid word that expressed an inspiring ideal. A century before, de Tocqueville had brilliantly described the debasement of fine words by the wear and tear of rough usage. He might have been describing the fate of ' appeasement ' since first the word came into current use.[1]

[1] Appendix, *Democracy in America*, Vol. 2, Chapter 16, 1862 Edition. French Edition 1850.

" L'expédient le plus ordinaire qu'emploient les peuples démocratiques pour innover en fait de langage, consiste à donner à une expression déjà en usage un sens inusité. Cette méthode-là est très simple, très prompte et très commode. Il ne faut pas de science pour s'en bien servir, et l'ignorance même en facilite l'emploi. Mais elle fait courir de grands périls à la langue. Les peuples démocratiques en doublant ainsi le sens d'un mot, rendent quelque fois douteux celui qu'ils lui laissent et celui qu'ils lui donnent.

" Un auteur commence par détourner quelque peu une expression connue de son sens primitif, et, après l'avoir ainsi modifiée, il l'adapte de son mieux à son sujet. Un autre survient qui attire la signification d'un autre côté; un troisieme l'entraîne avec lui dans une nouvelle route; et, comme il n'y a point d'arbitre commun, point de tribunal permanent qui puisse fixer définitivement le sens du mot, celui-ci reste dans une situation ambulatoire. Cela fait que les écrivains n'ont presque jamais

Appeasement did not mean surrender, nor was it a policy only to be used towards the dictators. To Chamberlain it meant the methodical removal of the principal causes of friction in the world. The policy seemed so reasonable that he could not believe that even Hitler would repudiate it. Hitler at the time seemed genuinely anxious to live on good terms with the British Empire. He had obtained equality of status for his country, and needed a period of peace to consolidate his political power. When, therefore, at Munich, he signed the pledge of perpetual friendship with Great Britain, he appeared not only to be acting in good faith, but to be embarking on a policy equally advantageous to himself and Germany. These were the considerations that influenced Chamberlain, and induced him to think that the Führer was more likely to keep his word than to break it. Supposing, however, that Chamberlain was mistaken, for he never regarded his opinion as infallible, he felt that he could fall back on the re-insurance policy that he possessed in the programme of British rearmament. The ink, indeed, was scarcely dry on the agreement when, as I have shown, he met the Service Ministers and Chiefs of Staff and agreed with them on a series of measures for accelerating re-armament, particularly the air programme of Spitfires and Hurricanes. Although Hitler was enraged at this reaction, Chamberlain none the less persisted with his double programme of peace if possible, and arms for certain. If I described his mind in a sentence, I would say that at the time of Munich he was hopeful but by no means sure that Hitler would keep his word, but that after Prague he came to the conclusion that only a show of greater determination would prevent him from breaking it.

---

l'air de s'attacher à une seule pensée, mais qu'ils semblent toujours viser au milieu d'un groupe d'idées, laissant au lecteur le soin de juger celle qui est atteinte."

"The most common expedient employed by democratic nations to make an innovation in language consists in giving some unwonted meaning to an expression already in use. This method is very simple, prompt and convenient; no learning is required to use it aright, and ignorance itself rather facilitates the practice; but that practice is most dangerous to the language. When a democratic people doubles the meaning of a word in this way, they sometimes render the signification which it retains as ambiguous as that which it acquires.

"An author begins by a slight deflection of a known expression from its primitive meaning, and he adapts it, thus modified, as well as he can to his subject. A second writer twists the sense of the expression in another way; a third takes possession of it for another purpose; and as there is no common appeal to the sentence of a permanent tribunal which may definitely settle the signification of the word, it remains in an ambiguous condition. The consequence is that writers hardly ever appear to dwell upon a single thought, but they always seem to point their aim at a knot of ideas, leaving the reader to judge which of them has been hit." (*Eng. Edit.*)

The Cabinet shared his views. I purposely emphasise a unanimity that, apart from Duff Cooper's resignation over the Munich Agreement, was steadily maintained from the early weeks of 1938 until the outbreak of war. We agreed with the Prime Minister ; we hoped with him that the Munich Agreement would succeed; and as we feared with him that it might not, we supported him in his many efforts to strengthen our defences.

He was not an autocrat who imposed his views upon doubting or hostile colleagues. Appeasement was not his personal policy. Not only was it supported by his colleagues; it expressed the general desire of the British people. This is a fundamental consideration in judging his action. Nothing is further from the truth than the myth that has been invented of his intolerant omnipotence. Whilst the prime mover, he was never the dictator of the Government's policy. The fact that throughout these years there were fifty or sixty meetings of the Foreign Policy Committee, almost all of which he attended, and that at the time of Munich he kept Halifax, Simon and myself in continuous conference, shows that, although he held the most definite opinions as to the action to be taken, his habit was always to consult his colleagues. If, nine times out of ten, he had his way, it was because his way was also the Cabinet's way. His colleagues supported him because they agreed with him, and in agreeing with him, they acted in accordance with the view of the great majority of his supporters in Parliament and a large body of public opinion in the country.

His personal influence was due to his mastery of facts, his clear head and his inherited gift of incisive speech. As Prime Minister, he took the closest possible interest not only in the Foreign Office, but in all the Departments of State. Being a remarkably quick worker, he was able to keep in touch with every important question, domestic as well as foreign, that concerned the Government. Ministers constantly visited Downing Street to discuss their affairs with him. His relations with the Foreign Office and the Foreign Secretary in no way differed from his relations with other Departments. With the Foreign Secretary, the meetings became particularly frequent in the days of Eden. With Halifax, the coming and going between the two sides of the street never slackened. From time to time, with the full approval of the Foreign Secretary, he would send for Cadogan, the Permanent Under-Secretary of State, just as he would send for the Permanent

heads of other offices, also with the full approval of the Departmental Minister, and discuss with him in detail some urgent
question. The Civil Servants would invariably find that he had
already read and mastered any papers that had been circulated
on the subject, and that he clearly wished to test and, if necessary,
modify his provisional conclusions with the help of their expert
knowledge. His reputation in Whitehall was of a Prime Minister
who kept abreast of everything that was happening, and was
always available to give his personal help in any departmental
difficulty. His private secretaries were amazed at his command
of intricate detail, and compared the atmosphere of perpetual
movement that pervaded Downing Street with the peaceful quiet
of his predecessor's régime.

In the Conservative Party, his qualities had much the same
influence as they had in Whitehall. Like his father before him, he
always kept his hand on the party machine. When the Party's
fortunes were at a low ebb in the days of MacDonald's second
administration, he reconditioned the organisation and appointed
new men to manage it. The Party's policy was constantly in his
mind, and no Conservative Minister ever took a more detailed
interest in election programmes. It was not, therefore, surprising
that his position in the Party was unassailable.

In the House of Commons, where it was no less secure, it was
further strengthened by his talent for debate. A party expects
fighting qualities in its leader. Chamberlain delighted his
followers not only with his gifts of clear statement and keen
argument, but still more, with the evident pleasure that he
showed in routing his enemies. Every offensive that the Opposition
launched against him he repelled with a devastating counter-
attack. Even Churchill's stirring eloquence he was able to meet
with close-knit arguments and ready retorts that justified the
Government policy and encouraged his followers. Whenever he
met the Conservative members of the House of Commons in the
Party meeting known as the 1922 Committee, and explained to
them his line of policy, he invariably received an overwhelming
vote of confidence. In the autumn of 1938, for instance, he
described to them in detail the steps that he intended to take to
reach an agreement, first with Mussolini, and next, with Hitler.
I was at the meeting, and I well remember the cheers that greeted
his speech. In 1939 there were similar demonstrations of support.

Perhaps the most significant was in March, 1939, when the Party was clamouring for conscription. Nothing could have better proved his hold upon his followers than their acceptance with scarcely a murmur of his plea for further delay, on the ground that it would be dangerous to disturb organised Labour until the crisis became more serious. The Government Whips and his intimate friends repeatedly assured him that no Conservative Prime Minister had ever had so strong a hold on his Party in the House of Commons.

If the great majority of Conservative members had not shared his views, the continuing international crisis in these years must have undermined his position. As it was, his change of front in March, 1939, was accepted for what it really was, namely, a new move in his fight for peace, rather than a reversal of his peace policy. Hitler's entry into Prague was not, as many declared, the end of the peace policy. Chamberlain and his colleagues never abandoned the hope of preventing a world war until it actually broke out in September, 1939. The lesson of Prague was not that further efforts for peace were futile, but rather that, without greater force behind them, negotiations and agreements with Hitler were of no permanent value. Thenceforth, rearmament took the first place in the Government's programme, and our approach to Hitler was changed from negotiation to explicit warning.

The swiftly moving events of the crisis throw a vivid light on his attitude. From the moment that he became Prime Minister, he had set himself the urgent task of exhausting every expedient for preventing the calamity of a European war. If, in spite of his efforts, war came, no one would be able to say that he had failed to take every step to avoid it. The sole fault would be unmistakably on Hitler's shoulders, and the whole Commonwealth would be solidly united in resisting the dictator's undisguised attempt to dominate the world.

In the twilight that followed Munich between October and March, he undoubtedly hesitated between hope and disillusionment. The outlook was obscure, but upon the whole, the forces of peace seemed to be gaining ground. Believing that his double policy was sound, and that the defence side of it was gathering volume, he hesitated to take any action that might deflect or delay it. This was the explanation of his reluctance to create a

Ministry of Supply. The programme of rearmament was at last producing results, and in particular, skilled labour was beginning to move to the aircraft industry. In these circumstances he believed that the creation of a new ministry would delay rather than expedite the programme. His attitude was another example of a passion for efficiency confronted by public sentiment. Whilst the public regarded a Ministry of Supply as the outward and visible sign of a resolute rearmament programme, he continued to believe that munitions could be produced as well or better without it. When at long last he accepted the demand, he gave the unfortunate impression that he was half-hearted about resistance. Unqualified efficiency has never been a popular quality in British Ministers.

I have checked my own impressions of the situation with many intimate letters that Chamberlain wrote during these months regularly every week to his sister, Miss Hilda Chamberlain. Comparing the letters with my memories, I am convinced that Chamberlain never regarded Munich as more than a step in his programme of peace. Far from being influenced by Hitler's wizardry, his personality repelled him. The fact that the Führer was a dictator made him instinctively doubt the permanence of any settlement with him. Chamberlain, who was really the last of the old Radicals, was deeply shocked at the very thought of unlimited power in any one man's hand. " How terrible," as he said more than once, " that the fate of millions of simple and peaceful men and women should depend upon one man's whims, and that man a paranoiac." Yet it was with this abnormal dictator that, for better or worse, he had to deal. From the first he was certain that the man was partially mad. He was equally sure that what Hitler said to-day, he might contradict to-morrow. None the less, he believed that he could be influenced, and that although his acts had been bad in the past, they might be better in the future. Schmidt, the interpreter, has described the noticeable impression that Chamberlain's frank and direct manner made on the Führer. Whilst it was worth trying to convince him that we were reasonable and genuinely anxious for a settlement of any dangerous differences, Chamberlain had no illusions about the possibility of failure. He saw from the first that his efforts would be widely open to misrepresentation. It would inevitably be said that he was either a weakling truckling to a dictator, or a semi-

Fascist influenced by a kindred spirit. Like Daladier in Paris, he was amazed at the welcome that greeted his return from Munich. Daladier, when he landed from his aeroplane, thought that the acclaiming crowds in Paris had come to lynch him. Chamberlain, as he said to Halifax on his way from Heston Aerodrome, was sure that the cheers in the streets would not last long. The chief reason that weighed with him for not taking Halifax with him to Berchtesgaden had been his reluctance to embroil one of his colleagues in what he thought would be an unpopular adventure.

Upon the question as to whether the Prime Minister should himself have flown to see Hitler at all, I had doubts when he first told me of his plan. Having myself suffered from my personal and direct negotiations with Laval in 1935, I was instinctively nervous of a discussion between principals at a distance from London. The crisis, however, was so acute, and the demand for the Prime Minister's intervention so general that, after a word of warning, I had to admit that his decision was both right and unanswerable. With the advent of the dictators, the diplomats had almost ceased to count. Since then, I have even more clearly realised how necessary in the circumstances were the meetings between the two men if anything was to stop war. After spending five years as Ambassador in Spain, I now see that the most effective way of influencing a dictatorship is a direct contact with the dictator himself. Churchill and Roosevelt reached the same conclusion as to the value of the direct approach. Indeed, Roosevelt was so enamoured of it that he came to believe that he alone could deal with Stalin. " I know you will not mind my being brutally frank," he wrote to Churchill in March, 1942, " when I tell you that I think I can handle Stalin personally better than either your Foreign Office or my State Department."[1]

In spite, however, of Roosevelt's failure to convert Stalin, the fact remains that dictators can often only be moved by personal visits and direct contacts. A dictator's ministers are shadowy figures who either obscure or faintly reflect his wishes. Upon

[1] The danger of the direct approach is shown in a later letter of Roosevelt of August 30, 1942, to William Bullitt, American Ambassador in Moscow. " I have just a hunch that Stalin doesn't want anything but security for his country, and I think that if I give him everything I possibly can and ask nothing from him in return, *noblesse oblige*, he won't try to annex anything and will work for a world of democracy and peace."

important questions that need a decision, the only useful course is to see the man whose word counts. As the autocrat tends to be elusive, an ordinary Ambassador, when he asks for an interview, is usually told to follow the protocol and go to the Foreign Minister. In my own case in Spain, it was only after a barrage attack of days and sometimes weeks that I was ever able to penetrate Franco's defensive lines. Once I remember I had an important communication to make to the Spanish Government, and the only way I could deliver it with effect was to pursue Franco to his summer resort, and to fly five hundred miles each way in a small military machine to reach him. Henderson in Berlin, and Perth and Loraine in Rome had a similar experience to mine, whilst Seeds in Moscow never, so far as I am aware, had any serious talk with Stalin. Chamberlain, therefore, if he was to penetrate the Iron Curtain that Hitler was building around himself, was forced into the direct approach. Being Prime Minister of Great Britain, and overwhelmed with official business of all kinds, the best approach was by aeroplane both to save time and impress the world. Here again, having as Secretary of State for Air, made many official journeys by air, I can appreciate some of the consequences of flights upon urgent business. Baldwin would never have flown to Munich. The very idea of his assuming the sole responsibility of a critical mission and jumping into an aeroplane for the first time in his life to carry it out, is so contrary to his character that it is altogether fantastic and ridiculous even to imagine it. Chamberlain was engaged upon a complete reversal of the quietism of recent years. He was determined to make a break both in the Government's procedure and his own habits of life. The new methods emphasised and perhaps exaggerated his natural inclination to take quick decisions. It is very difficult to regain one's complete balance immediately after leaving an aeroplane, particularly when it is the end of a first flight in a pre-war machine. Yet, in his case there is nothing to show that, even in the early moments of his talks with Hitler, he was rushed into unwise decisions, or confused by his unaccustomed surroundings. When Hitler insisted upon self-determination for the Sudeten Germans, Chamberlain at once realised the full implications of the demand, and insisted upon flying home to consult the Cabinet. Only in the last phase of his negotiations did he take a sudden and unexpected decision, when he drafted and

signed the declaration of Anglo-German reconciliation for the
future.

The British and German accounts of the conversations agree
that he walked warily, and knew that he was dealing with an
abnormal fanatic. It may be that his self-confidence misled him
into thinking that the Führer could be moved by arguments and
explanations that seemed to us unanswerable. British Ministers,
whether Grey, Asquith or Baldwin, have always been inclined to
think and act as if foreigners thought and acted like themselves.
Chamberlain evidently believed that there was at least a small
corner of Hitler's mind that was sufficiently like his own to respond
to British arguments. The belief was something more than wishful
thinking. The plan of the *blitzkrieg* against Czechoslovakia, for
instance, was dropped as the result of Chamberlain's insistence.
The truth seems to be that each of them was influenced by the
other, but that neither really understood the other's point of view.
Chamberlain failed to realise that Hitler wanted the whole
continent and not a few million more Germans. Hitler, when
he talked of perpetual peace between Germany and Great Britain,
always assumed that it would be based upon the division of the
old world between them.

The mistake that the Führer made was to think that Chamberlain had accepted the Munich terms from weakness. Whatever
may be said to the contrary, Chamberlain did not agree because
of our military unpreparedness. On the contrary, he sincerely
believed that it was necessary in the general interests of world
peace to let the Sudeten Germans unite with the Germans of the
Reich. The fact that we were militarily weak took a secondary
place in his mind. Extremely obstinate by nature, he would never
have submitted to a threat or surrendered through fear. He was
prepared to make an agreement only because he felt that it was
definitely wrong to plunge Europe into war to maintain what,
even in the negotiations of the Versailles Treaty, was regarded
as a precarious and vulnerable compromise. When he was told
that the loss of the Sudetenland would destroy the balance of
power in Europe, his answer was that a balance that depended on
Czechoslovakia was no longer reliable when the defences had been
turned by Hitler's occupation of Austria. Perhaps he underrated
the strength of Czech nationalism. Whilst his mind was insular
to the extent that he thought that foreigners thought like us, it was

cosmopolitan in its indifference to nationalist movements. It was only after the occupation of Prague that he saw that his detached reasonableness was insufficient to stop Hitler. The result was our guarantee to Poland, Greece, and Roumania, the introduction of conscription, and the intensification of rearmament.

Even after Prague, it would not have been right for him to abandon all hope of peace. There was still a chance that the certainty of Allied resistance would force Hitler to restrain his actions. We could not believe that the rantings of *Mein Kampf* were a practical manual of daily conduct from which he would never deviate, nor did we know of the definite plans that he had made with his Generals for an organised campaign of successive offensives. At the time, we were as much in the dark over Hitler's real intentions as later we were over Stalin's. Very little military intelligence slipped through to us from the German side. Now, as the result of the publication of the German secret papers, we know that Hitler was constantly planning acts of aggression. The so-called Hossbach Memorandum, in which a detailed account was given by Hitler's adjutant of a conference with his military commanders, shows that as early as November 5, 1937, he was preparing his future campaigns for the domination of Europe. General Jodl's plan of campaign, known as ' Operation Green,' described in further detail the tactics and strategy of an attack on Czechoslovakia. Yet, even if some cunning agent had obtained these documents and sent them to us, I do not believe that Chamberlain's action would have been different. He would have said, and we should have agreed with him:

" Here are two of the many schemes of this megalomaniac. Every general staff is asked to make plans for all sorts of emergencies. These may be plans of that kind. In any case, he may change his mind as quickly as he seems to have made it up, and in case he does not, we must make ourselves so strong that it will not be worth his while to start a world war of this kind. A world war is so immense a catastrophe that no British Prime Minister can abandon all hope of preventing it until it has actually started."

CHAPTER XXXIII

The Double Line

THE DOUBLE policy of peace and rearmament needed not only very skilful handling, but also a very subtle presentation. In a sense, the two aims were contradictory, often difficult and sometimes almost impossible to reconcile. So many balls had to be kept in play at once, the French, the Italian, the Russian, the German, the Polish, to say nothing of organised labour at home, and the Dominions overseas, that only the quickest and most delicate touch could prevent some of them dropping. Chamberlain certainly possessed sufficient quickness of hand. If his touch lacked anything, it was the sensitive feeling that gave the exact measure of strength to each of his efforts. When I listened to him explaining his two objectives, I could not help thinking of Balfour in my early political days, balanced on a tight-rope with protection in one hand and free trade in the other. If Balfour's feat was sometimes too subtle, Chamberlain's sometimes lost its balance and gave the impression that he was leaning to one side more than the other. I had every reason to appreciate his difficulties. Throughout the long controversy over the Indian Constitution, I had been continually explaining the two parallel objectives of security and independence, with the result that many Conservatives thought that I was sacrificing security, whilst many Indians were convinced that I was circumscribing their liberty. Such is always the fate of those who follow a double line. Chamberlain was singularly untroubled by the attacks to which he was exposed on two fronts. He had the clearest possible view of his objective, and from the moment that he became Prime Minister until his resignation three years later, never lost sight of it—peace upon reasonable terms and with any government that would carry them out, war in the last resort, when every attempt at peace had failed, and the whole Commonwealth had been united in an unbroken front of resistance, but above all, war that should be brought to an end before it had destroyed European civilisation.

" My critics," he wrote on July 30, 1939, to his sister, " think that it would be a frightful thing to come to any agreement with Germany without giving her a thorough thrashing ' to larn her to be a toad.' But I don't share that view; let us convince her that the chances of winning a war without getting thoroughly exhausted in the process are too remote to make it worth while. But the corollary of that must be that she has a chance of getting fair and reasonable consideration and treatment from us and others if she will give up the idea that she can force it from us, and convince us that she has given it up."

Even after war had started, he still hoped that the voice of reason would not be completely silenced. These were his words in another letter, on September 10, 1939, to his sister.

" One thing comforts me. While war was still averted I felt I was indispensable, for no one could carry out my policy. Half a dozen people could take my place while war is in progress, and I do not see that I have any particular part to play, until it comes to discussing peace terms, and that may be a very long way off. It may be, but I have a feeling that it won't be so very long. There is such a widespread desire to avoid war and it is so deeply rooted that it surely must find expression somehow. Of course the difficulty is with Hitler himself—until he disappears and his system collapses there can be no peace. But what I hope for is not a military victory —I very much doubt the feasibility of that—but a collapse of the German home front. For that it is necessary to convince the Germans that they cannot win. And the U.S.A. might at the right moment help this; on this theory one must weigh every action in the light of its probable effect on German mentality. I hope myself that we shall not start to bomb their munition centres and objectives in towns unless they begin it. If it must come, it would be worth a lot to us to be able to blame them for it. . . . It was of course a grievous disappointment that peace could not be saved, but I know my persistent efforts have convinced the world that no part of the blame can lie here. That consciousness of moral right which it is impossible for the Germans to feel must be a tremendous force on our side."

This intimate confession of faith goes far to explain both his public policy and his attitude of mind. It shows him conscious of his overwhelming responsibility, but at the same time sure of the course that he should follow in discharging it.

Was he too sure? Was he not too intolerant of criticism? Should he not have tried to form a national front with the help of the Opposition? For a fair answer to these questions, we must constantly remember the conditions of 1938 and 1939. Until September, 1939, there was still a chance of preventing war. To have brought into the Government the men who were opposing any negotiation with the dictators would have seemed to be the abandonment of the last hope of peace. In any case, the Opposition would not, I believe, have accepted an invitation to join a Government under Chamberlain. Although his advanced social views might have been expected to make a bridge between him and them, the leaders of the Opposition disliked him as much as he disliked many of them. Perhaps it was the debating skill that he had inherited from his father, and that he used to the full in the battles of the House of Commons, that left behind it bitterness and resentment. Just as in 1940 Attlee and his colleagues refused to serve under him, so in 1938 and 1939, with the Party disaster of 1931 in their minds, they would have undoubtedly rejected any suggestion of a coalition.

With Churchill it was different. According to Chamberlain and the Conservative Whips, Churchill was anxious to join the Government after Prague. Chamberlain by no means rejected the idea, but certain intractable obstacles made him hesitate. In the first place, the great majority of the Conservative Party in the House of Commons was solidly behind the double policy that he was pursuing. The stronger their support, the deeper was their resentment against the Conservative critics of the Government. Secondly, in the spring of 1939, not only the Party, but influential opinion in the Dominions was definitely opposed to Churchill's admission to the Cabinet. The critics maintain that this opposition was misguided and obscurantist. The fact remains that the bulk of the Party would have been restive if Chamberlain had at that time invited Churchill to join him, and the Dominion Governments would have regarded his appointment as the sign that war was inevitable. The invitation, therefore, was not made, but postponed until the crisis became more acute.

To the world at large, Churchill appeared to be the very embodiment of a policy of war. To have brought him into the Government when the balance between peace and war was still quivering, might have definitely tilted the scales on the side of war. This argument seemed to me to have been valid up to the time of the Prague *coup*. After Prague, I thought that Churchill's inclusion in the Government would have been more likely to impress Hitler with our firm resolution to resist further aggression, than provoke him to war. I had always been anxious to repair any breaches in the Conservative front, and Churchill's approval of our guarantee to Poland seemed to provide the chance not only for closing our ranks, but for adding greater vigour to the Government. The need of strengthening the Government had been constantly in my mind from the day that Chamberlain became Prime Minister in 1937, when I had strongly pressed him to renounce the Baldwin legacy of tired Ministers, and either to have a General Election or to make such sweeping changes in the Cabinet that the Government would appear new in more than name. " If you can," I wrote on June 3, 1937, " make all your changes at one moment. Baldwin destroyed his first Government by merely taking over the Bonar inheritance. Boredom is one of the chief enemies of governments, and the country will be bored from the start if it looks as if you are only continuing the Baldwin régime." To my regret he did not take my advice. Nor was he more inclined to make drastic changes when I repeated it immediately after the Munich crisis.

" I believe," I wrote on October 5, 1938 " that with the present House of Commons and with Parliament nearing its end, you will not get a fair run for a policy of peace. Every setback—there may be many—will be exploited against you, and with the House of Commons already breaking up into cliques, the situation may soon become untenable. These facts seem to point to an election. In any case, the reconstruction of the Government is urgent. I do not believe that there is any basis of a working agreement between Labour or Winston and ourselves. But as to Anthony, I would get him back if and when you can. As to the rest, I believe that the country demands new blood. The difficulty is to find it. . . . Is it not also worth considering whether you should not adopt for peace purposes the conception of the small War Cabinet? I believe that the country wants a change of this kind. People think that our present machinery is slow and obsolescent."

Some months later, the need of new blood seemed to me even more urgent. At the beginning of April, 1939, immediately after the Prague *coup*, I wrote to him: " The more people I see (among our best supporters), and the more I think of the position, the more I am sure that you must make big changes."

These examples of the advice that I consistently gave him over the whole period of his Premiership—for I persisted with it until the end of his administration—show how strongly I was in favour of broadening the Government front, and how reluctant he was to upset a machine that was not working badly. In spite of his perfectly legitimate fears that the inclusion of Churchill in the Cabinet would have compromised one side of his policy, I myself was prepared to take the risk. In the previous year immediately after Munich, I had been convinced that the gulf was too great for any alliance. The months, however, that had since passed had aggravated the crisis and made rearmament the predominant question. Whilst I can well understand Chamberlain's reluctance to complicate his overwhelmingly difficult task with the personal and political questions that Churchill's presence in the Cabinet would undoubtedly have raised, I thought at the time, and I think now even more than in the spring of 1939, that the advantage of his inclusion would have fully compensated for the risk.

It may be that, in alluding to Chamberlain's reluctance to make far-reaching changes in his Cabinet, I have touched on a fault of his qualities. He resented outside pressure. The more, therefore, the Press clamoured for Churchill's inclusion, the less likely he was to take any action. Again, over the demands that were made for a Ministry of Supply and the introduction of conscription, he was determined to take his own time and on no account to appear to be yielding to ill-advised agitation. Perhaps, also, his obstinacy influenced him in the choice of his Ministers. More than once at critical moments, when the public imagination needed stirring, he made the kind of routine appointments that would have been unexceptionable in normal times, but that in a crisis appeared altogether inadequate. Sure of himself and his programme, he was convinced that he could make almost any Ministers work well in his Cabinet, and was opposed to changes that might spoil his carefully laid plans.

The strain of three years of continuous crisis would have broken most Prime Ministers. An amazing feature of Chamberlain's

Premiership was his inexhaustible resiliency. Already over seventy, nearing the end of a hard and trying life, suffering intermittently from sharp attacks of gout, he none the less seemed to delight in accumulating all the Government's heaviest responsibilities on his own shoulders. Ready at any moment to draft a telegram or take a decision, or plunge into a Parliamentary debate, he was kept alive and alert by the unfaltering belief in his own mission. So firmly convinced was he of the rightness of his course, and so completely were his eyes fixed on the destination, that he did not always trouble himself about the details of the journey. He would not wait to find the exact word or phrase to describe his progress. " A quarrel in a far-away country between people of whom we know nothing "; " peace in our time "; " Hitler has missed the bus "—trite sentences such as these slipped out without his stopping to think out fine phrases and cautious formulas. This indifference to rounded periods and carefully considered statements was the very antithesis of Churchill's resounding eloquence. Unlike Churchill, he did not sufficiently appreciate the need for purple patches and inspiring perorations in a period of great emotional strain.

How different from his would have been Churchill's broadcast on the outbreak of war! Chamberlain's words sounded thin and uninspiring, and his critics attacked them for being egoistical. If he used the word ' I ' too frequently, it was not from any egoistical vanity. It was rather that he felt intensely his own personal responsibility. If he spoke dryly and even coldly, it was not that his feelings were not profoundly stirred, but rather that he felt so strongly that he did not dare unloose them.

For all his efforts, war came. Had, then, the three years of his Premiership been wasted? Worse than wasted, had they brought disaster upon the world? The evidence that I have produced from my many contacts with the problems that faced him, convinces me that the time was neither wasted nor a disaster aggravated by his double policy of peace, if humanly possible, and arms, if war became inevitable. The devastation, political, material and moral, that followed the failure of his crusade for peace does not prove that his policy was wrong, but rather that in face of a world war, it was right and necessary to try out every possible expedient for saving humanity from so terrible a catastrophe.

In his pursuit of peace he refused to accept the permanent division of the world into two hostile camps. The history of the post-war years seems to me to justify both his attempt to build bridges between the rival territories and his refusal to regard any gulf as insurmountable.

The other side of his policy I have also attempted to describe. In the conditions of his time there was no simple and easy way to British rearmament. General complacency, and sometimes active opposition, obstructed progress at every turn. None the less, although he would have been the first to admit that his programme was often subject both to delay and amendment, the two main objectives of his defence policy were achieved. When the crisis came, the Commonwealth was united, and the programme of rearmament within sight of great results that would, with time, become much greater. To create this unity of front it had been necessary to convince the Dominions of our profound desire for peace and our unshakable determination to resist an attack. The Grand Alliance of the League of Nations had been weighed in the balance and found wanting; America, North and South, stood aloof; Japan had broken adrift from it; the European neutrals feared to take their share of its obligations; Russia was only likely to adhere to it for selfish ends. With the Commonwealth it was altogether different. If the great Dominions accepted a policy and undertook its responsibilities, their material support was definitely assured, whilst their moral approval added incalculable weight to the British cause. The united front created during Chamberlain's Premiership was our first and indispensable line of defence. Secondly, our programme of rearmament, slow and inadequate as it may sometimes have been, remained the sound basis of our defence throughout the war. Without it, there would have been no victory in the Battle of Britain, no command of the air in later years, and no scope for the leadership of his great successor.

The disaster of 1940 was no fault of Chamberlain's. His plans had been inevitably, and as the military experts insisted, securely built upon the support of the French Army and Navy. So sure had the two staffs been that the French would hold that they were not even worried over the gap in the Maginot Line behind the Dutch and Belgian frontiers. Indeed, Gamelin had implied that he preferred to draw the German offensive on to ground of his own choosing by leaving the gap open. If the French Army had not collapsed and the French Fleet had kept command of the Western Mediterranean, Chamberlain's programme, sound in itself, would have been justified in the eyes of the world. His earlier approaches to Italy might well have convinced Mussolini that, with the French Army intact, it was unwise for Italy to enter the war. Italian neutrality might then have weighted the scales in favour of non-belligerency in Japan, and the result would have been a war of position, during which our programme would have developed according to the Staff plans, and given us the command of the air in 1942.

Are these fantasies from the feeble mind of one of his colleagues? I can at least claim that the evidence gathered since the war gives them some body and substance. The official volume on British War Production[1] brings out two striking facts, the first, that Chamberlain's rearmament programme was soundly conceived, the second, that it required no substantial change during the years of war. The plans were well laid. All that they needed was time for their fulfilment. It was the rout of the French Army and the immobilisation of the French Fleet that destroyed the breathing space upon which we had always relied.

[1] *British War Production*, by M. M. Postan (H.M. Stationery Office).

CHAPTER XXXIV

The Kind of War that was
not Expected

IN THE last chapter I was led on in my description of Chamberlain's mind to carry the story up to the dark days of 1940. To have stopped it short at Munich or Prague would have excluded some of the evidence most needed for a just verdict on his policy and character. The result has been that I have to some extent anticipated the end of these memoirs before I have described the final phase of the period with which I am dealing.

I must now, therefore, go back to the months before Chamberlain resigned, and say something of the experience of a member of the War Cabinet in a war that started so differently from what had been expected.

August, 1939, was the worst month that I have ever spent. The suspense was almost intolerable. War seemed practically certain, yet, until it actually started, there were still flickers of hope, and a few straws blowing about London and Berlin that fluttered in the direction of peace. According to various reports, Hitler had not finally abandoned his desire for an Anglo-German understanding. A delegation of British employers had returned from a visit to Germany with an optimistic account of the possibilities for mutual understanding and better trade. A Swedish business man, Birger Dahlerus, was in London describing Goering's efforts to prevent war. Vague rumours came to us of discontent among some of the German Generals. We had, however, reached the conclusion, after the Prague *coup*, that only Hitler counted, and that no opposition in Germany would deflect him from his decisions. The subsequent failure of the Generals' plot in 1944 seems to show that nothing would have been gained by relying on any effective opposition in September, 1939. The German war machine was unmistakably geared for an attack on Poland, and all the talks about peace were having no effect on its momentum. It was in this atmosphere of hope and fear that Chamberlain hurriedly returned to London from what he had intended to be a short holiday in Scotland. He at once asked me to see him, in order to hear my account of what had happened during his two days' absence. Whilst I could add little to the contradictory reports that we were receiving, I was able to tell him that, so far as the Home Office was concerned, the Bill was ready that conferred emergency powers on the Government in the event of war, and that I could put it into operation as soon as it was passed. He was pleased with the draft, and suggested that I should at once see the Labour and Trade Union leaders, and if possible, obtain their approval. I saw them on August 23, and found them ready to accept the Bill, provided that it was given a time limit. I readily agreed to this condition, and introduced it the next day in a quarter of an hour's speech, passed it through all its stages in the Commons, persuaded both Houses to suspend their Standing Orders, and obtained the Royal Assent the same evening at 10.15 p.m. No Bill, least of all a Bill that affected at every turn the liberties of the people, had ever been given a quicker passage. D.O.R.A. was, in fact, welcomed with open arms as the messenger of resistance against Nazi aggression.

In this twilight before the storm there were other urgent tasks to occupy me. Chamberlain and Halifax asked me to keep in personal contact with the leaders of the Press and the Lobby Correspondents and to give them guidance as to their general line. I at once held the first of many meetings with them, which were to continue until I left the Government in 1940.

During these days I also had two Audiences at the Palace. It was necessary for the King to have ready a broadcast for the moment when war was declared. The King very rightly took the view that his speech should avoid any attempt at rhetoric, and be as simple as possible. It was on this line that he approved the final draft. Another question that needed settling was where he and the Queen should live during the war. We had already arranged for a house in the west of England in the event of its being necessary for them to leave the London area. The house that we had selected was my wife's old home. It was interesting to remember, as an example of historic continuity, that the same house had been proposed as the possible refuge for George III and his family at the time of Napoleon's threat of invasion from Boulogne. Short, however, of the evacuation of the Government, the question had remained unsettled as to whether the King and Queen should remain at Buckingham Palace or go to Windsor. We agreed that for the time being they should use both.

Then, there was the delicate problem of the Duke of Windsor in wartime. If he could not remain in France, where should he live and what should he do? These questions we postponed until we saw how the war developed. The King was, however, ready at any moment to send the royal aeroplane to bring him to England if his position in France became dangerous.

Throughout these discussions His Majesty was completely cool and self-possessed. The crisis, so far from increasing his natural diffidence, had given him new strength and confidence.

As late as August 31 Hitler's decision still seemed in doubt. When, therefore, I was rung up from the Home Office early in the morning of September 1 to be told that Poland had been invaded, the news, although I had always expected it, came as a staggering blow. There followed a rush of events. Chamberlain immediately invited Churchill and Eden to join the Government, and they at once accepted the invitation. Mussolini intervened with a proposal for a standstill arrangement, and an international conference. Cabinet meetings followed in quick succession at which the decision was taken to bring into operation our guarantee to Poland and to send an ultimatum to Germany. It was at this point that serious and unexpected difficulties arose with the French. Whilst we were opposed to any international conference before the withdrawal of German troops from Polish territory, Bonnet was in favour of a meeting without any conditions. Whilst, also, we were anxious to put the shortest possible time limit in our ultimatum, the French pressed for delay on the ground that they needed more time to complete their mobilisation, and could not risk air attacks while it was still in progress. These differences placed the British Government, and particularly Chamberlain and Halifax, in a very difficult position when the two Houses met on September 1 and September 2. Chamberlain, who was unjustly suspected by the Opposition of planning a surrender, could not defend himself by saying that it was we who were pressing for quick action, and that it was our Allies who would not agree to it. The result was a general feeling that the Government was hesitating, and angry scenes in which totally unwarranted gibes were hurled at the Prime Minister. All the time we were insistently pressing the French to accept an early limit for the two ultimatums. Eventually, after many urgent messages, we persuaded them to agree to eleven o'clock the following day for ours, and five o'clock in the afternoon for theirs.

The next morning I was early at the Home Office to make a further check on our preparations for Civil Defence. I then went to Downing Street to be there when our time limit expired and Chamberlain broadcast to the nation. When I arrived, Rab Butler was just leaving, after giving the news that Hitler had made no answer to our ultimatum. I then sat in the hall, with two or three of Chamberlain's staff, and listened to the few and simple words in which, from the Cabinet Room next to us, he told the country of the destruction of his hopes, and his firm resolution to defeat the criminal who had plunged the world into war. Profoundly depressed at this end to our long efforts for peace, I hurried back to the Home Office as soon as he had finished, for the many pressing affairs that a state of war put upon me. A freakish providence started the tragic chapter with a comic turn. The first air-raid alarm was already sounding when I reached my office. We were at once hurried into the newly-built air-raid shelter, where we waited expectantly while nothing seemed to be happening. Eventually a message arrived that it was a false alarm. Radar had given us a backhander and warned us of two of our own civil machines that were flying over the Channel. Greatly relieved, I emerged from the shelter and hurried to the House of Commons to hear the Prime Minister's statement. I was met at the door by Lloyd George, very white and greatly excited. In answer to his questions, I was able to reassure him and tell him that the Germans were not raiding us. How strange, I thought to myself, was this great and courageous war leader's fear of air raids. It had become a by-word in the First World War, and it seemed to be as strong as ever in the Second.

As soon as the House adjourned, Chamberlain asked me to go

for a walk with him. When we reached the scene of our morning exercise in St. James's Park, he told me of his plans for a War Cabinet that was to consist of the Prime Minister, the Foreign Secretary, the Chancellor of the Exchequer, the Minister for the Co-ordination of Defence, the three Service Ministers and Hankey. Would I join it as Lord Privy Seal without any departmental responsibilities, or prefer to remain Home Secretary and Minister of Home Security without a seat in the Cabinet? I answered at once that whilst I should be very sorry to leave the Home Office, I could not resist his invitation to join the War Cabinet. At the same time, I raised with him a more general question. Would it not be wise, I asked, to have a really new Government? I reminded him of the fate of the Asquith Government in the First World War, and warned him of the demand that would eventually become irresistible for new men to meet the new emergency. I added that as far as I was concerned, I was perfectly ready to retire. His answer was a very definite negative. He was not willing to involve himself in all the personal troubles that were inevitable in forming a new administration, when his hands were already over full with the immediate problems of the war. Besides, he could not find the alternative Ministers. Churchill and Eden had already agreed to join the Government. Labour would certainly refuse an invitation. Where, then, should he find the new men? His mind was made up, and there was no use in continuing the argument.

Within a couple of hours I was sworn in as Lord Privy Seal, in a post that whilst it carried no departmental duties, stood very high in the hierarchy of political and social life. Its holder was still classed amongst the Great Officers of State, and took precedence over all the Dukes. These historical curiosities took my mind back to the Stuart and Tudor Kings who used the small seal, which was the symbol of the office, for transactions that were not sufficiently respectable for the Lord Chancellor's Great Seal.

After leaving the Palace, I took possession of the three or four upper rooms in the Treasury that had been allocated to me. One of my predecessors in them had been Nell Gwynne, whose bathroom still formed a part of my small suite. My official staff consisted of Hutchinson, formerly my excellent private secretary at the Home Office, an assistant, and two or three typists. As Chamberlain expected me to be a kind of general-purpose

Minister in the War Cabinet for undertaking duties that were
either not covered by the departmental chiefs or needed co-
ordination between them, I came to the conclusion that I must
strengthen my personnel. Accordingly, I persuaded R. B.
Bennett, the former Prime Minister of Canada, to join me as my
adviser on economic questions. Bennett, after a brilliant career
in Canada, had come to live in England. As he was consumed
with a burning zeal to do war work, he willingly accepted my
suggestion. Walter Layton also gave me most valuable advice as
to the need for better statistics and the form in which they should
be presented to the War Cabinet. When I proposed that he
should be given an official post, I found that the criticisms of the
News Chronicle, with which he was connected, still rankled in the
memories of Whitehall, and that the suggestion was unacceptable.

Lastly, I brought in Moore Brabazon, nominally as my
Parliamentary Private Secretary, actually as an old and intimate
friend whose advice, though I might not sometimes accept it, was
certain to be imaginative and stimulating.

It was equipped and assisted in this way that I started upon
my work as the Cabinet's man-of-all-work. I was soon to find that,
however tempting it might seem to have an interest in the affairs
of one's colleagues, the post of an overlord was beset with many
obstacles and dangers. The appointment of a co-ordinating
Minister was unexceptionable in theory. In practice, it was likely
to run counter to one of the fundamental principles of British
Cabinet Government—departmental responsibility. We had
found as the result of generations of political experience that one
of the essential conditions of Parliamentary Government was the
inescapable responsibility of a Minister for everything that went
on in his own department. This individual responsibility was, of
course, overshadowed by the collective responsibility of the
Cabinet under which every Minister was from time to time
compelled to accept the decision of his colleagues upon some
question for which his department was directly responsible.
Cabinet intervention of this kind was, however, very different
from the continuous supervision of an appointed overlord.

My regular sphere of influence was primarily to be Home
Affairs, but it was almost immediately extended to cover certain
questions of defence. From the first, however, I insisted that my
intervention should be specific for definite purposes rather than

continuous with any kind of overriding authority. Even so, the result was often to embroil me with one or other of my colleagues, and to drag me into debates in the House of Commons on subjects with which I was only indirectly concerned. For instance, I was instructed to find an answer to a question that has so far baffled everyone—the co-ordination of the work of the Ministries of Agriculture and Food. The result was that whenever the work of either of these departments came under attack in the House of Commons, the critics, and particularly Lloyd George, made great play with my obscure and anomalous position, and dragged me into controversies about which I knew little.

In the circumstances it seemed that my wisest course was to avoid any appearance of direct responsibility, and to concentrate my work upon the broad and simple issues that were often smothered in departmental detail. In the case of food and agriculture, the result was my recommendation to the War Cabinet of a ploughing programme of two million acres over and above the seven million acres already under cultivation.

I adopted the same line in an inquiry into our merchant shipping needs. The Board of Trade and the Admiralty were at the time engaged in a departmental war, the Board of Trade demanding more tonnage, and the Admiralty insisting that the trouble was not shortage of tonnage, but delays in turning round merchant ships. My inquiry showed that although submarine sinkings were at the time well below our pre-war estimates, there was urgent need not only for making better use of the Merchant Navy and for further restrictions in non-essential imports, but also for a greatly increased programme of new construction. Our target at the time was a yearly output of 800,000 tons, and that only to be reached at the end of August, 1940. I was convinced that this figure was altogether inadequate. I therefore proposed that it should be raised to a million and a half tons, and equal priority given for steel to both the Merchant and Royal Navies. The Cabinet accepted my recommendations early in January, and in order to allay Admiralty anxieties as to the reaction upon their own programme, made the First Lord responsible for all construction, whether for the Royal or the Merchant Navy. It was a matter of great satisfaction to me to have an all-important question, that might have led to both controversy and delay, settled amicably within a few weeks.

Of the other questions referred to me as Chairman of specially formed Committees in these early days of the war, the most likely to take time and excite controversy concerned the future strength of the Army. What kind of army should we create? What should be its strength? How long should we take to build it up? Questions of this kind involved not only a comprehensive estimate of our available resources, but also the very controversial allocation of them between the three Services. To each of them the answer depended upon whether we based our calculations upon a long or a short war. I saw at once that if we once started upon an exhaustive inquiry into all or any of them, we might take many months, and at the end be no nearer to the right solutions than if we had let our personal judgment give the answers at once. I wondered whether my colleagues in the Committee would accept this view. First and foremost, there was Churchill, brimming over with the expert knowledge gained in the First World War and in the Admiralty. Then, there were the other Service Ministers, Hore-Belisha at the War Office, and Kingsley Wood at the Air Ministry each suspicious lest the other should absorb too much, of our limited resources, and finally, Hankey, whose mind was a veritable *Encyclopædia Britannica* of all that had happened or might happen in any war.

The first meeting of the Committee confirmed my view that an immediate decision was needed which, even if it had afterwards to be substantially modified, would impress the world with our determination, and at the same time, suppress inter-departmental quarrels in Whitehall. In reaching it, the balance had to be held between the War Office, always prodigal of men, the Air Ministry, always suspicious of any army expansion, and the Board of Trade, always nervous of any diversion of man-power from the production of essential goods. Hankey's wise advice, supported by the brilliant mind of Humbert Wolfe at the Ministry of Labour, was of the greatest value to me, and enabled me, at the second meeting, to make a series of specific proposals. First, that we should assume that the war would last three years, and that the greatest possible publicity should be given to this assumption. An explicit declaration to this effect would, I felt sure, convince the world in general and Germany in particular that we intended to mobilise our total resources for victory. Secondly, that we intended to have an army of fifty-five divisions by the end of the second year of war, and a minimum of twenty divisions at the end of the first year. Thirdly, that the necessary priority for labour and materials for completing this programme should be guaranteed. Fourthly, that we would at once use every possible method, whether by foreign purchases or improvisation at home, to increase our strength in big guns. Lastly, that we would state categorically that our national effort would in no way fall behind the effort that we made in the First World War, and that the immediate programme of Army expansion would only be the first chapter of still greater developments. All these proposals were unanimously accepted, first by the Committee, and subsequently, subject to the limitations of labour and industry, by the Cabinet. The Committee had only been appointed on September 6, and it was on September 8 that our report received Cabinet approval. Were grave decisions ever taken with greater speed? When I compared them with the hesitant and tentative proposals that trickled out of Downing Street in the early years of the First World War, I felt that we had put a new drive into the complicated machine of government. What was more important, five years of war did not invalidate the strength of our recommendations.

I have quoted these instances of three of my interventions as Lord Privy Seal as evidence of my general outlook upon war questions. I was convinced that a totally new volume in British history had commenced, and that, so far from making it look like a continuance of the old book, it was essential, if the public was to be impressed by it, to make it appear as different as possible when once war had started. " Business as usual " seemed to me to be the worst of all mottoes. Business certainly as much as possible, but business with new methods and, if possible, with new men, if we were to excite the country's imagination and maintain its morale.

The difficulty was to make striking changes in the curious kind of war that had just begun. Our preparations had been for Armageddon, and it had not started. We were ready with millions of gas-masks for gas attacks that had been expected in the first few days of war, and not one had been needed. A quarter of a million emergency beds were waiting in the hospitals for the casualties that did not appear. As the outward and visible sign of our unexpected security, the Government remained in London, when we had plans ready for dispersing it in the country.

In the meanwhile, the state of the French front recalled the tranquillity of the winter quarters during Louis XIV's campaigns in the Low Countries. No doubt, this strange chapter of waiting, which became known as ' the phoney war,' was of great value to a country in which total mobilisation had hitherto been impracticable, but it brought with it the difficult problem of maintaining at the highest point the will to resist, when there was little to resist. A period of suspense seemed to some people almost worse than an attack that would brace the country's nerves and harden its morale. In this no-man's-land between peace and war, the new D.O.R.A. restrictions seemed to many people not only irksome, but unnecessary. What, for instance, was the need for the depressing black-out when enemy raids were so intermittent and ineffective? Why should meat and sugar be rationed when stocks were known to be substantial and ships were arriving regularly in British ports? Questions such as these gave ample scope to the Opposition for criticism of the Government.

It was during these months of waiting that my very old friend Lothian, who had recently taken up his post as British Ambassador in Washington, and was already exercising great influence upon official and non-official opinion in the United States, started with me a correspondence that continued unbroken until the crisis of the following spring. It began with a letter from him on September 15. I quote it in full and follow it with extracts from the later letters that describe the course of events as we saw them from London and Washington during the first months of the war that we had expected to start so differently.

" *British Embassy,*
" *Washington, D.C.*
" *September 15, 1939.*

" If I am to have any real effect here it is essential that I should understand thoroughly the British view of the future of the war. Most people here have not much comprehension of strategics and they are still inclined to think in terms of the last war. Yet the attitude they will take to the Neutrality Act, our blockade measures, and their own relationship to the war will largely depend upon their knowledge of the true facts and the true situation.

" The line I have taken hitherto with the people to whom I can talk frankly—not the Press—has been this. The defection of Russia has made impossible the creation now of that Eastern front, compelling Germany to fight a long war on two fronts and to suffer an effective blockade, which was the core of our strategic position during the first three years of the late war. We are therefore being driven back to the method by which we beat Napoleon—and Germany itself, in the last year of the late war—the long-distance or rationing blockade. From here there seems now little or no chance of the military defeat of Germany by direct assault. It seems clear that the Polish resistance must before long be overcome and that it will be vital, on a long view, for the French and our-selves to conserve our forces and not destroy them in a new Pas-schendael against the Siegfried line.

" The blockade, however, can still in the long run be effective partly because Germany starts short of money, supplies, and partly because it is not going to be at all easy for her to secure large supplies—except of oil from Roumania—from Russia, and because Italy, even if she comes in on her side, will be an economic liability rather than a source of strength. This prospect, however, depends upon the Navy defeating the submarine, and in the future, a possibly highly organised attack on commercial shipping from the air.

" Nobody, however, can yet tell what Germany will do if and when she overcomes Polish resistance. She may organise south-eastwards or attack the west. Nor do we know what Italy will do —whether she can be induced or compelled to come over as her people probably want—or whether she will join the general attempt to loot the British and French Empires as her Fascist leaders probably want.

" Nor can we prophesy what Japan will do. She may refuse commitments in Europe, but she is certain to try to exploit England and France's difficulties in Europe for her own ends in Asia.

" The consequence of the serious position in which the Russo-German pact and the forthcoming defeat of Poland are going to place England and France is beginning to come home to thinking Americans and instinctively the mass of Americans feel that Hitler is a mortal enemy of all they stand for. But at the moment they are obsessed with the desire to keep out of war—a desire which naturally grows stronger as they feel the abyss drawing nearer. Their moral preparedness is about that of England during the Baldwin period. If the only issue in the Neutrality Act were whether they would allow England and France to buy implements of war, the embargo would be lifted at once. But the fight is more and more going to take the form of a debate whether this war is also America's war or not. For that will increasingly be seen to be the real issue.

" I suppose if we press things to their logical conclusion, the issue of the war will depend on two things. The first is on our keeping control of the seas, including the Mediterranean and everything except the China seas, which we can afford to abandon so long as we do not lose Singapore. The second is, if the unlimited air war starts, on our being able to destroy the machine industry of Germany, now mostly in the Ruhr—on which Germany's war effort really depends—and weaken her economy by blockade before she can destroy our industry and France's, or cut off our seaborne supplies by submarines and air blockade. In the long run, the United States of America holds the decisive cards in both respects. Her fleet can make the Pacific, Australia and Singapore secure, as against Japan. And her machine industry can produce a volume of munitions, especially bombers from a base which cannot be attacked, which will eventually be decisive both against Germany and Italy. Some Americans already see this clearly, but the majority don't.

" Could you drop me a line to tell me whether this diagnosis is correct, or tell me what your view is, and also any facts and figures which I can use to bring home the real issues and the real facts to Roosevelt and other leaders here. Believe me, there is nothing more important you can do than to equip me with the facts and the arguments which will bring home to the United States the real situation which confronts us."

I answered this letter on September 25

" 25th September, 1939

" Your letter of the 15th and its duplicate have just arrived and I hasten to write to you in reply. I entirely agree with your last sentence in which you say that if we can equip you with the facts and arguments which will bring home to the United States the real situation which confronts us, we shall be doing as useful work as we can. I will, therefore, try to write to you every week and give you my most intimate and personal impressions. It may well be that by the time you get my letter, my comments will have proved to be foolish or groundless. It is inevitable when we are dealing with a completely uncharted world and with irresponsible and un-principled leaders like Hitler and Stalin. None the less, I will take the risk of being wrong and will not hesitate to send you my guesses.

" The line that you have been taking seems to me to be entirely sound.

" It looks to me as if a German advance in the Balkans has now been blocked by Russia. If this is so, Hitler will have to decide in the next fortnight between an attack through Holland and Belgium, or a long period of defensive warfare in the West. I would guess that it is impossible to penetrate the Maginot Line without terrific losses, and I should be very much surprised if Hitler attempts it. His only chance in the West, therefore, for quick results is a lightning attack through Holland and Belgium. It is now very late in the year to begin such an attack, particularly as it must take a considerable amount of time to transfer large forces from the East to the West. None the less, he may take this risk on the ground that he cannot face a long war. If he does, there will be a terrible chapter of destruction in which inevitably many civilians will be killed in the air bombing. Keep this last and grimmest point in your mind, as it may be well to prepare the minds of your friends for it. If it takes place, it will be Hitler's violation of Holland and Belgium that will have started it.

" The more likely contingency, it seems to me, is that the Armies will face each other in the West, and nothing much will happen with them until next spring. As to whether in this period there will be great air attacks or not, I am very uncertain. If there are air attacks, I believe that they will be upon the British and French aircraft industries rather than upon ostensibly open towns.

" Upon the general question as to which of these contingencies would suit us best, it seems to me that the broad consideration is that if Hitler wants a short war, we ought to go for a long war. If we go for a long war, it is obviously unwise to risk our resources, particularly in the air and on the sea, until we reach a decisive moment. Remember that our bombers are now very like our Battle Fleet. It is essential that the two Fleets should be kept in being until the decisive moment. This, you will remember, is the basic principle of fighting upon which Mahan insisted, and it may be worth your while to press this point upon your important friends.

" With this consideration in our minds we came out with the statement about the three years' war. It was my idea, and it emerged from a very important Committee of which I am Chairman for the settlement of the Air Force and Army programmes. The second statement that we intend our war effort to be the maximum effort not less than the effort of 1918, I also inspired with a view to meeting the propaganda in France that we are only on a limited liability basis.

" This is the broad background as I see it, and it is a background that is not very easy to hold with the world and the country.

Everyone will be expecting dramatic events, and instead, there will
be a war of nerves constantly playing upon the weaker side of
human nature. I am sure, however, that short of air attacks upon
us, this is the line that we must hold. The issues of life and death
are too grave to be played with. I do not know whether your friends
realise the magnitude of the task that we have undertaken and the
tremendous risks that we are facing. If they wish Anglo-American
civilisation to continue, they will have to give us what help they
can, moral and economic, or we may both be destroyed.

" The country here is very resolute. Indeed, one of the dangers
is that the man in the street is impatient, and thinks that we are
acting too slowly. We cannot tell him that in every respect we have
been keeping step with the French General Staff who are even more
cautious about dangerous risks than are we. As you will have seen,
we have been going through the difficult period of transition from
peace to war conditions. This has meant a considerable dislocation
of labour. I am sure, however, that our big munition programmes
that are now beginning to move quickly forward, will absorb all
the labour in the country. It is, however, essential that we should
get the necessary machine tools from the U.S.A. and Canada. This
is one of the key factors of the war and somehow or other we must
have, and have quickly, what we want. Over these questions of
supply, Labour is at present very touchy as, rightly or wrongly, they
think that they have not been sufficiently consulted in the matter.
. . . I wish very much that Labour had come into the Government.
Sooner or later they will, and the sooner the better, as this nagging
upon supply questions, much of it unjustified, does nothing but
harm.

" There can be no question of our rising to Mussolini's peace
fly. The Government and public opinion here are solid on this
matter. It seemed to me in some of the talks that I have had, as
if some of our Dominions friends and also some of our American
friends were wondering whether we should not do well to have a
peace by negotiation. All that I can say is that any such suggestion
is totally impracticable. . . .

P.S.—Since starting this letter I have heard a description of events
in Poland that comes through Carton de Wiart, the head of our
Military Mission. He says that the *débâcle* was not due to the
great efficiency of the German advance, to the German mechanised
divisions, or, most surprising of all, to the German Air Force. It
was due to the complete breakdown of the Polish communications.
The result was that nobody knew what to do, and great bodies of

troops were left without orders. This was particularly the case with the Polish Air Force, which seems never to have received any effective orders at all. The Polish Air Force was not destroyed by the German Air Force as, according to him, about three-quarters of the machines flew off during the collapse to neighbouring countries, and are now interned. As to the German mechanised transport, it was constantly breaking down and the ground is strewn with broken down cars and tanks. The Polish Air Force, however, having had no orders, does not seem to have made any use of this confusion. I tell you this not to disparage the Poles, but rather to warn you or anyone else from deducing that what happened in Poland will necessarily happen in the West."

A fortnight later I brought my appreciation up to date:

" 7th October, 1939

" I hope that my letter of last week was what you wanted. I have waited for Hitler's speech before I wrote you another. The speech is not what I expected. I had imagined that he would take one of two courses. Either he would make a very attractive peace offer, possibly going to the point of offering to retire himself in the interests of peace, with a view to enlisting the support of the neutrals and damaging morale in France and England; or he might have made a truculent speech ending with some kind of ultimatum under which he called upon the Allies to give an answer within a certain time. He has done neither of these things and instead, has made a long and confused statement that does not seem to end anywhere. It may be that he is not sure of his own mind, or that there are rival forces behind him. Whatever be the reason, we must, I am sure, act with great care and foresight. I feel that our line should be that our own position is clear, and that nothing that has been said or done since the war started, has in any way altered it, but that what is not clear is Hitler's position, and that before we even contemplate the possibility of a peace conference, we must have it much more clearly explained than has been done in his speech. This would seem to be a wiser course for us to take rather than to meet his speech with a curt and immediate refusal. If there is anything genuine in the offer, we shall discover it by this means, and if there is not, we shall prove to this country and the world the emptiness of his words. I can imagine that this elucidation may take some time. In the meanwhile, no one here or in America should have any anxiety as to the country's morale or the Government's determination. There are, of course, a number of people who are asking whether it is worth while going on with a war that started to save Poland and has seen Poland's destruction in the course of three or four weeks. There are also people who are bewildered with the situation created by the Russian entry upon the West. There is a further class of those who are irritated by the smaller vexations of war, and who have not been braced up to them by any great demand for patriotic sacrifice. These classes of people must be constantly kept in mind. They do not, however, alter the fact that the morale of the country as a whole is good. Lloyd George would not agree with me when I say this. He is out of touch with things; he hates the Government in general and Neville in particular, and feels bitterly that he has little or no chance of altering the course of things. The mistake that he made in the House on Tuesday was not that he came out for peace proposals, but that he implied that we were certain to be defeated, and that we must make peace from weakness and not from strength. I imagine that the discontented in the country will rally round him, but I am sure that there is no big body of support that would influence the conduct of events in this direction.

" The more I follow daily events, the more I am sure that our strategy is right, namely, that we should not fritter away our resources, but have them concentrated ready for the decisive moment. This means a strain upon everyone's nerves, but it is a strain that must be maintained. I suppose that it will affect the Opposition in particular. It will make them more prone to criticise the Government, and now that Attlee is back, the criticism will become more persistent and perhaps more bitter. It is very easy for an Opposition in wartime to make capital out of the nation's discontents and, in the present case, Attlee cannot bear Neville, with the result that there is a personal antipathy added to the natural propensity of the Opposition to criticise the Government.

" So far as the Cabinet is concerned, it is working well and there are no signs of a rift. . . ."

There followed a letter from Lothian on October 20 in which he thanked me for my two reports, and added further details to the American picture that he had outlined in his first letter.

I replied on October 30:

" *30th October, 1939*
" I have just got your letter of 20th October and it reminds me that I have not written to you for more than a week. I imagine that you are, on the whole, well satisfied as to the way the Neutrality

legislation is going. Here, in the meanwhile, the situation is still as uncertain as it was when I wrote to you ten days ago. There are rumours on all sides of an impending air and sea offensive against us, and there is also the large concentration of German divisions on the Western Front and the difficulty of keeping them there doing little or nothing. Judged by all the military rules it ought to be too late for a military offensive, but Hitler of course may do anything. As to the air and the sea, I feel sure that he will do everything in his power. No doubt the sinking of the *Royal Oak* has greatly encouraged him. On the other hand, the significant fact has emerged that our fighters walk round his bombers.

" Naturally so many uncertainties in the future make people rather irritable. This shows itself in constant criticism of D.O.R.A. regulations and small muddles. What is really happening is that the Government machine, prepared for a devastating series of air raids, has been too comprehensive for this period of comparative inaction. Almost everything was ready for a great climax and the climax did not come. Scores of people who wanted jobs, found that the staffs were already chosen and on the spot. The same kind of thing has shown itself in the field of trade and industry. With none of the preliminary period of muddle and preparation that there was in the last war, the full control came into operation at once. In fact, the machine has been too big for the small output of the war. If, however, we are now beginning a new chapter of much greater activity and possible ruthlessness, the machine will, I believe, prove to be very effective. If, on the other hand, the period of inaction goes on, we shall no doubt have to relax many of the restrictions. . . .

" As to the Government here, it is of course abused as is every War Government, but it is not going on badly. Neville shows amazing vitality and Winston a plethora of imaginative ideas. . . ."

My next letter was on November 11.

" I am afraid that it is some days since I wrote to you. However, to-day I am on Sunday duty and have a certain amount of unbroken time. Accordingly I send you these stray comments on the present situation.

" For the last two days, we have been in almost constant session over the possibility of a Dutch invasion. Two days ago it looked as if Hitler had made up his mind to occupy Holland. Now, this morning there is a flood of tendentious communiqués from Berlin implying that he never had any such intention. By the time this letter reaches you, we shall be able to judge better what is really going to happen. It certainly looks as if once again there are divisions in Hitler's councils. There were divisions over the proposal to attack the Maginot Line, there were divisions over the proposal to turn the Line by attacks through Belgium and Switzerland, and now, I would guess, there have been divisions over the invasion of Holland. I do not imagine that anything further is needed in the U.S.A. to intensify feeling against Hitler. If it were, I would guess that it would be the invasion of Holland for the express purpose of making intensive and ruthless air attacks upon England. As you know, the German occupation of Holland would mean that the German short-range bombers would be brought within range of the key points in Great Britain, and that bomber raids could be escorted by fighters. There is also the further fact that the shorter the range, the more intensely an air attack could be maintained. On the other side of the picture, there is the fact that as we should presumably blockade Rotterdam and Antwerp, two of Germany's principal sources of supply would be stopped. This is a fact of considerable importance when we are chiefly engaged upon an industrial rather than a food blockade. However, it is scarcely worth while guessing about these things. From all accounts Hitler now sees no one except two or three sycophants and is more irresponsible than ever.

" It looks as if the U-boat campaign is well under control. At the same time, it must be remembered that convoys and restrictions of various kinds mean great delays, and that these delays must inevitably have their effect upon the import of food stuffs and raw materials. We shall certainly want all the neutral shipping that we can get, and all the help that we can have from neutral markets, if we are to maintain standards here and carry through the gigantic programmes of the three fighting services. I hope that you will keep this all-important point constantly in mind when you are talking to our American friends. I do not believe that it is fully realised that we have undertaken far bigger programmes than were contemplated in the early years of the last war, and that these programmes are much more complicated and expensive to carry through.

" The Dominions seem to be playing up well. They have sent over a good lot of representatives and, as far as I can judge, there are no difficult questions between us. Our old friend Zafrullah[1] whom I have seen two or three times is not worried over Congress, but he gives me the impression that in his view Hopie[2] has been

[1] Sir Zafrullah Khan, the Indian Moslem leader.
[2] The Second Marquess of Linlithgow, Viceroy of India.

too Olympian and remote.   Crozier of the *Manchester Guardian*, who came to see me about Indian questions, agreed with me that sooner or later they will all have to come back to All-India Federation and that if Hopie were wise he would make another effort to push it now, particularly through four or five of the big Princes.

" In the field of Home affairs, the Government's fortunes have been going rather better.   It was inevitable that in a war in which there was little or no fighting, all the criticism would be concentrated upon the Home Front.   The Opposition would not have been human if they had not seized every opportunity for discrediting the Government, and the Press, deprived of their advertisements and betting news, found anti-Government stunts the best way to sell their papers.   On the Government's side, there was little or no reply to these attacks.   Everyone was working so hard that the defence went by default.   Things have lately been going rather better.   Some of the papers realise that they have overdone the criticism and, as a result of ten weeks of experience, the Government has been able to relax a number of the more irritating restrictions. One of the troubles is that the House of Commons has nothing to do except to criticise the Government two or three days a week, and as the Government's legislative programme takes little or no time in the House, it means that the fullest possible opportunity is given for nagging.   I dare say that this criticism does not do much harm here, and I hope that you will make it clear to our American friends that it is a part of the regular game and does not mean that the war is being incompetently carried on.   As a matter of fact, an impartial observer would probably say that the war organisation has been too good rather than not good enough, and that the result has been that people have been annoyed by the working of a great machine whose full volume is only needed in a time of a hundred per cent war.

" As to the personal side of the picture, you will have seen that Neville has had his first attack of gout for nearly two years.   Horder, whom I have seen once or twice, tells me that it is going along normally and that, in his view, the rest may really do him good. It is amazing that Neville has stood up to the strain so long.   I never knew anyone so physically hard and so mentally alert.

" Winston has been through a rough sea over the Scapa incidents.[1]   Being for the moment the war hero, he has come through it fairly well.   I shudder to think what would have happened if there had been another First Lord and he had been in

[1] The sinking of the *Royal Oak*.

Opposition. As it is, the Navy have had a shake up, and I am sure that there is no risk of such mistakes being made again."

It was after sending the second of these letters that I received a very full reply to my letter of October 7.

" *Washington, D.C.*
" *November 3rd, 1939*

" This is a reply to your very interesting and useful private and confidential letter of October. I want some guidance, and the best way to get it, I think, is to put a thesis up to you for criticism.

" The repeal of the arms embargo will open a new phase in the relation of the United States to the war. The net outcome of the six weeks' debate is that the United States has decided to place its industrial resources behind the Allies, on the ' cash and carry ' basis, and at the same time has also decided with practical un-animity that it is utterly against being drawn into the war in Europe. Public opinion, by overwhelming majority, wants the Allies to defeat Hitler—and more recently to keep Russia at bay—partly for ideological reasons, partly because the success of the Allies will remove the Hitlerian menace to American security, especially in South America, while their defeat would leave the United States face to face with a totalitarian Europe. But especially since the expected anti-Comintern war against the democracies, which, with the entry of Japan, would have immediately confronted the United States with very grave decisions in the Pacific, has disappeared, the war has become an internal European war, not even involving Spain and the Mediterranean so long as the Allied front remains intact and does not challenge in any immediate way the vital interests of the United States. Public opinion, therefore, is far more confident that it can and ought to keep out of the war than it was. Both the President and the isolationists have had a partial victory, and the present Neutrality Act represents very fairly the compromise between the two.

" If there were any evidence of an impending collapse of the North Sea-Maginot Line front, either through a successful attack on France, or through a successful aerial offensive on the British Fleet and shipping, or through an aerial attack on the industrial plant of France and Britain, or if Russia were to begin to move through Scandinavia or to come to terms with Japan in the Pacific, the present complacency would rapidly disappear, and the question of whether or not the vital interests of the United States would require some form of intervention would revive. But there seems, from here, to be much less probability of an attempted *blitzkrieg* against the Allies than there was a month ago. The weather seems likely to prevent an attempt at a decision this winter, though there will probably be continued attacks by air and submarine on the fleet, and in the spring, with the improved allied defences and a steady stream of armaments beginning to cross the Atlantic from the United States, and with Japan, Italy and Spain determined neutrals, Hitler may well have to decide that the *blitzkrieg* then also is too dangerous to attempt, with Russia waiting in the East to profit from the exhaustion in the West. The position of Germany is clearly becoming extremely dangerous, between a strengthened Russia in the East and a strengthening allied front in the West. This may force her either to try something desperate against us or it may lead to a terrific internal struggle between those who want to throw in their lot for good with Bolshevism and Russia and those who want to come to terms with the West and save Germany from Bolshevism.

" If this estimate proves to be true it is very difficult to foresee the effect on the United States. On the one hand, the present boredom with the stalemate war—amounting in places almost to resentment that the expected ' drama ' of world war is not after all going to be played—is likely to increase so that domestic politics, such as the Presidential election of 1940 and the question of the third term for Roosevelt, will once more take first place in the news. On the other hand, now that the United States has decided to back the Allies ' short of war ' and subject to ' cash and carry,' as the fear of war, which has underlain the more hysterical phase of the isolationist opposition to repeal, lessens, and as the underlying discontent with the ' save our skins at any rate ' aspect of the campaign begins to find expression, there may quite easily be a move towards a more forward international policy, especially in the Far East, and unless the war is intensified soon, there will almost certainly be much discussion here this winter as to how a peace can be brought about on terms which will give a guarantee of security both to the democracies and against an early return of world war. The one thing which will leave the United States comparatively indifferent will be developments in the Balkans. . . .

" If they " (i.e. American questioners) " do talk to me I should be inclined to reply somewhat as follows. The prospects of an early peace—assuming that no complete collapse of the Hitlerite régime is in sight this winter—really depends upon the neutrals, that is, in essence, on the United States. If they stand aloof, it is difficult to see how a fight to a finish can be avoided, and a fight to a finish probably means the eventual involvement of the United

States in the war and the collapse of civilisation. Left to ourselves we cannot afford to make what will only be a truce with Hitler. Nor, confronted only by us, will Hitler abandon his dreams of world power. But if the democratic neutrals—with the United States in the lead—are prepared to throw their weight behind the Allies, so that the preponderance of power behind the free world of the United States, the British Commonwealth, France, Scandinavia, Switzerland, Belgium, Holland, is overwhelming, we can probably convince Germany that victory is permanently out of reach, and that if eventual Bolshevism of all Central Europe is to be avoided, there must be a sufficient movement to the right inside Germany to make possible a negotiated peace on the lines outlined above, while the existence of such a loose confederacy of democracies would in itself be security against a renewal of the war. This would not mean that the United States would go to war, or promise to do so. Nor does it mean that the United States would entangle itself in the internal affairs of Europe. But it would mean that she decides on a unilateral policy of her own to stand behind the Allied system, as, in a measure the repeal of the embargo implies, to the point that nobody will dream of challenging it. It means the restoration of the nineteenth century peace system, based on sea and air power but with the United States as an active support of the control of the seas everywhere, or at least in the Pacific, as we are in the Atlantic. I attach my Pilgrim speech here last week, which tentatively develops this idea."

I replied to his request for my comments on November 21.

"I have just received your most interesting letter of 3rd November and the report of your excellent speech at the Pilgrims' Dinner. Let me congratulate you upon the speech and say something about the questions that you ask me in your letter, but first let me begin with a word about the present situation.

"A week ago all the evidence seemed to show that Germany had decided to invade the Low Countries. It was not a case of alarmist rumours or interested propaganda, it was the genuine view of most people who were closely following the course of events. Hitler, who must get on or get out, had found it impossible to make an offensive in the Balkans, to attack the Maginot Line and to invade France through Switzerland and Belgium. Baulked of these chances, his obvious alternative seemed to be Holland, both as a means of winning a quick success and also of obtaining an advanced air base against Great Britain. I suppose that we shall never know accurately why he has not yet taken this obvious step.

The Belgians tell us that it is because the constant air reconnaissance of German machines showed the strength of the Belgian defences. Others declared that it was the intervention of Italy and Spain that stopped him. My own view is that he could not make up his own mind, and that he could not make up his own mind because, for all his reputation to the contrary, he is, when faced with really dangerous decisions, weak and undependable. No one can say that the Low Countries project is finally off. My guess would be that he will now concentrate upon his new mines and trust to sinking a large amount of British and neutral shipping. It is certainly true that his Naval Staff have shown much more versatility than they did in 1914. The mines will be formidable weapons. I have no doubt of this, but I feel sure that we shall get the measure of them, and that in the meanwhile, their use will draw neutral opinion more and more towards us.

" But I must come now to your questions. I say at once that I agree with your view about the Far East. I feel sure that if the U.S.A. maintain the kind of policy that you outline, there will be no difference between us about it.

" As to Europe, the first and predominant war aim is to win the war. Upon this central objective the French and we are completely united. The time must come when we must define more closely our further war aims. If we start prematurely upon them, we may well start a wrangle between them and ourselves. Some people are saying in Paris already, that we are contemplating what they call a ' professors' peace.' Keep this French anxiety in your mind when you are pressed, as you will be, in the U.S.A. to define precisely our aims. As to the kind of Germany with which we could make peace, I am inclined to think, however, that we can be rather more definite than you are in your letter. For instance, I believe that we should need more than the autonomy of Poland and Czechoslovakia. If there are to be safeguards for peace in the future, surely Poland and Czechoslovakia must be independent. I think also that we must be careful to know what we mean when we say that we cannot make peace with the ' Hitler gang.' We must surely be satisfied that the new men will not be the old men under different names. You say that we must not impose a democratic system upon authoritarian Germany. I agree. It is a fatal mistake to try to impose any system of government upon a foreign country. At the same time, I am convinced that the form of German Government, whether it be republican or whether it be monarchical, must be very different from what it is to-day. There surely must be a constitution of some kind. There is none to-day. I hope, myself, that with the fall of Hitlerism, some of the peaceful forces in Germany will regain their former influence, but it is essential that these forces should come from within Germany rather than have the appearance of being imposed upon Germany from outside. For instance, it would be a great mistake on our part to press for the dismemberment of Germany or for a monarchist restoration. If, however, either emerge from Germany itself, it might be a real guarantee of peace for the future. As to a monarchist restoration, it would be doubly dangerous for us to sponsor it. Our intervention would turn the new Germany against it, and would, I imagine, alienate great bodies of opinion in the United States and on the Left in Europe. It may come of itself, as it already seems to be coming in Spain, and if Poland is restored, in Poland. As to Poland, Zaleski, next to whom I was sitting at luncheon on Friday, told me that even the Poland of the Left was turning towards a monarchy as an essential symbol of unity, both for themselves and for a Central and Eastern Europe federation.

" I do not know whether these disconnected comments will be of use to you. Perhaps they may have the effect of giving a more concrete form to some of the problems that are facing us. The fact remains that whether in the East or in the West, the ultimate future of peace will depend to a great extent upon the U.S.A. and the more concrete can be their influence on the side of it, the sooner the war will be over and the firmer the peace that will be established."

The letters led to a further and more detailed survey of the American attitude from Lothian on February 1.

" *British Embassy.*
" *Washington, D.C.*
" *February 1st, 1940*

" Before the war broke out, American public opinion, thanks to the newspapers and the radio, had watched events in Europe with all the keenness and intimate knowledge of the personalities and the moves in the diplomatic game characteristic of spectators at a football match. On the one hand, it constantly shouted to the British and French players that unless they stood up to the dictatorships they would themselves be devoured. On the other hand, it was believed that if the war came, it would take the form of frightful air attacks on the great cities of Western Europe and the immediate entry into the war on Germany's side of Japan, Italy and possibly Spain. There was, therefore, a widespread conviction, as revealed in the Gallup and Fortune polls, that if and when war came, America would fairly rapidly be drawn into it. The experience of the war has falsified these expectations. There has been no serious air war on cities in Europe, Japan was driven out of the anti-Comintern Pact by the Germano-Russian Treaty, Italy and Spain, largely for the same reason, have pursued a policy of determined neutrality. The war itself has become a purely internal European war beyond the Rhine. In its actual 1939 form the war was clearly not America's immediate concern. And the long view that intervention now would prevent far greater sacrifices later is one which most democracies find it extremely difficult to take. At the same time, American public opinion itself, suddenly realising that it was watching not a gigantic football show but a game in which the footballs were immensely destructive bombs, was swept by a wave of emotional pacifism, springing at first largely from mothers and wives who, in the interest of their children and husbands, demanded that at all costs the United States itself should be kept out of the war. At one time it looked as if this wave might defeat the President's policy of repealing the arms embargo in order to place American machine industry at the disposal of the Allies. But gradually the recognition prevailed among all clear-sighted people that the best way of keeping America out of the war was to help Great Britain and France to defeat Hitler by selling them arms, and at the same time to remove some of those causes which had led to the entry of America into the last war, e.g. torpedoing of American ships and the increasing dependence of American industry on vast war orders financed by American loans, by enacting the ' cash and carry ' provisions. In the end, the President got his bill by larger majorities than at one time seemed likely.

" Industrial assistance to the Allies, subject to the most rigid conditions designed to prevent the United States from being drawn into the war, thus became the settled policy of the United States, as the result of the long Neutrality debate.

" Since the repeal of the arms embargo American public opinion has been slowly developing in response to events in Europe and the Far East. It gradually became convinced that the risk of its being drawn into the European war was rapidly lessening, that Hitler had made a profound mistake in his pact with Stalin, which had lost him all his old allies and had imprisoned Germany between the rapidly strengthening French and British forces and a Russia whose ostensible friendship really concealed long-distance suspicion and hostility. With the New Year therefore American public opinion began to turn with gusto to the always entertaining drama of the Presidential election. . . .

" The attack of Russia on Finland has stirred American emotions to the depths. The Finns have long been regarded as the most outstanding small democracy in Europe. The popularity it has won by its achievements has been increased because alone among the nations of the world, it had performed that most acceptable of all public acts to the American democracy, it had paid its debts. . . .

" In the last week or two there has been the sudden outburst against British interferences with American trade and communications. This has been brewing for some time. . . .

" This resentment has been increased by the suspicion that Great Britain is using the war as an excuse to transfer trade from the United States of America to its own Empire and to foreign countries or in favour of countries like Italy who have more nuisance value. . . .

" All these grievances came to a head at the same time as our rejection of the American protest about examining the mails. The State Department then deliberately ' turned the heat on us ' for three or four days, partly to compel us to pay attention, and partly to prove to offended elements in Congress and the country that it was not, as a Senator said, a ' mere doormat ' for the British. . . .

" The United States to-day is less afraid of being drawn against its will into the European war, and is emerging from the somewhat humiliating attitude of abandoning all its rights which it adopted when the fear of war was strongest upon it. It is therefore beginning to reassert itself as a positive influence in the international situation. The danger to us lies in the fact that the Neutrality Act has eliminated almost all points of friction with Germany, so that minor American grievances and controversies are almost exclusively against ourselves. In the last war, however irritated the United States got through the arbitrary exercise of our command of the sea, we could be certain that the Germans would do something far more exasperating. To-day this factor no longer exists. This imposes upon us the necessity of walking extremely warily in our interferences with American trade, and of doing everything we can to convince the Administration beforehand that what we propose to do is really an important contribution towards winning the war. . . .

" In the past the United States has been inclined to expect us to take the lead in the Far East on the ground that our interests there were far greater, without promising any support. That phase is passing away. Both the Administration and public opinion realise that we are fully preoccupied in Europe. They are beginning to lose the suspicion, deeply ingrained since the events of 1931, that we are only awaiting a favourable opportunity to abandon the Chinese and sell out to the Japanese. They have come to recognise that the main initiative and responsibility there now rests squarely upon their own shoulders. . . .

" If the U.S.A. presses on with its policy of commercial pressure, it may find itself confronted with the necessity of taking simultaneous action in both oceans, if Great Britain and France get into difficulties, or of beating a somewhat humiliating diplomatic retreat with consequential depressing effects on China and encouragement to Japan. The probabilities will become clearer during the Congressional discussions of the next few weeks. . . .

" The present unwritten and unnamed naval alliance with Great Britain is almost as essential to the United States of America if it is to continue to enjoy the kind of existence it has led since 1814 as it is to ourselves. Public opinion is instinctively aware of this, but no politician of importance—even the President, especially in election year—can point openly to these facts for the reason that the logical conclusion is that America must abandon isolation for good and make a permanent naval arrangement with ourselves, with the commitment to war which that implies. . . .

" At the moment, therefore, and unless some of the contingencies involved in the foregoing paragraphs mature, the United States will do everything in its power to keep out of war. But there is another possibility more difficult to assess. Some of the best judges of American opinion are convinced that behind the surface façade of isolationism the people of the United States are slowly making up their minds that, if their own future and a free civilisation are to be maintained, they have got to intervene. That is my own conviction. . . .

" There is the rising feeling that the United States is playing an unworthy part in one of the greatest dramas of history, and is in danger of losing her soul unless she shoulders her share of the burden.

" In the last war America re-elected Wilson in November, 1916, on the ticket ' He kept us out of war.' In April, 1917, after the unlimited German submarine campaign, he took a united but fundamentally ignorant country into the war. To-day, if the United States decides that victory for the Allies is essential, that a deadlock is fatal to its own future, and that it must cast its own weight into the scale, it will do so because public opinion itself, now extraordinarily well informed about world affairs, has gradually itself come to the conviction that, on a long view of its

O

own interests, it must act. If it does so, isolationism will be over for good. But the developments in this direction cannot be pre-meditated. They depend on the march of events. . . .

" The number of individuals and societies who realise that, if the world is to get peace, the United States must be willing to contribute responsibility to its maintenance not merely by dis-armament, but by helping to supply the overwhelming force which must stand behind any just settlement, is steadily growing. . . .

" One final word about Anglo-American relations. The one fatal thing is for us to offer the United States advice as to what she ought to do. We have never listened to the advice of foreigners. Nor will the Americans. They only differ in that we ignore such advice, and the Americans get extremely angry when it is offered to them by any Briton. She is going to work out the problem for herself. She is glad of information. She is quite ready to listen—indeed is anxious to listen—to our views, provided they are expressed as our own opinions and do not include any expression of opinion as to what the United States should do. But just because the British have a power of emotional appeal, due to common ancestry, common language, common ideals, anything which looks like British propaganda designed to influence American policy creates a cold fury in the American mind."

I have quoted these letters at length as they give a contem-porary picture of the early months of the war both here and in America, and show how the world was astonished and almost disappointed that the *blitzkrieg* had not started. In the States, the effect was the strengthening of the conviction that the American continent could and should be kept out of the war. The tendency, in the absence of any dramatic crisis, was to resent any British action that interfered with American shipping or the transmission of American cables from England to the States. British difficulties were not yet fully realised. For instance, there was a widespread misunderstanding of our policy in the Far East, where our cautious attitude towards Japan was believed to be based on sympathy with an aggressor rather than our military inability to carry on simul-taneous wars in the Pacific and the Atlantic.

The surprise of the war that was not yet a war put an even greater strain upon British nerves. The British public was ready and prepared to accept great sacrifices, but not minor irritations. The compelling force of immediate danger that stirred and united the whole country in the following year was absent. Members of the House of Commons, with practically no legislative business to occupy them, would not, as I told Lothian, have been human if they had not justified their existence by exploiting to the full the many small grievances about which their constituents complained. To add to the general *malaise*, the Government machine, that had been so carefully planned for a totally different war, appeared as a kind of juggernaut that was quite unnecessarily stifling the life of the nation.

CHAPTER XXXV

The Scrapping of a Plan

T HE HISTORY of the war-time Ministry of Information illustrates in a particularly vivid way this chapter of war that was not of the expected kind, and of waiting that, although of great value to our military preparations, seemed to the world at large to be a sign of confusion and hesitation.

Much against my wish, I had been involved in the Ministry's creation from the start. Hankey's great War Book, which covered the whole field of preparations for war, contained an important chapter on the need of a central department for dealing with news in war time. Accordingly, shortly before I went to the Home Office in 1937, a committee composed of the permanent chiefs of the principal offices in Whitehall was appointed to draw up a plan for bringing into operation a Ministry of Information with a special Minister at its head as soon as war started. The Committee, after making a detailed examination of the control and distribution of news in the First World War, came to the conclusion that centralisation rather than decentralisation should be the basis of the new organisation. In the First World War, there had been five separate organisations concerned with controlling and distributing news, and although great efforts were made to remedy the confusion that ensued, the position was still unsatisfactory when hostilities ended. Centralisation involved a single department for information and the readiness of the other departments, including the Service Ministries, to accept it as the channel for their news and the controlling authority on their publicity. Whilst it might have been expected that the fighting services would have objected to this delegation of an important part of their public relations to another office, it was the representative of the Air Ministry who actually made the proposal of centralisation to the Committee. The Committee's report was unanimous, and was at once approved by the Committee of Imperial Defence and the Cabinet. The question then arose as to which Minister and Department should be responsible for working out the details of the proposed organisation. None of my colleagues wished to undertake the work, with the result that the Home Secretary, the residuary legatee of the Government, had it thrust upon him. This meant a further responsibility in addition to my many duties connected with Air Raid Precautions, and with almost daily attendances at the Committee of Imperial Defence and the Foreign Policy Committee.

The new work involved many interviews with leaders of the Press and experts of all kinds in the world of publicity. Although it took much of my time, the result seemed to make it worth while. I found both in Whitehall and Fleet Street a general desire to co-operate on the lines that had been proposed. The representatives of the Press, London, Provincial and Scottish, approved of the plan, and appointed a representative for liaison with the Government. Agreement was reached as to the staff that would be required, and the names of the many journalists who were earmarked for it. When I described the scheme in the House of Commons on July 28, five weeks before the outbreak of war, it was received with general approval. The war started, the Ministry began its work with little apparent friction in the new buildings of the University of London, and a Minister, Lord Macmillan, universally respected for his ability and impartiality, became the first Minister.

The plan had rightly been prepared to cover the risks of an all-out war. As it seemed likely that air raids would disrupt communications with the provinces, provision had been made for information officers to be attached to the headquarters of the Regional Commissioners, who had already been appointed for Civil Defence. A staff in London which, though it appeared very large, was yet much less than the various staffs in 1918, was ready for non-stop work by shifts. A centre was available for the Press with every kind of facility for quick communication, both within the country and overseas. In fact, the Ministry assumed at once the bodily form that months of discussion with those best qualified to give their opinion had recommended, and that the experiences of the First World War suggested. The trouble, which soon showed itself, was that there were no devastating air attacks to prove the value of a regional organisation, and no war news of first-class value to dispense through a great machine of publicity. The result was general irritation. The American correspondents were restive under any restrictions. The British Press complained that broadcasting was given a favoured position. Still more serious, the Service Departments, although they had agreed to pool their news, showed that in practice they were determined to keep control of their communiqués and censorship. Lastly, the public was convinced that the absence of news did not mean that nothing was happening, but that information was being withheld by the Government for sinister reasons.

Upon this growing heap of inflammable discontent descended on September 12 a high explosive bomb. The Expeditionary Force was at the moment being transported across the Channel. Its safe passage was of critical importance, not only to us, but to our French allies. In view of the great issues at stake, it was felt in London that there should be no public reference to the operation until it was complete. Accordingly, the Press censorship prohibited the publication of any reports of the movement. Much to our surprise, however, the French authorities published the news late on the evening of the 12th, before all our troops were across the Channel. The story was cabled to America and spread at once over the world. In the circumstances the Ministry of Information, with the approval of the War Office, told the British Press that the embargo was removed. The papers therefore printed their morning editions with the news prominently featured. The authorities at the War Office at this eleventh hour became suddenly nervous, and demanded that all publicity should once again be prohibited. The Ministry could not ignore so serious a representation upon a question of military security, and re-imposed the embargo. In the meanwhile, the early editions of the papers had gone out with the news in them. There followed several hours of complete confusion, in the midst of which an official of the War Office, without any authority, instructed Scotland Yard to seize any papers that contained the news. Upon the strength of this instruction, the police visited the newspaper offices and waylaid early morning travellers in order to obtain possession of the papers. Scarcely, however, was the perquisition completed, when the French Director of Information released a further and fuller account of the transport of the Expeditionary Force that made our embargo more than ever futile. Almost, therefore, before the editions had been suppressed, the papers were once again given liberty to publish their stories. Could there have been confusion worse confounded, and could any incident have given a better handle for the criticisms against the new Ministry?

I myself knew nothing about the seizure of the papers, or the sudden change in the minds of the authorities at the War Office. The first news was given to me on the telephone on the following morning. Although I was no longer directly responsible, since a Minister of Information had already been appointed, I hurried off to the Ministry to see what could be done. A long conference showed that the changes over the embargo were entirely due to the War Office, and that the Ministry of Information had had nothing to do with the visitations of the police. Parliament and the Press were already in an uproar, and it was left to me, as the Ministry's spokesman in the House of Commons, to make the best story that I could on the following day. " You have a terribly difficult job," Simon said to me as I was collecting my notes at the table. I could not have more fully agreed with him. My main difficulty was that I could not say that the whole trouble was due first, to the French, and then, to the War Office. All that was possible was to apologise and to promise that it would never happen again. The House, having lectured the Ministry officials for a crime that they had not committed, never afterwards abandoned its prejudice against the new office. The criticism continued unabated, and within a fortnight, the Prime Minister was forced to announce that the principle of centralisation had been abandoned, and that in future the Service Departments would be responsible for the control and distribution of their own news. I was convinced that this sudden change was a mistake, and that when once the war became intensified, it would be necessary to return to the original plan. But as there was now a Minister of Information, and I was no longer responsible for the Ministry's activities, I could not press my view beyond telling Chamberlain that some time in the future there would certainly be a reaction in favour of the original conception of the office.

The reaction came sooner than I expected. When the

Chamberlain Government fell, and Bracken became the very popular and able Minister of Information in Churchill's Government, the tide turned again in favour of centralisation. By the end of the war, the broken bits had been stuck together again, and the Ministry recreated in much the same form as it had been given at the beginning.

There could be no better illustration for the first chapter of the war, with its irritations, frustrations and apparent failures, than the big building in Bloomsbury, the future seat of the University of London, prepared in every way for the control and distribution of vast quantities of world-shaking news, and appearing for the moment as an unnecessary excrescence, for the simple reason that the war, with which it was to deal, had not yet started. In the meanwhile, the general public behaved like people in a dark waiting-room, uncomfortably expecting a train that did not arrive.

The thundery atmosphere of expectancy had its effect upon the War Cabinet. We met every morning, and regularly began our proceedings with reports from the three Chiefs of Staff. For the first few days we hoped and expected upon the best military advice that the Poles would be able to resist until the autumn rains stopped the German advance. We were sadly disabused by the speed of the German victory. Then came the news of the Russian occupation of Polish territory, the sinking of the battleship *Royal Oak*, and our heavy losses in the small air raids that we were attempting. Lloyd George was quick to make use of these misfortunes for a very defeatist speech in the House of Commons on October 3. On the other hand, the Chief of the Imperial General Staff had been to Paris for a conference with Gamelin, and had returned in an optimistic mood, but as uncertain about Hitler's plans as when he went. Soon afterwards, the Luftwaffe launched the first attack by magnetic mines upon our sea approaches, and if it had not been for the superb bravery of the naval officers who dismantled one of the mines in the Thames and discovered the mechanism, very great damage must have been inflicted on British shipping. Although this success was some compensation for the sinking of the *Royal Oak*, it was a shock to everyone that a battleship had been sunk with such ease in home waters.

Upon the home front, the question of profiteering was creating a demand for legislation, but no two people were agreed as to what the legislation should be. While we were discussing the question, we suddenly found ourselves in a coal crisis. Although I was Chairman of the Home Affairs Committee, I had been given no warning of the shortage of rolling stock for transporting coal to London, and I only heard of the trouble when London was faced with an immediate coal famine. I at once intervened, and arranged for a concentration of all the available rolling stock on the single objective of supplying London. Whilst this rough and ready action saved the situation, it cut across a network of complicated plans that Sir Josiah Stamp was working out in a very expert Economic Committee.

CHAPTER XXXVI

Premature Action, and the End
of the Government

I T WAS not unnatural that in the kind of atmosphere typified
by incidents such as these, the public demand became insistent
for more active and resolute military operations. Its first
notable expression was over the Finnish war. The Russian
invasion of Finland and the gallant resistance of the Finns had
made a profound impression upon public opinion both here and
in the United States. It seemed to many intolerable to stand by
inactive and see a small democracy destroyed by an unscrupulous
dictator. Intervention was pressed from another angle. Had we
not been given an opportunity to drive a wedge between Hitler
and Stalin by supporting the Finns, with whom several German
Generals and Admiral Raeder were known to be in sympathy?
The result of this pressure was a conference with the French
and an agreement to organise a joint expeditionary force
to help the Finns. The most difficult problem was, however,
unsolved—the movement of any such force to the scene of war.
It was clear that the right of passage through Sweden was indispensable. The Swedish Government, true to its habitual policy
of neutrality and its permanent fear of Russia, refused it. The
result was an impasse, and the suggestion of a special Mission to
Stockholm for a further attempt to persuade the Swedes to withdraw their refusal. It was out of this discussion that there emerged
a proposal that I should go to Stockholm and avail myself of a
long-standing friendship with King Gustav V for influencing his
Government. I doubt whether my Mission would have been of
any use. In any case, the proposal was dropped, as the war took

a sudden turn for the worse when Finnish resistance broke down before the overwhelming force of Russian reinforcements. The Anglo-French plan was discarded, and with it, our first attempt to win the initiative in the ' phoney ' war.

The demand for action of some kind became stronger than ever. Churchill in particular was straining at the leash. Not a week passed without some imaginative proposal from his fertile and brilliant mind. The plan upon which he chiefly insisted was the blockade of the Norwegian waters through which Swedish iron ore was transported to Germany when the Swedish route was blocked by winter ice. Mines were to be laid in the narrow channel interspersed with inlets and islets that was affording safe passage for the ore. The plan that had been carefully prepared for several weeks seemed likely to succeed. Churchill and Oliver Stanley, the Secretary of State for War, who dined with me on April 3, when it was on the point of being launched, were very optimistic. Within a few hours of their leaving the house, however, I was awakened by a telephone message from the Chief of the Air Staff to say that Hitler had forestalled us by occupying Denmark and invading Norway. What next happened is a matter of history, and I need only allude to the events with which I had some special and personal connection.

It was in the previous week that, once again after a tour of most of the great offices of Whitehall, I had returned to the Air Ministry. Kingsley Wood had worked himself almost to death since he left the Ministry of Health and succeeded Swinton in a department that was very new to him. It was clear to both the House of Commons and the Cabinet that he was a tired man who needed a change. For a time, Chamberlain persuaded him to go on, but eventually, towards the end of March, he insisted upon leaving. Chamberlain then asked me to change places with him, and to return to a post that I had held three times before. At first I asked to be excused, but eventually, and with considerable reluctance, I accepted the exchange. The result was that, after an interval of more than ten years, I found myself back in my old office. Instead of being at home in surroundings where I had spent many years, I felt myself a stranger in a new world. The Air Ministry and Air Force that I had known had been a new and struggling department and a small *corps d'élite* that Trenchard and I had managed almost as a family party. The

Department was now one of the largest in Whitehall, and the Air Force fast becoming the predominant fighting service. Aircraft production, not yet allocated to a special department, which in early days had meant little more than the ordering of a few score machines, had become the most complicated and urgent of the Government's responsibilities. Whilst in the past the Secretary of State had been able to control practically all the details of the administration, he now seemed little more than a passenger in a coach driven by staff officers and technical experts. It was inevitable that in time of war the main duties of a Service Minister should pass to the Service Staff. I had therefore become not so much an initiator of Air policy as an interpreter of air operations, first to the Cabinet, and next, to the House of Commons and the public. Kingsley Wood's ill health and his inexperience of Service questions had tended to obscure the activities of the Air Force in a war that did not seem to be real war. I did my best to remedy the lack of understanding, and both in the Cabinet and on the wireless, to tell the story of its great achievements in the face of heavy odds. I soon realised how much I had come to need this new and very human task. I had been sitting week days and Sundays in the War Cabinet amidst a mass of papers and expert opinions, and through no want of sympathy or human feeling, had begun to feel very remote from what was actually happening on the battle-front. My return to the Air Minsitry brought me back to the grim and moving realities of war. To the world outside, the war was the " phoney war," the *drôle de guerre* of the French, in which nothing was happening. To the Air Force in the winter of 1939 and the spring of 1940, it was a chapter of heroic bravery, of forlorn hopes, of brilliant improvisation that at great sacrifice surmounted one difficulty after another and laid the foundation of ultimate victory. Scarcely a day passed without some act of incredible skill or courage, whether in the attacks on German shipping, or the laying of mines, or even in the dropping of leaflets in the face of cold, bad visibility, and primitive guides to navigation. The climax was reached during the Norwegian operations, when the Squadrons, without landing grounds and against overwhelming odds, fought incomparable battles that could only end in certain defeat. There, indeed, was the evidence of the superb quality of our air crews. It had not been in vain that Trenchard had year after year insisted upon an almost unattainable standard of quality for Air Force personnel. Having worked with him for six years. I could well appreciate the results that were visible in 1940. His work had stood the test of war, not only in the matter of training, but no less in the field of tactics and strategy. My colleagues on the Air Council had all graduated in his school. The doctrine of attack as the best defence, and of concentration of force rather than of dissipation of local effort was firmly held. I did my best to explain it to the Cabinet, where there was sometimes a tendency to call upon the Air Force for little packets of local help. Still more, did I need to press it upon the French when I went to the Supreme War Council in Paris and urged the necessity of the stragetic bombing of military targets in Germany. Gamelin and his staff, tied down to the traditional conception of war on the ground, could never envisage the new possibilities of long-distance air action, and it was only with the greatest reluctance that they eventually agreed to the bombing of German marshalling yards and oil installations. Between them and our Air Staff was a gulf of opinion that was never fully bridged and that continually impeded sound decisions until the French collapse ended the chapter of argument.

These few weeks at my old Ministry taught me another lesson. They showed me the result of a unity of purpose that had persisted unbroken for many years. Whether it was Trenchard or the Salmond brothers or Ellington or Newall, the broad policy had remained the same. Although controversy with the older Services had often impeded its fulfilment, the central objectives had never been altered. If the immediate results shown in more numerous squadrons and machines had often seemed disappointing to the world in general, the solid foundations that had been firmly dug, had made it possible to build upon the remnant left after the First War a Force capable of winning the command of the air. The Air Staff was therefore able to look to the future with sober confidence, provided that the growing Force was not dissipated in futile and unsound operations. Only once in 1939 was there a deflection from this policy—in the Norwegian expedition—and then under great pressure from outside influences. I was indeed fortunate to be reminded at first hand of this fine record. Many of Trenchard's successors had added their names to it. Not least Newall, the Chief of Staff during my short term of office, who never wavered in his defence of the true faith, and within a few weeks was to join with Dowding in saving our fighter force from extinction in the French collapse.

Having interposed the story of my return to the Department, I must take up the thread of the history of the Norwegian expedition. As soon as I re-entered the Air Ministry, I found myself in a whirl of quick changes and sudden decisions. The preparations for the expedition had been rushed to meet the German move. The Admiralty relied upon submarines to close the Kattegat to German reinforcements. In Norway, no air base was available from which our aircraft could operate. The three Chiefs of Staff, though they had reluctantly acquiesced in the decision to send an expedition, were obviously doubtful about its success. Looking back at the many discussions that then took place, some of them continuing far into the night, I have since come to the conclusion that if we had not been influenced by the persistent demand for action of some kind, we should not have proceeded with the plan. As it was, we went from disaster to disaster, and within a few weeks were forced to make the first of the evacuations that were later to be followed by the much greater withdrawal from Dunkirk. The result was to present Hitler with a resounding success at a time when German morale was uncertain and the war unpopular in Germany. Supposing that we could have firmly maintained a waiting policy, concentrated upon rearmament, and abjured all minor operations, we could have gathered our strength for decisive action at the opportune moment, and deprived Hitler of the chance not only of an easy victory, but of consolidating the German people behind a leader who seemed always able to give them a swift success.

When I say that the expedition was one of the chief mistakes of the war, I do not in the least wish to absolve myself from the responsibility of having agreed to it. Like many others, I was impatient at the long period of waiting, and sensitive to the criticisms that were made against the Government's inaction.

When the news of our withdrawal was announced, Amery, always ready for a fight to the end, rang me up in great distress. " The Government must go," were his last words on the telephone. He was right, but not for the same reason that convinced me. For him, the fault was our failure to continue the campaign and to push home our attack on Trondjhem. For me, it was the rashness of undertaking a military operation for which we were not prepared, and in failing to resist the outcry for action when waiting was the only wise course. The result was a disastrous failure. A Government in war time must be overwhelmingly strong if it is to withstand failure. After six months of a war without movement, Chamberlain's Government was too weak to survive such a disaster. I remember well that after doing my best to defend the operation in the House of Commons in the debate that followed the evacuation, I said to my wife in the car as we drove home: " That is not only the last speech that I shall make as a Minister, but it is the last speech that I shall make in the House of Commons." It was the end of eighteen years of almost continuous office. Four times Secretary of State for Air, Secretary of State for India, Foreign Secretary, First Lord, Home Secretary, Lord Privy Seal—I suppose that I had filled as many great posts in Whitehall as any of my contemporaries. Not one of them had been free from fierce controversy. With Trenchard, I had fought the battle of the independent Air Force against the Army and the Navy. Throughout the long years of my Indian work I had, night after night, met Churchill's attacks in the House of Commons. In the Foreign Office, I had inherited the insoluble controversy over Abyssinia, and in the Home Office, my Criminal Justice Bill had brought me into bitter conflict with many members of my own party. If, on that Wednesday night, I had thought of my controversial past, I might well have wondered why anyone of so peaceful a disposition as myself should have been thrown into so many scenes of bitter controversy.

Naturally enough, none of these thoughts entered my mind as I left the House of Commons. There were other and much graver issues at stake than the fortunes of an individual Minister. The Government's majority had fallen to eighty, and I was not surprised when Chamberlain told me after the division that he would resign. In the meanwhile, Hitler's long-threatened offensive had begun. On the following morning, a telephone message from the Air Ministry woke me at 5 a.m. with the news of the invasion of Holland. Within an hour Stanley, the Secretary of State for War, and I were at the Admiralty to discuss the position with Churchill who, a week before, had become the Chairman of a Committee of the Service Ministers. Churchill, whose spirit, so far from being shaken by failure or disaster, gathered strength in a crisis, was ready as always with his confident advice. I shall never forget the breakfast that we had with him. It was six o'clock in the morning, after a fierce House of Commons debate and a late sitting. We had had little or no sleep, and the news could not have been worse. Yet there he was, smoking his large cigar and eating fried eggs and bacon, as if he had just returned from an early morning ride. Physically as well as mentally, he was in splendid training for the events that made him Prime Minister within a few days, and the champion of European freedom within a few weeks.

Chamberlain's first inclination was to withhold his resignation until the French battle was finished. The landslide, however, in favour of an all-party Government soon swept away the possibility of delay, and, as I had always expected, the Labour Party refused to serve in any Government of which he was Prime Minister. Churchill, therefore, succeeded at once to the kingdom that had so obviously been reserved for him. Soon afterwards, I was at the Palace to surrender my seals, and messengers were at my house to collect the keys of my Cabinet boxes.

Chamberlain would not have been human if he had not been overwhelmed by the *débâcle*. When I went to see him in the rambling eighteenth-century rooms of the Lord President's office, I found none of his old resiliency and obstinacy. What had shattered his spirit had not been the fall of his Government. He had often contemplated his own withdrawal from office when once the war was under way. Nor was it the apparent failure of his policy. He was still convinced that the policy had been right, and that no alternative had been possible. The overriding reason for his depression was very different. It was the collapse of the French Army, and with it, the disruption of all our carefully considered strategy. Supported by the best available military advice, he had relied on the French to withstand an invasion, although he had always realised that they were not strong enough to launch an offensive. I had myself been given a memorable illustration of French confidence. Three months before the collapse, Hankey and I had made a tour of the French front. When we reached the ill-famed section of Sedan, General Corap, commanding the ninth French army corps, had taken us to the Meuse and shown us the wooded banks and rushing waters. " Look at the *terrain*," he had said to us, " no German army can get through here," It was at this very point that German air and armour had broken the front in the space of a few hours. The unexpectedness of the collapse made the blow all the more crushing for Chamberlain. For the first time he saw the spectre of defeat approaching through the black clouds. Even the distant sight of it seemed to have almost paralysed him. When I left him, I was sure that whether in or out of the Government, he would not survive much longer. He would continue to devote himself body and soul to the service of the State and the conduct of the war, but his life, with its mainspring broken, was certain to run down very quickly.

As for myself, Churchill neither wanted me in his Government, nor, after the first feeling of frustration at the loss of absorbing work, did I wish to join it. And so, within a fortnight, I found myself Ambassador in Spain, once again plunged into a hotbed of controversy, but this time at least engaged in daily combat with the enemy, rather than in controversy with many of my fellow countrymen.

APPENDIX

The Zinoviev Letter

THE ZINOVIEV LETTER was a confidential communication sent by Zinoviev, the President of the Third International, to the British Communist Party. Its object was twofold: first, to instruct British Communists to bring pressure to bear on the Ramsay MacDonald Government to ratify the Anglo-Russian Treaty; secondly, to stir up trouble in the ranks of the fighting services and labour. In the words of the letter:

> " It is indispensable to stir up the masses of the British proletariat, to bring into the movement the army of unemployed proletarians. . . . It is imperative that the group in the Labour Party sympathising with the Treaty should bring increased pressure to bear upon the Government and Parliamentary circles in favour of the ratification of the Treaty.
>
> " Armed warfare must be preceded by a struggle against the inclination to compromise. . . . Only then will it be possible to count upon complete success of an armed insurrection.
>
> " From your last report it is evident that agitation-propaganda work in the army is weak, in the navy, very little better. . . . It would be desirable to have cells in all units of the troops, particularly among those quartered in the large centres of the country, and also many factories working on munitions and at military store depots. We request that the most particular attention be paid to these latter."

Lastly, the British Communists were explicitly instructed to turn any imperialist war into a class war, and at once to select military leaders for the revolution.

A copy of the letter was taken to the Foreign Office on October 10, 1924. Sir Eyre Crowe, the Permanent Under-Secretary of State, at once took steps to verify its authenticity. Not only was he convinced by his inquiries that it was authentic, but he also discovered that it had already been secretly discussed by the British Communist Party. These disclosures came at the end of a long chapter of unscrupulous Soviet propaganda, against which we had frequently protested. As our official protests had been ignored, Sir Eyre Crowe rightly believed that what was needed was a public exposure of the methods that the Soviet was adopting against the British Government. Ramsay MacDonald, Foreign Minister as well as Prime Minister, agreed. " I favour publication of such things," was his comment on the minute. The procedure to be adopted was the dispatch of a stiff note of protest to Rakovsky, the Soviet Ambassador, and the publication of the note in the Press as soon as the Ambassador had received it.

In the meanwhile, the *Daily Mail* had obtained a copy of the letter, and the editor told the Foreign Office that he intended to publish it at once. As Sir Eyre Crowe rightly wished to forestall the publication in the *Daily Mail*, and to follow the established method of dealing direct with the Ambassador, he gave instructions for the British note to be sent at once to Rakovsky and to be published simultaneously in the Press. Being under the impression that his chief had approved of this procedure, he was taken aback when MacDonald, who at the time was electioneering in the provinces, told him that he was expecting to see the papers again before he gave any final directions for publication. By this time, the note to Rakovsky and our protest were already in the hands of the Press.

The General Election was then in full blast. Inevitably, therefore, the disclosure of revolutionary propaganda was exploited by the Opposition. It is doubtful, however, whether the publication of the letter made any material difference to the result. The Government was already discredited, and the Opposition certain to win. In any case, there was no kind of plot or intrigue behind the disclosure. Sir Eyre Crowe sincerely believed that he was carrying out a normal process approved by the Foreign Secretary. MacDonald himself fully exonerated him from any charge of disloyalty, and declared that his confidence in him was unabated.

In the meanwhile, Rakovsky replied to the note with the charge that it was a forgery, and that the Soviet Government was not responsible for the Presidium of the Third International. MacDonald refused to accept the note, as it contained an unwarranted charge against the British Government. At this point, the position seemed clear. The Ministers, however, smarting under the electoral defeat, insisted upon a further examination of the authenticity of the letter. An inquiry took place, and ended in a finding that the authenticity could not be proved, as the original of the letter was not available for inspection. This was on the eve of the Cabinet's resignation. One of Baldwin's first acts on taking office was to appoint a very strong Cabinet Committee to re-examine the question of authenticity. The result was a clear and unanimous conclusion that the letter was genuine.

It is only necessary to add that on many subsequent occasions the same kind of propaganda has been launched against us by the Soviet, and that no serious and impartial observer has ever doubted the connection between the Politbureau and the Third International.

INDEX